The Son of Man

The Son of Man

A Verse-by-Verse Commentary on the Gospel According to Luke

by

John R. Rice

SWORD of the LORD
PUBLISHERS
P.O.BOX 1099, MURFREESBORO, TN 37133

Printed and bound in the United States of America

Table of Contents

LUKE, CHAPTER 3

LUKE, CHAPTER 4

LUKE, CHAPTER 5

LUKE, CHAPTER 9

LUKE, CHAPTER 10

LUKE, CHAPTER 11

LUKE, CHAPTER 12

LUKE, CHAPTER 13

LUKE, CHAPTER 14

LUKE, CHAPTER 15

LUKE, CHAPTER 16

LUKE, CHAPTER 17

LUKE, CHAPTER 18

LUKE, CHAPTER 19

LUKE, CHAPTER 20

LUKE, CHAPTER 21

LUKE, CHAPTER 22

LUKE, CHAPTER 23

LUKE, CHAPTER 24

12 LUKE

Introduction

Although Luke has only 24 chapters to 28 in Matthew, the Gospel of Luke is longer than the Gospel of Matthew, as you can see by counting the pages in a Bible without notes.

In *The International Standard Bible Encyclopaedia* Dr. A. T. Robertson says that the Canon of Muratori, Irenaeus, Tertullian, and Clement of Alexandria name Luke as the author of the third Gospel. Harnack and Dr. Robertson agree with nearly all the conservative scholars that Luke was the author of the book of Luke and of Acts of the Apostles.

Matthew Henry reminds us that Jerome says Luke was born in Antioch. Origen and Epiphanius say he was one of the seventy whom Jesus sent out in Luke 10. That is unlikely. He seems to have been a Gentile. In Colossians 4:10,11 Paul names Aristarchus, Mark and Justus, *"who are of the circumcision,"* that is, Jews who are Paul's *"fellow workers."* Then he names Epaphras and Luke and Demas (vss. 12-14) as helpers, not listed as *"of the circumcision,"* that is, not Jews as we understand it. Some think that in II Corinthians 8:18 when Paul speaks of *"the brother, whose praise is in the gospel throughout all the churches,"* he speaks of Luke, his traveling companion much of the time. And some suggest that *"the brother"* has connection with Titus who had just been mentioned and that the man mentioned, possibly Luke, was a brother of Titus. That is not proven, of course.

When was Luke written? Dr. A. T. Robertson in the I.S.B.E. says, "The Gospel was certainly written before Acts (Acts 1:1) and while Paul was alive, if I Tim. 5:18

be taken as a quotation from Lk. 10:7, which is by no
means certain, however.   But it is true that the most
natural way to interpret the sudden close of Acts, after
2 years in Rome (Acts 28:31), is the fact that Luke
finished the book at that time. . . . Harnack says: 'It
seems now to be established beyond question that both
books of this great historical order were written while
St. Paul was still alive.'" Very probably, then, it was
written before A. D. 66.

Ellicott thinks that Luke was perhaps about the age
of the Apostle Paul, since "St. Paul, e.g., never speaks
of him as he does of younger disciples, like Timothy
or Titus, as his *'child,'* or *'son, in the faith.'*"

If we believe that every word in the Scripture is "God
breathed" (the word for *"inspired"* in II Tim. 3:16),
and that *"every word. . . proceedeth from the mouth of
God"* (Matt. 4:4), then we do not need to speculate that
Luke copied from Mark or from some mysterious,
mythical, never-seen manuscript "Q."   And in Luke
1:3 Luke tells us that he had *"perfect understanding of
all things from the very first,"* but more literally *"from
above"* (the Greek word is *anothen*). So we can believe
that the material came not from scholarly investigation
and chasing down of sources but by direct revelation
from God.[1]

Dr. Robertson, though prone to follow those who believed in the documentary hypothesis of the Synoptic
Gospels, yet says in the I.S.B.E., "But, if it is true that
Luke made use of Q as of Mk, he was no mere copyist.
No solution of the synoptic problem can ever be obtained
on the idea that the Gospels are mere reproductions of
previous documents."   Again he said, "The point of all
this is that a great deal of criticism of the Gospels is
attempting the impossible, for many of the variations
cannot possibly be traced to any 'source.'"

---

[1] See the author's volume, *Our God-Breathed Book--THE BIBLE,* chapter VIII.

And Bishop Ryle says in his *Expository Thoughts on the Gospel,* "It would be mere waste of time to inquire from what source St. Luke obtained the information which he has given us in his Gospel. We have no good reason for supposing that he saw our Lord work miracles, or heard Him teach. To say that he obtained his information from the Virgin Mary, or any of the apostles, is mere conjecture and speculation. Enough for us to know that St. Luke wrote by inspiration of God. Unquestionably he did not neglect the ordinary means of getting knowledge. But the Holy Ghost guided him, no less than all other writers of the Bible, in his choice of matter. The Holy Ghost supplied him with thoughts, arrangement, sentences, and even words. And the result is, that what St. Luke wrote is not to be read as the '*word of man,*' but the '*word of God.*' (I Thess. ii.13.)"

And again he says, "There is no encouragement here for those who place confidence in unwritten traditions, and the voice of the church. St. Luke knew well the weakness of man's memory, and the readiness with which a history alters its shape both by additions and alterations, when it depends only on word of mouth and report. What therefore does he do? He takes care to 'write.'"

Some Clear Differences in the Gospel According to Luke

The genealogy of Jesus in Luke 3 traces Jesus right back to "*Adam, which was the son of God.*" That is evidently the genealogy of Mary, but it pictures Jesus as the Son of mankind, the Second Adam, the Pattern Man, the Perfect Man. Thus it shows more about the compassion of Jesus, His interest in women and children, in the poor, in the sick. The parables of the Widow Before the Unjust Judge, of the Unjust Steward, of the Good Samaritan, of the Prodigal Son, of the Great

Supper, and of the Pounds, are not repeated in other Gospels.

In the book of Luke, Jesus is not pictured particularly as the coming King of the Jews, as in Matthew, nor even as the suffering Servant of God, as in Mark, nor as the Son of God, as in John, but as, the Son of man, the pattern for all Christians. Therefore, there is more in the book of Luke about soul winning. There is the man who goes to his friend at midnight to get three loaves for another friend—surely picturing a Christian seeking the Bread of Life for sinners. The fifteenth chapter of Luke, with its stories of the Lost Sheep, the Lost Coin, and the Prodigal Son, shows how Christ loves sinners and seeks to win them. So does the Great Supper, recorded in Luke 14. Only in Luke are we told the wonderful story of the salvation of the dying thief.

Luke had far more emphasis on the Holy Spirit than do the other Gospels. Where Matthew mentions the Holy Spirit twelve times, and Mark fewer yet, the Gospel according to Luke mentions the Holy Spirit seventeen times. Only Luke gives the story of Spirit-filled Zacharias and Elisabeth and their prophecies and the marvelous story of the birth of John the Baptist. And there we learn that John the Baptist was to be *"filled with the Holy Ghost, even from his mother's womb."* Only in Luke is it told that after Jesus was baptized with the Holy Spirit, or after the Holy Spirit came on Him when He was baptized and prayed, He went into the synagogue in Galilee and quoted to them Isaiah 61:1 and 2, and told them, *"This day is this scripture fulfilled in your ears,"* that is, *"The Spirit of the Lord is upon me, because he hath anointed me to preach the gospel. . . ."* Only Luke has the promise of Luke 11:13, that God will *"give the Holy Spirit to them that ask him,"* and the command of Luke 24:49, *"But tarry ye in the city of Jerusalem until ye be endued with power from on high."*

In connection with the plea for Bread for sinners, Ellicott reminds us:

"Lastly, we cannot fail to note, as we read his Gospel, the special stress which he, far more than St. Matthew or St. Mark, lays upon the prayers of the Christ. It is from him we learn that it was as Jesus was 'praying' at His baptism that the heavens were opened (iii. 21); that it was while He was praying that the fashion of His countenance was altered, and there came on Him the glory of the Transfiguration (ix. 29); that He was 'praying' when the disciples came and asked Him to teach them to pray (xi. 1); that He had prayed for Peter that his faith might not fail (xxii. 32). In the life of prayer, no less than in that of self-chosen poverty, His was the pattern-life which His disciples were—each in his measure and according to His power—to endeavour to reproduce" (Vol. 6, p. 242).

Since the book of Acts is to be the story of the mighty power of God coming upon disciples as they carry out the Great Commission, so Luke gives Jesus, our Pattern, filled with the Holy Spirit, as our Example. And Jesus is our Example also in prayer.

The Son of Man

A Verse-by-Verse Commentary
on the
Gospel According to Luke

LUKE 1

VERSES 1 — 4:

FORASMUCH as many have taken in hand to set forth in order a declaration of those things which are most surely believed among us,

2 Even as they delivered them unto us, which from the beginning were eyewitnesses, and ministers of the word;

3 It seemed good to me also, having had perfect understanding of all things from the very first, to write unto thee in order, most excellent Theophilus,

4 That thou mightest know the certainty of those things, wherein thou hast been instructed.

Luke's Introduction

There were "many" uninspired accounts of the life of Christ. The term *many* here could not mean the two inspired accounts — Matthew and Mark — which may have been written before Luke. The Gospel of John was written considerably later. There were many other uninspired accounts to which Luke refers.

These accounts by many honest Christians who spread the Gospel depended on the reports of the apostles and other ministers of the Word who reported the various incidents in the life of Christ which they had seen, or of which they had heard. They were "hearsay" accounts, relying on the reports of others, and the accounts were

sifted, as best men could, from a multitude of varying
and often conflicting accounts.   They had written "*a
declaration of those things which are most surely believed among us,*" verse 1 says.

However, we must bear in mind that they were not
inspired accounts.   Naturally enough men could not,
from these human and imperfect accounts, know "*the
certainty*" of the things they had heard.   What Luke
would write is from "*perfect understanding of all things.*"
That no uninspired writer could have, so there is a need
for an orderly, inspired, perfect account of the life of
Christ written with a particular color and emphasis
which God will give to Luke.

Note carefully the distinction between the fallible, uninspired accounts mentioned by Luke and the inspired
account which he will write from "*perfect understanding,*" so that Theophilus and others "*mightest know
the CERTAINTY of those things, wherein thou hast been
instructed.*"   The Gospel of Luke claims an infallibly
perfect report of the things it records.   That is a claim
for divine inspiration.   Human writings, not inspired of
God, are not infallibly perfect.

Luke's Perfect Sources Were "From Above"

In verse 3, Luke says, "*It seemed good to me also,
having had perfect understanding of all things from the
very first, to write unto thee in order, most excellent
Theophilus.*"

But the term "*from the first*" is an inadequate trans-
lation of the Greek word *anothen* used here. Sir William
Ramsey and many others who followed that distinguished
English scholar thought that Luke had talked with
Mary and thus learned about the virgin birth and that
he had carefully traced out by research, the things
about which he writes in the Gospel according to Luke.
That is wrong, in the first place, because it leaves out

the perfection of divine revelation and leaves the impression that we have here simply the human and thus
imperfect report of a fallible human writer who did the
best he could, searching out sources, talking to eyewitnesses and then writing his Gospel.   That could not
possibly fit the report that Luke *"had perfect understanding of all things."* Excepting Jesus Christ alone,
no man in all this world since Adam's sin ever *"had
perfect understanding of all things"* except as it was
divinely revealed. All the labor, all the investigation, all
the weighing of evidence by men never resulted in *"perfect understanding of all things,"* relating to the birth,
life, ministry, atoning death and resurrection, teaching
and ascension of Jesus Christ.

Again, that does not fit in with what the Bible so often
and so clearly teaches about what God means by inspiration.   And II Timothy 3:16 declares, *"All scripture is
given by inspiration of God,"* that is, literally *theopneus-
tos,* that is, God-breathed. In Matthew 4:4, Jesus, quoting Deuteronomy 8:3, says of the Scripture that *"every
word...proceedeth out of the mouth of God."* And if
Luke's Gospel is Scripture, and is God-breathed and if
every word came from the mouth of God, as it did, then
the words are not the result of human investigation and
research, simple human reporting.

First Corinthians 2:9 expressly denies that God's
revelation could come by what eyewitnesses have seen or
what ears have heard or what entered into the heart of
man: *"But as it is written, Eye hath not seen, nor ear
heard, neither have entered into the heart of man, the
things which God hath prepared for them that love him."*
And how did they come? Verse 10 tells us: *"But God
hath revealed them unto us by his Spirit,"* and verse 13
says that these revelations from God, in the Scripture,
come *"not in the words which man's wisdom teacheth,*

*but which the Holy Ghost teacheth; comparing spiritual
things with spiritual."*

If the *"eye hath not seen, nor ear heard, neither have
entered into the heart of man"* the matters written in the
Scriptures, then Luke did not learn what he wrote from
eyewitnesses. Nor was the book of Acts material learned
by Luke from Paul, and church father, Papias, was
mistaken in thinking Mark wrote what Peter reported to
him. Human research, or eyewitnesses, or memory,
cannot account for the inspired Scripture.

When God said to Isaiah, in Isaiah 51:16, *"I have put
my words in thy mouth..."* and told Jeremiah, in Jeremiah 1:9, *"Behold, I have put my words in thy mouth,"*
then we may be sure that if the Gospel of Luke is inspired Scripture like the other Scriptures, then God
Himself gave the words which Luke wrote. Human
wisdom, human observation, human judgment, human
weighing up of the witnesses and sources, could never
produce any part of this infallible Word of God and
they cannot account for the Gospel of Luke. If it is
inspired of God by the Scripture's own definition of
inspiration, then Luke did not search out all things
diligently from the first and know them *"perfectly"* so
that one might *"know the certainty"* of what he reads.

But the Word **Anothen** Clearly Means
"From Above"

Instead of the translation of the King James Version
which says, *"...having had perfect understanding of all
things from the very first,"* it should read, *"...having
had perfect understanding of all things from above;"* for
the word here translated *"from the first"* literally means
from above, as it is shown in other places in the New
Testament.

In John 3:31 we read, *"He that cometh from above is
above all: he that is of the earth is earthly, and speaketh*

of the earth: he that cometh from heaven is above all."
But the term *from above,* used twice here, is the translation of the repeated Greek word *anothen.* Christ
came *from above,* so did Luke's Gospel then come *from
above.*

In John 19:11, Jesus answers Pilate, "*Thou couldest
have no power at all against me, except it were given
thee from above.*" And the term "*from above*" here is
a translation of the Greek word *anothen,* as used in
Luke 1:3. In James 1:17, James 3:15 and 17, the
Greek word *anothen* is translated *from above,* and
obviously could not be translated to mean "from the
first."

Great scholars, including Erasmus, Gaussen, B. H.
Carroll, C. I. Scofield, James M. Gray, Spurgeon, and
many others, agree that that term should be translated
"from above." The Greek word *anothen* is the word in
John 3:3 translated "again" — "*Except a man be born
again....*" And in John 3:7, "*Ye must be born again,*"
the word "again" is a translation of *anothen* and obviously means one must be born "from above," not
"from the first."

The Greek word *anothen* is not translated anywhere
else in the Bible as "*from the first,*" except in this mis-
translation in Luke 1:3. It is translated "*from the beginning*" one time in Acts 26:5.

The meaning in Luke 1:3 demands the translation
"from above." Only if Luke received his "*understanding
of all things from above*" could it be "*perfect understanding,*" and only then could the reader "*know the
certainty of those things, wherein thou hast been instructed,*" correcting uncertain, uninspired accounts by others.

"*It seemed good to me also*" (vs. 3). It seemed good
to Luke because it seemed good first to God. In Acts
15:28, apostles and elders, after the council at Jerusalem,
wrote that "*it seemed good to the Holy Ghost, and to*

us, to lay upon you no greater burden than these neces-sary things." So Luke, inspired of God, was moved to feel the need for his Gospel and was inspired to write it with a perfect understanding of all things from above.

"To write unto thee in order" (vs. 3). Then, we may expect in the book of Luke, as in Matthew and in Mark, a more orderly account of the things God wants us to know about the birth, life, ministry, death and resurrection of Jesus Christ. Thus Luke is one of the "synoptic Gospels." The Gospel of John does not follow the same order, and does not, in most cases, intend to give the same material.

We will find that many of the same events in the life of Christ are told in the same order as in Matthew and in Mark.

_____

VERSES 5—12:

5 THERE was in the days of Herod, the king of Judæa, a certain priest named Zacharias, of the course of Abia: and his wife *was* of the daughters of Aaron, and her name *was* Elisabeth.

6 And they were both righteous before God, walking in all the commandments and ordinances of the Lord blameless.

7 And they had no child, because that Elisabeth was barren, and they both were *now* well stricken in years.

8 And it came to pass, that while he executed the priest's office before God in the order of his course,

9 According to the custom of the priest's office, his lot was to burn incense when he went into the temple of the Lord.

10 And the whole multitude of the people were praying without at the time of incense.

11 And there appeared unto him an angel of the Lord standing on the right side of the altar of incense.

12 And when Zacharias saw *him,* he was troubled, and fear fell upon him.

Zacharias and Elisabeth

"...in the days of Herod, the king of Judaea." This was Herod the Great, the first of the Herod family, a strong, intelligent sub-king under the Roman Empire. He was wicked, guilty of many murders, including the murders of the little innocent boy children in Bethlehem two years old and under (Matt. 2:16). He built at great expense the beautiful Temple which existed in the lifetime of Christ. Herod died while the Baby Jesus was in Egypt (Matt. 2:19). Archelaus, son of Herod, succeeded his father Herod the Great until 6 A.D. and was deposed and followed by another son of Herod the Great, Herod Antipas, called *"Herod the tetrarch"* (Matt. 14:1; Luke 3:19). This was the Herod who beheaded John the Baptist, the Herod who agreed with Pilate to the death of Christ (Luke 23:7; Acts 4:27). A third Herod, Herod Agrippa, a grandson of Herod the Great, reigned as sub-king in Judaea, and persecuted the church (Acts 12:1-4). His death is told in Acts 12:23.

A fourth man named Herod, Herod Agrippa II, was the son of the Herod of Acts 12:1 and the grandson of Herod the Great, the man before whom Paul was brought in Acts 25:13-27 and in Acts 26. These rulers were all appointed as sub-rulers as a part of the Roman Empire.

Zacharias was a priest. He was descended from Aaron, and his wife Elisabeth was also of the priestly line of Aaron. *"And they were both righteous before God,"* we are told. And that must indicate here a heart-righteousness, not simply ceremonial correctness. Abraham was righteous before God: *"And he believed in the Lord; and he counted it to him for righteousness"* (Gen. 15:6). Romans 4 tells us very explicitly that thus Abraham is a pattern for all in the matter of salvation, and we are reminded in Genesis 15:5-8:

"And he brought him forth abroad, and said, Look

now toward heaven, and tell the stars, if thou be able to number them: and he said unto him, So shall thy seed be. And he believed in the Lord; and he counted it to him for righteousness. And he said unto him, I am the Lord that brought thee out of Ur of the Chaldees, to give thee this land to inherit it. And he said, Lord God, whereby shall I know that I shall inherit it?"

That is righteousness before God. Old Testament saints then were saved just as people are saved now, by trusting in the Saviour that God would provide. So, Acts 10:43 tells us, *"To him give all the prophets witness, that through his name whosoever believeth in him shall receive remission of sins."*

To an Old Testament saint, just as to us today, Jesus Christ is *"THE LORD OUR RIGHTEOUSNESS"* (Jer. 23:6). And Romans 10:4 tells us, *"For Christ is the end of the law for righteousness to every one that believeth."*

These two, Zacharias and Elisabeth, *"were both righteous before God, walking in all the commandments and ordinances of the Lord blameless."* Then when they kept the ceremonial commandments, the ceremonies were not an empty form but pictured the coming Saviour. The passover lamb pictured Christ our Passover. The circumcision of a baby boy pictured the circumcision of heart, regeneration. The work of a priest pictured the priestly work of the coming Saviour. They kept these ceremonies, pointing to Christ, in simple obedience and faith, just as good Christians today take the Lord's Supper, pointing back to the death of Christ but not relying upon the ordinance, the ceremony itself, for salvation.

"And they had no child, because that Elisabeth was barren, and they both were now well stricken in years." Here we have a case like that of Abraham and Sarah.

It would take a miracle to restore Sarah, ninety years old, to the youthful condition of a child-bearing woman. And Abraham, a hundred years old (Gen. 21:1-7), was *"as good as dead"* as far as fathering a child was concerned (Heb. 11:12). So it will take a miracle in the case of Elisabeth and Zacharias. Elisabeth had been for years shamed with the reproach of barrenness (vs. 25), but now this godly, righteous couple, this couple who have so earnestly prayed for a son, will see their prayers answered.

It is significant that Zacharias was, *"according to the custom of the priest's office,"* given the lot to burn incense at the altar of incense in the Temple. That incense represented the praise and prayer offered to God. It was made of sweet spices, a perfume described in Exodus 30:34-38. For any to be made like it for private use was forbidden. But now, since so many prayers are to be answered, and since there will be great rejoicing and praise to God, at the time of the offering of the incense the angel of God appeared to Zacharias. While *"the whole multitude of the people were praying without at the time of incense,"* the angel appeared.

Angels Had a Happy Part in the Events Surrounding the Birth of the Saviour

First, the angel appears to Zacharias in verse 11. Then the Angel Gabriel appeared to Mary in verse 26 to announce the birth of Jesus. And *"the angel of the Lord"* appeared to Joseph in a dream telling him that Mary was with child by the Holy Ghost (Matt. 1:20).

When Jesus was born, the angel announced the glad tidings to the waiting shepherds in the field near Bethlehem (Luke 2:8-12) and a great multitude of the heavenly host joined in the glorious chant (Luke 2:13,14).

Then *"the angel of the Lord appeareth to Joseph in a dream, saying, Arise, and take the young child and his mother, and flee into Egypt"* (Matt. 2:13). It is strange but significant that when an angel appeared to men, usually his first words must be "fear not," so unused are we to these heavenly messengers, these ministers to us who, unseen, surround us! *"The angel of the Lord encampeth round about them that fear him, and delivereth them"* (Ps. 34:7).

VERSES 13, 14:

13 But the angel said unto him, Fear not, Zacharias: for thy prayer is heard; and thy wife Elisabeth shall bear thee a son, and thou shalt call his name John.

14 And thou shalt have joy and gladness; and many shall rejoice at his birth.

The Birth of John the Baptist Announced

"Thy prayer is heard." We may well suppose that for thirty years and more, probably all through the years of their marriage, Zacharias and Elisabeth had pleaded with God for a son. And now their prayer was heard. It is a frequent theme in the Old Testament that barren women prayed most earnestly for a child. In Genesis 11:30 we read, *"But Sarai was barren; she had no child."* Distraught Sarai, wanting a child even by proxy, gave to her husband her handmaid Hagar, to bear for her a child (Gen. 16:1-4). And Abraham, with hope so long deferred, could hardly believe that God would give a son through Sarah: *"Then Abraham fell upon his face, and laughed, and said in his heart, Shall a child be born unto him that is an hundred years old? and shall Sarah, that is ninety years old, bear?"* (Gen. 17:17). But God fulfilled His promise.

Strangely enough, Rebekah was for a season barren. *"And Isaac intreated the Lord for his wife, because she was barren: and the Lord was intreated of him, and*

Rebekah his wife conceived" (Gen. 25:21).

And Rachel pleaded with Jacob, "*Give me children, or else I die*" (Gen. 30:1). At last God answered and gave her Joseph and Benjamin.

For a time Leah was barren after the birth of some sons, "*And God hearkened unto Leah, and she conceived, and bare Jacob the fifth son*" (Gen. 30:17).

The story of how Hannah prayed and bargained with God that He might in her barrenness give a child, and of the birth of Samuel, lent to the Lord as long as he should live, is wonderfully told in I Samuel, chapter 1.

The "*great woman*" of Shunem was barren until the Prophet Elijah interceded for her and God gave the child (II Kings 4:8-17).

Now Zacharias and Elisabeth have sought the Lord and their prayer is heard! Elisabeth, an old woman, is to bear a son through the miraculous touch from God.

We must remember that this was not a virgin birth like the birth of Jesus, but that God simply miraculously restored youthful fertility to a couple too old normally to bear children.

Zacharias and Elisabeth would rejoice at the birth of John the Baptist, and so should many others, as we see in Luke 1:58: "*And her neighbours and her cousins heard how the Lord had shewed great mercy upon her; and they rejoiced with her.*" But symbolically uncounted multitudes later would rejoice in the ministry of this man sent from God!

VERSES 15—17:

15 For he shall be great in the sight of the Lord, and shall drink neither wine nor strong drink; and he shall be filled with the Holy Ghost, even from his mother's womb.

16 And many of the children of Israel shall he turn to the Lord their God.

17 And he shall go before him in

the spirit and power of Elias, to
turn the hearts of the fathers to
the children, and the disobedient
to the wisdom of the just; to make
ready a people prepared for the
Lord.

The Greatness of John the Baptist

John the Baptist was *"great in the sight of the Lord."*
He was not unanimously received by the religious leaders
of his day. He called the scribes and Pharisees, *"O*
generation of vipers" (Matt. 3:7). To these religious
leaders Jesus asked the question, *"The baptism of John,*
whence was it? from heaven, or of men? And they
reasoned with themselves, saying, If we shall say, From
heaven; he will say unto us, Why did ye not then believe
him? But if we shall say, Of men; we fear the people;
for all hold John as a prophet" (Matt. 21:25,26).

John angered Herod Agrippa, telling him plainly,
when he took his brother Philip's wife, *"It is not lawful*
for thee to have her," and Herod imprisoned John.
And eventually, at the instigation of the adulterous wife
of Philip he had stolen, he had John beheaded in prison
(Matt. 14:1-12; Mark 6:14-29; Luke 9:7-9). But he was
great in the sight of the Lord and probably all the greater because he offended men whom he ought to offend
and condemned sin that ought to be condemned.

John was *"great in the sight of the Lord."* What a
tribute Jesus gave to John in Luke 7:24-29! Jesus
praised his rugged steadfastness, said he is a prophet
"and much more than a prophet" —he is the promised
messenger of Malachi 3:1, and, *"Among those that are*
born of women there is not a greater prophet than John
the Baptist." The Pharisees and lawyers rejected the
baptism of John and said, *"He hath a devil"* (Luke
7:30,33).

John the Baptist was *"great in the sight of the Lord,"*
great in moral purity. He drank neither wine nor
strong drink. He had evidently taken the *"vow of a*

Nazarite," as men and women did *"to separate them-selves unto the Lord"* (Num. 6:2). We see in that sixth chapter of Numbers that the Nazarite separated himself from wine and strong drink or even vinegar or grapes or raisins, did not cut his hair but was separated to the Lord, *"because the consecration of his God is upon his head."* The Nazarite vow was sometimes, as we think it was in the case of John the Baptist and in the case of Samson (Judges 13:5), for a lifetime. In other cases it might be for a limited time, as we think it was with the Apostle Paul (Acts 21:23-26). So John never married, gave up the ordinary pleasures and comforts of life and went boldly unto his death as a martyr.

But John was *"great in the sight of the Lord,"* we understand, principally as a mighty, Spirit-filled soul winner. With what power he preached to the whole multitude so that there *"went out to him Jerusalem, and all Judaea, and all the region round about Jordan, And were baptized of him in Jordan, confessing their sins"* (Matt. 3:5,6)! And we are told that *"many of the children of Israel shall he turn to the Lord their God"* (vs. 16). He is likened to Spirit-filled Elijah, the mighty prophet and preacher at Mount Carmel.

As Elijah, one man, temporarily halted the course of idolatry of a whole nation, so we are told of John that *"he shall go before him* [Jesus] *in the spirit and power of Elias."* So the prophecy in Malachi 4:5 and 6 which foretells about Elijah, John the Baptist fulfilled in its first great fulfillment. So Jesus said, *"Elias is come already, and they knew him not, but have done unto him whatsoever they listed"* (Matt. 17:12).

Note the moral revolution in the revivals under John the Baptist. He would *"turn the hearts of the fathers to the children, and the disobedient to the wisdom of the just; to make ready a people prepared for the Lord."*

See Luke, chapter 3, where the publicans, or public servants, were turned to honesty, the lewd and violent soldiers turned to integrity. In some moral sense, the prophecy of Isaiah about John the Baptist, in Isaiah 40:3-5, was fulfilled in that "*every valley shall be exalted, and every mountain and hill shall be made low: and the crooked shall be made straight, and the rough places plain: And the glory of the Lord shall be revealed, and all flesh shall see it together: for the mouth of the Lord hath spoken it.*"

A genuine revival means a moral revolution. So it was in the days of Wesley and of Moody, R. A. Torrey, Billy Sunday, Sam Jones and Bob Jones, Sr., and so it was nationwide under John the Baptist.

John the Baptist Was "Filled With the Holy Ghost"

Here is an amazing and unique statement. Of no one else in the Bible is it ever said that he was "*filled with the Holy Ghost, even from his mother's womb.*" At Pentecost the apostles and others of the hundred and twenty were "*filled with the Holy Ghost*" in answer to their own persistent prayer. John the Baptist was filled with the Holy Ghost, evidently, in answer to the persistent prayers of Zacharias and Elisabeth, his father and mother. Isaiah 44:3 says, "*For I will pour water upon him that is thirsty, and floods upon the dry ground: I will pour my spirit upon thy seed, and my blessing upon thine offspring.*"

"*I will pour my spirit upon thy seed,*" says the Scripture. So, because of the thirst of Zacharias and Elisabeth, we believe, God poured out the Holy Spirit upon the child, John the Baptist, from the time of his birth. How wholly dedicated to God was the baby John, that God had the unborn child leap in his mother's womb when Mary saluted Elisabeth (vs. 41)! The unaccountable child, not knowingly a sinner, could be filled with the Holy Spirit at God's choice, as he was, but if he continued filled with the Spirit, then the moment he came to know himself as a guilty, lost sinner he would have turned to the Lord and trusted Him. God would not continually fill a rebellious, unrepentant sinner, of course.

John the Baptist was *"filled with the Spirit."* That is not mentioned in Matthew, Mark or John. The Gospel of Luke has a special emphasis on the Holy Spirit. So Elisabeth (vs. 41), so Zacharias (vs. 67), and so old Simeon (Luke 2:25-27), are mentioned in Luke alone as *"filled with the Spirit."* So only Luke has the parable about a friend seeking heavenly Bread for sinners (Luke 11:5-8), and the wonderful promise of Luke 11:13, *"If ye then, being evil, know how to give good gifts unto your children: how much more shall your heavenly Father give the Holy Spirit to them that ask him?"* Only Luke of the four Gospels has the command to *"tarry ye in the city of Jerusalem, until ye be endued with power from on high"* (Luke 24:49).

The most important emphasis here is that the fullness of the Spirit made John a great soul winner: *"And many of the children of Israel shall he turn to the Lord their God"* (Luke 1:16). That is the inevitable result of Spirit-filled witnessing. So it was in Acts 2:4 and Acts 4:31. That is the promise of Acts 1:8, *"But ye shall receive power, after that the Holy Ghost is come upon you: and ye shall be witnesses unto me."* So it was with Barnabas: *"For he was a good man, and full of the Holy Ghost and of faith: and much people was added unto the Lord"* (Acts 11:24). The fullness of the Spirit is simply 'an enduement of power from on high' for the specific purpose of winning souls. So John the Baptist had what all Christians are commanded to have in Ephesians 5:18. We are commanded there, *"Be filled with the Spirit."*

VERSES 18—25:

18 And Zacharias said unto the angel, Whereby shall I know this? for I am an old man, and my wife well stricken in years.

19 And the angel answering said unto him, I am Gabriel, that stand in the presence of God; and am sent to speak unto thee, and to shew thee these glad tidings.

20 And, behold, thou shalt be dumb, and not able to speak, until the day that these things shall be performed, because thou believest not my words, which shall be fulfilled in their season.

21 And the people waited for Zacharias, and marvelled that he tarried so long in the temple.

22 And when he came out, he could not speak unto them: and they perceived that he had seen a vision in the temple: for he beckoned unto them, and remained speechless.

23 And it came to pass, that, as soon as the days of his ministration were accomplished, he departed to his own house.

24 And after those days his wife Elisabeth conceived, and hid herself five months, saying,

25 Thus hath the Lord dealt with me in the days wherein he looked on me, to take away my reproach among men.

Zacharias Struck Dumb for His Unbelief

The angel who brings the announcement about John the Baptist to Zacharias is "*Gabriel, that stand in the presence of God.*" There are millions of angels — "*ten thousand times ten thousand, and thousands of thousands*" (Rev. 5:11). Except the fallen angel, Lucifer (Isa. 14:12), only two of them are named in the Bible: Gabriel, when announcing the birth of John the Baptist and announcing the birth of Jesus to Mary (Luke 1:26) and appearing to Daniel in Daniel 8:16, Daniel 9:21; and the archangel Michael "mentioned as having a particular relation to Israel and to the resurrections," Scofield says (Dan. 10:13-21; 12:1; Jude 9; I Thess. 4:16).

From the context here, we learn of Gabriel standing before God intimately, as a particularly favored messenger of God. Angels are "*all ministering spirits, sent forth to minister for them who shall be heirs of salva-tion"* (Heb. 1:14).

It seems likely that *"the angel of the Lord"* who an-nounced the birth of Christ to the shepherds in Luke 2:9 was the same Gabriel; not "an angel" but *"the angel."*

"Behold, thou shalt be dumb, and not able to speak," Zacharias is told, because of his unbelief. First, that illustrates the sin of unbelief. It was natural. Zacharias said, *"Whereby shall I know this? for I am an old man, and my wife well stricken in years."* It would take a miracle. Abraham and Sarah doubted also when a similar miraculous birth of Isaac was promised them (Gen. 16:1-4; Gen. 17:17; Gen. 18:11-15). But being dumb until the birth of John the Baptist was not pri-marily punishment but rather assurance. Every day Zacharias, who could not speak, had the evidence that God would fulfill the promised answer to his long beseeching prayer. The silent months until John the Baptist was born worked a wonderful development of faith and fullness of the Spirit in Zacharias, as we see from verses 62 to 79.

"And the people waited for Zacharias, and marvelled ...." Verse 10 has told us, *"And the whole multitude of the people were praying without at the time of incense."* To many of these it was not a mere form or ceremony. Many surely understood that the sweet incense offered within the Temple pictured the prayers and praises of God's people and many must have prayed. No doubt some of them were looking for the Messiah. It was not hard for some of them to believe in spiritual and miraculous things, because *"they perceived that he had seen a vision in the temple"* (vs. 22).

We are reminded of old Simeon who waited to see the promised Saviour before he should die (Luke 2:25-35), and of the spiritual widow Anna, in Luke 2:36-38. We remember Jews who sent priests and Levites from Jerusalem to ask John the Baptist if he were the Messiah (John 1:19-21), and those thoughtful priests and scribes who knew from Micah 5:2 that the Messiah should be born in Bethlehem (Matt. 2:4-6). And even the Samaritan woman said, "*I know that Messias cometh, which is called Christ...*" (John 4:25). And the wise men from the East were looking for the Saviour. Doubtless there were many saved people who had, through the ceremonies and teachings of the prophets, learned to trust in the coming Messiah and were saved.

Zacharias' days of service in the Temple were finished. He went to his home and Elisabeth conceived. She had great joy in that her reproach of barrenness was taken away.

VERSES 26—30:

26 And in the sixth month the angel Gabriel was sent from God unto a city of Galilee, named Nazareth,

27 To a virgin espoused to a man whose name was Joseph, of the house of David; and the virgin's name *was* Mary.

28 And the angel came in unto her, and said, Hail, *thou that art* highly favoured, the Lord *is* with thee: blessed *art* thou among women.

29 And when she saw *him*, she was troubled at his saying, and cast in her mind what manner of salutation this should be.

30 And the angel said unto her, Fear not, Mary: for thou hast found favour with God.

Gabriel Appears to Mary

So the same exalted Angel Gabriel brings the message to Mary. Nazareth remains to this day. Despite Queen Helena, mother of Constantine, who selected a supposed site of the annunciation to Mary in a cave and had thereon built a church, followed by a tremendous building now being built by Rome, there are really no known buildings or places identifiable as especially connected with the holy family. The Church of St. Joseph is built over the cave supposedly the home of Joseph and Mary, with no evidence. A "hill of precipitation" outside the city is probably the place mentioned in Luke 4:29.

And why would Jesus be born in Nazareth instead of Jerusalem or some other better known city? Doubtless He was to take on whatever reproach of poverty and ignominy that would make Him representative of this poor, sinning and suffering race. Ever since Tiglath-pileser, king of Assyria, took the inhabitants of Galilee into captivity (II Kings 15:29) and then took the rest of the northern tribes into captivity (II Kings 17:6), Galilee had been a portion of the land in reproach. After that captivity, godly Jews centered in or about Jerusalem, when Jerusalem and Judaea were restored in the days of Ezra and Nehemiah. Meantime, that area of the northern tribes had been repeopled by heathen people (II Kings 17:24-41). The Jews had scattered and although the ancestral home of the descendants of David was in Judaea, about Jerusalem, Mary and Joseph lived in Nazareth in Galilee, that backwoods province in reproach among good Jews.

Mary Was "a Virgin"

The angel came *"to a virgin."* This matter is so important in God's plan and such a majestic miracle that we are not surprised it was foretold. God promised Eve that *"her seed"* should bruise the serpent's head, that is, the seed of a woman, not of a woman and a man (Gen. 3:15). Jeremiah told of the wonder that *"a woman shall compass a man"* without the normal process of reproduction (Jer. 31:22). And Isaiah 7:14 promised, *"Behold, a virgin shall conceive, and bear a son, and shall call his name Immanuel."*

The translators of the Revised Standard Version tell us that the Hebrew word *almah* in Isaiah 7:14 should be translated simply "young woman," and that the real word for virgin is *bethulah*. However, they are wrong. *Bethulah* does not always mean virgin. Joel 1:8 says, *"Lament like a virgin girded with sackcloth for the husband of her youth."* The word translated virgin here is *bethulah* and refers to a widow, not a virgin. The term *bethulah,* translated virgin, is often used symbolically for idolatrous cities guilty of spiritual adultery and so would not symbolize virginity.

On the other hand, the word *almah* in the Hebrew, in every single case, appears necessarily to mean virgin wherever used in the Old Testament. But the best proof that the lexicons and the liberals are wrong is this:

1. The translators of the King James Version, the English Revised Version and the American Revised Version translated the word in Isaiah 7:14 *"virgin."*

2. More important still, the Septuagint translation of the Old Testament in the Greek, completed long before Christ, when Hebrew was a living language, translated the word *almah* into the Greek *parthenos,* which everybody admits must mean virgin.

3. Stronger proof yet is that God Himself quotes Isaiah 7:14 in the New Testament (Matt. 1:23), and quotes it, *"Behold, a virgin shall be with child, and shall bring forth a son, and they shall call his name Emmanuel...."* Those who believe that Mary was a virgin, as the Bible says, ought to have no difficulty in believing that God foretold the virgin birth ahead of time.

Mary was *"highly favoured...blessed...among women."* Here we understand that Mary was a devout, converted child of God. The angel said, *"The Lord is with thee."* She had *"found favour with God."* So we feel sure that she had sought the favor of God and so gained it. It is apparent that she immediately accepted the will of God, that she believed what the angel told her, that she gladly faced whatever reproach and trouble should come to her as the mother of the coming Saviour.

VERSES 31—35:

31 And, behold, thou shalt conceive in thy womb, and bring forth a son, and shalt call his name JESUS.

32 He shall be great, and shall be called the Son of the Highest: and the Lord God shall give unto him the throne of his father David:

33 And he shall reign over the house of Jacob for ever; and of his kingdom there shall be no end.

34 Then said Mary unto the angel, How shall this be, seeing I know not a man?

35 And the angel answered and said unto her, The Holy Ghost shall come upon thee, and the power of the Highest shall overshadow thee: therefore also that holy thing which shall be born of thee shall be called the Son of God.

The Saviour's Birth Announced

The virgin Mary is to conceive a son. Had Mary been praying for this? She had *"found favour with God."* Is this the favor she sought? Her quickness to believe and willingness to take the heartbreak and shame that were inevitable, indicate she may have prayed for this very thing. At least her seeking the favor of God had gained her this boon.

His name is to be called JESUS. That name had been given for Him to Joseph also by the angel who said, *"...for he shall save his people from their sins"* (Matt. 1:21). The word *Jesus* means Saviour. So the angel will tell the shepherds in Luke 2:11, *"For unto you is born this day in the city of David A SAVIOUR...."* So Mary is to say, *"My spirit hath rejoiced in God my SAVIOUR"* (vs. 47). And Spirit-filled Zacharias will praise the Lord that *"he hath visited and redeemed his people, And hath raised up an HORN OF SALVATION for us"* (vss. 68,69). So when the holy Baby is born, He is given this blessed human name, JESUS (Luke

2:21). And old Simeon will rejoice, "*For mine eyes have seen thy SALVATION*" (Luke 2:30). And Spirit-filled Anna the prophetess gave thanks and "*spake of him to all them that looked for REDEMPTION in Jerusalem*" (Luke 2:38).

Make no mistake, the reason Jesus Christ came to this world was to save sinners. So the Apostle Paul wrote in I Timothy 1:15. So Jesus said, "*I came not to call the righteous, but sinners to repentance*" (Luke 5:32; Matt. 9:13; Mark 2:17).

We do not wonder that the songwriters rejoice in the name of Jesus. They say:

> "Jesus! the very thought of Thee
>   With sweetness fills my breast."
>
> "Jesus, Jesus, Jesus—
>   Sweetest name I know."
>
> "The name of Jesus is so sweet,
>   I love its music to repeat."
>
> "My Jesus I love Thee,
>   I know Thou art mine. . . ."
>
> "Take the name of Jesus with you. . . ."
>
> "Precious name, O how sweet!
>   Hope of earth and joy of Heav'n."

"*He shall be great, and shall be called the Son of the Highest.*" Do not separate the two phrases. They surely refer to the actual deity of Jesus Christ. "*In the beginning was the Word, and the Word was with God, and the Word was God*" (John 1:1). "*Who, being in the form of God, thought it not robbery to be equal with God: But made himself of no reputation, and took upon him the form of a servant, and was made in the likeness of men"* (Phil. 2:6,7). He is not called here *a* Son of God but *THE* Son of the Highest. The greatness of Jesus is not simply human greatness, with its limitations and frailties, relative greatness. No, He has all the power and righteousness and wisdom of God, this Baby to be born! Jesus is *"Son of man,"* but that is taken for granted here: what is clearly stated is that He is the Son of God. He is the promised *"Son"* of Psalm 2:7 and 12.

To Inherit the "Throne of David"

"And the Lord God shall give unto him the throne of his father David." This simply takes up the wonderful covenant God made with David, in II Samuel 7:16: *"And thine house and thy kingdom shall be established for ever before thee: thy throne shall be established for ever."*

That promise is given also in I Chronicles 17:11-14:

"And it shall come to pass, when thy days be expired that thou must go to be with thy fathers, that I will raise up thy seed after thee, which shall be of thy sons; and I will establish his kingdom. He shall build me an house, and I will stablish his throne for ever. I will be his father, and he shall be my son: and I will not take my mercy away from him, as I took it from him that was before thee: But I will settle him in mine house and in my kingdom for ever: and his throne shall be established for evermore."

Note carefully that this promise is not immediately all to Solomon but to *"thy seed after thee,"* after David was to die, *"when thy days be expired that thou must go to be with thy fathers."* Solomon was not established forever. Note also that the promise is future. David already had his throne but it was not then established forever. In the future, under his greater Seed, Jesus, the

throne shall be established forever. That is the promise
given in Isaiah 9:6 and 7:

*"For unto us a child is born, unto us a son is given:
and the government shall be upon his shoulder: and his
name shall be called Wonderful, Counsellor, The mighty
God, The everlasting Father, The Prince of Peace. Of
the increase of his government and peace there shall be
no end, upon the throne of David, and upon his kingdom, to order it, and to establish it with judgment and
with justice from henceforth even for ever. The zeal of
the Lord of hosts will perform this."*

In Isaiah 11 we are told how a sprout will come out
from the stump of the Davidic dynasty, the tree cut
down for a time but later *"a Branch shall grow out of
his roots."* That is Jesus. The Second Psalm is definitely about Jesus, and while verses 1 to 3 speak of
the trial and crucifixion of Jesus, verses 6 and 7, speaking of the future return and reign of Christ, says, *"Yet
have I set my king upon my holy hill of Zion. I will
declare the decree: the Lord hath said unto me, Thou
art my Son; this day have I begotten thee."* Thus we
find the principle, often followed in the Old Testament,
that both the first and second comings of Christ are
mentioned in the same passage. Surely God intended us
to remember that the crucifixion of Christ and even His
ascension, leaving this world full of sin with a corrupt
civilization, a race of Christ-rejecters, is not the end!
Christ will come again to reign on David's throne.

Perhaps, too, the Lord wanted to keep it clear that the
space of time between the first and second comings of
Christ was never foretold, was unpredictable in length,
and all of God's people should be looking continually
for His Second Coming.

That promise that God will *"raise unto David a righteous Branch, and a King shall reign and prosper, and*

shall execute judgment and justice in the earth"—that this King will be *"THE LORD OUR RIGHTEOUS-NESS,"* is foretold in Jeremiah 23:3-6. The restoration of the Davidic kingdom is prophesied further in Ezekiel 34:11-31 and in Ezekiel 37:24 and 25. And Micah 5:2 tells us of the ruler in Israel who will be born in Bethlehem. We know from many Scriptures that this reign of Christ must wait until Christ comes to receive His own in the air, as promised in I Thessalonians 4:16,17 and in I Corinthians 15:51 and 52. And after a honeymoon in Heaven while the Great Tribulation takes place on earth, the Lord will return *"with ten thousands of his saints"* (Jude 14) to destroy His enemies and set up His kingdom on this earth.

Christ's Earthly Kingdom Unending

"And he shall reign over the house of Jacob for ever; and of his kingdom there shall be no end" (vs. 33). The kingdom of the Lord Jesus on earth will be on *"the throne of his father David."* It will involve the regathering of Israel from all countries (Deut. 30:1-6; Isa. 11:10-12; Matt. 24:31 and elsewhere). In Ezekiel 20:33-38, we will find that the remnant of Israel left alive after the tribulation will be brought out of all countries into the *"wilderness of the people,"* and that God will *"purge out from among you the rebels, and them that transgress against me,"* and then establish His kingdom on earth.

Details of Christ's return and the gathering and conversion of Israel are given in Zechariah 12:10; also Israel's mourning and repentance in 12:10; the fountain of salvation opened in the house of David for the inhabitants of Jerusalem in 13:1; Jews facing the wounds in the hands of Jesus in 13:6; Christ's feet on the Mount of Olives in 14:4; His rule over all the earth in 14:9.

The reign of Christ will be *"over the house of Jacob*

for ever.'' Forever? Then how about the one-thousand-
year reign? Is it a set time or is it everlasting? Is it
for a limited time or is it everlasting? It is both! Christ
first will reign on the throne of David in the restoration
of the Davidic kingdom, and the reign is more particularly *"over the house of Jacob"* but worldwide.
After that, the blessed millennial reign of a thousand
years, *"then cometh the end, when he shall have delivered
up the kingdom to God, even the Father"* (I Cor. 15:
24). Then the heavens and the earth will be purged.
They are *"reserved unto fire against the day of judgment and perdition of ungodly men"* (II Pet. 3:7). That
is the time of the last judgment pictured in Revelation
20:11-15. And the new heavens and the new earth,
planted anew like a Garden of Eden, will find that the
heavenly Jerusalem will come down from God out of
Heaven and the tabernacle of God will be with men and
God the Father Himself will join in the eternal reign
(Rev. 21:1-4).

'How should the birth of the Saviour come,' said
Mary, "seeing I know not a man?" The Holy Ghost
would come miraculously upon her and, without a
human father, the Baby would be conceived. And then
again the statement, *"that holy thing which shall be born
of thee shall be called the Son of God."*

So Jesus is called the *"only begotten Son"* (John 3:16),
that is, He is the only one physically begotten of God,
without a human father. Our spiritual birth, when one
is born of God, is a birth of the Spirit (John 3:5). Jesus
is the only one conceived *physically* by the Holy Ghost.

VERSES 36 — 40:

36 And, behold, thy cousin Elisabeth, she hath also conceived a son
in her old age: and this is the sixth
month with her, who was called
barren.
37 For with God nothing shall

be impossible.

38 And Mary said, Behold the handmaid of the Lord; be it unto me according to thy word. And the angel departed from her.

39 And Mary arose in those days, and went into the hill country with haste, into a city of Juda;

40 And entered into the house of Zacharias, and saluted Elisabeth.

Elisabeth and Mary

"*Thy cousin Elisabeth....*" Elisabeth "*was of the daughters of Aaron*" (vs. 5), and Mary is "*of the house of David*" that is, the tribe of Judah (vs. 27). How would they be cousins? Probably because their mothers were from the house of Aaron and the tribe of Levi, but Mary's mother had married a man of the house of David, of the tribe of Judah. If the word literally means cousins in the strict sense which we now usually us it, that could well be.

Mary and Elisabeth seem to have been very close, and both very spiritual, devoted and godly women.

"*For with God nothing shall be impossible.*" That is about the same argument that God used with Abraham and Sarah about the same kind of promised miracle: "*Is any thing too hard for the Lord?*" (Gen. 18:14). And God is here not only stating the miracle of the virgin birth but that God is a God of miracles and Christianity is a religion of miracles.

Mary said, "*Behold the handmaid of the Lord.*" She meant, of course, absolute surrender to the will of God. She said, "*Be it unto me according to thy word.*" In a moment she believed all that the angel told her and s urrendered to the will of God, which was sweet to her.

We are reminded of the words of Saul of Tarsus, converted on the road to Damascus, "*Lord, what wilt thou have me to do?*" (Acts 9:6).

It is not surprising that Mary felt she must see Elisabeth and tell her the blessed news. These two godly women must have greatly influenced and comforted one

another through the years. To Zacharias and Elisabeth
the angel had said, *"for thy prayer is heard"* (vs. 13),
and to Mary he said, *"Thou hast found favour with
God"* (vs. 30). Had they joined in prayer in connection
with the coming Messiah? Was that in their hearts —
Elisabeth that she should bring forth a son who would
be a mighty prophet who never drank but won a multitude of souls, and Mary that mayhap she should become
the mother of the Saviour? There was some sweet tie,
some kinship in their heart's desire and in their prayers.
So in the time of greatest spiritual blessing they sought
each other.

Mary went from Nazareth, up in Galilee, down to the
hill country of Judaea, near Jerusalem. Whether she
went alone, whether she walked or rode a donkey or
camel, we are not told. It is very possible that she
could have gone along in a caravan with some of those
who regularly went as pilgrims to Jerusalem. It is
striking that she did not tell Joseph to whom she was
engaged (vs. 27) but went to tell Elisabeth, of her blessing. To Joseph it became apparent later that Mary
was with child. Then an angel assured him that the
Child was conceived of the Holy Ghost (Matt. 1:20-23).
The indication is that Mary and Elisabeth had been
often together and had shared their faith and their
prayers.

VERSES 41 — 45:

41 And it came to pass, that, when Elisabeth heard the saluta-tion of Mary, the babe leaped in her womb; and Elisabeth was filled with the Holy Ghost:

42 And she spake out with a loud voice, and said, Blessed *art* thou among women, and blessed *is* the fruit of thy womb.

43 And whence *is* this to me, that the mother of my Lord should come to me?

44 For, lo, as soon as the voice of thy salutation sounded in mine

ears, the babe leaped in my womb for joy.
45 And blessed *is* she that be-lieved: for there shall be a perform-ance of those things which were told her from the Lord.

Elisabeth Filled With the Holy Ghost

Mary greeted Elisabeth and the babe, John, leaped in her womb. This amazing child — 'never a greater born of woman,' Jesus said — seems to have been, as far as humanly possible, wholly dedicated to his place as a forerunner of Jesus Christ and to win souls to Him. No drinking, no excesses, no money-making, no marriage, as far as we know, preaching to multitudes with mighty power, and then martyred for Jesus! He was filled with the Holy Ghost from his mother's womb. How marvelous that the unborn child should be moved of God, knowing that Mary was to become the mother of Jesus. So was Mary greeted at Elisabeth's home.

"Elisabeth was filled with the Holy Ghost: And she spake out with a loud voice."

To be filled with the Spirit, uniformly in the Bible, means a special enduement of power to witness for God. So it is in the promise quoted from Joel 2:28-32 in Acts 2:15-18, that the Holy Spirit would come on old men, young men, servants, handmaids, and they would prophesy and witness for God. So did Elisabeth.

She spoke *"with a loud voice,"* with some abandon of her own normal, modest, retiring way, we suppose. So the emotions, divinely stirred and controlled, are used in the witness. So people filled with the Spirit may have a boldness in witnessing which is not usual. In a Free Church in Chicago, we are told that in the midst of a great revival the Swedish saints, praising God, reverted to the mother-tongue of the old country, for the moment not laboring in the hardly learned English language.

So those saved in the house of Cornelius, filled with

the Spirit, praised God *"with tongues"* or literally "with
languages." We suppose it was with various languages
that these Italians living in Palestine and knowing the
Aramaic and using the Aramaic and Greek language
also, praised the Lord. So in Acts 19:1-7, when the
disciples at Ephesus were filled with the Spirit in that
cosmopolitan many-racial city, they spake with tongues
and prophesied, that is, spoke with several languages
and prophesied. No miraculous gift of tongues is
mentioned or necessary in these cases. We are saying
that the freedom and boldness of the fullness of the
Spirit caused Elisabeth to praise the Lord with a loud
voice.

Elisabeth's Spirit - Filled Message

Spirit-filled Elisabeth said to Mary, *"Blessed art thou
among women, and blessed is the fruit of thy womb.
And whence is this to me, that the mother of my Lord
should come to me?"* Notice that this is just as soon as
"Elisabeth heard the salutation of Mary." When Mary
greeted Elisabeth, Elisabeth instantly, by the Holy Spirit,
knew that Mary would be the mother of the Saviour.
You see, to be filled with the Spirit is to *"prophesy,"* that
is, to speak in the power of God, witnessing for Him.
To prophesy is to speak beyond human wisdom, as did
Elisabeth. She witnessed for the coming Messiah and
this indicates to us that Elisabeth was spiritually tuned
to God through much prayer and devotion, so God could
quickly reveal to her His good news.

Elisabeth calls the unborn Child Jesus *"my Lord."* So
we understand her heartfelt trust and surrender to the
coming Saviour. Elisabeth was a born-again child of
God.

We know that spiritually-minded people in the Old
Testament time understood the same Gospel which is
taught in the New Testament. In Acts 10:43 Peter said

to Cornelius, "*To him give all the prophets witness, that through his name whosoever believeth in him shall receive remission of sins.*" So Elisabeth evidently knew the coming Saviour as her own Lord and her surrendered, happy heart, filled with the Spirit, praised Him!

See again verse 44. Verse 41 says, "*the babe leaped in her womb.*" Verse 44 says that the baby, John the Baptist, "*leaped in my womb for joy.*" We must believe that God gave the unborn baby John joy in the prospect of the Saviour whom he would serve.

Through the Holy Spirit, Elisabeth saw this wonderful truth: that Mary had trusted God's Word and fully surrendered to Him. "*Blessed is she that believed.*" We suppose long before this both Elisabeth and Mary had trusted that God would provide the Sacrifice, the Saviour, and now Mary believed the particular promise that she should be the mother of this Saviour and Elisabeth had full assurance of this truth also, though Mary had not yet had a chance to tell her!

VERSES 46 — 56:

46 And Mary said, My soul doth magnify the Lord,

47 And my spirit hath rejoiced in God my Saviour.

48 For he hath regarded the low estate of his handmaiden: for, behold, from henceforth all generations shall call me blessed.

49 For he that is mighty hath done to me great things; and holy is his name.

50 And his mercy is on them that fear him from generation to generation.

51 He hath shewed strength with his arm; he hath scattered the proud in the imagination of their hearts.

52 He hath put down the mighty from *their* seats, and exalted them of low degree.

53 He hath filled the hungry with good things; and the rich he hath sent empty away.

54 He hath holpen his servant Israel, in remembrance of *his* mercy;

55 As he spake to our fathers, to Abraham, and to his seed for ever.

56 And Mary abode with her | to her own house.
about three months, and returned |

The Heartfelt Praise of Mary

Mary said, "*My soul doth magnify the Lord.*" The
term *Lord* is used throughout the New Testament as a
title for Jesus Christ. In the Old Testament it may have
referred sometimes to God the Father or as in Deuteronomy 30:3, "*The Lord...will return...,*" to Jesus
Christ. The loving, surrendered heart of Mary praises
Christ as Lord.

Mary rejoiced in Jesus as "*God my Saviour.*"

She did not say "*the* Saviour," but "*MY Saviour.*"
The only people who need saving are sinners, so Mary
takes her place with the whole human race as a sinner
who must be saved. The idea of Mary being sinless is
not hinted in the Bible. The so-called "Immaculate
Conception," the Romish doctrine that Mary was born
without sin, is a human invention to make Mary an
idol. No, Mary was a sinner like all others, and needed
a Saviour, and here she is praising the unborn Jesus as
"*God my Saviour.*"

Mary was greatly blessed in that she bore the Saviour.
But that was an earthly blessing. The blessing of
eternal life, given to her because she trusted Christ and
so is to be forever with Him and all the saved in
Heaven, is immensely more important than that she
bore the Saviour in her body.

Romish Mariolatry Is Unscriptural

Any effort to make Mary more than just a good
Christian woman, saved by the blood of Christ, is idolatrous and wicked and takes glory from Jesus Christ and
puts it on His mother and that is wrong.

In the Bible, no one was ever encouraged to pray to

Mary. Mary was never recognized as a mediator between Jesus and others. Mary was never called "Mother of God." She was the mother of the human body of Jesus but not the mother of God.

More than once Jesus plainly compared His mother with others who did the will of God.

In Luke 8:19-21 we find that when Jesus' mother and His half brothers wanted to see Him and could not because of the press, and *"it was told him by certain which said, Thy mother and thy brethren stand without, desiring to see thee,"* Jesus answered and said unto them, *"My mother and my brethren are these which hear the word of God, and do it."* This statement is even stronger in Matthew 12:46-50 and in Mark 3:31-35. In Luke 11:27,28 we read, *"And it came to pass, as he spake these things, a certain woman of the company lifted up her voice, and said unto him, Blessed is the womb that bare thee, and the paps which thou hast sucked. But he said, Yea rather, blessed are they that hear the word of God, and keep it."*

It is a greater blessing that anyone should hear the Word of God and keep it, than if one should be physically the mother of Jesus. St. Augustine was right when he said *"that Mary was more blessed in that she believed in Christ than in that she had given Him birth."* (Quoted in the New Confraternity Translation of the Bible, by Catholic scholars.)

Mary had no more special place of honor among the New Testament Christians than other women. The idea that she can answer prayer, that she is the way to Christ, the silly falsehood that her body was taken bodily to Heaven—all these are superstition and idolatry.

Mary took part in the prayer meeting before Pentecost (Acts 1:14). She is never again mentioned in the New Testament and God seems to have taken particular

pains to see that those who would worship Mary have
no excuse for it in the Bible.

Mary rejoiced *"in God my Saviour,"* she said. That
put her in the same blessed class with all poor sinners
who put their trust in Jesus Christ as Saviour.

Christ Came Specially to the Poor Masses

Note the praises of Mary in verses 48 and 49. She
was of a low estate from *"Galilee of the Gentiles"* (Matt.
4:15). Poor, unlettered, of an unknown family, and a
town of poor repute—*"Can any good thing come out of
Nazareth?"* (John 1:46). Now she is exalted and selected
to be the mother of Jesus!

In verses 50 to 53, her praises are for such a God
and such a Saviour who lifts up the poor who trust Him
and brings down the mighty who are arrogant and
proud.

Mary here praises God for the continual process by
which God evens things up for men. The rulers, the
doctors, the lawyers, the prophets of God come principally from the masses of the poor. I think of the pastors
of two of the largest churches in the world—the one was
the son of a small-town barber, now president of his
11 million-member denomination; the other a coal miner,
no college or special training, who came from a humble
home. President Dwight D. Eisenhower came from a
small farm home in Kansas. Lincoln came from a log
cabin. President Nixon came from poverty and obscurity.

On the other hand, the rich man's sons enjoy his
money, his grandchildren spend it and usually the
fourth generation is back in mediocrity. Only where
there is a strong Christian character built in, do riches
and great usefulness extend beyond the third generation.
The success that leads to pride then leads to decline.

Christ came *"to preach the gospel to the poor"* (Luke 4:18). Christ said, *"Blessed be ye poor."*

That He selected Mary to be the mother of Jesus gives encouragement to all the humble and poor and unlettered in the world. The heart of God is open to you if you will but seek His face and please Him, as did Mary.

Mary Knew the Old Testament Promises

But Mary's praises were also for her people, Israel. She is thinking of the salvation of many. She remembers the Abrahamic covenant (see verse 55) that through Abraham's seed all nations of the earth should be blessed. She rejoices that through the Lord Jesus Christ, God's mercy to Israel shall be extended to all the world and forever.

Mary's praises to God for raising her out of obscurity and poverty and giving her great blessing remind us of the praises of Hannah, when God, in answer to prayer, gave her a son. Read I Samuel 2:1-10. She, too, said, *"My heart rejoiceth in the Lord."* She, too, told how God lifts up the humble and how He brings down the proud; how *"He raiseth up the poor out of the dust, and lifteth up the beggar from the dunghill, to set them among princes..."* (I Sam. 2:8). We wonder if Mary may not have been familiar with that wonderful passage. The gratitude of a heart who receives a Son from the Lord is kin to that of barren Hannah who was made so glad after long delay, by the birth of Samuel.

VERSES 57 — 66:

57 Now Elisabeth's full time came that she should be delivered; and she brought forth a son.

58 And her neighbours and her cousins heard how the Lord had shewed great mercy upon her; and

they rejoiced with her.

59 And it came to pass, that on the eighth day they came to [h]circumcise the child; and they called him Zacharias, after the name of his father.

60 And his mother answered and said, Not so; but he shall be called John.

61 And they said unto her, There is none of thy kindred that is called by this name.

62 And they made signs to his father, how he would have him called.

63 And he asked for a writing table, and wrote, saying, His name is John. And they marvelled all.

64 And his mouth was opened immediately, and his tongue *loosed*, and he spake, and praised God.

65 And fear came on all that dwelt round about them: and all these sayings were noised abroad throughout all the hill country of Judæa.

66 And all they that heard *them* laid *them* up in their hearts, saying, What manner of child shall this be! And the hand of the Lord was with him.

The Birth of John the Baptist

Mary stayed three months with Elisabeth, after Elisabeth was six months pregnant (vss. 36,56). Evidently that brought her right to the time of the birth of John and perhaps Mary stayed for that event. After her return to her own house at Nazareth (vs. 56), it would become obvious to her neighbors and to Joseph, her espoused, her fiance, that she was with child and then would follow the distress of Joseph and the revelation by the angel, in a dream to Joseph, as we are told in the first chapter of Matthew.

We are not told the praises of Elisabeth, after the birth of her son, but we know the gladness of her heart when her neighbors and her cousins *"rejoiced with her."* Her rejoicing over the child continued from the first word she had that John was to be given her (vs. 25).

The child was named John. First the mother insisted upon it (vs. 60); then the father, when kindly relatives and friends wanted to name the child Zacharias after his father or some other relative, *"asked for a writing table, and wrote, saying, His name is John."* He did not say his name *shall* be John. His name was *already* John. John is the English way of saying the Hebrew word Johanan and the word means "Jehovah is gracious." But most of the world knows the meaning of the name according to John 1:6, *"There was a man sent from God, whose name was John,"* so the word to most people means *"a man sent from God."* This commentator was named John at my birth and later I learned that my father and mother gave me to God to be a gospel preacher then. In an old, old Bible left by my father, I found heavily underlined in ink these words in Luke 1:63, *"His name is John."*

Now that the baby was born, Zacharias' tongue was loosed and how he praised God! Rumors went through all the country about this wonderful child, born of a father and mother long after they were too old to expect a child naturally, a child filled with the Holy Ghost from his mother's womb, promised to be a forerunner of the Messiah!

And we read, *"The hand of the Lord was with him."* It would have to be so since he was *"filled with the Holy Ghost, even from his mother's womb."*

We are reminded about Joseph, *"And the Lord was with Joseph, and he was a prosperous man."* And again, *"And his master saw that the Lord was with him, and that the Lord made all that he did to prosper in his hand"* (Gen. 39:2,3). And again, *"But the Lord was with Joseph, and shewed him mercy, and gave him favour in the sight of the keeper of the prison. And the keeper of the prison committed to Joseph's hand all the prisoners that were in the prison; and whatsoever they did there, he was the doer of it. The keeper of the prison looked not to any thing that was under his hand;*

*because the Lord was with him, and that which he did,
the Lord made it to prosper"* (Gen. 39:21-23).

So it was with David, too, when he was anointed king,
the shepherd boy, not yet known and approved as
destined to be king of Israel and ancestor of the coming
Saviour.   When David was anointed, *"The Spirit of
the Lord came upon David from that day forward"*
(I Sam. 16:13).

VERSES 67 — 80:

67 And his father Zacharias was filled with the Holy Ghost, and prophesied, saying,
68 Blessed be the Lord God of Israel; for he hath visited and redeemed his people,
69 And hath raised up an horn of salvation for us in the house of his servant David;
70 As he spake by the mouth of his holy prophets, which have been since the world began:
71 That we should be saved from our enemies, and from the hand of all that hate us;
72 To perform the mercy *promised* to our fathers, and to remember his holy covenant;
73 The oath which he sware to our father Abraham,
74 That he would grant unto us, that we being delivered out of the hand of our enemies might serve him without fear,
75 In holiness and righteousness before him, all the days of our life.
76 And thou, child, shalt be called the prophet of the Highest: for thou shalt go before the face of the Lord to prepare his ways;
77 To give knowledge of salvation unto his people by the remission of their sins,
78 Through the tender mercy of our God; whereby the dayspring from on high hath visited us,
79 To give light to them that sit in darkness and *in* the shadow of death, to guide our feet into the way of peace.
80 And the child grew, and waxed strong in spirit, and was in the deserts till the day of his shewing unto Israel.

Spirit- Filled Zacharias

"Zacharias was filled with the Holy Ghost," says

verse 67.   We come again to the theme so prominent in Luke. John was to be *"filled with the Holy Ghost, even from his mother's womb"* (vs. 15). *"Elisabeth was filled with the Holy Ghost"* (vs. 41). We should look then for the emphasis through the book of Luke on people being filled with the Spirit to witness for Christ.

"Zacharias was filled with the Holy Ghost, and prophesied." Witnessing, in the power of the Spirit, always follows people filled with the Spirit. Not till the resurrection of Jesus would the Holy Spirit take up His abode in the bodies of Christians (John 7:37–39; 20:22; Rom. 8:9; I Cor. 3:16,17; I Cor. 6:19,20) but the Holy Spirit came *"upon"* Christians in power to witness for God in prophecy or to act for God, all through the Old Testament. To the seventy elders selected to help Moses, God promised, *"I will take of the spirit which is upon thee, and will put it upon them; and they shall bear the burden of the people with thee, that thou bear it not thyself alone"* (Num. 11:17). And verse 25 tells us that God did so. Then verse 26 reminds us of Eldad and Medad: *"And the spirit rested upon them; and they were of them that were written, but went not out unto the tabernacle: and they prophesied in the camp. And there ran a young man, and told Moses, and said, Eldad and Medad do prophesy in the camp."*

We know that the Spirit of the Lord came upon the great prophets from time to time. Elisha begged that a double portion of the Spirit that was on Elijah should rest on him and received the blessing (II Kings 2:9-15). Of Samson we read more than once that *"the Spirit of the Lord came mightily upon him"* (Judg. 14:6,19; 15: 14). And the angel's promise that John the Baptist would be *"filled with the Holy Ghost, even from his mother's womb,"* was enlarged: *"And he shall go before him in the spirit and power of Elias."* So Spirit-filled Elijah was a pattern for Spirit-filled John the

Baptist. Thus Elisabeth and Zacharias were filled with
the Spirit on occasion and prophesied for God.

Zacharias said, "*Blessed be the Lord God of Israel;
for he hath visited and redeemed his people, And hath
raised up an horn of salvation for us....*" He knew
that the great central theme of John the Baptist should
be salvation, and that the birth of John the Baptist
guaranteed the birth of the Saviour soon thereafter.

Zacharias was mindful of the covenant which God had
made to David and his seed (vs. 69). He was aware
that this promise was repeated in many of the prophecies
of the Old Testament (vs. 70). He remembered the
promise that Israel should be restored, and the covenant
with Abraham (vs. 73); so by faith and by the illumi-
nation of the Spirit, he looked forward to the time of the
millennium when Christ is to reign, when Israel is to be
restored.

Is all this connected with salvation? Oh, yes. The
resurrection of the Christian's body is a part of salvation. Now we have only the firstfruits, but we will
have the finished salvation. Romans 8:23 and 24 tells
us, "*And not only they, but ourselves also, which have
the firstfruits of the Spirit, even we ourselves groan within ourselves, waiting for the adoption, to wit, the redemption of our body. For we are saved by hope: but hope
that is seen is not hope: for what a man seeth, why doth
he yet hope for?*" Salvation is not only a present
possession; it is a blessed hope of the future when salvation shall be completed in the resurrection of the body
and then in the restoration of a righteous government in
the world, and eventually in the Garden of Eden restored
on the earth!

Note from verse 75 that Zacharias understands that
the kingdom of Christ on David's throne and the restoration of Israel will be "*in holiness and righteousness.*"
And John the Baptist was to be "*the prophet of the*

Highest" going before the Lord (vs. 76). And verse 77 foresees the tremendous evangelistic ministry of John the Baptist winning thousands as is promised by the angel. Note in verse 78 the name for Jesus, *"dayspring from on high."* Oh, what mercy that God should send His Son!

The world is in such darkness of sin, but Christ is to *"give light to them that sit in darkness and in the shadow of death, to guide our feet into the way of peace."*

This wonderful child John *"grew, and waxed strong in spirit, and was in the deserts till the day of his shewing unto Israel,"* we suppose when he was about thirty years old.

LUKE 2

VERSES 1, 2:

AND it came to pass in those days, that there went out a decree from Cæsar Augustus, that all the world should be taxed.

2 (*And* this taxing was first made when Cyrenius was governor of Syria.)

God Has an Emperor Help Fulfill Prophecy

Caesar Augustus was emperor at Rome. In a strong, sensible rule he had brought a large degree of peace throughout the Roman Empire and now he made a decree that "*all the world should be taxed.*" "*All the world*" is from a Greek term used thirteen times in the New Testament for the habitable earth, primarily the Roman Empire. It did not include the Far East, Northern Europe, and other outlying districts but it did include Southern Europe, even including Southern England, North Africa, Palestine and the Balkan States, Persia and even down to India.

It was probably in the year 4 or 5 B.C. when Jesus was born. Although our calendar is based on time since the birth of Christ, those who long later calculated the time of Christ's birth missed it a few years as is now generally known.

"*To be taxed.*" But the American Standard Version says "enrolled." Actually they went to register for taxation.

How wonderful that the world emperor, without knowing it, was used of God to fulfill the Scriptures! It is written in Micah 5:2, "*But thou, Beth-lehem Ephratah, though thou be little among the thousands of Judah, yet out of thee shall he come forth unto me that is to be ruler in Israel; whose goings forth have been from of old, from everlasting.*" So the Saviour must be born in Bethlehem. Joseph and Mary are of the house and lineage of David, so they must go back to Bethlehem, David's ancestral home, to register for the taxation and thus the Scripture will be fulfilled. The Lord Jesus will bear the reproach of growing up in that half-Gentile country province of Galilee, away from the great center of religious leadership in Jerusalem and away from the great centers of learning and commerce, Damascus, Athens, Ephesus, Corinth, and Rome. But He must be born in Bethlehem, the ancestral home of David. We remember that *"the king's heart is in the hand of the Lord, as the rivers of water: he turneth it whithersoever he will"* (Prov. 21:1).

By seven years of awful debasement, Nebuchadnezzar learned *"that the most High ruleth in the kingdom of men, and giveth it to whomsoever he will, and setteth up over it the basest of men"* (Dan. 4:17,25,30,32). So a decree of a world emperor is made to help bring to pass the human birth of the Baby Jesus, the Creator and Saviour of the world!

We are reminded that Pilate had Jesus scourged (John 19:1), not knowing that he was fulfilling Isaiah 53:5, *"...and with his stripes we are healed."* The high priest and members of the Sanhedrin spit in Jesus' face *"and buffeted him; and others smote him with the palms of their hands."* The soldiers crowned Him with thorns and *"spit upon him, and took the reed, and smote him on the head"* (Matt. 26:67; 27:29,30 and John 19:2 and 3) and so abused and bruised the poor, swollen face of Jesus that Isaiah 52:14 was fulfilled saying, *"...many were astonied at thee; his visage was so marred more than any man, and his form more than the sons of men."* And when the chief priests insisted that they should break the legs of Jesus and of the two thieves so that the crucifixion would be over by sundown when the high Sabbath would begin, one soldier finding that Jesus was dead already disregarded their plea and *"with a spear pierced his side, and forthwith came there out blood and water"* (John 19:34), not knowing that he was thus fulfilling Psalm 34:20 and Zechariah 12:10, *"They shall look upon me whom they have pierced,"* and the passover lamb ruling, *"neither shall ye break a bone thereof"* (Exod. 12:46; Num. 9:12).

Oh, we may be sure that in all the universe there is none so mighty or strong that he can resist the plan of God. God makes alike the emperor, the angry priests and the illiterate soldier to bring about the fulfillment of the Scriptures. So when Caesar Augustus decrees it, Mary and Joseph will go to Bethlehem and there the Saviour will be born, fulfilling Micah 5:2.

Cyrenius, Governor of Syria

"(And this taxing was first made when Cyrenius was governor of Syria.)" Cyrenius is the Greek spelling of Quirinius, a Latin name. He was governor of Syria, which then included Phoenicia and Judaea and so was above King Herod of Judaea. Some have objected that they know of no governorship by Cyrenius until some years later. But Norval Geldenhuys in *The New International Commentary on the Gospel of Luke,* page 100, says:

> Luke describes this taxing as "the first" and states that it took place when Quirinius was governor of Syria. He calls it "the first enrolment" to distinguish it from the well-known enrolment in A. D. 6 of which he makes mention in Acts v. 37. Of this "first enrolment" we have no other direct mention outside the New Testament. There is, however, no cogent reason why doubt should be cast on Luke here. There is inscriptional evidence. Quirinius was governor of Syria for some time in the first decade B C. as well as from A. D. 6 to 9.

Scholars will remember that Sir William Ramsey proved that Luke was the most reliable historian of that century, even by human standards. And Bishop Ryle says:

> Some say that there were two taxings, in both of which Cyrenius was officially concerned, though not exactly in the same capacity on both occasions, -- and that St. Luke was aware of this, and expressly inserts the word "first" to show which of the two taxings he meant. In favour of this view, it must be remembered that St. Luke was infinitely more likely to be correct about a matter of fact, than any uninspired historians, and that we have no right to assume, where he differs from them, that they are correct, and he incorrect. Moreover, it is a striking fact, that Justin Martyr, who lived in the second century, distinctly asserts three times that Christ was born under Cyrenius. Wordsworth says that, "the researches of Zumpt have enhanced the probability that Quirinius, who was governor of Cicilia, was also governor of Syria at the time of the nativity."

But our confidence is in the simple statement of the inspired Word of God itself and we are certain it is absolutely accurate.

VERSES 3 — 5:

3 And all went to be taxed, every one into his own city.
4 And Joseph also went up from Galilee, out of the city of Nazareth, into Judæa, unto the city of David, which is called Bethlehem; (be-cause he was of the house and lineage of David:)
5 To be taxed with Mary his espoused wife, being great with child.

Joseph and Mary to Bethlehem

Joseph and Mary left Nazareth to go seventy-five or eighty miles or more down to Bethlehem, south of Jerusalem. If they came over to the Jordan River valley and down that water-level route which was easier traveling, as most people did, it was further. We do not know whether they walked or whether, as we are accus-

tomed to seeing it pictured, Mary rode a donkey while
Joseph walked beside her.   They may have come in a
caravan, since many went to Jerusalem.

Joseph was *"of the house and lineage of David."*   The
lineage of David is given in Matthew 1:1-16, where we
are told that *"Jacob begat Joseph the husband of Mary,
of whom was born Jesus, who is called Christ."*   Joseph
was not named here as the actual father of Jesus but as
the legal parent.   The Scripture takes care here not to
say that Joseph begat Jesus, so acknowledging the virgin
birth.   From Ruth 1:2 we read of Elimelech and his wife
Naomi and their two sons *"of Beth-lehem-judah."*   When
Elimelech and the sons died, Naomi returned from the
country of Moab with Ruth.   But when Boaz took Ruth
as a wife, he bought also *"a parcel of land, which was
our brother Elimelech's"* near Bethlehem (Ruth 4:3).
Then of Boaz and Ruth was born Obed, the father of
Jesse and grandfather of David.   So back to Bethlehem
in the province of Judaea, the city of David, must come
Joseph and Mary to be enrolled for taxation.

Note verse 5 says that Mary was Joseph's *"ESPOUSED
wife, being great with child."*   She was still only in status
as engaged to Joseph, not being actually a wife.   The
marriage had not been consummated.   For it was
prophesied in Isaiah 7:14 and quoted in Matthew 1:23,
*"Behold, a virgin shall be with child, and shall bring
forth a son."*   And we are told that when Joseph *"took
unto him his wife,"* Mary, he *"knew her not till she had
brought forth her firstborn son"* (Matt. 1:24,25).   The
Baby Jesus was conceived in the womb of a virgin and
born while Mary was still a virgin.   She was only
Joseph's *"espoused"* or engaged wife.

How long were they in Bethlehem before the Saviour
was born?   We do not know.   Probably not long.

One commentator thinks probably God had so arranged
it and possibly Joseph and Mary had that in mind that
if they were away from all their relatives and friends

when the Saviour was born, it would not be particularly noted that the Baby was born only six months after the marriage ceremony and thus Mary may have escaped much of the scorn and gossip which she would have suffered had the Saviour been born in Nazareth. In truth, it seems impressive that only once is the suspicion recorded that Jesus was *"born of fornication"* (John 8:41).

VERSES 6, 7:

6 And so it was, that, while they were there, the days were accomplished that she should be delivered.
7 And she brought forth her firstborn son, and wrapped him in swaddling clothes, and laid him in a manger; because there was no room for them in the inn.

Jesus Born in a Stable, No Room in the Inn

David had many descendants and many of them were more wealthy and prominent than Joseph and Mary. The inn in the place was crowded. So the Lord Jesus was born in a stable and laid in a manger. We suppose that the inn was a khan or caravansary, a stone rectangle of buildings with a wide gate, where caravans stopped. There would be mangers to feed their animals and inn rooms for the people. But these rooms were all full. In the *International Standard Bible Encyclopedia,* Christie thinks that at this time of the year most of the animals were in the fields and so there was room in a stable for Mary and Joseph and where the Baby Jesus was born and laid in a manger. Tourists now see the ruins of one such "inn" near "Solomon's Pools," below Bethlehem.

In Bethlehem today a cave is shown as the place where the Saviour was born and two churches, one Greek and one Roman Catholic, are built above it.

About the year 324 A.D. St. Helena, mother of Emperor
Constantine, came to Palestine and selected this cave as
the birthplace of the Saviour and over it was built the
Church of the Nativity.   However, in the more than
three centuries that had elapsed since the birth of the
Saviour, war had devastated the land again and again.
In A.D. 70 and again in A.D. 135, Jerusalem was utterly
destroyed.   Jews had been scattered out to all the nations;
not a house in Jerusalem had been left standing and it
is unlikely that any was left in Bethlehem six miles away.
About the year 324 A.D. Helena selected the site for the
Church of the Holy Sepulchre in Jerusalem, also claimed
to stand over the place of the crucifixion and tomb of
Jesus.   She claimed supernatural signs showed her
where to build. And again she selected the place for the
Church of the Annunciation in Nazareth. Of course, no
history, sacred or secular, names the spot of the annunciation.   Roman tradition is notoriously unreliable.
The Scripture says nothing about Jesus being born in a
cave.   In Matthew 2:11 the wise men found the Baby
Jesus in a house.

It seems likely that the Lord deliberately planned it
so none could ever know the exact spot of the birth of
Jesus nor of His crucifixion nor of His burial. It
seems probable to me that Gordon's Calvary and the
Garden Tomb nearby were the real sites of the death of
Christ and His burial, but centuries of tradition and the
weight of Rome denies it and so people generally are
not sure.   God knew, no doubt, that people would
worship a place instead of the Saviour and such a
place would become a snare and an idol, even as it was
with the brazen serpent of Numbers 21:5-9, which in the
days of Hezekiah must be broken in pieces because *"the
children of Israel did burn incense to it: and he called
it Nehushtan"* (II Kings 18:4).   And Jesus told the
woman of Samaria that *"the hour cometh, when ye shall
neither in this mountain, nor yet at Jerusalem, worship*

the Father....But the hour cometh, and now is, when the true worshippers shall worship the Father in spirit and in truth: for the Father seeketh such to worship him" (John 4:21,23).   It is heart worship God wants, not place worship.   It is interesting to see the cave in Bethlehem where rich kings have made their gifts, where church dignitaries and monks and priests have fought over the right to have processions and burn candles and hang expensive lamps.   But Jesus was born to all the world, and the fact is far more important than a cave or a house.

"No Room in the Inn"

"There was no room for them in the inn."   So this world is revealed as not favoring the Saviour.   Here is symbolized the fact of John 1:11, *"He came unto his own, and his own received him not."*   He is to be *"despised and rejected of men; a man of sorrows, and acquainted with grief"* (Isa. 53:3).   King Herod will try to kill the Baby Jesus.   Pharisees will seek to stone Him and be supernaturally restrained (John 8:59). And the furious townsmen of Nazareth where He was brought up later tried to rush Him to the hill to cast Him down headlong (Luke 4:29,30).   And at last Herod and Pontius Pilate and the rulers of the Jews and the mob of people will all combine to have Him scourged and crowned with thorns and crucified.   It is symbolic that *"there was no room for them in the inn."*

I wonder, did the Baby Jesus, pricked by the straw in that rough bed and wrapped in swaddling clothes, know that there was no room for Him in this wicked world?

When this writer was a boy four years old, in a country church Sunday school a good man gathered us little ones around his knees in the "card class" and taught us this lesson.   On the colored picture card was a picture of Joseph, Mary, a manger, the Baby Jesus and, I think, a donkey, and the hay was about.   And the

"Golden Text" was, "*There was no room for them in the inn.*" And some way my four-year-old heart burned with an awful sense of the wickedness of mankind. My sister and I had a little trundle bed which in the daytime folded up and rolled under Mother's and Daddy's bed and everybody at our house slept in comfortable beds, but there was no bed for the Baby Jesus! What a wicked world it must be that had no room for Jesus!

And, oh, before we leave this pungent phrase from the Scripture, let everyone make sure—have you made room in your heart for Jesus?

No beautiful chamber, No soft cradle bed,
No place but a manger, Nowhere for His head;
No praises of gladness, No tho't of their sin,
No glory but sadness, No room in the inn.

No sweet consecration, No seeking His part,
No humiliation, No place in the heart;
No tho't of the Saviour, No sorrow for sin,
No pray'r for His favor, No room in the inn.

No one to receive Him, No welcome while here,
No balm to relieve Him, No staff but a spear;
No seeking His treasure, No weeping for sin,
No doing His pleasure, No room in the inn.

No room, no room for Jesus,
    Oh, give Him welcome free,
Lest you should hear at Heaven's gate,
    "There is no room for thee."

Mary Was to Have Other Children

Mary's "*firstborn son.*" If the Scripture had said,

"She brought forth her son," the indication might mean her only son. But when she brought forth her *"firstborn son,"* the indication is there were to be others. Actually, after Jesus was born, Mary and Joseph had a normal life as husband and wife and had a family of children. The Catholic tradition that Mary was a perpetual virgin and had no other children is wrong. The children of the family are mentioned in Matthew 13:55 and 56: *"Is not this the carpenter's son? is not his mother called Mary? and his brethren, James, and Joses, and Simon, and Judas? And his sisters, are they not all with us?"* These four men are called his brothers in Matthew 12:46; Mark 3:31; Luke 8:19. Catholic tradition would like to make these "brethren" simply kinsmen, cousins. But the Messianic Psalm 69, in a passage referring to Jesus, says, *"I am become a stranger unto my brethren, and an alien unto my mother's children."* So James, Simon, Joses and Judas (or Jude), were children of Joseph and Mary, half brothers of Jesus. The sisters are not named.

James, the Lord's brother (Gal. 1:19), is the apostle who seems to have presided in the council at Jerusalem in Acts 15:13. James, the brother of John, was killed by Herod in Acts 12:2. This James wrote the book of James, and his brother (the Lord's half brother) Jude wrote the book of Jude (Jude 1). All the efforts to deify Mary, to make her a mediator, one who hears prayers, is idolatry and unscriptural.

VERSES 8, 9:

8 And there were in the same country shepherds abiding in the field, keeping watch over their flock by night.

9 And, lo, the angel of the Lord came upon them, and the glory of the Lord shone round about them: and they were sore afraid.

The Shepherds

They were "*in the same country,*" that is, near Bethlehem. It may well have been the "Shepherds' Field" now shown to us when we visit there. Some tradition says that this was the field of Boaz where Ruth gleaned (Ruth 2), perhaps the field where David kept his father's sheep. We cannot be sure of any of that but it was near Bethlehem. The shepherds were "*abiding in the field.*" There are caves in that traditional field where the shepherds might have camped very comfortably, keeping watch over their flocks, caring for baby lambs, etc.

Is it not wonderful that God chose to announce the birth of the Saviour to humble shepherds? Not to the chief priests, the Sanhedrin, religious leaders in Jerusalem; not to King Herod, not to Emperor Augustus, not to the wealthy, not to the wise, but to the humble shepherds, His birth was announced.

It is true the message of salvation is "*good tidings of great joy, WHICH SHALL BE TO ALL PEOPLE*" (vs. 10), but if the announcement were to the select elite, it would not seem to be for all people. No, it was for the masses, the poor, the illiterate, the sinful, the nobodies.

How often does this emphasis appear, and particularly in Luke's Gospel! So in Mary's praises she said, "*He hath regarded the low estate of his handmaiden*" (Luke 1:48), and "*He hath put down the mighty from their seats, and exalted them of low degree. He hath filled the hungry with good things; and the rich he hath sent empty away*" (vss. 52,53). So Jesus came, especially anointed to "*preach the gospel to the poor...heal the brokenhearted, to preach deliverance to the captives, and recovering of sight to the blind, to set at liberty them that are bruised*" (Luke 4:18). So, blessed, Jesus said, are the poor, the hungry, the weeping, the hated (Luke 6:20-22). And Jesus, in the parable of the man who made a great supper, and some invited would not come, said the master of the house commanded, "*Go out quickly into the streets and lanes of the city, and bring in hither the poor, and the maimed, and the halt, and the blind*" (Luke 14:21). God wanted to make it clear, even in His announcement to the shepherds, that God loved the whole world and that salvation was for "whosoever." How that fits with the character of Jesus who is "*meek and lowly in heart*" (Matt. 11:29) to all who approach Him! We do not wonder that we read in Luke 15:1, "*Then drew near unto him all the publicans and sinners for to hear him,*" and in Mark 12:37, "*The common people heard him gladly.*" Oh, it is good that the angels brought the message to the shepherds. Jesus came not just for good people, not just for educated people, not just for leaders, but to the multitudes.

The Angel

Note it is "*THE angel,*" not simply "AN angel," probably the same Angel Gabriel who came to Mary (Luke 1:26), and to distressed Joseph (Matt. 1:20).

VERSES 10–14:

10 And the angel said unto them, Fear not: for, behold, I bring you good tidings of great joy, which shall be to all people.

11 For unto you is born this day in the city of David a Saviour, which is Christ the Lord.

12 And this *shall* be a sign unto you; Ye shall find the babe wrapped in swaddling clothes, lying in a manger.

13 And suddenly there was with the angel a multitude of the heavenly host praising God, and saying,

14 Glory to God in the highest, and on earth peace, good will toward men.

The Angel's Message: A Saviour

The angel's message was "*tidings of great joy.*" So we do not wonder that the Gospel is the "Good News," as the Greek word literally means. Then the preacher, the Sunday school teacher, the personal soul winner, the seminary professor, ought always to remember this is not a dry-as-dust theology, but this is a glorious, heart-warming, soul-rejoicing thing we deal with when we teach the Word of God and preach the Gospel. Oh, shame that for some preachers and teachers the glow has gone, the honeymoon is over, the thrill has long since given way to the routine matter-of-factness which is far less than the "*good tidings of great joy.*"

This message is "*to all people.*" Not to an elite group included, some suppose, in a "limited atonement." No, the "*whosoever*" in the Gospel is an honest one and the love and grace of God is not limited nor is His invitation limited. So, it is "*to all people.*"

And this good news is that a Saviour is born! The angel does not announce that this Baby Jesus will change the course of human history. That is incidental. He does not mention that the art, the literature, the education, the benevolences of the whole world will be colored, influenced, and formed by this same Baby Jesus. The angel does not mention that slavery will tend to disappear, that monogyny will take the place of plural wives, that schools, hospitals, orphanages and relief programs around the world will flow forth from the influence of the Child born that day in Bethlehem. Oh, no, all these are incidental to the one great end—the Lord Jesus came to be a Saviour. Christian workers should put first what God puts first. This is why the human name, Jesus, was given Him by the angel, both in speaking to Mary (Luke 1:31) and to Joseph (Matt. 1:21,25), because *Jesus* means "Saviour." And we miss the whole point of the Scriptures and of the incarnation of the Saviour, and His work, if we do not remember that the one thing dearest to the heart of God is to save sinners, and the one principal work of Christians is to win souls to know the Saviour. So one lost sheep is to get more attention than ninety-nine that are safe in the fold, and one sinner repenting brings more joy in Heaven than ninety-nine just persons who need no repentance (Luke 15:1-8).

No good news could ever come to any man like the good news of forgiveness of sin, salvation, redemption, being reconciled to God, having a home in Heaven, and everlasting life!

"Christ the Lord"

This Saviour is *"Christ the Lord."* The word *Christ* is the Greek form of the Hebrew *Messiah,* meaning "the anointed." The term *Christ* had become familiar to the Jews, from the Old Testament prophecies, first in Psalm 2:2, *"...Lord, and against his anointed,"* and then from the type of the high priests anointing David to be king and the frequent reference to *"mine anointed."* Among Jewish leaders accustomed to the terminology *"mine anointed,"* referring to kings, priests, to Cyrus (Isa. 45: 1), and prophets, it indicated to the spiritually minded that a Messiah, an anointed Christ, the Lord, would come.

Now we may expect to find hundreds of times throughout the New Testament that Jesus is called *"the Lord."* The Greek term is *kurios,* Lord, Sir, Master. And the very term involves that claim of the resurrected Christ to His disciples, *"All power is given unto me in heaven and in earth,"* that is, all authority.

"The glory of the Lord shone round about them," when the angel appeared. We are reminded of the Shekinah glory in the Tabernacle and the Temple, over the Ark of the Covenant; of the pillar of fire in the night and the glorious cloud by day that led the children of Israel. We are reminded of the transfiguration of Jesus when *"his face did shine as the sun, and his raiment was white as the light"* (Matt. 17:2). And we are reminded of the shining face of Moses when he

came down from Mount Sinai (Exod. 34:29,30). We
are reminded that when *"the angel of the Lord descended
from heaven, and came and rolled back the stone from
the door, and sat upon it, His countenance was like
lightning, and his raiment white as snow: And for fear
of him the keepers did shake, and became as dead men"*
at the empty tomb of Jesus (Matt. 28:2-4)! It may be
part of that light was what made the face of the martyr
Stephen like the face of an angel (Acts 6:15). We
remember that when the resurrected Jesus appeared to
John on the isle of Patmos giving the revelation, *"His
eyes were as a flame of fire; And his feet like unto fine
brass, as if they burned in a furnace. . .and his countenance was as the sun shineth in his strength"* (Rev. 1:
14-16).

They Could Find the Baby Jesus!

*"Ye shall find the babe wrapped in swaddling clothes
. . . ."*
They need not doubt the message for they can prove
it to themselves.   They can go and see the Baby in a
manger, wrapped in swaddling clothes!
So, doubting Thomas, who could not believe that
Christ was risen from the dead, was met a week later by
the resurrected Saviour and was sweetly invited to *"reach
hither thy finger, and behold my hands; and reach
hither thy hand, and thrust it into my side: and be not
faithless, but believing"* (John 20:27). So, the man who
wills, or chooses to *"do his will, he shall know of the
doctrine, whether it be of God"* (John 7:17). And
"Then shall we know, if we follow on to know the Lord"
(Hos. 6:3). Here is the blessed truth: *"Draw nigh to
God, and he will draw nigh to you"* and *"humble
yourselves in the sight of the Lord, and he shall lift you
up"* (Jas. 4:8,10).
Thank God, one can always know whether the Bible
is true, whether Christ is a Saviour, whether God keeps

His promises. So Jesus said to Andrew, and Philip said to Nathanael, "*Come and see*" (John 1:39,46).

"Let All the Angels of God Worship Him"

"*And suddenly there was with the angel a multitude of the heavenly host.*" Of the millions of angels, "*ten thousand times ten thousand, and thousands of thousands*" (Rev. 5:11), multitudes of them were present to praise the Lord. Their glory would fill the sky! Here is fulfilled the statement which Hebrews 1:6 quotes from the Old Testament, "*And again, when he bringeth in the firstbegotten into the world, he saith, And let all the angels of God worship him.*" That quote is from Deuteronomy 32:43, in the Septuagint translation into the Greek. And if all these millions of angels of God did not take part in the presence of the shepherds in the hallelujah that a Saviour was born, then wherever they were in all the universe of God they made it glorious with their praises of the Saviour! The birth of the Saviour meant glory to God in the loving praise of forgiven millions who will be in Heaven.

And the message is, "*And on earth peace, good will toward men.*" It is true that God here shows His goodwill to men, and His eventual promise of peace when Christ the "*Prince of Peace*" (Isa. 9:6) begins to reign. But the translation of the American Standard Version is probably better, "*Peace to men of good will.*" For "*there is no peace, saith my God, to the wicked*" (Isa. 57:21), but only to men of good will. And to the believer here is all the sweet comfort of John 14:1, "*Let not your heart be troubled,*" and of 14:27, "*Peace I leave with you, my peace I give unto you: not as the world giveth, give I unto you. Let not your heart be troubled, neither let it be afraid.*" There is a way of perfect peace for the Christian who takes his burdens to God and thus lays aside his cares (Phil. 4:6,7). It is not surprising that nearly all the epistles in the New

Testament give in the salutation, "*Grace be unto you, and peace, from God our Father, and from the Lord Jesus Christ,*" or some similar statements.   The angel host offers peace to men of good will.

VERSES 15—20:

15 And it came to pass, as the angels were gone away from them into heaven, the shepherds said one to another, Let us now go even unto Bethlehem, and see this thing which is come to pass, which the Lord hath made known unto us.

16 And they came with haste, and found Mary, and Joseph, and the babe lying in a manger.

17 And when they had seen *it*, they made known abroad the saying which was told them concerning this child.

18 And all they that heard *it* wondered at those things which were told them by the shepherds.

19 But Mary kept all these things, and pondered *them* in her heart.

20 And the shepherds returned, glorifying and praising God for all the things that they had heard and seen, as it was told unto them.

The Shepherds Hasten to See
the Baby Jesus and Tell It

Why were these particular shepherds selected out of all the multitude of the poor and unlettered and unknown? Probably because these were believing shepherds.   They may have already come to know the Lord through faith in the coming Messiah.   Note how instantly they believed and said, "*Let us now go even unto Bethlehem, and see this thing which is come to pass, which the Lord hath made known unto us.*"   No doubting, no questioning!

Note also that *they wanted to see the Saviour.*   Not like the chief priests and scribes of Matthew 2:4-6 who could tell the wise men that the Saviour would be born in Bethlehem as promised in Micah 5:2, but they themselves went not to see Him.   Not like King Herod himself who heard and was troubled and not joyful but sent soldiers to kill the Baby Jesus! Oh, these shepherds had a heart to hear the Gospel and you may be sure that God's good news goes to those who have hearts for it.

How often did Jesus say, "*Who hath ears to hear, let him hear*" (Matt. 13:9; 13:43; Mark 4:9; 4:23; 7:14; Luke 8:8; 14:35; and eight times in the book of Revelation)! And how often the Scripture complains that people's ears are dull of hearing! These shepherds heard gladly because they delighted in the thought that they could now see the Saviour Himself.

"*They came with haste.*" What a glad urgency! So when the angel of the Lord told Philip to join himself to the chariot of the Ethiopian eunuch, he ran (Acts 8:30). So Peter and John ran to the sepulchre when they heard of the resurrection of Jesus (John 20:4). So it was that when Jesus told Zacchaeus, who was up a sycamore tree waiting to see Him, "*Make haste, and come down; for to day I must abide at thy house,*" he "*made haste, and came down, and received him joyfully*" (Luke 19:4-6).

A lukewarm attitude among God's people is disgusting to God (Rev. 3:15,16). It was no mistake that God chose these shepherds to whom He could tell first the glad news that a Saviour was born.

And after they saw the Baby Jesus, what did they do? "*They made known abroad the saying which was told them concerning this child. And all they that heard it wondered at those things which were told them by the shepherds.*" They told not only that they had seen the Baby Jesus themselves, but they told the message of the angel, that He was the Saviour—good news to all people. So everybody who meets the Saviour ought to tell it gladly. Those who know Him should claim Him.

And after telling everybody they could, "*The shepherds returned, glorifying and praising God for all the things that they had heard and seen, as it was told unto them.*" It was all true. And the Saviour was their Saviour.

The good news was to all people who take Him to their own hearts!

What a deeply spiritual woman was Mary: *"But Mary kept all these things, and pondered them in her heart."* So deeply ran the current of joy and faith and pain and glory in the soul of this woman who had found favor with God and who offered herself gladly as the handmaid of the Lord!

VERSES 21 — 24:

21 And when eight days were accomplished for the circumcising of the child, his name was called JESUS, which was so named of the angel before he was conceived in the womb.

22 And when the days of her purification according to the law of Moses were accomplished, they brought him to Jerusalem, to present *him* to the Lord;

23 (As it is written in the law of the Lord, Every male that openeth the womb shall be called holy to the Lord;)

24 And to offer a sacrifice according to that which is said in the law of the Lord, A pair of turtledoves, or two young pigeons.

The Circumcision of Jesus

Galatians 4 tells us that *"when the fulness of the time was come, God sent forth his Son, made of a woman, made under the law, To redeem them that were under the law, that we might receive the adoption of sons."* So the Lord Jesus, *"made under the law,"* is to be circumcised after eight days, after the command of God to Abraham, *"And he that is eight days old shall be circumcised among you, every man child in your generations..."* (Gen. 17:12). At this circumcision the child was officially named just as on the eighth day when they circumcised John they named him (Luke 1:59). So they officially gave Him the name *"JESUS, which was so named of the angel before he was conceived in the womb."* Circumcision pictured the new birth. So to the Colossians Paul was inspired to write, *"In whom also ye are circumcised with the circumcision made without hands, in putting off the body of the sins of the flesh by the circumcision of Christ"* (Col. 2:11).

And in Deuteronomy 30:6 is the clear promise that at His second coming and the regathering of Israel, *"The Lord thy God will circumcise thine heart, and the heart of thy seed, to love the Lord thy God with all thine heart, and with all thy soul, that thou mayest live."* You see, circumcision was only an object lesson, as were the other ceremonies of the law and just as the Lord's Supper and baptism are now object lessons.

However, now that Christ is come, the body which all the shadows of the ceremonial law pictured, the handwriting of ceremonial ordinances, is nailed to the cross and out of the way. So Colossians 2:14-17 says:

"Blotting out the handwriting of ordinances that was against us, which was contrary to us, and took it out of the way, nailing it to his cross; And having spoiled principalities and powers, he made a shew of them openly, triumphing over them in it. Let no man therefore judge you in meat, or in drink, or in respect of an holyday, or of the new moon, or of the sabbath days: Which are a shadow of things to come; but the body is of Christ."

And so now we *"have put on the new man... Where there is neither Greek nor Jew, circumcision nor uncircumcision"* (Col. 3:10,11).

And now, *"For in Jesus Christ neither circumcision availeth any thing, nor uncircumcision; but faith which worketh by love"* (Gal. 5:6). And those Jewish Christians who had been taught at Galatia to go back and take up circumcision and the ceremonies were thus missing the point that Christ is already here, missing the point of the new heart and being born again and putting themselves under *"the yoke of bondage."* And thus if

they should depend on the ceremonies of the law it would
be wrong. The law *"was our schoolmaster to bring us
unto Christ, that we might be justified by faith"* (Gal.
3:24). So after Christ came and the plan of salvation
was so abundantly manifested, then to go back to the
law would be going back to the schoolmaster and turning away from the Christ which it had proclaimed. In
that sense, Paul could say to these troubled Christians
going back to the law, *"that if ye be circumcised, Christ
shall profit you nothing"* (Gal. 5:2). But it was proper
for Christ Jesus to be circumcised as a baby, since
He was born under the law and came to fulfill the law.

This bringing the Baby Jesus to the Temple when He
was forty days old had a twofold purpose. First, He
was to be presented to the Lord, as the firstborn son,
according to Exodus 13:2,13 and Exodus 22:29. The
second purpose was for Mary to offer a sacrifice for her
ceremonial cleansing, after the birth of a child and the
period of ceremonial uncleanness following. According
to Leviticus 12:6-8, the command was:

*"And when the days of her purifying are fulfilled, for
a son, or for a daughter, she shall bring a lamb of the
first year for a burnt-offering, and a young pigeon, or
a turtledove, for a sin-offering, unto the door of the
tabernacle of the congregation, unto the priest: Who
shall offer it before the Lord, and make an atonement
for her; and she shall be cleansed from the issue of her
blood. This is the law for her that hath born a male
or a female. And if she be not able to bring a lamb,
then she shall bring two turtles, or two young pigeons;
the one for the burnt-offering, and the other for a sin-
offering: and the priest shall make an atonement for
her, and she shall be clean."*

But Mary and Joseph were very poor so they brought
the poor offering, not a lamb but two birds. How fitting

that the Saviour should be born in poverty when most of this poor, sad world is in that condition!

VERSES 25—35:

25 And, behold, there was a man in Jerusalem, whose name *was* Simeon; and the same man *was* just and devout, waiting for the consolation of Israel: and the Holy Ghost was upon him.

26 And it was revealed unto him by the Holy Ghost, that he should not see death, before he had seen the Lord's Christ.

27 And he came by the Spirit into the temple: and when the parents brought in the child Jesus, to do for him after the custom of the law,

28 Then took he him up in his arms, and blessed God, and said,

29 Lord, now lettest thou thy servant depart in peace, according to thy word:

30 For mine eyes have seen thy salvation,

31 Which thou hast prepared before the face of all people;

32 A light to lighten the Gentiles, and the glory of thy people Israel.

33 And Joseph and his mother marvelled at those things which were spoken of him.

34 And Simeon blessed them, and said unto Mary his mother, Behold, this *child* is set for the fall and rising again of many in Israel; and for a sign which shall be spoken against;

35 (Yea, a sword shall pierce through thy own soul also,) that the thoughts of many hearts may be revealed.

Adoration and Prophecy of Simeon

Tradition has said that this Simeon was the son of the famous rabbi, Hillel, and father of Gamaliel. The records do not show that. He waited for *"the consolation of Israel."* And what a name that is for the Saviour! We remember that Barnabas was orginally named Joses but the disciples named him Barnabas, *"The son of consolation"* (Acts 4:36)—a sweet name for one who reminded them of the Lord Jesus.

We are reminded again that many godly people were looking forward to the coming of the Saviour, so often foretold in the Scriptures. Some spiritual people certainly

knew that the time was at hand for the fulfillment of
the prophecy of Daniel 9:25. And since the time of the
first coming was already set and announced, it is not
surprising that the Lord should reveal by His Holy
Spirit to this spiritual man that he would live to see the
Saviour. Since Christ's second coming for His own will
be at a time kept strictly secret (Acts 1:7; Mark 13:32-37),
it is not likely that the Spirit of God would reveal to
anyone now any matter that would tend to date or
make immediately certain the rapture of the saints.

Now the Lord Jesus is brought to the Temple and
the Holy Spirit brings Simeon to the Temple to meet
Him! With what tender care does God deal with His
beloved and believing saints!

Now the old man is ready to die and perhaps soon
would die. He said, "*Lord, now lettest thou thy servant
depart in peace, according to thy word.*" *The Biblical
Illustrator* says:

Many a hoary seer longed for the dayspring, but saw it
not. A sweet Welsh evangelist has a very striking illustration on this point. About Christmas time, John, the elder
brother, is expected home from London by the midnight
train. All the younger children are in ecstasy, and they
all wish to stay up until his arrival. "Pray, father, let us
stay up to wait John home," is the universal petition. But
the reply is, "No, my dear ones, it will be too long for
you to wait; you must go to rest; you shall see John in
the morning--not sooner."

Friends, the ancient prophets expected a Saviour--their
Elder Brother Jesus. How delighted they would be to see
Him in the flesh; but they were compelled to enter the
cold bed of the grave before His arrival. David cried,
"Father, let me see the Horn of Salvation of which I sang
so well." "No, My child, you must retire." Job implored,
"Father, let me see my living Redeemer." "No, My child,
you must retire; but you shall see him after you awake
on the resurrection morning." Malachi cried, "Father, I
am about the last of them all; do let me see the Sun of
Righteousness of which I sang so sweetly." "No, My
child, you must retire to rest; it will be too long for you

to wait." And they silently retired into their cold graves to rest. But at last, hoary-headed Simeon advanced, and earnestly implored, "Oh! my Father, the train is nearly in, according to my brother Daniel's table; do let me stay up to see the Consolation of Israel." "Yes, My child, thy request is granted," said the Father, and the old saint was allowed to see the daybreak, and so delighted was he with its splendor that he prayed for death – (what a strong saint!) – "Lord, now lettest Thou Thy servant depart in peace, for mine eyes have seen Thy salvation." -- *Bib. Illus.* -- (From *Gray and Adams Bible Commentary, pages 298,299.*)

Read again the Spirit-filled praise of Simeon! Christ is called "*Thy salvation,*" which God "*prepared before the face of all people.*" By the Holy Spirit he knew that Christ was "*a light to lighten the Gentiles*" as well as Israel. He knew that the coming of Jesus was as a Saviour, that His purpose was salvation, that it was for all people, Gentiles and Jews.

Note the prophecy of Simeon to Mary, "*Behold, this child is set for the fall and rising again of many in Israel.*" Christ is set for the fall of the Herodians and Pharisees and Sadducees and all who rejected the Saviour, holding on to the ceremonies of the law but set for the rising of all who trust in Him.

And now notice the words to Mary: "*Yea, a sword shall pierce through thy own soul also.*" Doubtless, he meant the sorrows of seeing the Saviour denied, rejected, tried and crucified.

"*...that the thoughts of many hearts may be revealed.*" Only when put up beside Christ and the Gospel does the shallowness, insincerity and fruitlessness of formal Christianity appear.

VERSES 36 — 38:

36 And there was one Anna, a prophetess, the daughter of Phan- | uel, of the tribe of Aser: she was of a great age, and had lived with an

husband seven years from her virginity;

37 And she *was* a widow of about fourscore and four years, which departed not from the temple, but served *God* with fastings and prayers night and day.

38 And she coming in that instant gave thanks likewise unto the Lord, and spake of him to all them that looked for redemption in Jerusalem.

Adoration of Anna

Anna was a prophetess, not a preacher. Prophetesses never were preachers. A prophet or prophetess is one who speaks in the power of the Holy Spirit. But the rules of the Bible are still applicable. "*The spirits of the prophets are subject to the prophets*" (I Cor. 14:32). In God's command, "*Let your women keep silence in the churches: for it is not permitted unto them to speak; but they are commanded to be under obedience, as also saith the law*" (I Cor. 14:34); and the command in I Timothy 2:11 and 12, "*Let the woman learn in silence with all subjection. But I suffer not a woman to teach, nor to usurp authority over the man, but to be in silence*"—that rule was founded on a fact going back to Adam and Eve and the nature of men and women. So a prophetess witnessed to individuals, never to mixed congregations as such. And prophets witness sometimes to individuals and occasionally to congregations.

Anna was of the tribe of Asher. As a group, that tribe had not returned from the captivity, but many of all the twelve tribes were included now in the area of Judaea. How old was she? The Scripture seems to say that she was married seven years and then a widow for eighty-four years, which would make her over one hundred years old. Some think that verse 37 means her total age was eighty-four, but she "*served God with fastings and prayers night and day.*" So it is not surprising that the Spirit of God was upon her and revealed to her that this Baby was the Lord and she "*spake of him to all them that looked for redemption in Jerusalem.*" This indicates there must have been many, many people who looked for a Saviour, who saw themselves guilty sinners and many of them, no doubt, had trusted in God's Redeemer who had not yet appeared.

Now the events of Matthew 2, the appearance of the wise men, etc., had not occurred till after these forty days and after the presentation of the Baby Jesus in the Temple. They would hardly have gone to the Temple after the warning of the angel in Matthew 2:13. And, in fact, the next verse, verse 14, plainly says that "*he took the young child and his mother by night, and departed into Egypt.*"

Then the coming of the wise men was not immediately at the birth of Jesus. They may have seen a star appearing at the time of the birth: they may have spent some weeks en route. We do not know. We know that when the wise men appeared the Baby Jesus was not in a stable but in a house (Matt. 2:11). We know that Herod "*slew all the children that were in Bethlehem, and in all the coasts thereof, from two years old and under, according to the time which he had diligently enquired of the wise men*" (Matt. 2:16). It seems likely that the two years was simply Herod's effort to make sure that he would get the Baby Jesus and that "*according to the time which he had diligently enquired of the wise men*" referred to the time of the appearing of the star and so the earliest time at which the Child would have been born. Most likely the wise men came not long after the appearance of Jesus in the Temple.

VERSES 39, 40:

39 And when they had performed all things according to the law of the Lord, they returned into Galilee, to their own city Nazareth.

40 And the child grew, and waxed | and the grace of God was upon
strong in spirit, filled with wisdom: | him.

The Return to Nazareth

The Gospel of Luke does not give the story of the
flight into Egypt. We do not know how long that time
was, until the death of King Herod.

Verse 39 says, "*And when they had performed all
things according to the law of the Lord....*" This refers
not only to the presentation in the Temple but doubtless
includes also the Old Testament prophecy, "*And called
my son out of Egypt*" (Hos. 11:1). That was a part
of the law (that is, the Old Testament), and must be fulfilled, too. But that matter of coming out of Egypt, and
of Israel coming out of Egypt as a type of Christ coming
out, was more particularly a lesson for Jews and so is
included in Matthew and so it was not necessarily included in the book of Luke.

Returning from Egypt and fearing Archelaus, son of
Herod, reigning in Judaea, they "*turned aside into the
parts of Galilee*" (Matt. 2:22). And now Joseph and
Mary are back to their own city Nazareth and there
they will live and the Saviour with them, until He is
about thirty years old.

The Lord Jesus, as a child, grew in body. But isn't
it strange that He "*waxed strong in spirit, filled with
wisdom*"? We do not know how much the Lord Jesus
knew, as a Child, but we do know that He must go
through the apprenticeship picturing all mankind. And
we know that He must learn obedience through suffering
(Heb. 5:8). And we must remember that the dear
Lord Jesus "*made himself of no reputation, and took
upon him the form of a servant, and was made in the
likeness of men: And being found in fashion as a man,
he humbled himself, and became obedient unto death,
even the death of the cross*" (Phil. 2:7,8).

So whatever it took to make Jesus, who was without sin, fit in with the rest of us, whatever poverty and initial ignorance, and a need to study and learn and grow, the dear Lord Jesus gladly took on Himself. We find in John 13:4 that the Lord Jesus "*laid aside his garments*": that was only a simple likeness to the way He came into this world. He laid aside the heavenly garments of deity, the shining glory that was His equal with the Father, and humbled Himself and took on Himself whatever limitations and poverty and sufferings were necessary to make Him a model Man, the proper example for those of us who would follow Him after we are saved.

VERSES 41 — 52:

41 Now his parents went to Jerusalem every year at the feast of the passover.

42 And when he was twelve years old, they went up to Jerusalem after the custom of the feast.

43 And when they had fulfilled the days, as they returned, the child Jesus tarried behind in Jerusalem; and Joseph and his mother knew not *of it*.

44 But they, supposing him to have been in the company, went a day's journey; and they sought him among *their* kinsfolk and acquaintance.

45 And when they found him not, they turned back again to Jerusalem, seeking him.

46 And it came to pass, that after three days they found him in the temple, sitting in the midst of the doctors, both hearing them, and asking them questions.

47 And all that heard him were astonished at his understanding and answers.

48 And when they saw him, they were amazed: and his mother said unto him, Son, why hast thou thus dealt with us? behold, thy father and I have sought thee sorrowing.

49 And he said unto them, How is it that ye sought me? wist ye not that I must be about my Father's business?

50 And they understood not the saying which he spake unto them.

51 And he went down with them, and came to Nazareth, and was subject unto them: but his mother kept all these sayings in her heart.

52 And Jesus increased in wisdom and stature, and in favour with God and man.

Jesus When Twelve Years Old

The silent years go by. It is remarkable that between
the time Jesus was forty days old and the time He was
thirty years old (Luke 3:23), we have only this one
single incident in His life.

Each year Mary and Joseph went to Jerusalem. A
caravan of people usually went together, devout Jews
going up to the Temple, they went *"in the company"*
(vs. 44).

They did not fret, starting out from Jerusalem, seventy-
five or eighty miles back to Nazareth: the Boy Jesus
had never caused them any grief, had never disobeyed
them, had never been even thoughtless about them, so
they had no fret to start on their journey back. But at
the end of the first day's journey (it would take several
days on foot), they went among the company, probably
camped together or at an inn together, and sought
Jesus but could not find Him.

We may be sure that the Lord Jesus had planned
this incident. Even now He knows that *"I must be
about my Father's business,"* and He knows that Joseph
and Mary must be impressed again that Joseph is not
His father but that God is His Father; His life is not to
be ordinary. Besides that, we may be sure that His deep
and passionate concern about the Scriptures was real.
So they found Him in the Temple after three days
*"sitting in the midst of the doctors, both hearing them,
and asking them questions."* We do not wonder that
*"all that heard him were astonished at his understanding
and answers"* (vs. 47).

The rest of us may be taught, but we learn so poorly.
We read but we do not understand it all. We read but
we soon forget. Our minds are limited and worse still,
our devotion is limited, our attention is distracted, our
interest is divided. Not so with the Lord Jesus. We

will not wonder later when we find in every incident, and applying to every situation, His mind remembers some Scripture, some prophecy that must be fulfilled, some lesson to be applied.

Note verse 48. Mary was distressed; "*Why hast thou thus dealt with us? behold, thy father and I have sought thee sorrowing.*" But it must not be left as if He is accepting Joseph as His father. Others may not know but He and Mary and Joseph know that He is the only begotten Son of God, the only One physically begotten, born of a virgin mother, and is God in human form.

They did not fully understand it then. But we are not surprised that His mother "*kept all these sayings in her heart.*" She must have remembered the warning of Simeon that a sword should pierce through her soul (vs. 35). And in verse 19 we read, "*But Mary kept all these things, and pondered them in her heart.*" This godly, spiritual woman gladly took her place and gladly still counted herself the handmaid of the Lord. We will not be surprised later in John, chapter 2, that she, before anyone else, expected Jesus to work a miracle, and He did.

Now compare verse 52 with verse 40: "*Jesus increased in wisdom and stature, and in favour with God and man.*" We know that Jesus had consciously and intentionally humbled Himself. Now He learned perfectly where we learned imperfectly. He grew in stature. It is probable that He was a tall Man, for in the Garden Tomb, in Gordon's Calvary at Jerusalem, it appears that the grave, intended first for a shorter man, needed to be dug out more at the foot to make room for the taller Jesus. But He grew "*in favour with God and man.*"

How could the Lord Jesus grow in favor with God? He who had pleased God in everything!

There is a sense in which God's love is all of grace and so He loves the wicked and not only the good.

But there is also some sense in which "*God loveth a cheerful giver*" (II Cor. 9:7) more than one who does not give cheerfully.   It is true that God loved the world but Jesus especially loved the rich young ruler (Mark 10:17-22), and He loved Mary and Martha and Lazarus (John 11:5).

So if Mary earns the love of God and the dear Lord Jesus "*increased...in favour with God,*" the capacity of God to love His Son would grow more and more as the dear Lord Jesus unfolded in His righteousness and beauty as the perfect Man, the second Adam, the Substitute for all the sinning race.

He grew "*in favour with...man.*" So we find in Luke 4:16,17 that He went to the synagogue as His custom was on the Sabbath and evidently, according to custom, they asked Him to read the Scriptures.   He was the model young Man.   Until He was filled with the Spirit, until He began to preach and His burning words convicted and offended, He was all that was admirable. But Spirit-filled witnessing goes against the grain for sinful people.   The Lord Jesus earned the admiration and love of all good people.   But later He also earned the reproaches that wicked men have for God and for righteousness.

LUKE 3

VERSES 1, 2:

NOW in the fifteenth year of the reign of Tiberius Cæsar, Pontius Pilate being governor of Judæa, and Herod being tetrarch of Galilee, and his brother Philip tetrarch of Ituræa and of the region of Trachonitis, and Lysanias the tetrarch of Abilene,

2 Annas and Caiaphas being the high priests, the word of God came unto John the son of Zacharias in the wilderness.

Roman Emperors of the New Testament

John the Baptist began preaching *"in the fifteenth year of the reign of Tiberius Caesar."* He had followed Caesar Augustus, emperor of Rome at the time of Christ's birth. Tiberius was now seventy or seventy-one years old. He died in 37 A.D., about seven years later. The little city of Tiberias, on the west coast of the Sea of Galilee, was named for him, mentioned in John 6:23. The Sea of Galilee is sometimes called *"the sea of Tiberias"* (John 6:1;21:1). When Tiberius died in 37 A.D., he was followed by Caligula as Roman emperor, who was not mentioned in the New Testament. And then in 41 A.D. he was followed by Claudius Caesar, mentioned in Acts 11:28. In 54 A.D. Nero became emperor at Rome and reigned until 68 A.D. This is the Caesar under whom Paul was imprisoned and beheaded about the year 66 A.D.

Pilate was now governor in Judea. Judea has been reduced from a kingdom to a province and has a governor instead of a king, as in the days of Herod the Great when Christ was born. The Herod mentioned here in Luke 3:1 is tetrarch of Galilee, son of Herod the Great and Philip, the tetrarch of Ituraea. Ituraea was a province north of Galilee and of the Sea of Galilee, and Abilene was a province still further north.

Annas and Caiaphas — Two High Priests?

In verse 2 we are told, "*Annas and Caiaphas being the high priests.*"   Actually Caiaphas was the high priest that year legally (John 11:49). And John 18:13 tells us that the officers of the Jews took Jesus and "*led him away to Annas first; for he was father in law to Caiaphas, which was the high priest that same year.*" So Annas, with great influence over his son-in-law, took some of the authority of the high priest's office. After His arrest Jesus was first taken to Annas, and then Annas "*sent him bound unto Caiaphas the high priest*" (John 18:24).

After Thirty Years John the Baptist Appears

In Luke 1:80 we left the baby, John the Baptist, with the simple statement, "*And the child grew, and waxed strong in spirit, and was in the deserts till the day of his shewing unto Israel.*"

We leap now to the beginning of John's ministry, at the age of thirty (John was six months older than Jesus — Luke 1:36 — and Jesus, when baptized by John, was "*about thirty years of age*" — vs. 23).   He had been living a life of separation as a Nazarite. "*In the wilderness*" simply means an uninhabited area, perhaps we would say in the back country, avoiding the cities and people.   The habits of John were simple and rustic: "*And John was clothed with camel's hair, and with a girdle of a skin about his loins; and he did eat locusts and wild honey*" (Mark 1:6). His simple raiment was evidently a matter of comment, for Jesus said about him, "*What went ye out into the wilderness to see? A reed shaken with the wind? But what went ye out for to see? A man clothed in soft raiment? behold, they that wear soft clothing are in kings' houses. But what went ye out for to see? A prophet? yea, I say unto you, and more than a prophet"* (Matt. 11:7-9).

VERSES 3—6:

3 And he came into all the country about Jordan, preaching the baptism of repentance for the remission of sins;
4 As it is written in the book of the words of Esaias the prophet, saying, The voice of one crying in the wilderness, Prepare ye the way of the Lord, make his paths straight.
5 Every valley shall be filled, and every mountain and hill shall be brought low; and the crooked shall be made straight, and the rough ways *shall be* made smooth;
6 And all flesh shall see the salvation of God.

John, a New Testament Gospel Preacher

John the Baptist has been greatly mistreated by the commentators. In his Scofield Bible notes on Acts 19:1-7, Dr. Scofield seems to have wholly missed the point of John's preaching and baptism. He says about these who had believed and been baptized, these "disciples" as the Bible calls them: "Paul was evidently impressed by the absence of spirituality and power in these so-called disciples. Their answer brought out the fact that they were Jewish proselytes, disciples of John the Baptist, looking forward to a coming King, not Christians looking backward to an accomplished redemption." When God says disciples, then no one has the right to say "so-called disciples." And one who thinks that John the Baptist was simply making Jewish proselytes, not Christians, wholly misunderstands his ministry.

And that has been the trend among some great dispensationalists. So, Dr. Scofield's note on John 1:17 says, "As a dispensation, grace begins with the death and resurrection of Christ.... The point of testing is no longer legal obedience as the condition of salvation, but acceptance or rejection of Christ, with good works

as a fruit of salvation..." (the older edition of the
Scofield Bible). But "legal obedience as the condition
of salvation" is not taught anywhere in the Bible, not
in the Mosaic Law and certainly not in the preaching
of John the Baptist.

The tendency of some commentators to make a different plan of salvation before the coming of Christ, or
even up to the time of the crucifixion, is wrong. It
stems partly, perhaps, from the disposition to make
Pentecost the time of the origin of the church instead of
understanding that that "*general assembly and church
of the firstborn, which are written in heaven*" (Heb.
12:23) includes all the saved of all ages. Scofield
cannot even imagine why Jesus came to John to be
baptized as the note in Matthew 3:15 implies: "Why
one who needed no repentance should insist upon receiving a rite which signified confession (v. 6) and
repentance (v. 11) is nowhere directly explained." A
pedo-Baptist, who did not see baptism as being buried
with Christ, picturing His burial and resurrection and
the believer's symbolic burying of the old man and
rising to live in newness of life, missed the point of
Christ as our Pattern-Example when Jesus said, "*Thus
it becometh us*" to be baptized.

John came "*preaching the baptism of repentance for
the remission of sins*"; not *baptism* for the remission of
sins but *repentance* for the remission of sins and baptism
that pictured that transaction. But repentance is no
different from the plan of salvation given everywhere in
the Bible.

It is interesting that the message of John the Baptist
and the message of Jesus is summed up in exactly the
same words. Of John it is said that he preached, "*Repent ye: for the kingdom of heaven is at hand*" (Matt.
3:2). Of Jesus it is said, "*From that time Jesus began
to preach, and to say, Repent: for the kingdom of*

heaven is at hand" (Matt. 4:17). And Jesus continues to preach repentance as the way of salvation in Luke 13:3 and 5. And Paul preached repentance as the plan of salvation in ,Acts 17:30,31. Peter preached the same thing in Acts 2:38; Acts 3:19. And II Peter 3:9 says that God would *"that all should come to repentance."* So repentance and saving faith are simply different ways of expressing the same truth. One turns from his sin and rebellion to trust in Jesus Christ.

In John 3:16-18 we have the plan of salvation in the words of the Saviour: one who believes in Christ shall not perish but have everlasting life. But in the same chapter, beginning with verse 27, we hear John the Baptist speaking and in verse 36 he says, *"He that believeth on the Son hath everlasting life: and he that believeth not the Son shall not see life; but the wrath of God abideth on him."* John preached exactly the same Gospel as Jesus preached and as all the other preachers in the Bible preached.

But necessarily this must be so. There has never been but one plan of salvation. In Acts 10:43 we read, *"To him* [Christ] *give all the prophets witness, that through his name whosoever believeth in him shall receive remission of sins."* Every prophet in the Old Testament preached the same plan of salvation—faith in Christ. So Abraham *"believed in the Lord; and he counted it to him for righteousness"* (Gen. 15:6). And in Romans 4 Abraham is held up to all New Testament Christians as an example of salvation by simple faith in Christ.

Mark 1:1 starts the story of John the Baptist with these words, *"The beginning of the gospel of Jesus Christ, the Son of God."* So John was a New Testament preacher. His baptism was New Testament baptism. Nowhere in the Old Testament is there ever a hint of baptism, as one's public profession of faith in Christ,

as John preached it and practiced it. Jesus Himself
was baptized by John. All the apostles were baptized
by John. When the other eleven apostles prayerfully
selected another man to take the place of Judas as a
witness of the resurrection of Christ, it must be one "*of
these men which have companied with us all the time
that the Lord Jesus went in and out among us, Beginning from the baptism of John....*" And the baptism
which John the Baptist administered was Christian baptism, having exactly the same meaning as Bible baptism
has today for believers.

Of John the Baptist, Jesus said there was never a
greater born of woman, and that puts him equal to
Moses, Abraham, David, Elijah, Peter, John, and Paul.
Of all the men, only John the Baptist was "*filled with
the Holy Ghost, even from his mother's womb.*" And
it may well be that John the Baptist was the greatest
soul winner of all the Bible. It was promised, "*Many
of the children of Israel shall he turn to the Lord their
God*" (Luke 1:16). And we are told, "*Then went out to
him Jerusalem, and all Judaea, and all the region
round about Jordan, And were baptized of him in
Jordan, confessing their sins*" (Matt. 3:5,6). Peter and
other apostles at Pentecost and immediately following,
in Jerusalem, may have had such crowds and large
numbers of penitent sinners converted, but as far as we
know, no other evangelist in the New Testament had
such great crowds or as many converts.

Isaiah's Prophecy About John

Verses 4 to 6 here quotes that marvelous passage
from Isaiah 40, verses 3 to 5, so wonderfully set to
music in Handel's Oratorio, *The Messiah.* The part
of the quotation from Isaiah given in verse 4 is quoted
in Matthew 3:3 and is the part that applies most directly
to John the Baptist. Verses 4 and 5 here must refer not

only to Christ's first coming but to the completion of His wonder work at His second coming, for surely only then will every valley be filled, every mountain and hill be brought low, the crooked made straight, etc., and only then shall "*all flesh. . . see the salvation of God.*"

Note in this passage that the ministry of John the Baptist is definitely connected with the whole New Testament age. He is a New Testament preacher, not an Old Testament prophet. As Joel 2:28-32 foretold the pouring out of the Holy Spirit on all kinds of people through this whole New Testament age, "*the last days,*" so Isaiah foretells the coming and complete final triumph of the Lord Jesus. And as Peter in Acts 2:14-16 quotes Joel, quotes prophecy when the event begins to take place, so here John the Baptist quotes Isaiah's prophecy when the event begins to take place. John is not only the forerunner of Christ in His first coming, but in Christ's final triumph and reign.

It is interesting that in many, many Old Testament Scriptures the first and second comings of Christ are mentioned together as parts of one great general, historical fact. So Isaiah 61:1 and 2 foretells the anointing of Jesus Christ, following His baptism, to preach the Gospel to the poor but in the same sentence, has "*and the day of vengeance of our God.*" Let no one think that the work of Christ is done until after the rapture when Christ returns in glory to reign over the earth and then to see the earth itself made into a new garden of Eden (Isa. 51:3; Ezek. 36:35). That is the "regeneration" of Matthew 19:28, "*the times of restitution of all things*" of Acts 3:21. So the term "*the day of the Lord*" used so many times in the Bible refers not to His first coming but to His triumphant second coming.

VERSES 7 — 9:

7 Then said he to the multitude that came forth to be baptized of him, O generation of vipers, who hath warned you to flee from the wrath to come?

8 Bring forth therefore fruits worthy of repentance, and begin not to say within yourselves, We have Abraham to *our* father: for I say unto you, That God is able of these stones to raise up children unto Abraham.

9 And now also the axe is laid unto the root of the trees: every tree therefore which bringeth not forth good fruit is hewn down, and cast into the fire.

The Great Truths of God's Plan of Salvation

Here John calls the unconverted, "*O generation of vipers.*" This is the same thing that Jesus meant when He said to Nicodemus, "*Ye must be born again.*" Here in pungent language is described the depravity of the unregenerate heart, the inherent taint of sin. He insisted that those who came to be baptized, professing that they were repenting of their sins and trusting the Saviour, "*bring forth. . .fruits worthy of repentance.*" He demanded there should be a changed life following heart repentance.

Here he preaches clearly the miraculous new birth. Just because these Jews were descendants of Abraham did not make them children of God. "*God is able of these stones to raise up children unto Abraham.*" This teaches that salvation is "*Not by works of righteousness which we have done, but according to his mercy he saved us, by the washing of regeneration, and renewing of the Holy Ghost*" (Titus 3:5). Only God can make a lost sinner into a child of God. And that is the miraculous new birth which takes place instantly when one turns his heart from sin to trust the Saviour.

"*The axe is laid unto the root of the trees.*" That is, judgment is coming for unrepentant sinners. The fruit mentioned here is the penitent heart turning from sin.

It does not mean good works as a plan of salvation, but repentance itself is a turning to Christ for mercy. "...*cast into the fire*": We must take that to mean just what Jesus meant in His story of the rich man and Lazarus recorded in Luke 16:19-31. This reminds us of the warning of torment "*with fire and brimstone*" in Revelation 14:10 and the lake of fire in Revelation 20:15. And why should we think that when God says "*fire*" so often He did not mean fire?

VERSES 10 — 14:

10 And the people asked him, saying, What shall we do then?
11 He answereth and saith unto them, He that hath two coats, let him impart to him that hath none; and he that hath meat, let him do likewise.
12 Then came also publicans to be baptized, and said unto him, Master, what shall we do?

13 And he said unto them, Exact no more than that which is appointed you.
14 And the soldiers likewise demanded of him, saying, And what shall we do? And he said unto them, Do violence to no man, neither accuse *any* falsely; and be content with your wages.

The Fruits of Repentance

John the Baptist was clear on the plan of salvation. "*God is able of these stones to raise up children unto Abraham.*" He taught a supernatural new birth and repentance, a heart change of attitude against sin, a turning to God as the way to receive the new birth. This does not contradict salvation by faith which He taught in John 3:36.

But repentance is to be followed by certain fruits of repentance. Good works is not the way of salvation, but good works should follow. So the Bible says again and again. Ephesians 2:8 and 9 tells us, "*For by grace are ye saved through faith; and that not of yourselves:*

it is the gift of God: Not of works, lest any man should boast." But then it adds in the next verse, "*For we are his workmanship, created in Christ Jesus unto good works, which God hath before ordained that we should walk in them.*" We are saved by grace but saved "*unto good works.*" And though Romans 8:1 says, "*There is therefore now no condemnation to them which are in Christ Jesus,*" verse 4 says, "*That the right-eousness of the law might be fulfilled in us, who walk not after the flesh, but after the Spirit.*" A new heart in-evitably means a change in attitudes and motives. So there ought to be a marked change in one's life after salvation.

The Scripture never indicates that we can tell who is saved and who is not by the way they live. The state-ment of Jesus in Matthew 7:16, "*Ye shall know them by their fruits,*" applies to false prophets. In verses 15 and 16 the Lord said, "*Beware of false prophets, which come to you in sheep's clothing, but inwardly they are ravening wolves. Ye shall know them by their fruits. Do men gather grapes of thorns, or figs of thistles?*" One can tell a false prophet by his teaching. One who denies the virgin birth, the deity of Christ, His blood atonement, and the bodily resurrection of Jesus Christ, is a false prophet, and one who does not believe the Bible doctrine about Jesus Christ "*hath not God,*" is not saved, according to II John, verses 9 to 11. But we are not to judge whether one is saved or not. We must remember that "*man looketh on the outward appearance, but the Lord looketh on the heart,*" and the stern warning about judging the heart of men, which we cannot see, is given by Jesus: "*Judge not, that ye be not judged*" (Matt. 7:1).

But as far as a witness to people, Christians should so live that they are obviously known as Christians. Jesus said, "*By this shall all men know that ye are my*

disciples, if ye have love one to another" (John 13:35).
Christians who do not love one another as they ought
are not always recognizable as Christians.

As far as a witness to others is concerned, *"Even so
faith, if it hath not works, is dead, being alone. Yea,
a man may say, Thou hast faith, and I have works:
shew me thy faith without thy works, and I will shew
thee my faith by my works."* As a witness to men, a
Christian life is the only way to prove that we are
Christians.

That does not change the fact that in the sight of God
one who trusts in Christ is instantly justified; and so in
Galatians 3:11 we read, *"But that no man is justified
by the law IN THE SIGHT OF GOD, it is evident: for,
The just shall live by faith."* And again Romans 3:20
says, *"Therefore by the deeds of the law there shall no
flesh be justified in his sight: for by the law is the
knowledge of sin."* Yes, salvation is wholly by grace
and instantly one is justified in the sight of God when
he turns to Him with a penitent heart, trusting Jesus for
forgiveness.   So one is justified in the sight of God
wholly by faith and without works. But one is justified
in the sight of men by his works also.

The preaching of John the Baptist that people should
repent and be made into children of God and *"bring
forth therefore fruits worthy of repentance"* (vs. 8), was
like the preaching of the Apostle Paul. In Acts 26:20 he
tells King Agrippa the manner of his preaching: *"But
shewed first unto them of Damascus, and at Jerusalem,
and throughout all the coasts of Judaea, and then to the
Gentiles, that they should repent and turn to God, and
do works meet for repentance."*

So when people asked John, *"What shall we do then?"*
following repentance, *"He answereth and saith unto
them, He that hath two coats, let him impart to him
that hath none; and he that hath meat, let him do*

likewise." And publicans who repented were told, "*Exact no more than that which is appointed you.*" Soldiers were commanded, "*Do violence to no man, neither accuse any falsely; and be content with your wages.*"

This is simply a practical application of the command, "*Thou shalt love thy neighbour as thyself*" (Lev. 19:18; Matt. 22:39). Here is taught the practical outworking of love one for another. Here John gives the outworking of the Golden Rule: "*Therefore all things whatsoever ye would that men should do to you, do ye even so to them*" (Matt. 7:12). This here is the teaching as Jesus expressed it in the parable of the Good Samaritan (Luke 10:30-37). And notice that this kindness and generosity and thoughtfulness for others is not to be confined only to friends, nor only to good people.

Oh, when we turned to Christ for mercy, a Christian life ought to shine out with the fruits of repentance. In God's sight no man is justified by the deeds of the law or by works, but in the sight of men, the evidence of a changed heart is a changed life.

VERSES 15—18:

15 And as the people were in expectation, and all men mused in their hearts of John, whether he were the Christ, or not;
16 John answered, saying unto *them* all, I indeed baptize you with water; but one mightier than I cometh, the latchet of whose shoes I am not worthy to unloose: he shall baptize you with the Holy Ghost and with fire:
17 Whose fan *is* in his hand, and he will throughly purge his floor, and will gather the wheat into his garner; but the chaff he will burn with fire unquenchable.
18 And many other things in his exhortation preached he unto the people.

John the Baptist Announces the Coming of Jesus Christ

The above passage is very much like that in Matthew

3:1-12 and Mark 1:1-8. But in John's Gospel considerably more is given (see John 1:15-37).

Note in verse 15, *"And as the people were in expectation, and all men mused in their hearts of John, whether he were the Christ, or not."* So we see there were many looking for the appearing of the Saviour. We are reminded of Simeon and of godly Anna, in the Temple looking for the Saviour's coming (Luke 2:25-37). It is not surprising that *"the people were in expectation"* about the Messiah's coming. Even King Herod seemed to have known about the prophecies of Christ's coming, for he demanded of the scribes and Pharisees where Christ should be born (Matt. 2:4), and the chief priests and scribes told him that according to Micah 5:2 Christ would be born in Bethlehem. They expected the Messiah because Moses had told them, *"The Lord thy God will raise up unto thee a Prophet from the midst of thee, of thy brethren, like unto me; unto him ye shall hearken"* (Deut. 18:15). So the people asked John the Baptist, *"Art thou that prophet?"* And he answered, *"No"* (John 1:21). They were expecting "the prophet" promised by Moses.

They had a promise in Malachi 4:5, in the next to the last verse in the Old Testament, *"Behold, I will send you Elijah the prophet before the coming of the great and dreadful day of the Lord."* And so in the same verse they said to John, *"Art thou Elias?"*

They had the prophecies of Isaiah 53, of Psalm 2, of Psalm 22, and many others. And Daniel 9:25 had set the time of sixty-nine weeks of years, from the commandment to rebuild Jerusalem under Cyrus to the coming of *"the Messiah the Prince"*; and thus the Wise Men from the East evidently knew the time was at hand and looked for the star which announced Christ's coming. All the people were *"in expectation."* This, no doubt, was a part of the whole plan of God that *"when the fulness of the time was come, God sent forth his Son"* (Gal. 4:4).

John's Baptism and the Prophesied "Baptism With the Holy Ghost"

John said, *"I indeed baptize you with water. . . ."* It is clear that John's baptizing with water had a definite part in announcing Christ's ministry. Baptism in water pictured nothing of the ceremonial law; it pictured Christ's burial and resurrection, pictured the Christian's leaving all for Christ, counting the old sinful man dead and buried, raised out of the watery grave to live the new Christ-life. John, rising centuries after the last Old Testament prophet, is definitely New Testament in message.

As God's messenger, a man may administer baptism to a new convert as John did and as God's ministers today may do. But the Lord Jesus, pictured and announced here, is beyond comparison, mightier even than John, one of the greatest ever born of women. And Jesus *"shall baptize you with the Holy Ghost and with fire."* All four of the Gospels emphasize the statement of John the Baptist that Jesus was to baptize with the Holy Ghost. See Matthew 3:11; Mark 1:8; John 1:33. The emphasis the Scriptures place on the statement indicates its importance. And Jesus stated the matter again, and with the same emphasis, in Acts 1:4 and 5: *"And, being assembled together with them, commanded them that they should not depart from Jerusalem, but wait for the promise of the Father, which, saith he, ye have heard of me. For John truly baptized with water; but ye shall be baptized with the Holy Ghost not many days hence."*

Dr. Scofield thinks that **"every believer is . . . baptized by the Spirit,"** in the note on Acts 2:4, where the Scripture says, *"And they were all filled with the Holy Ghost,"* and he gives the reference here, I Corinthians 12:12,13.

Thus he teaches that "potentially" every Christian in the world was baptized into the body of Christ at Pentecost, making the baptism of the Holy Ghost simply a dispensational matter, the forming of the church at Pentecost. That position, we think, was common with Plymouth Brethren teachers. Now it is true that I Corinthians 12:13 states that the Christians at Corinth were baptized into the body of Christ by the Spirit, that is, the Holy Spirit works a miracle of regeneration and so puts the convert into that group that will be called out at the rapture, that "*general assembly and church of the first-born, which are written in heaven*" (Heb. 12:23). The Holy Spirit, as agent, baptizes or submerges each convert into the group to be raptured. First Corinthians 12:12 and 13 makes no reference to Pentecost nor to the origin of the church, so Dr. Scofield's position seems a very strange interpretation.

Actually the Scripture does not even discuss Pentecost as the time of "the founding of the church." And we believe that that church which will be called out at the rapture, when Christ comes, will include all the saints of all ages to be called out and assembled in Heaven and so a true *ecclesia*, a true "church."

At any rate, here, in the teaching of John and of Christ, is unusual emphasis on "baptized with the Holy Ghost" and pointing toward Pentecost in the plain words of Jesus in Acts 1:4 and 5. We believe it refers to the pouring out of the Holy Spirit upon God's people. Baptism means an immersion or an overwhelming or a covering, and surely the Holy Spirit poured out at Pentecost did cover and surround the people of God who waited in that upper room and were "*filled with the Spirit.*"

So we believe the promise that Christ is to "*baptize with the Holy Ghost*" simply means that the Lord Jesus Himself is the One who pours out the Holy Spirit

upon His people when they meet His requirements. And
that is the way Peter explains the wonderful outpouring
at Pentecost. In Acts 2:32 and 33 he said, "*This Jesus
hath God raised up, whereof we all are witnesses. Therefore being by the right hand of God exalted, and having
received of the Father the promise of the Holy Ghost,
he hath shed forth this, which ye now see and hear.*"
It is Christ who "sends" His disciples to win souls,
even as the Father sent Him (John 17:18; John 20:21,
22). It is Christ who gave them the indwelling of the
Holy Spirit and now gives every Christian at conversion
the Holy Spirit to dwell within, but it is Christ also who
gives Holy Spirit power to those who wait upon Him
and witness for Him. So when a soldier with a spear
pierced the side of Jesus, "*forthwith came there out
blood and water*" (John 19:34). The blood picturing
an atonement for sin, the water picturing the Holy Spirit
power purchased for every Christian.

Christ Baptizes With Fire

But the statement in Mark or John mentions only the
promise, "*He shall baptize you with the Holy Ghost,*"
while in Matthew and Luke he adds, "*and with fire,*"
and the term is explained in the following verse, that
Christ "*will gather the wheat into his garner; but the
chaff he will burn with fire unquenchable.*" Christ who
will pour out the Holy Spirit upon His people is the
Christ who has the authority of judgment. It is Christ
who will send people to Hell. But remember that He
said, "*All power is given unto me in heaven and in
earth,*" that is, all authority (Matt. 28:18). And
Jesus said in John 5:22 that God "*hath committed all
judgment unto the Son.*" So it is Christ Himself who
will say to those unsaved on His left hand, at the judgment of the living Gentiles when He shall return to set
up His kingdom, "*Depart from me, ye cursed, into*

everlasting fire, prepared for the devil and his angels"
(Matt. 25:41). And Matthew 13:41 and 42 tells us that
it is the Son of Man Himself who *"shall send forth his
angels, and they shall gather out of his kingdom all
things that offend, and them which do iniquity; And shall
cast them into a furnace of fire: there shall be wailing
and gnashing of teeth."* Those slander and misrepre-
sent Jesus who picture Him only as love and never as
in wrath against rebellious sinners, picture Him as a
Saviour but do not picture Him also as a Judge. The
Christ who will gather the wheat into His garner is the
same Christ who will burn up the chaff in Hell, *"with
fire unquenchable."*

VERSES 19, 20:

19 But Herod the tetrarch, being reproved by him for Herodias his brother Philip's wife, and for all the evils which Herod had done, 20 Added yet this above all, that he shut up John in prison.

John the Baptist Put in Prison

Because the Scripture has been giving John's message,
it adds here events that happened later after Jesus was
baptized. Wicked Herod, who had seduced and taken
his brother Philip's wife, was sternly rebuked by John
for that and *"for all the evils which Herod had done."*
Eventually this will result in John's death through the
spite of wicked Herodias, the adulterous woman, as we
read in Matthew 14:1-12 and Mark 6:14-29. It is
thought that John's imprisonment, and later his be-
heading, was at Herod's winter palace at Machaerus
east of the Dead Sea. It was John the Baptist who
baptized Jesus, before John's imprisonment, though the
imprisonment is mentioned first here.

VERSES 21, 22:

21 Now when all the people were baptized, it came to pass, that Jesus also being baptized, and praying, the heaven was opened, 22 And the Holy Ghost de- scended in a bodily shape like a dove upon him, and a voice came from heaven, which said, Thou art my beloved Son; in thee I am well pleased.

The Baptism of Jesus

More detail is given in Matthew 3:13-17:

"*Then cometh Jesus from Galilee to Jordan unto John, to be baptized of him. But John forbad him, saying, I have need to be baptized of thee, and comest thou to me? And Jesus answering said unto him, Suffer it to be so now: for thus it becometh us to fulfill all righteousness. Then he suffered him. And Jesus, when he was baptized, went up straightway out of the water: and, lo, the heavens were opened unto him, and he saw the Spirit of God descending like a dove, and lighting upon him: And lo a voice from heaven, saying, This is my beloved Son, in whom I am well pleased.*"

We suppose that Jesus walked from Galilee to Jordan where John was baptizing. John was naturally self-conscious and reluctant about baptizing One so much greater than himself, but Jesus there teaches that baptism is for all Christians: "*Thus it becometh US to fulfill all righteousness.*"

Note that Luke tells that "*the Holy Ghost descended in a bodily shape like a dove upon him.*" And Matthew says, "*He saw the Spirit of God descending like a dove, and lighting upon him.*" We are not told whether others saw this manifestation when the Holy Spirit came upon Jesus. Certainly John, who baptized Jesus, saw that, for John says in John 1:31-34:

"And I knew him not: but that he should be made manifest to Israel, therefore am I come baptizing with water. And John bare record, saying, I saw the Spirit descending from heaven like a dove, and it abode upon him. And I knew him not: but he that sent me to baptize with water, the same said unto me, Upon whom thou shalt see the Spirit descending, and remaining on him, the same is he which baptizeth with the Holy Ghost. And I saw, and bare record that this is the Son of God."

John the Baptist had been in the deserts until the showing to Israel (Luke 1:80); so he had little, if any, touch with Jesus, though their mothers seemed very close. But Jesus grew up in Nazareth. It is possible that John had never known Jesus, or it is possible that he knew Jesus, knew of His godliness and holiness, even though he did not know until the heavenly dove appeared to rest upon Him that this was really the Son of God. Here the voice of God spoke aloud from Heaven. So did it when Jesus was on the Mount of Transfiguration (Matt. 17:5; Mark 9:7; Luke 9:35). It did again in John 12:28.

We will note in verse 23 that Jesus was about thirty years old. Up till this time He had never preached a sermon, never worked a miracle, never won a soul. In John, chapter 2, following His baptism, we see that Jesus went to Cana of Galilee and at the wedding turned water to wine and *"this beginning of miracles did Jesus in Cana of Galilee"* (John 2:11). So Jesus did not begin His public ministry until He was filled with the Spirit and we will find that all His miraculous work He did as our Example through the power of the Holy Spirit which came upon Him, and not simply as the Son of God. See the discussion on Luke 4:16-21.

VERSES 23—38:

23 And Jesus himself began to be about thirty years of age, being (as was supposed) the son of Joseph, which was *the* son of Heli,

24 Which was *the son* of Matthat, which was *the son* of Levi, which was *the son* of Melchi, which was *the son* of Janna, which was *the son* of Joseph,

25 Which was *the son* of Mattathias, which was *the son* of Amos, which was *the son* of Naum, which was *the son* of Esli, which was *the son* of Nagge,

26 Which was *the son* of Maath, which was *the son* of Mattathias, which was *the son* of Semei, which was *the son* of Joseph, which was *the son* of Juda,

27 Which was *the son* of Joanna, which was *the son* of Rhesa, which was *the son* of Zorobabel, which was *the son* of Salathiel, which was *the son* of Neri,

28 Which was *the son* of Melchi, which was *the son* of Addi, which was *the son* of Cosam, which was *the son* of Elmodam, which was *the son* of Er,

29 Which was *the son* of Jose, which was *the son* of Eliezer, which was *the son* of Jorim, which was *the son* of Matthat, which was *the son* of Levi,

30 Which was *the son* of Simeon, which was *the son* of Juda, which was *the son* of Joseph, which was *the son* of Jonan, which was *the son* of Eliakim,

31 Which was *the son* of Melea, which was *the son* of Menan, which was *the son* of Mattatha, which was *the son* of Nathan, which was *the son* of David,

32 Which was *the son* of Jesse, which was *the son* of Obed, which was *the son* of Booz, which was *the son* of Salmon, which was *the son* of Naasson,

33 Which was *the son* of Aminadab, which was *the son* of Aram, which was *the son* of Esrom, which was *the son* of Phares, which was *the son* of Juda,

34 Which was *the son* of Jacob, which was *the son* of Isaac, which was *the son* of Abraham, which was *the son* of Thara, which was *the son* of Nachor,

35 Which was *the son* of Saruch, which was *the son* of Ragau, which was *the son* of Phalec, which was *the son* of Heber, which was *the son* of Sala,

36 Which was *the son* of Cainan, which was *the son* of Arphaxad, which was *the son* of Sem, which was *the son* of Noe, which was *the son* of Lamech,

37 Which was *the son* of Mathusala, which was *the son* of Enoch, which was *the son* of Jared, which was *the son* of Maleleel, which was *the son* of Cainan,

38 Which was *the son* of Enos, which was *the son* of Seth, which was *the son* of Adam, which was *the son* of God.

The Genealogy of Jesus Through Mary

Compare this with the genealogy give in Matthew 1:1-17. That genealogy is of Christ as King of the Jews, and goes back to David and Abraham and is obviously the genealogy through Joseph, a legal parent, because Matthew 1:16 says, "*And Jacob begat Joseph the husband of Mary, of whom was born Jesus, who is called Christ.*" Dr. Scofield says in his note on Luke 3:23:

> In Matthew, where unquestionably we have the genealogy of Joseph, we are told (1. 16) that Joseph was the son of Jacob. In what sense, then, could he be called in Luke "the son of Heli"? He could not be by natural generation the son both of Jacob and of Heli. But in Luke it is not said that Heli *begat* Joseph, so that the natural explanation is that Joseph was the son-in-law of Heli, who was, like himself, a descendant of David. That he should in that case be called "*son* of Heli" ("son" is not in the Greek, but rightly supplied by the translators) would be in accord with Jewish usage (cf. 1 Sam. 24. 16). The conclusion is therefore inevitable that in Luke we have Mary's genealogy; and Joseph was "*son* of Heli" because espoused to Heli's daughter. The genealogy in Luke is Mary's whose father, Heli, was descended from David.

It is interesting also that the genealogy through Joseph goes back through Solomon, David's son (Matt. 1:6,7), and through Jechonias (Matt. 1:11), while the literal genealogy of Jesus Christ through Mary goes back through Nathan, another son of David and leaves out Solomon's descendants, including Jechonias. This Jechonias is the Coniah of Jeremiah 22:28-30 and verse 30 says, "*Thus saith the Lord, Write ye this man childless, a man that shall not prosper in his days: for no man of his seed shall prosper, sitting upon the throne of David, and ruling any more in Judah.*" That was true then in the captivity, but if Jesus were literally the Son of Joseph and so descended through Coniah or Jechonias, then He could not reign as He will do when He returns to sit on the throne of David according to the promise of Luke 1:33 and many other Scriptures.

It is suggestive also that the genealogy here in Luke goes all the way back to Adam and to God, and that indicates that the Gospel according to Luke is written about Jesus as the Son of Man, the pattern Man. We will find that Jesus is called "*Son of man*" eighty times in the New Testament: twenty-nine times in Matthew, fourteen times in Mark, twenty-six times in Luke, ten times in John and one in the book of Acts. He who is the Son of God, and the King of Glory, loved to call Himself the "*Son of man.*"

How the humanity of the incarnated Christ shines out in these genealogies in Luke and in Matthew! He is the Son of all mankind, not only the Son of Abraham, and of Jewish race, but the Son of Rahab the harlot and the Son of Ruth the Moabitess and so the Saviour of Gentiles as well as Jews. He is the Son of man, of King David, on the one hand, and of all those who preceded David and those who followed him through the line of Nathan, not a king. So humble Mary, in a peasant home in Nazareth, is the mother of the Saviour.

Christ is the Son of the rich and the poor. Abraham and David were rich, but for the humble Mary, there was no room in the Inn, and her Baby, our Saviour, was born in the stable.

Whatever taint of sin is in poor, fallen mankind, was close to Jesus, though never in Jesus. He who never sinned came from the line of Judah and his daughter-in-law Tamar when she played the harlot. He came from the line of Rahab the Canaanite harlot at Jericho, who was converted and saved alive and married Salmon from whom was born Boaz, grandfather of David. He came from the line of David and Bathsheba after David had seduced Bathsheba and had her husband slain.   Oh, the Lord Jesus, who knew no sin, loved mankind and put Himself down in the midst of our poor, fallen sinful race.   He made Himself truly the "*Son of man.*"

So the Lord Jesus rose from the dead, still with a human body, a glorified body, with a body such as we will have, a body that ate and drank before His disciples and, we believe, a body like the perfect body of Adam in the Garden of Eden before sin came.   And as a Man, the perfect Man, the God-Man, Christ will return to sit on David's throne and rule over the house of Jacob as the angel promised Mary, before His birth, (Luke 1:32,33) and over the whole world (Dan. 2:44). Oh, and truly, Hebrews 4:15 tells us:

"*For we have not an high priest which cannot be touched with the feeling of our infirmities; but was in all points tempted like as we are, yet without sin.*"

And again, Hebrews 7:26-28 comforts us with these blessed words:

"*For such an high priest became us, who is holy, harmless, undefiled, separate from sinners, and made higher than the heavens; Who needeth not daily, as those high priests, to offer up sacrifice, first for his own sins, and then for the people's: for this he did once, when he offered up himself. For the law maketh men high priests which have infirmity; but the word of the oath, which was since the law, maketh the Son, who is consecrated for evermore.*"

How fitting that the angels should announce to the shepherds, "*UNTO YOU is born this day in the city of David a Saviour, which is Christ the Lord.*"   Yes, to the shepherds, to the poor, the weak, the ignorant, the sinful, to the high and the low, the Jew and the Gentile, to the king and the slave, Jesus is Son of Man and a fit Saviour and a fit High Priest for all the sinning race.

LUKE 4

VERSES 1, 2:

AND Jesus being full of the Holy Ghost returned from Jordan, and was led by the Spirit into the wilderness,

2 Being forty days tempted of the devil. And in those days he did eat nothing: and when they were ended, he afterward hungered.

The Temptation of Christ

Jesus *"being full of the Holy Ghost."* Since He had now been baptized and set out to be a pattern for Christians and to enter His public ministry in the power of the Holy Spirit, Jesus must be tempted to the very limit in order to make Him a fit Substitute for sinning man. So, He was *"in all points tempted like as we are, yet without sin"* (Heb. 4:15). If the Spirit-filled Saviour is to work wonderful things in the power of the Holy Spirit, then He must show that one can be tempted, yet resist successfully and still be filled with the Spirit and carry on God's work.

"Forty days." Forty seems to be a special number for testing. Israel was forty years in the wilderness. Jonah preached *"forty days, and Nineveh shall be overthrown,"* a delay of forty days in which Nineveh could repent (Jonah 3:4). Forty stripes in a beating was the limit (Deut. 25:3; II Cor. 11:24). God seems to have made much of the forty years' testing for Israel (Exod. 12:35; Num. 14:33; Ps. 95:10). And three times in the reign of the judges, after great apostasy and then divine deliverance, Israel had rest forty years before further testing (Judg. 3:11; 5:31; 8:28). So Jesus had all the limit of temptation, yet without sin.

VERSES 3, 4:

3 And the devil said unto him, If thou be the Son of God, command this stone that it be made bread.
4 And Jesus answered him, say- ing, It is written, That man shall not live by bread alone, but by every word of God.

The First Temptation: The Desires of the Body

Note that when we speak of the temptation of Jesus, we should mean not only the three particular temptations mentioned in verses 3 to 12, but He was *"forty days tempted of the devil"* before these three temptations, and then temptation ceased only *"for a season"* (vs. 13).

The temptation was first for bread when Jesus was desperately hungry after forty days of fasting, but Jesus would not succumb to that temptation. He could have made the bread as He originally made these very stones and made all things, but He could not rightly do so. First, He was led of the Spirit to fast and He must obey. Second, He must resist all the temptations and go to whatever degree of hunger any other poor, frail human might suffer, and yet Jesus must reject the temptation. How much more important than food to eat, it was to live by the Word of God!

Here in verse 4 Jesus quoted from Deuteronomy 8:3 *"that man shall not live by bread alone, but by every word of God."* This quotation as given in Matthew 4:4, reporting the same incident, says, *"but by every word that proceedeth out of the mouth of God."* Jesus is putting His endorsement on the claim of Scripture that every word in the original manuscript came from the mouth of God. That is verbal inspiration beyond cavil.

The temptation here is to the physical man — the gnawing pain and desire of hunger. Every Christian must decide continually whether he will *"mortify the deeds of the body"* (Rom. 8:13). He must learn to *"deny himself*

... and follow me" (Matt. 16:24), Jesus said. No Christian worker will ever be of much service for God until he is willing to be poor, to be hungry, to be sick, to lack fine clothes or a pleasant home, and the comforts and luxuries that other people take for granted. So Jesus is tempted on this matter of His fleshly needs — normal, bodily cravings.

Concerning times of temptation, I John 2:16 seems to give an outline under three heads, *"For all that is in the world, the lust of the flesh, and the lust of the eyes, and the pride of life, is not of the Father, but is of the world."* When Eve sinned, she *"saw that the tree was good for food":* that is the lust of the flesh. *"And that it was pleasant to the eyes":* there is the lust of the eyes, the appeal of beauty, desirable and attractive things. *"And a tree to be desired to make one wise":* that is the pride of life, the desire for pre-eminence, and so naturally attainment and popularity. So Eve was tempted and fell, and so Adam fell.

The three temptations listed here seem to follow somewhat the same outline. Jesus was tempted by *"the lust of the flesh,"* the natural bodily needs and desires. He was tempted by *"the lust of the eyes,"* that is, He saw all the beautiful kingdoms and nations of this world over which He will sometime righteously reign. Oh, He must have longed for that beautiful perfection, that glorious righteousness and holiness and eternal goodness, even as good Christians today long for it. And the next temptation was to *"the pride of life,"* to have the acclaim of the multitude, the praises and worship which is His due.

But Jesus turned down this temptation to supply the natural needs of the body for food. No, that must not come first. The Spirit-filled Son of God must seek first the kingdom of God, so He answered Satan with a Scripture, quoting from Deuteronomy 8:3. Man is

never to put bread first, bodily needs first, the flesh
first. The tempted Saviour knew that now, in this awful
testing time, He must not take His thoughts or His
desires from the will of the Father. Oh, let every Christian remember that he needs more to feed every day on
the Word of God than to supply his bodily needs for
food.

VERSES 5—8:

5 And the devil taking him up
into an high mountain, shewed unto
him all the kingdoms of the world
in a moment of time.
6 And the devil said unto him,
All this power will I give thee, and
the glory of them: for that is
delivered unto me; and to whomsoever I will I give it.
7 If thou therefore wilt worship
me, all shall be thine.
8 And Jesus answered and said
unto him, Get thee behind me, Satan: for it is written, Thou shalt
worship the Lord thy God, and
him only shalt thou serve.

The Second Temptation: The Lust of the Eyes,
Attainment, Success, Happiness

Here the temptation is for Jesus to go on to His
glorious reign in power, without going to the cross.
He could avoid the shame, the poverty, the abuse, the
spittle and Gethsemane, the bloody sweat, the mocking
crowds, the public condemnation, the scourging, the
humiliation and the pain that killed Him on the cross.
He could avoid the long delay while the Gospel is
preached before the Second Coming.

You see, what Satan offered Jesus is really what He
is going to have without Satan, and Jesus Christ is to
be *"the faithful witness, and the first begotten of the
dead, and the prince of the kings of the earth"* (Rev.
1:5). He is the *"Alpha and Omega, the beginning and
the ending. . .the Almighty"* (Rev. 1:8). Now He has
the keys of Hell and death (Rev. 1:18). Oh, He will

come riding a white horse, followed by the angels and all the hosts of Heaven, and "*out of his mouth goeth a sharp sword, that with it he should smite the nations: and he shall rule them with a rod of iron: and he treadeth the winepress of the fierceness and wrath of Almighty God. And he hath on his vesture and on his thigh a name written, KING OF KINGS, AND LORD OF LORDS*" (Rev. 19:15,16). He is "*the blessed and only Potentate, the King of kings, and Lord of lords; Who only hath immortality. . .*" (I Tim. 6:15,16). So to Him every knee shall bow in Heaven and earth and Hell and "*every tongue should confess that Jesus Christ is Lord, to the glory of God the Father.*" See Philippians 2:10,11. So all things that were created in Heaven and earth "*visible and invisible, whether they be thrones, or dominions, or principalities, or powers: all things were created by him, and for him: And he is before all things, and by him all things consist*" (Col. 1:16,17), so that "*in all things he might have the preeminence*" (vs. 18).

Oh, what Satan promised Jesus is not as much as God the Father has already put aside for Him. But Satan wanted Him to take it the easy way. Satan offered the crown without a cross; offered Jesus a reign without dying.

But let us remember that if Christ had gone to reign without dying, then the rest of us would have gone to Hell. For the only Gospel by which anybody can be saved is that "*Christ died for our sins according to the scriptures; And that he was buried, and that he rose again the third day according to the scriptures*" (I Cor. 15:3,4).

How Satan hated the matter of Christ's atoning death! So he had Herod try to kill Him when He was a baby, as he killed the other boy babies of Bethlehem (Matt. 2:16). So the Pharisees took council to destroy Jesus ahead of time (Matt. 12:14), but could not. John 10:31 tells us how *"the Jews took up stones again to stone him,"* but could not. And here in Luke 4:28,29 we learn how His own neighbors in Galilee rose up in wrath in the synagogue and *"thrust him out of the city, and led him unto the brow of the hill whereon their city was built, that they might cast him down headlong,"* but He slipped away.

Oh, if Satan could only kill Jesus before He fulfilled the Scriptures! If it could be on some other day besides the day of the killing of the passover! If He could die somewhere else besides on a tree, as was prophesied. If He could die some other way than with wounds in His hands and His feet, some other way than with a spear piercing His side, as foretold. If He could die somewhere without fulfilling the prophecies of Psalm 22, or without the stripes and beating of Isaiah 53! Satan wished to defeat the scriptural plan. For if Jesus were to be a Saviour, it had to be that He died *"according to the scriptures."*

So the night before His crucifixion in Gethsemane Satan tried to kill Him and Jesus said, *"My soul is exceeding sorrowful, even unto death"* (Matt. 26:38; Mark 14:34). When Jesus prayed, *"Let this cup pass from me,"* He was not praying against the will of God but in the will of God. Hebrews 5:7 tells us about it: *"Who in the days of his flesh, when he had offered up prayers and supplications with strong crying and tears unto him that was able to save him from death, and was heard in that he feared."*

Oh, here in this temptation Satan tries to get Jesus to ruin the Gospel and go to a reign without crucifixion and without saving sinners! And the weight of all the souls in the universe hung in the balance that fateful day when the tempted Saviour turned down the invitation in order to go to the cross and pay sin's debt and invite to Himself a multitude who would call Him Saviour!

VERSES 9—13:

9 And he brought him to Jerusalem, and set him on a pinnacle of the temple, and said unto him, If thou be the Son of God, cast thyself down from hence:

10 For it is written, He shall give his angels charge over thee, to keep thee:

11 And in *their* hands they shall bear thee up, lest at any time thou dash thy foot against a stone.

12 And Jesus answering said unto him, It is said, Thou shalt not tempt the Lord thy God.

13 And when the devil had ended all the temptation, he departed from him for a season.

The Third Temptation: The Love and Honor and Praise of the People

The third temptation is to *"the pride of life."* It is not wrong for one to crave love and friendship, to have one's character admired, one's righteousness known, one's beauty and goodness praised. So we may be sure the dear Jesus longs for the joyful day when people will come from the north and east and south and west to sit down with Abraham and Isaac and Jacob in the kingdom of God. He longs, I am sure, for that day when all the hosts of Heaven and on earth and in Hell will bow the knee to Him, and when the Hallelujah Chorus will be sung out more gloriously than it has ever been sung according to that which John in prophecy foretold: *". . . I heard a great voice of much people in heaven, saying, Alleluia; Salvation, and glory, and honour, and power, unto the Lord our God"* (Rev. 10:1).

So will the Lord Jesus show miraculous power to get the acclaim of the multitude? Will He prove Himself, His deity, His power, by showing His marvelous works to everyone? Shall He show them He is not bound by human limitations and human frailty and weakness?

Let Him leap down from the pinnacle of the Temple, that corner of the Temple platform where the wall of Jerusalem rears seventy feet high in a sharp corner above the Valley of Kidron.   He could cast Himself down.   And Satan reminds Him of the promise of Psalm 91:11 and 12, that *"He shall give his angels charge over thee, to keep thee: And in their hands they shall bear thee up, lest at any time thou dash thy foot against a stone."*

No, Jesus is not to show His power simply to gain followers. He will feed five thousand starving people out of His compassion, and again four thousand.   But again and again when He works some great miracle He will insist that it not be told.   Out of His compassion He healed the sick, He raised the dead, He did mighty works when people trusted Him, but all this He did not to show His strength but out of the compassion of His heart He set all of us an example.   When He was before Pilate, the Roman governor was astonished that He would make no defense.   Jesus answered not a word (Matt. 26:11-14; Mark 15:2-5).   Jesus could have so pleaded His case that there would have been no possibility for Him to be condemned and crucified.   He could have called twelve legions of angels to His defense, but He did not.   No, *"as a sheep before her shearers is dumb, so he openeth not his mouth"* (Isa. 53:7).

Oh, Jesus will have time for the plaudits and praise and adoration of the throngs.   But first He must be the meek and lowly Jesus, despised and rejected of men. The cross and its shame, with the spitting, His betrayal by Judas, His murder by the Pharisees and Romans, His being forsaken even by His disciples — all this must come first.

So Christ turned down the invitation, the temptation to *"the pride of life,"* and He answered Satan's false use of Scripture with another Scripture, "*Thou shalt not tempt the Lord thy God*" (Deut. 6:16).

Let us remember then that no one ought ever try to demonstrate supernatural powers in order to impress men. Those who would talk in tongues or work miracles or take up snakes, or those who would have some other marvelous spiritual successes to gain the applause of men, thus fall to the temptation where Jesus did not succumb.

And Satan "*departed from him for a season.*"

How well the Lord Jesus illustrates Psalm 119, verses 9 and 11 which say, "*Wherewithal shall a young man cleanse his way? by taking heed thereto according to thy word.*" And again, "*Thy word have I hid in mine heart, that I might not sin against thee.*"

So Jesus, filled with the Scriptures and thoroughly committed to please His Father, and atone for sin, answered Satan and answered the probings in His own heart with Scripture, and so may we.

There have been great controversies over whether Jesus could have sinned. Let us remember the Scripture says that He was "*in all points tempted like as we are, yet without sin*" (Heb. 4:15). I think we may simply say that He could not consent to sin. He was tempted to sin but He was so moral and good and righteous and so wholly committed to the Father's will that He would never consent to sin. He could have sinned if He could have consented to sin, but He could not sin because He would not be willing to sin.

VERSES 14, 15:

14 And Jesus returned in the power of the Spirit into Galilee: and there went out a fame of him through all the region round about. 15 And he taught in their synagogues, being glorified of all.

Jesus Still Filled With Holy Spirit

Jesus returned "*in the power of the Spirit.*" Note carefully that since the Holy Ghost descended in a bodily shape upon Jesus in Luke 3:23, at His baptism, then Jesus, full of the Spirit, returned from Jordan where He was baptized (Luke 4:1) and "*was led by the Spirit into the wilderness*" to be tempted (same verse). So, now, we find that still the mighty enduement of God is upon Him. For what came at His baptism was not simply a temporary blessing, not simply the public acknowledgement of God the Father but it was a holy enduement of power. And from that moment of His baptism on to His death and on to His resurrection and beyond, through His millennial reign on earth, the dear Lord Jesus will be filled without limit with the power of the Holy Spirit. He is the Model, the perfect Pattern, the Spirit-filled Man, the Son of man.

John, who himself had been filled with the Holy Ghost since his mother's womb, tells us in John 3:34 concerning Jesus, "*For God giveth not the Spirit by measure unto him.*" Oh, the perfect sinless Saviour, sold out in every detail to do the will of the Father in paying sin's debt and redeeming sinners, is fit to be filled continually, perfectly without measure with the Holy Spirit of God.

VERSES 16 — 21:

16 And he came to Nazareth, where he had been brought up: and, as his custom was, he went into the synagogue on the sabbath day, and stood up for to read.

17 And there was delivered unto him the book of the prophet Esaias. And when he had opened the book, he found the place where it was written,

18 The Spirit of the Lord *is* upon me, because he hath anointed me to preach the gospel to the poor; he hath sent me to heal the broken-hearted, to preach deliverance to

the captives, and recovering of sight to the blind, to set at liberty them that are bruised,

19 To preach the acceptable year of the Lord.

20 And he closed the book, and he gave it again to the minister, and sat down. And the eyes of all them that were in the synagogue were fastened on him.

21 And he began to say unto them, This day is this scripture fulfilled in your ears.

Jesus, Our Pattern, Did All His Ministry and Preaching and Miracles in the Power of the Holy Spirit

In the above passage we have a marvelous truth made clear. Jesus came back to Nazareth where He had spent nearly thirty years and as was His custom, He went to the synagogue on a Sabbath day. He was widely known as the best Bible student, the most righteous and godly among them, and so, of course, they asked Him to read. He took the scroll of Isaiah and turned until He found Isaiah 61:1,2 and read, "*The Spirit of the Lord is upon me, because he hath anointed me to preach the gospel.*"

The Lord Jesus is anointed to preach. Thirty years old and He had never preached until that holy anointing came. He had never worked a miracle until after His baptism and then He went, as John, chapter 2, tells us, to Cana of Galilee and there turned the water to wine at the wedding and "*this beginning of miracles did Jesus in Cana of Galilee*" (John 2:11).

Let us face it: when Jesus preached a sermon He did not preach it in the perfection of wisdom as the Son of God, but He preached it as a good Man, a sinless Man, a Man filled with the Holy Spirit. It is true that Jesus is God, but He had humbled Himself and taken on Himself the form of a servant. He had laid aside the garments of deity and the appearance of deity to appear as a man. He called Himself "*the Son of man.*" And so all His work is to be done in the same way that we can do it, for He said in John 14:12,

"*Verily, verily, I say unto you, He that believeth on me, the works that I do shall he do also; and greater works than these shall he do; because I go unto my Father.*" He had said in John 8:12, "*I am the light of the world.*" And again, "*As long as I am in the world, I am the light of the world*" (John 9:5). But in Matthew 5:14 He said, "*Ye are the light of the world.*" We, too, are the same kind of light that Jesus is. In fact, Christ is within us and He and we are saviours together of sinners.

In the high priestly prayer, Jesus prayed to the Father, "*As thou hast sent me into the world, even so have I also sent them into the world*" (John 17:18). And the day that He arose from the dead He breathed on the disciples and said to them, "*As my Father hath sent me, even so send I you. And when he had said this, he breathed on them, and saith unto them, Receive ye the Holy Ghost*" (John 20:21,22). This truth that Jesus is a Spirit-filled Son of man and that all His ministry was in the power of the Holy Spirit is expressed here. He was anointed to preach the Gospel to the poor. It is expressed even more clearly in Acts 10:37,38:

"*That word, I say, ye know, which was published throughout all Judaea, and began from Galilee, after the baptism which John preached; How God anointed Jesus of Nazareth with the Holy Ghost and with power: who went about doing good, and healing all that were oppressed of the devil; for God was with him.*"

God was with Jesus, that is, the Holy Ghost was with Him. God the Father anointed Jesus of Nazareth with the Holy Ghost and all His miracles, all His preaching, all His soul winning was done in the power of the Holy Spirit.

That is why the second Psalm calls Him the "*anointed.*"

The Hebrew word for it is *Messiah,* the Greek word is *Christos* or *Christ.*

And so when David was anointed to be king, he was thus typifying this greater Son of David who will be anointed King. And when Aaron was anointed to be high priest, he was only typifying our great High Priest. It is significant that such a volume of oil was poured upon Aaron's head that it *"ran down upon the beard . . . that went down to the skirts of his garments"* (Ps. 133:1,2). You see, it pictures the limitless power of the Holy Spirit given the Lord Jesus, since *"God giveth not the Spirit by measure unto him"* (John 3:34). Jesus had not the frailty and sinfulness that often limit the Holy Spirit's power on us.

So we are told in Hebrews 9:14 that when Jesus went to the cross He *"through the eternal Spirit offered himself without spot to God."* Acts 1:2 says that before ascending, *"He through the Holy Ghost had given commandments unto the apostles whom he had chosen."* And when He comes back to reign, He will come *"a rod out of the stem of Jesse, and a Branch shall grow out of his roots: And the spirit of the Lord shall rest upon him, the spirit of wisdom and understanding, the spirit of counsel and might, the spirit of knowledge and of the fear of the Lord. . ."* (Isa. 11:1,2). And so in the Holy Place of the Temple, the golden lampstands burning pure olive oil pictures Jesus, the Light of the world, burning in the power of the Holy Spirit. So Jesus, our blessed Pattern, did not preach until He was anointed to preach. What shame ought to fill the hearts of all who try to do God's work without God's power!

We remember Nadab and Abihu, sons of Aaron, who were ordained to be priests but who put common fire on the altar when God had forbidden and said that He would furnish supernatural fire. Leviticus 10:1 and 2 tells how *"there went out fire from the Lord, and*

devoured them, and they died before the Lord." Oh,
in how many pulpits, in how many classes there is a
strange fire instead of the divine fire! How God despises
it and curses it! Not human wisdom nor talent nor
personality put the anointing power of the Holy Spirit
is what all God's people need.

But let us stop to savor all the riches Christ came to
bring. He came anointed *"to preach the gospel to the
poor; he hath sent me to heal the broken-hearted, to
preach deliverance to the captives, and recovering of
sight to the blind, to set at liberty them that are bruised,
To preach the acceptable year of the Lord."* Oh, the
poor have the Gospel preached to them! God wanted
publican and harlot. He wanted us to scour the highways and hedges to get them. He wanted that one lost
sheep, and so should we.

Oh, there is healing for the brokenhearted. There is
deliverance for the captives of sin! How often have we
seen God take the thirst from the drunkard and the
habit from the dope addict! How often have we seen
Him make the adulterer and the harlot pure, make the
infidel into a believing saint! Oh, you who are blinded
and imprisoned and bruised, Jesus came for you.

It is significant that Jesus, quoting from Isaiah 61:1
and 2, stopped in the middle of a sentence. The rest
of the sentence is, *". . . and the day of vengeance of our
God; to comfort all that mourn." "The day of vengeance
of our God"* is not now but is at the second coming, so
Jesus did not read that part. Note carefully verse 21,
*"And he began to say unto them, This day is this
scripture fulfilled in your ears."* Now, for the first time
they heard Jesus speak when He was filled with the Holy
Spirit.

VERSES 22—30:

22 And all bare him witness, and wondered at the gracious words which proceeded out of his mouth. And they said, Is not this Joseph's son?

23 And he said unto them, Ye will surely say unto me this proverb, Physician, heal thyself: whatsoever we have heard done in Capernaum, do also here in thy country.

24 And he said, Verily I say unto you, No prophet is accepted in his own country.

25 But I tell you of a truth, many widows were in Israel in the days of Elias, when the heaven was shut up three years and six months, when great famine was throughout all the land;

26 But unto none of them was Elias sent, save unto Sarepta, *a city* of Sidon, unto a woman *that was* a widow.

27 And many lepers were in Israel in the time of Eliseus the prophet; and none of them was cleansed, saving Naaman the Syrian.

28 And all they in the synagogue, when they heard these things, were filled with wrath,

29 And rose up, and thrust him out of the city, and led him unto the brow of the hill whereon their city was built, that they might cast him down headlong.

30 But he passing through the midst of them went his way,

What Happened When Jesus Spoke First to Neighbors in the Power of the Holy Spirit?

Isaiah 61 is now fulfilled for the first time, and they see Jesus now not simply as a pure and moral and model young Man, righteous and clean and good, but there is a burning to His words that cuts them to the heart. Human goodness will never take the place of divine power. Now Jesus has the power of the Holy Spirit.

And let us learn the lesson that no matter how moral and upright you are, how kind to your neighbors; you may tithe your income, you may be faithful in church, have family devotions, pay honest debts, love and read the Bible—but all that will not win souls. Unless you are anointed with the power of God, you cannot do the work of God. Even the Lord Jesus had never worked a miracle nor preached a sermon nor won a soul until He was filled with the Holy Spirit at His baptism.

But now they are astonished: "Is not this Joseph's son? Is this the same young Man we have known these twenty-odd years?" How strange it seemed to them! Oh, what a difference the power of God makes!

But the witness and prophesying in the power of the Holy Spirit is not all sweetness and light. Sometimes there is the ax in the hand of John the Baptist, there is a scourge as Jesus drives out the moneychangers in the Temple. Now His words burn the hearts of these, His townsmen. Why does He not show His power here and do the miracles He did in Capernaum? "We are your neighbors!" But their unbelief, their lack of repentance, made it unsuitable for Him to do any miracles there. He reminds them that Elijah was sent only to one widow and only Naaman the Syrian was cleansed among many lepers because of the awful wickedness and unbelief of the people.

This kind of preaching aroused the anger of men. It does now. John the Baptist's plain preaching led to his imprisonment and his murder. Paul's plain preaching got him in jail many times. He was beaten; many times he caused riots and tumults and was without food, without friends. He had scars upon his body. And at last, after long imprisonment, he was beheaded. The right kind of preaching will bring opposition. Jesus is despised and rejected of men; and that is the part of those who are filled with the Holy Spirit.

They "led him unto the brow of the hill whereon the city was built, that they might cast him down headlong," verse 29 says. But it was not the time for His death, so He slipped away. They still call a point of a hill there "the hill of precipitation," which tradition says is the hill from which they would have cast the Saviour down.

From now on we follow the steps of a Spirit-filled Saviour, the "*Son of man*," through the Gospel of Luke.

VERSES 31, 32:

31 And came down to Capernaum, a city of Galilee, and taught them on the sabbath days.

32 And they were astonished at his doctrine: for his word was with power.

Jesus Now Makes Capernaum His Home

Jesus had visited Capernaum before and had done mighty works there preceding His return to His "own country," Nazareth (vs. 23). His townsmen had heard of it, blamed Him that He did not do as great works in Nazareth as at Capernaum. But now He moves to Capernaum to live. Matthew 4:13 says, "*And leaving Nazareth, he came and dwelt in Capernaum, which is upon the sea coast, in the borders of Zebulon and Nephthalim.*" We take for granted that with him went his mother, Mary, and her other children. Joseph we suppose to be dead since he has not been mentioned in the Scripture since that trip to Jerusalem when Jesus was twelve years old (Luke 2:41-51).

Making Capernaum His home, He "*taught them on the sabbath days,*" we suppose regularly. And from now on "*most of his mighty works*" would be done in the towns around the north end of the Sea of Galilee: Chorazin, Bethsaida and Capernaum (Matt. 11:20-23). What a marvelous blessing for Capernaum that Jesus should live there, that all the people could see Him, His miracles, hear Him, talk to Him! The city was "*exalted unto heaven,*" as Jesus said in Matthew 11:23. We are not surprised then that the judgment of God has blotted it out until nothing remains but the ruins of an old synagogue and even the town was unidentified for centuries.

The people "*were astonished at his doctrine: for his word was with power.*" There is a burning, condemning, awakening, cyclonic power in the Word of God when it is carried by the Holy Spirit. And since Jesus received His anointing power at His baptism (Luke 2:22), He has been filled continually with the Spirit (Luke 4:1,14, 18) and that would be true from now on. Not all would like His teaching but it would be powerful, mighty everywhere He went. There was no ebb to that mighty power because, "*For he whom God hath sent speaketh the words of God: for God giveth not the Spirit by measure unto him*" (John 3:34).

Let all the powerless throw away their excuses, that they cannot get crowds, that people will not listen, that there are no life-changing results. "*His word was with power*" was true of Jesus. It was also true of many other Bible preachers and of many since Bible times. We, too, are commanded, "*be filled with the Spirit*" (Eph. 5:18). The promise of the gift of the Spirit "*is unto you, and to your children, and to all that are afar off, even as many as the Lord our God shall call*" (Acts 2:39).

VERSES 33 — 35:

33 And in the synagogue there was a man, which had a spirit of an unclean devil, and cried out with a loud voice,
34 Saying, Let *us* alone; what have we to do with thee, *thou* Jesus of Nazareth? art thou come to destroy us? I know thee who thou art; the Holy One of God.
35 And Jesus rebuked him, saying, Hold thy peace, and come out of him. And when the devil had thrown him in the midst, he came out of him, and hurt him not.

Jesus Casts Out Devils

This poor man *"had a spirit of an unclean devil."* The Greek word is *daimon,* that is, a demon, not *diabolos,* who is *"the Devil and Satan,"* the accuser, the fallen Lucifer (Isa. 14:12), the *"prince of the power of the air"* (Eph. 2:2), the tempter of the Saviour, and the greater enemy of our souls. Not that god of this world (II Cor. 4:4), the Devil, Satan, but a demon, evil spirit, like those that often possessed men then and often, no doubt, possess men now. Some thirty times in the Gospel is the casting out of devils or unclean spirits mentioned; so we must account this one of the principal works of the Lord Jesus, in preaching the Gospel to the poor, healing the brokenhearted, preaching deliverance to the captives, recovering of sight to the blind and setting at liberty them that are bruised, as He was anointed to do and did (see vs. 18; Isa. 61:1,2). These evil spirits sometimes caused sickness (*"a spirit of infirmity,"* Luke 13:11). Some rendered people deaf and therefore dumb (Mark 9:17,25). And sometimes evil spirits made people insane, mentally ill like the Gadarene demoniac (Luke 8:27-38). Sometimes they gave people more than human wisdom about the future or revealing of secrets, like *"a certain damsel possessed with a spirit of divination. . . which brought her masters much gain by soothsaying"* of Acts 14:16. It seems clear that the prohibition in Deuteronomy 18:10,11 of *"one that. . . useth divination, or an observer of times, or an enchanter, or a witch, Or a charmer, or a consulter with familiar spirits, or a wizard, or a necromancer,"* refers to consulting with such evil spirits. So spiritists and fortunetellers are always evil, are sometimes devil-possessed now, certainly so if they are able to foretell the future or reveal unknown secrets.

Jesus gave the twelve disciples *"power against unclean*

*spirits, to cast them out, and to heal all manner of
sickness and all manner of disease"* (Matt. 10:1; Mark
6:7; Luke 9:1,2).   And that commission to cast out
devils is someway given along with the Great Commission in Mark 16:15-18.   Among the signs that shall
follow them that believe is, *"In my name shall they cast
out devils"* (Mark 16:17).   That certainly does not mean
that everyone who is saved will cast out devils, but only
those who have faith for this power may have it.

In these sophisticated times, we think that demon-possession is not as obvious among enlightened people.
And yet a maniac senselessly murders eight nurses in
Chicago.   Two days ago at Manchester, Tennessee, a
sheriff and deputy were gunned down by a mental patient
without reason.   Surely much crime, much of alcoholic
and dope enslavement, much of the rage of communism,
is the work of demons on men.   A more subtle work of
devils is to act as the angels of light and to deceive
God's people, so we are commanded to *"try the spirits
whether they are of God"* (I John 4:1).   There is a
kinship between apostate false teachers and evil spirits,
*"false apostles, deceitful workers, transforming them-
selves into the apostles of Christ"* (II Cor. 11:13).   So
it is not surprising that Hell, which is prepared for the
Devil and his angels, will also be the home of Christ-
rejecting sinners.

But demon-possession such as we see in Bible times,
is often found in heathen nations now.   Early missionaries in China reported many such cases and witch
doctors in Africa seem often to be really demon-possessed.

Oh, but the Gospel in the power of God is for these,
too, and Christians need to have power to free the
enslaved and darkened who want to be free.

Note that the demons (plural) knew Jesus.   Verse 34
says that they cried out, *"Saying, Let us alone; what
have we to do with thee, thou Jesus of Nazareth? art*

*thou come to destroy us? I know thee who thou art;
the Holy One of God.*" Other demons showed that they
knew Jesus Christ (vs. 41), so the legion of devils in the
Gadarene demoniac pleaded, "*What have we to do with
thee, Jesus, thou Son of God? art thou come hither to
torment us before the time?*" (Matt. 8:29). They recognized Jesus as Master and Ruler of the universe, knew
that He would one day cast them into the lake of fire
prepared for the Devil and his angels. James 2:19
says, "*Thou believest that there is one God; thou doest
well: the devils also believe, and tremble.*" Demons
may make men into infidels and religious liberals but
they themselves know Jesus and believe in Him. Remember that the evil spirit whom the sons of Sceva tried
to cast out answered and said, "*Jesus I know, and Paul
I know; but who are ye?*" (Acts 19:15).

VERSES 36, 37:

36 And they were all amazed, and spake among themselves, saying, What a word *is* this! for with authority and power he commandeth the unclean spirits, and they come out.

37 And the fame of him went out into every place of the country round about.

The Word With Power

Verse 32 says, "*They were astonished at his doctrine:
for his word was with power.*" There was authority and
power in Jesus Christ. And the man of God who can
cast out devils, making the drunkard sober, making
the harlot pure, making the infidel into a humble believer, making the criminal into a saint, can get attention and respect and hearers. Billy Sunday, Sam
Jones, Bob Jones, Spurgeon, Wesley and other mighty
soul winners have been able to get the attention of
people and crowds because of the obvious power of

God that commanded respect and attention by this poor, hungry-hearted, distraught world!

VERSES 38, 39:

38 And he arose out of the synagogue, and entered into Simon's house. And Simon's wife's mother was taken with a great fever; and they besought him for her.

39 And he stood over her, and rebuked the fever; and it left her: and immediately she arose and ministered unto them.

Jesus Heals Peter's Wife's Mother

Leaving the synagogue, Jesus "*entered into Simon's house.*" Peter's home was at Bethsaida (John 1:44). He may have moved to Capernaum, but it is not mentioned, and we suppose Bethsaida was only about four miles east. Bethsaida is mentioned as one of the cities wherein most of these mighty works were done (Matt. 11:20,21). So, possibly this miracle and the others in verses 40 and 41 and many more were at or near Bethsaida.

"*Simon's wife's mother. . . .*" So Peter was married and the Roman requirement of unmarried priests is wholly artificial and unscriptural. They pleaded for Jesus to heal the fever-stricken woman and He did, immediately! God does not always heal the sick, but He often does. God usually uses human means to heal bodies or to win souls, but He certainly sometimes does heal the sick without any medicine or doctors, in answer to believing prayer. So James 5:13-16 teaches us to have prayer for the sick, but only "*the prayer of faith*" is promised to heal the sick. If God gives the faith, He can give the healing and will. But Paul's thorn in the flesh was not removed (II Cor. 12:1-10). Timothy's unhealed weak stomach needed the vitamins of fruit juices (I Tim. 5:23), and often God's best blessings come through sickness.

VERSES 40—44:

40 Now when the sun was setting, all they that had any sick with divers diseases brought them unto him; and he laid his hands on every one of them, and healed them.

41 And devils also came out of many, crying out, and saying, Thou art Christ the Son of God.   And he rebuking *them* suffered them not to speak: for they knew that he was Christ.

42 And when it was day, he departed and went into a desert place: and the people sought him, and came unto him, and stayed him, that he should not depart from them.

43 And he said unto them, I must preach the kingdom of God to other cities also: for therefore am I sent.

44 And he preached in the synagogues of Galilee.

The Attraction of a Saving, Healing Christ

Many people were healed.   We judge that in every case they wanted to be healed and they came for that purpose and others interceded for them.   Every such an one was healed, verse 40 tells us.   But His words at Nazareth in verses 25 to 27 indicate that where there is little faith there is little healing and little blessing.

Oh, the crowd that gathered in the twilight when blessing came.   No doubt the Saviour was late getting to rest but when day came "*he departed and went into a desert place,*" that is, a place with no people.   For one thing, He needed to be alone to pray.   For another, He had such a burning burden for all the people of Galilee.   So, despite the pleadings that He remain, He went and preached in the other synagogues of Galilee.

LUKE 5

VERSES 1—3:

AND it came to pass, that, as the people pressed upon him to hear the word of God, he stood by the lake of Gennesaret,

2 And saw two ships standing by the lake: but the fishermen were gone out of them, and were washing *their* nets.

3 And he entered into one of the ships, which was Simon's, and prayed him that he would thrust out a little from the land. And he sat down, and taught the people out of the ship.

Outdoor Preaching

"*The lake of Gennesaret*" is the little Sea of Galilee. The great preaching of Wesley and Whitefield was "field preaching." No church could contain the people. And Wesley, after a struggle, would go away from his formal Anglican tradition and go to preach where the people, the poor, the unchurched, the illiterate, the sinful would come in crowds to hear him. So Spurgeon went to Surrey Music Hall and other great auditoriums, and then had built the tabernacle seating 5,000 which was always crowded to standing room, to hear him. So the great revivals have taken place in tents, in big auditoriums, in crude tabernacles.

One who follows Jesus must go to get the crowds and perhaps go where the crowds are. Paul preached in a loft, in people's homes, by the seaside, on shipboard. The ministry of Jesus was with the multitudes, usually in the open air, or wherever they could be assembled. John the Baptist preached to the multitudes by the River Jordan. Not a single church building is mentioned in the New Testament! And of the church at Jerusalem we are told that, "*daily in the temple, and in every house, they ceased not to teach and preach Jesus Christ*" (Acts 5:42).

Blessed is that preacher and that Christian who will not confine his witness to a church house but takes it to the people everywhere.

Two ships were *"standing by the lake,"* that is, possibly tied to a wharf or pulled slightly out of the water. The fishermen had worked in the night when it was thought they were more likely to catch fish (See John 21:1-3).

VERSES 4 — 11:

4 Now when he had left speaking, he said unto Simon, Launch out into the deep, and let down your nets for a draught.

5 And Simon answering said unto him, Master, we have toiled all the night, and have taken nothing: nevertheless at thy word I will let down the net.

6 And when they had this done, they inclosed a great multitude of fishes: and their net brake.

7 And they beckoned unto *their* partners, which were in the other ship, that they should come and help them. And they came, and filled both the ships, so that they began to sink.

8 When Simon Peter saw *it*, he fell down at Jesus' knees, saying, Depart from me; for I am a sinful man, O Lord.

9 For he was astonished, and all that were with him, at the draught of the fishes which they had taken:

10 And so *was* also James, and John, the sons of Zebedee, which were partners with Simon. And Jesus said unto Simon, Fear not; from henceforth thou shalt catch men.

11 And when they had brought their ships to land, they forsook all, and followed him.

Jesus Calls Peter, Andrew, James and John

Jesus will call four men here to be His disciples, learners, to be made into apostles, to witness and speak with authority for Him in the churches until the Scriptures should be written. But He will teach them that the ministry means fishing for men. What an object lesson! As they had toiled all night without results (vs. 5), now, when they let down their newly washed nets "*they in-closed a great multitude of fishes.*" The unusual load was enough to break their nets. James and John, sons of Zebedee, and Peter's partners, were called. Both ships were filled: "*filled. . . so that they began to sink,*" that is, that the waves lapped water over the sides.

Obviously this was a miracle of God. This was no ordinary good catch of fish but of fish miraculously assembled. Before such a miracle Peter was conscience-smitten: "*He fell down at Jesus' knees, saying, Depart from me; for I am a sinful man, O Lord.*" Ah, but to the four of them but primarily to Simon, Jesus said, "*Fear not; from henceforth thou shalt catch men.*"

What lessons are here!

1. Serving God is fishing for men. It is like a shepherd who goes after the lost sheep. It is like a woman who seeks the one lost coin at any cost. It is like the father eagerly receiving the prodigal son. It is like the servant bidding men to the dinner who went to the poor, the lame, the blind, and in highways and hedges to compel people to come in.

2. But working for God is a miracle business. D. L. Moody said, "It is foolish to try to do God's work without God's power." It is no Bible kind of ministry that does not have the power of Jesus Christ to catch the fish.

3. And surely the lesson is, too, that we should expect the power of God to reach the great multitudes. Some may be content with small crowds and small results and only a few people saved, but Jesus was not content and we ought not to be.

Now, they brought the ships to land and the four of them "*forsook all, and followed him.*" Their hearts are forever given over now from making money and providing for their families, to following the Saviour and fishing for men.

Some additional details are given in the account of the call of these four in Matthew 4:18-22. Probably Jesus before this had said to Peter and Andrew, "*Follow me, and I will make you fishers of men*" (Matt. 4:18,19). And then a little further He had made the same call to James and John who were in a ship with Zebedee their father, mending their nets: "*And they immediately left the ship and their father, and followed him.*" And we suppose that then Jesus preached in Peter's ship, and they launched out for the great draught of fishes. And in the thrill and impact of that mighty event they left all to follow Jesus. Peter and Andrew left their nets. James and John left their father and the ship. One must always give up some things to follow Jesus.

We are greatly impressed with the fact that they went without any promise of support for their families. It was a step of faith gladly taken.

And this event of the wonderful catch of fish was re-enacted after Peter had gotten backslidden and denied Christ and quit the ministry, when the resurrected Saviour appeared by the seaside in John 21. Again after that great net full of fish, Peter was called afresh and started again to follow Jesus, to wait in the Upper Room, and to preach with power at Pentecost and afterward.

VERSES 12—16:

12 And it came to pass, when he was in a certain city, behold a man full of leprosy: who seeing Jesus fell on *his* face, and besought him, saying, Lord, if thou wilt, thou canst make me clean.

13 And he put forth *his* hand, and touched him, saying, I will: be thou clean. And immediately the leprosy departed from him.

14 And he charged him to tell no man: but go, and shew thyself to the priest, and offer for thy cleansing, according as Moses commanded, for a testimony unto them.

15 But so much the more went there a fame abroad of him: and great multitudes came together to hear, and to be healed by him of their infirmities.

16 And he withdrew himself into the wilderness, and prayed.

Jesus Heals the Leper

A simple, moving and beautiful story here. Faith and need cried out, *"Lord, if thou wilt, thou canst...,"* and Jesus answered, *"I will."* The instant healing of leprosy was a miracle. Leprosy is often used as a type of sin. And this shows how the Lord can, in a moment, make the black heart white, make one who is a child of Hell into a child of God with a home in Heaven and a new heart on earth.

Jesus had the man go show himself to the priest and *"offer for thy cleansing, according as Moses commanded, for a testimony unto them."* We may see in Leviticus 14:4 the small testimonial sacrifice required. And that indicates that even in Old Testament times a leper was sometimes miraculously healed and it also indicates that Jesus was not healing in order to prove Himself deity. He healed out of great compassion which He and the Father have for troubled and sick and sinning people.

The Saviour's fame increased. Many more came to be healed. *"And he withdrew himself into the wilderness, and prayed."*

How often Jesus went aside and prayed! And so we need to do.

VERSES 17 — 26:

17 And it came to pass on a certain day, as he was teaching, that there were Pharisees and doctors of the law sitting by, which were come out of every town of Galilee, and Judæa, and Jerusalem: and the power of the Lord was *present* to heal them.

18 And, behold, men brought in a bed a man which was taken with a palsy: and they sought *means* to bring him in, and to lay *him* before him.

19 And when they could not find by what *way* they might bring him in because of the multitude, they went upon the housetop, and let him down through the tiling with *his* couch into the midst before Jesus.

20 And when he saw their faith, he said unto him, Man, thy sins are forgiven thee.

21 And the scribes and the Pharisees began to reason, saying, Who is this which speaketh blasphemies? Who can forgive sins, but God alone?

22 But when Jesus perceived their thoughts, he answering said unto them, What reason ye in your hearts?

23 Whether is easier, to say, Thy sins be forgiven thee; or to say, Rise up and walk?

24 But that ye may know that the Son of man hath power upon earth to forgive sins, (he said unto the sick of the palsy,) I say unto thee, Arise, and take up thy couch, and go into thine house.

25 And immediately he rose up before them, and took up that whereon he lay, and departed to his own house, glorifying God.

26 And they were all amazed, and they glorified God, and were filled with fear, saying, We have seen strange things to day.

The Paralytic Healed

This story is wonderfully told in Mark 2:1-12. There we learned there were four friends which carried the paralyzed man. Note some lessons here:

1. Often a number of Christians, working together, can bring one to Christ who could not be brought by one.

2. Often the general crowd of church people are a hindrance instead of a help. The onlookers, the nominal church members, those who take no active part in the winning of souls, hinder the work, as they did here.

3. But to get the man to Jesus was worth the extra trouble it took to carry him, to get him on the housetop, to break up the roof. Doubtless it caused a good deal of criticism. Most likely the replacing of the tile roof cost money or work. Any effort at winning souls

without tears, without burden, without giving up over some failures and obstacles, is not likely to be successful.

4. The man was a paralytic but he came first of all not to be healed but to get saved. So Jesus first said, "*Man, thy sins are forgiven thee.*" More important than all healing and all of the blessings is to know the forgiveness of sins. This forgiveness is the first of the six great blessings in Psalm 103:1-6.

5. When Jesus "*saw their faith.*" Not simply the faith of the man, but the faith of those four men, looking down to Him from the hole in the roof! Their's was a faith that could be seen. Their efforts, their patience, their willingness to pay whatever it cost, was such an expression of faith that Jesus could see.

It is interesting to see in Hebrews 11 that by faith Noah built an ark, and by faith Abraham and all the other heroes did certain things. Faith that works can be seen. Honest, hard work to get sinners to Jesus is faith in action. We sometimes wonder, Why cannot a lost sinner trust Jesus Christ? It may be a greater question: Why cannot Christians trust Him as these men did, working to get men to Jesus?

6. The healing of the man proved that "*the son of man hath power upon earth to forgive sins.*" Saving power, and some wonderful manifestation of healing frequently went together in Bible times and so they do now. In times of great revival I have often seen God give a rain in time of great drought, seen Him heal the sick, or I have seen God show His power in other ways. God backs up those who trust Him.

The result of the miracle was amazement and glory to God, and holy fear. So it ought to be.

VERSES 27 — 29:

27 And after these things he went forth, and saw a publican, named Levi, sitting at the receipt of custom: and he said unto him, Follow me.

28 And he left all, rose up, and followed him.

29 And Levi made him a great feast in his own house: and there was a great company of publicans and of others that sat down with them.

The Call of Matthew the Publican

The same event is recorded in Matthew 9:9 and in Mark 2:13,14. From Mark we learn that this Levi was the son of Alphaeus. And from the account in Matthew we learn that Levi's other name was Matthew. He later wrote the book of Matthew and there used his other name.

He was the son of Alphaeus, says Mark 2:14. But Mark 3:18, Luke 6:15, Acts 1:13 mention "*James the son of Alphaeus.*" This was the disciple, James the Less, not the brother of John. Very possibly, then, James the Less and Matthew were brothers, as were James and John, the sons of Zebedee, and as were Andrew and Peter.

What a heartwarming example is this man Matthew! He hears the call of Jesus, and immediately leaves his profitable career as a tax collector and follows Jesus.

He lived in Capernaum where the previous events of the chapter occurred. It is certain he had heard Jesus before and had been moved by His marvelous ministry. It seems probable he had already trusted Christ as Saviour or at least had come to face clearly the problem of turning from sin and committing himself to Jesus and trusting Jesus. And now in a moment the whole matter is settled for certain and the dye is cast. He is not only saved but is definitely surrendered to be a disciple or learner under Jesus, then an itinerate preacher of the Gospel, an apostle, "*one sent.*"

And how can Levi quickly use his wide influence for the Lord? He is not poor, he has wide acquaintance. So, in his own home he makes a *"great feast,"* and invites *"a great company"* of publicans and the associates of publicans to the feast where they can meet and hear the Lord Jesus!

How wise it is to use every contact and every influence of love and friendship and business, to get people to hear the Gospel! How wise are those who set up tract stands and pulpits at fairs, and festivals, to witness for Jesus! Every father-son banquet, every mother-daughter banquet, every "bring-a-friend" dinner one can give that will bring Christians in loving contact under proper circumstances where the Gospel can be preached, is good.

Once the writer was invited to a football banquet given by a small church. Two or three members of the strong high school football squad were members of the church. They made a big dinner. All the football squad, their fathers, their mothers, their coach, their sweethearts, were invited. The team was honored as a civic matter and then I preached the Gospel and every member of the squad not already saved claimed the Saviour openly. The loving influence of coach and classmates and fathers and mothers were all combined in a happy social event to win to Christ. Bravo, Levi! You used all your social and business connections to get people to hear the Gospel!

VERSES 30—32:

30 But their scribes and Pharisees murmured against his disciples, saying, Why do ye eat and drink with publicans and sinners?

31 And Jesus answering said unto them, They that are whole need not a physician; but they that are sick.

32 I came not to call the righteous, but sinners to repentance.

Why Jesus Seeks Sinners First

Such a *"great company"* of publicans and their friends who met at Matthew's house for the feast stirred the indignation of the Pharisees and scribes, the religious people. Were not the publicans, those tax collectors for the Romans, hated enemies of the Jewish people? The government required of a tax collector in a certain area only a certain amount of money. All he could collect beyond that was his own. So most publicans became rich and most were oppressive. So Zacchaeus, when converted, said, *"Behold, Lord, the half of my goods I give to the poor; and if I have taken any thing from any man by false accusation, I restore him fourfold."* So the publicans were not good Jews, usually not good men. Their companions would usually be bad people according to the strict standards of the Jewish law. So the Pharisees would ask Jesus, *"Why do ye eat and drink with publicans and sinners?"* If the Lord Jesus was a good man, why would He not prefer to associate only with the moral, religious people like the Pharisees and scribes?

But the answer reveals the heart of Jesus. The main concern of His heart was to get sinners saved. Those who were well did not need a physician and those who thought they were well would not heed one. So Jesus said, *"I came not to call the righteous, but sinners to repentance."*

Note carefully the one great overpowering aim of the Lord Jesus Christ is *"to save sinners."* So in I Timothy 1:15 Paul tells of that good and worthy proverb that was going around, *"This is a faithful saying... that Christ Jesus came into the world to save sinners; of whom I am chief."* Do not ever mistake it: Jesus did not come into the world to improve society, to establish benevolent institutions, to raise the standards of womanhood, to do away with slavery and polygamy, to refine the arts and cultures. No. It is true that all these things stem from Christ and His influence and from Christianity. If you take out the impact of Christ on literature, art, public morals, and laws and government, you would strike out the very best of our civilization. But that is not what Jesus came for. These things are the incidental by-products. What He really came for is to save sinners! So the Great Commission is all centered on this one main thing—getting people saved and getting them committed, and teaching them to win others.

How clear this is made in the parables of the lost sheep, the lost coin, the prodigal son, in Luke 15! How clear it is made in the parable of the man who made a great supper and bade many, in Luke 14 and in Matthew 22! Pastors, churches, Sunday school teachers, and all Christians who do not make the winning of sinners to Christ the main business thus miss the point of the Saviour's coming into this world.

Jesus a Friend of Sinners but Never Yoked With Them

The Lord Jesus always called sinners to His position. He never joined them on theirs. The dear Lord Jesus would never "do wrong to get a chance to do right." He would never "*do evil that good may come.*" Paul, who was inspired to write, "*Be ye not unequally yoked together with unbelievers*" (II Cor. 6:14), wrote for Jesus. The Apostle John said, "*Whosoever transgresseth, and abideth not in the doctrine of Christ, hath not God. He that abideth in the doctrine of Christ, he hath both the Father and the Son. If there come any unto you, and bring not this doctrine, receive him not into your house, neither bid him God speed: For he that biddeth him God speed is partaker of his evil deeds*" (II John 9-11). But it was really Christ speaking, for the Spirit of God who wrote the Scriptures is the Spirit of Christ. The Pharisees and scribes will ask Jesus to put His new wine in their old bottles but He never will. The unconverted Temple authorities were shocked when Jesus overturned the tables of the moneychangers and upset the routine of the Temple and the money-making sale of cattle there. He scorned their religious traditions. He held no meetings under their sponsorship, never sought nor had their commendation.

The publicans and sinners with whom He associated and for which He was so scorned by the scribes and Pharisees were penitent ones like Levi, like the weeping woman who wept over His feet (Luke 7:36-50). Like Zacchaeus the publican at Jericho converted and making restitution (Luke 19:1-10), other sinners often heard Him gladly, crowds of common people, but found no compromise, no excusing their sins. Jesus never hinted that anyone could be a servant of God without being born again. Those who have unbelieving professors in colleges and seminaries, those who receive unconverted members in churches, those who have religious liberals or infidels to help sponsor and control revival campaigns or denominations, have no excuse for their disobedience in either the words or the example of Jesus. Jesus preached to unbelievers; did not preach jointly with them. Unconverted sinners should be in the congregation hearing the preacher, not on the platform being honored or counted as religious leaders.

VERSES 33—35:

33 And they said unto him, Why do the disciples of John fast often, and make prayers, and likewise *the disciples* of the Pharisees; but thine eat and drink?
34 And he said unto them, Can

ye make the children of the bride-
chamber fast, while the bridegroom is with them?
35 But the days will come, when
the bridegroom shall be taken
away from them, and then shall
they fast in those days.

Is Fasting for New Testament Christians?

Both the disciples of John and the disciples of the
Pharisees *"fast often,"* the Pharisees and scribes told
Jesus. We remember that the self-righteous Pharisee in
the parable in Luke 18:12 said, *"I fast twice in the
week."* Now it was not wrong to fast, but these unsaved
men did not fast for a good purpose. In Matthew 23:5
Jesus said about the scribes and Pharisees, *"But all
their works they do for to be seen of men...."* Millions
of others like them go through religious exercises, thus
satisfying their conscience that they are good men, thus
hoping to have favor with God for their religiousness.
In Matthew 6 Jesus gave plain instructions that people
are not to give their alms, nor to say their prayers, nor
to do their fasting, in order to impress people or *"to
be seen of men."*
Some devout people set out to fast one day a week.
They do not thus necessarily make themselves better
Christians.
However, as a matter of earnestly waiting on God and
seeing that one puts all the lesser matters out of mind in
order to more wholly give oneself to prayer and waiting
upon God, fasting is good. One might for a time give
up sleep in order to pray. One might for a time give
up food in order to pray. In I Corinthians 7:1-6, hus-
bands and wives are plainly warned that they belong to
each other, and one should not defraud the other of the
normal marriage affection and duty. But they are permitted to withhold themselves from this natural comfort
if it be *"with consent for a time, that ye may give yourselves to fasting and prayer; and come together again,*

that Satan tempt you not for your incontinency" (I Cor. 7:5). There is no spiritual virtue in fasting itself but only in the attitude of mind that seeks to find God's will and blessing, and thus gladly for a time leave off normal enjoyments and comforts.

So the Lord Jesus fasted forty days when He was tempted in the wilderness (Luke 4:2). Thus a group of earnest Christians fasted and prayed before Paul and Silas were set apart for their missionary journeys (Acts 13:2,3).

The widow Anna *"served God with fastings and prayers night and day"* (Luke 2:37), and that was good, as was the fastings of the disciples of John. Jesus indicated, after the wonderful healing of the devil-possessed boy, *"Howbeit this kind goeth not out but by prayer and fasting"* (Matt. 17:21). The earnestness in prayer, which is indicated by fasting, is a part of successful prayer. So in II Corinthians 6:4 and 5 Paul lists fastings as a part of the evidence of a good minister of Christ, and in II Corinthians 11:27 he says that he himself was *"in fastings often."* And he may mean that if one were true to Christ, not having food to eat was sometimes the reason for fasting.

So here in verse 35 Jesus said, *"But the days will come, when the bridegroom shall be taken away from them, and then shall they fast in those days."* So, after the ascension, when the disciples gather in the Upper Room for those ten days of waiting on God, no doubt some or all of them fasted while they continued in prayer and supplication (Acts 1:14).

VERSES 36—39:

36 And he spake also a parable unto them; No man putteth a piece of a new garment upon an old; if otherwise, then both the new mak-

eth a rent, and the piece that was *taken* out of the new agreeth not with the old.

37 And no man putteth new wine into old bottles; else the new wine will burst the bottles, and be spilled, and the bottles shall perish.

38 But new wine must be put into new bottles; and both are preserved.

39 No man also having drunk old *wine* straightway desireth new: for he saith, The old is better.

Parables of the Garment and Bottles

The Pharisees and scribes were disturbed that Jesus did not follow their pattern and fit in with the customs they had developed. They wanted to continue the Jewish priesthood, the animal sacrifices, and their own places of leadership. They did not want an atoning Saviour to die an atoning death and fulfill all the ceremonies and types and prophecies of the Old Testament.

But Jesus tells them in two parables that God loves to start anew. He would not cut out a piece of the new garment to patch it onto an old garment. They would not match and that would not succeed. God's dealings with Israel had been a pattern: now, through the Jewish people come a Saviour and the Scriptures so that through Christ, Abraham's seed, should come blessings to all the world.

Jesus had new fruit juice. It must not be put into old wine skins which could not stretch with the new wine, lest it burst the old leather containers.

Here is a great principle of God's work. Some greatly anointed man of God founds an institution, starts a denomination, a school, a mission board, or local church. After poverty and struggle and fidelity comes security, approval of men, complacency. So God diminishes His blessing on the complacent one, starts with another Spirit-filled man, another institution. God for a time put mighty power on John Wesley and the

Methodist movement. It got rich and powerful and officially turned away from the Gospel and the soul-winning emphasis and the loyalty to the Bible and the Spirit-filled zeal of early Methodists. So God takes His hand off the institution and starts over with new groups of fervent souls. They are sometimes in small groups, not always sound on every detail but always with fervor and holy concern.

The Northern Baptist Convention, now the American Baptist, was once about the strongest soul-winning and missionary influence in the world and in one foreign field baptized 2,222 converts in a day. Then the zeal and faithfulness declined and the number of churches and the number of missionaries and the number of converts. God starts over.

Spurgeon's Metropolitan Tabernacle in London, which was regularly jammed with over 5,000 people on Sunday, now has, an authority of the church in London told me, regularly only about 100 in attendance! The church went back into the liberal connection Spurgeon had left for its unbelief, but it does not prosper.

The churches mentioned and praised in the New Testament times have all disappeared and the only remnant is the monstrosity that grew out of that little faithful group in Rome.

So we may expect that the places God blesses will be new schools and young churches. And the greatest revivals will be in new auditoriums or tents or open air. God leaves the formal, the ritual, the stylized worship, the groups set in traditional ways and puts His new wine in new bottles.

LUKE 6

VERSES 1 — 11:

AND it came to pass on the second sabbath after the first, that he went through the corn fields; and his disciples plucked the ears of corn, and did eat, rubbing *them* in *their* hands.

2 And certain of the Pharisees said unto them, Why do ye that which is not lawful to do on the sabbath days?

3 And Jesus answering them said, Have ye not read so much as this, what David did, when himself was an hungred, and they which were with him;

4 How he went into the house of God, and did take and eat the shewbread, and gave also to them that were with him; which it is not lawful to eat but for the priests alone?

5 And he said unto them, That the Son of man is Lord also of the sabbath.

6 And it came to pass also on another sabbath, that he entered into the synagogue and taught: and there was a man whose right hand was withered.

7 And the scribes and Pharisees watched him, whether he would heal on the sabbath day; that they might find an accusation against him.

8 But he knew their thoughts, and said to the man which had the withered hand, Rise up, and stand forth in the midst. And he arose and stood forth.

9 Then said Jesus unto them, I will ask you one thing; Is it lawful on the sabbath days to do good, or to do evil? to save life, or to destroy *it?*

10 And looking round about upon them all, he said unto the man, Stretch forth thy hand. And he did so: and his hand was restored whole as the other.

11 And they were filled with madness; and communed one with another what they might do to Jesus.

Hungry Disciples Eat Grain in the Fields on the Sabbath

The Scripture says this happened "*on the second sabbath after the first.*" We suppose the "*first*" Sabbath refers to the one in the synagogue at Nazareth (Luke 4:16). The "*disciples*" here are simply followers: the twelve were not yet chosen till verses 12 and 13 afterward.

It seems likely that these disciples who were following Jesus were hungry indeed. Perhaps they often were hungry and we should take literally what Jesus said in Matthew 8:20 and Luke 9:58, *"Foxes have holes, and the birds of the air have nests; but the Son of man hath not where to lay his head."* From Matthew 27:55 we know that some women of Galilee followed Jesus even to Jerusalem *"ministering unto him."* And as He went through the villages and towns of Galilee also some women were named who *"ministered unto him of their substance"* (Luke 8:1-3).

We can understand why Jesus discouraged the faint-hearted from becoming regular disciples of His. If we connect John 7:53 with the first verse of the following chapter, we find, *"And every man went unto his own house. Jesus went unto the mount of Olives,"* and then *"early in the morning he came again into the temple."* Did Jesus sleep, perhaps, on the ground, in the Garden of Gethsemane? We think He probably did.

However, Jesus Did Not Really Break the Sabbath Command

Rubbing out a handful of wheat in the hands and blowing the chaff away so one could eat the grain was not work in the Bible sense. Even in the two high annual Sabbaths, beginning and ending the feast of the passover and of unleavened bread in Exodus 12:14-16, the command simply specified *"no manner of work shall be done in them, save that which every man must eat, that only may be done of you"* (Exod. 12:16).

The Pharisees would have made this a violation of the Sabbath by rabbinical rules. But it was not and Jesus here calls attention to a case in I Samuel 21:6 when David was given the showbread for himself and his men to eat, though by Exodus 25:30, and Leviticus 24:5-9, it was intended only for the priests. But it is clear that the command is a ceremonial command not intended to make hardship in an emergency. Jesus, accused of breaking the Sabbath again in the healing of an afflicted woman, reminded the ruler of the synagogue, *"Thou hypocrite, doth not each one of you on the sabbath loose his ox or his ass from the stall, and lead him away to watering?"* And wasn't it more important to heal this woman (Luke 13:15,16).

And again, in Luke 14:1-4, when Jesus healed a man of dropsy the lawyers and Pharisees looked accusingly at Him. He said, *"Which of you shall have an ass or an ox fallen into a pit, and will not straightway pull him out on the sabbath day?"* (Luke 14:5). We do not wonder that *"they could not answer him again to these things."*

No, Jesus did not do wrong to heal on the Sabbath day. And Jesus properly asked them in verse 9, *"Is it lawful on the sabbath days to do good, or to do evil? to save life, or to destroy it?"* Here is a case where *"the letter killeth, but the spirit giveth life"* (II Cor. 3:6). Without any understanding of the spiritual impact of the ceremonial law and the teaching under it, lawyers and Pharisees made their rules, interpreting the law.

"The Son of Man Is Lord Also of the Sabbath"

This does not mean, as Seventh-Day Adventists say, that *"the Lord's day"* of Revelation 1:10 was the Jewish Sabbath. No, it means that the Lord Jesus is Master not only of all the other days but of the Sabbath days, too. When Christ had the first Sabbath, He had finished creation and *"he rested on the seventh day from all his work which he had made"* (Gen. 2:2). He blessed the Sabbath day then because a great spiritual meaning was involved in it, though the Sabbath was not made known to man until it became part of the ceremonial law later. When God looked on the world He had made and found it good, then He could rest and Christ could rest. But soon God's Sabbath of rest was broken: man sinned! Now, God must start to work again, with all the prophecies, the Scriptures, the ceremonial laws and types pointing to the Saviour, then the coming of the Saviour Himself and finally His atoning death and resurrection. So Jesus said in John 5:17, *"My Father worketh hitherto, and I work."* Then when the atonement was finished Jesus could cry out triumphantly on the cross, *"It is finished"* (John 19:30). At least the atonement was finished, although the work of getting the Gospel to sinners everywhere remained for us (Col. 1:24), then and now.

But Jesus, Lord of the Sabbath, had a right to give it in the first place when He gave the ceremonial law, and to end it, in the second place, when He ended the ceremonial law.

The Saturday Sabbath Was Ceremonial Law

This truth is clear from several evidences:

1. The Sabbath was never commanded to anyone until God gave it to Moses and Israel in Exodus 16:23-30. *"So the people rested on the seventh day"* (vs. 30) and that was the first time that men ever observed the Sabbath on earth. It is never mentioned that Adam, Abel, Seth, Noah, Abraham, Isaac, or Jacob ever knew about the Sabbath or observed it. It was never commanded before Exodus 16.

2. The Sabbath was never commanded in the New Testament. The moral commands of the Old Testament are repeated concerning idolatry, profanity, murder, adultery, stealing, covetousness, and lying. But there is no New Testament command about the Sabbath. In all the list of virtues and good works, the Sabbath-keeping is never mentioned, and in all the list of sins of the flesh, Sabbath-breaking is never mentioned in the New

Testament.   The ceremonial law was never commanded
to anybody but to Jews.

3. It is true the Sabbath is in the Ten Commandments.
But God does not separate the Ten Commandments
from the rest of His law.   In the context of the Ten
Commandments God gives both moral and ceremonial
laws.   The Ten Commandments in Exodus 20 start out,
*"I am the Lord thy God, which have brought thee out
of the land of Egypt."* And in Deuteronomy 5 where
the Ten Commandments are repeated, the passage starts
off, *"And Moses called all Israel, and said unto them,
Hear, O Israel, the statutes and judgments which I
speak in your ears this day, that ye may learn them,
and keep, and do them."* The Ten Commandments
were addressed primarily to Israel.

4. Nehemiah 9:12-14 plainly tells us that the Sabbath
is a part of the ceremonial law, made known at Mount
Sinai.

*"Moreover thou leddest them in the day by a cloudy
pillar; and in the night by a pillar of fire, to give them
light in the way wherein they should go.   Thou camest
down also upon mount Sinai, and spakest with them
from heaven, and gavest them right judgments, and
true laws, good statutes and commandments: And
madest known unto them thy holy sabbath, and com-
mandedst them precepts, statutes, and laws, by the hand
of Moses thy servant."*

5. Exodus 31:12-14 says plainly that the Sabbath
was a sign between God and Israel and it is repeated
in verse 17.   Then Ezekiel 20:12 says, *"Moreover also
I gave them my sabbaths, to be a sign between me and
them, that they might know that I am the Lord that
sanctify them."* So Israel was set apart from the Gentiles,
with a Sabbath given them as a sign of their separation.

6. And Colossians 2:13,14 tells us how Christ *"having*

forgiven you all trespasses; Blotting out the handwriting of ordinances that was against us, which was contrary to us, and took it out of the way, nailing it to his cross." So the ceremonial law is not now binding. And verses 16 and 17 give some details: *"Let no man therefore judge you in meat, or in drink, or in respect of an holyday, or of the new moon, or of the sabbath days: Which are a shadow of things to come; but the body is of Christ."* So the Sabbath is a part of that handwriting of ordinances that was nailed to the cross, it was a shadow of things to come, it was a ceremonial picture, object lesson of spiritual truth in Christ. Now Christ is come and a New Testament Christian is not to be judged about the ceremonial Sabbath of the Jews.

It is very suggestive that Matthew 28 begins the story of the resurrection of Christ with *"In the end of the sabbath."* It was not only the end of the annual high Sabbath on Thursday (the day that followed 'the day of the preparation' on the passover—John 19:14,31, which we think was on Thursday that year), but also of the weekly Saturday Sabbath. Jesus was in the grave *"three days and three nights"* (Matt. 12:40) but the resurrection of Christ was also *"the end of the sabbath,"* in a sense, the end of the ceremonial law for those who understood.

The Sabbath Was "a Shadow of Things to Come"—Col. 2:17

What was the meaning then of the ceremonial Sabbath? There are two kinds of Sabbaths in the ceremonial law, with two kinds of meaning. First, the Saturday weekly Sabbath was a picture of Heaven earned by good works. The Sabbath command was not simply that the Jews must rest the seventh day, but *"six days shalt thou labour, and do all thy work,"* and then no work on the Sabbath. Six, in the Bible, is in some sense the number of man. Seven pictures deity and perfection, and thus Heaven. So God puts seven days in a week, and He put the number seven in nature; seven notes in the scale before the eighth which begins another seven, another octave. The eggs of various kinds of fowls hatch in 14, 21, 28, 35 days — all multiples of seven. The moon goes about the earth four times in seven days, and so is a woman's usual menstrual cycle.

Now, if one perfectly fills in all the work he ought to do in the six days of life, he would earn Heaven. If one were not born wrong the first time, he would never need to be born again. If one never sinned, he would never need forgiveness. If Adam and every other person had perfectly fulfilled the law of God, then there would have been no need of the atonement. Ah, then, the ceremonial Sabbath pictures the awful frustration that the natural man has. As a sinner he cannot earn Heaven! So in this matter, *"the law was our schoolmaster to bring us unto Christ"* (Gal. 3:24). No one ever earned Heaven, pictured by the Sabbath, because he never perfectly did all the work of God. The Sabbath commandment in the Decalogue requires perfection; no man has ever attained it since the fall but Jesus.

But there was another Sabbath given before the weekly Saturday Sabbath. Exodus 12:14-16 tells us that the day they ate the passover lamb, beginning the seven days feast of unleavened bread, was a day of *"holy convocation"* and so was the seventh day and *"no manner of work shall be done in them, save that which every man must eat"* (Exod. 12:16). That first Sabbath, beginning at sundown the day of the slaying of the passover lamb, was that *"high day,"* the annual Sabbath mentioned in John 19:31. *"For even Christ our passover is sacrificed for us"* (I Cor. 5:7) on the day that had been prophesied by the slaying of passover lambs for nearly 1500 years!

This is a different Sabbath from the weekly Saturday
Sabbath. This is an annual Sabbath but it pictures
salvation by grace, not salvation by works. The very
day one eats of the passover lamb, he has entered into
a Sabbath. That means that one has forgiveness and
peace with God and salvation without works and before
he has done any work. Then, in the days that follow,
he may work because he is saved but he does not work
in order to get saved.

But the seventh day of that feast is a Sabbath, too,
and that still pictures Heaven. I have heaven in my
heart now, Christ in my heart now, peace in my heart
now, but this will be made perfect in Heaven. So, in
Hebrews 4:9 and 10 we are told, "*There remaineth
therefore a rest to the people of God. For he that is
entered into his rest, he also hath ceased from his own
works, as God did from his.*" One has ceased to trust
himself and ceased from relying on his own works, and
so enters into rest here. But "*there remaineth. . . a rest.*"
And the word "*rest*" here is the Greek word *sabbatismos,*
Sabbath. We have rest now and will have rest in
Heaven.

Why Did Satan Use Lawyers and Scribes and Pharisees to Oppose Jesus So Strongly on This Sabbath Question?

Why did Jesus press the matter and insist upon healing on the Sabbath day? The issue was joined about
the disciples plucking corn on the Sabbath in Luke 6:1-
5, and in the companion passages: Matthew 12:1-8;
Mark 2:23-28. And again when Jesus healed the man
with the withered hand (Luke 6:10 and the companion
passages: Matthew 12:9-14; Mark 3:1-6). In Luke
13:10-17 the issue came up over the woman loosed
from her infirmity on the Sabbath and in Luke 14:1-6

the case of the man Jesus healed of dropsy on the
Sabbath.   John, chapter 5, tells how Jesus healed the
man by the pool of Bethesda on the Sabbath (John 5:9).
And verse 16 tells us, *"Therefore did the Jews persecute
Jesus, and sought to slay him, because he had done
these things on the sabbath day."* And again in verse
18, *"Therefore the Jews sought the more to kill him,
because he not only had broken the sabbath, but said
also that God was his Father, making himself equal
with God."*

You see, the very deity and authority of Christ was at
stake.   He is the Lord of the Sabbath.   And again, the
plan of salvation was involved.   People were never
saved by the ceremonial law, and Jesus must make that
clear that there is now a new covenant.   Ceremonies
could only picture Christ and salvation and they must
pass away.   They are the *"shadow of things to come;
but the body is of Christ"* (Col. 2:17).

The Lord's day, Sunday, is recognized among Christians ever since Christ rose from the dead.   It is not the
Sabbath changed to another day, as many suppose.
It is grace, not law; is voluntary, not commanded.   We
need the Lord's day for rest and for worship, but there
is no command to observe it.

VERSE 12:

12 And it came to pass in those days, that he went out into a mountain to pray, and continued all night in prayer to God.

The Prayer Life of Jesus

Jesus is our Pattern and we should walk in His steps
(I Pet. 2:21).   He has sent us even as the Father sent
Him into the world (John 17:18; John 20:21).   Jesus
is the Light of the world (John 8:12; John 9:5).   But

we are the light of the world also (Matt. 5:14). We are to have the same mind and surrender and unselfish devotion which Christ had (Phil. 2:5-8). And the very work that Jesus did we are to do also (John 14:12). So our prayer life ought to be much patterned after Jesus.

Mark 1:35 tells us, *"And in the morning, rising up a great while before day, he went out, and departed into a solitary place, and there prayed."* We ought to put God first in our lives, first in our giving, first in our love, and so first in every day. Before any other work Jesus prayed. He went into a solitary place to be alone with God.

Jesus prayed at His baptism (Luke 3:21,22). Evidently He prayed for Holy Spirit power to begin His ministry and to fulfill the promise and prophecy, made in His baptism, and that holy enduement came.

Jesus fasted for forty days during and before His temptation (Luke 4:1,2). We may be sure that the fasting was not a matter of pharisaical righteousness but included an honest heart-seeking after God, His will, His power. He said to Peter, *"Watch and pray, that ye enter not into temptation"* (Matt. 26:41). Surely His own success in resisting temptation came in answer to prayer.

In Luke 5:16 we learn when great fame came to Jesus and great multitudes came together to hear and be healed, *". . . he withdrew himself into the wilderness, and prayed."* We may need to pray more in success than in failure. Popularity is a great temptation. Success should be a time of earnest heart-searching and waiting on God lest our hearts be too much lifted up and we lose our burden and concern.

So here in Luke 6:12 we find that Jesus *"went out into a mountain to pray, and continued all night in prayer to God."* Blessed example! Often prayer is more important than sleep, more important than food, more important than work.

In Luke 9:18 we find that *"as he was alone praying, his disciples were with him."* Every Christian is somewhat alone with Christ when he prays. Here, the disciples about Him, Jesus was alone.

In Luke 9:28 we find that Jesus went up to the Mount of Transfiguration to pray, and verse 29 tells us that *"as he prayed, the fashion of his countenance was altered. . . ."* The result may not be so obvious and visible with us but a result there is, the reservoir of power is filled again, the waiting upon God renews strength for the burden (Isa. 40:30,31).

In Luke 11:1 we find that Jesus was praying in a certain place and when He ceased the disciples, greatly impressed with the compassion and burden for others and for Holy Spirit power, asked Him, *"Lord, teach us to pray."*

We may be sure that the Lord Jesus not only sometimes prayed all night, or rose up a great while before day to pray, or prayed alone or in the presence of others, but surely He did that which all of us are commanded to do. He prayed without ceasing (I Thess. 5:17). So we may be sure that His prayer connection with the Heavenly Father was maintained continually, so He could say, *"Father. . . I knew that thou hearest me always"* (John 11:41,42). And He surely must refer to a continual contact in prayer.

Here in Luke 6:12, Jesus prayed all night before selecting the twelve disciples who would be called apostles, and would be understudies and learners under Him for some three years. In Gethsemane He prayed again and again (Luke 22:42,44,45). And Hebrews 5:7 tells us, *"Who in the days of his flesh, when he had offered up prayers and supplications with strong crying and tears unto him that was able to save him from death, and was heard in that he feared."* One can never understand the continued blessing and power on Jesus' ministry unless we remember that He was a Man, the God-Man, but One who had limited Himself to human limitations, and the power of the Holy Spirit which we may have, too, and He prayed!

VERSES 13—16:

13 And when it was day, he called *unto him* his disciples: and of them he chose twelve, whom also he named apostles; 14 Simon, (whom he also named Peter,) and Andrew his brother, James and John, Philip and Bartholomew, 15 Matthew and Thomas, James the *son* of Alphæus, and Simon called Zelotes, 16 And Judas *the brother* of James, and Judas Iscariot, which also was the traitor.

The Twelve Apostles

Note carefully these apostles. Peter heads the list every time they are named. There are three sets of brothers: Andrew and Peter, James and John, and James the Less and Judas (not Iscariot). There are two Simons: Simon Peter and Simon called Zelotes. There are two Judases: Judas the brother of James the Less and Judas Iscariot. Jesus nicknamed James and John Sons of Thunder. Simon He surnamed Peter, the rock. Matthew had another name, Levi (Luke 5:27). The lesser Judas, not Iscariot, was also called Lebbaeus, and with a surname Thaddaeus. Perhaps he preferred not to use the name Judas after the betrayer was known.

Verses 12 and 13 suggest that Jesus was still in the mountain where He prayed all night when He sent for a group of disciples. From them He selected the twelve to be called "apostles," that is, *ones sent,* and gave them marvelous powers to cast out devils and heal the sick, as we are told in the companion Scripture, Matthew 10:1.

These twelve were specially commanded to go before Jesus *"to the lost sheep of the house of Israel,"* in the cities and towns where Jesus would follow. Detailed instruction for that tour of cities was given, with warnings of persecution.

The twelve are to be witnesses to Jesus' resurrection after His crucifixion and ascension; must have been with Him in all His ministry from the baptism of John to His resurrection (Acts 1:22). There must be twelve, as witness to Israel, so Matthias was elected after Judas' death.

Others called apostles later are Paul and Barnabas (Acts 14:14), James the brother of our Lord (Gal. 1:19), and Jesus Himself (Heb. 3:1).

VERSES 17 — 19:

17 And he came down with them, and stood in the plain, and the company of his disciples, and a great multitude of people out of all Judæa and Jerusalem, and from the sea coast of Tyre and Sidon, which came to hear him, and to be healed of their diseases;

18 And they that were vexed with unclean spirits: and they were healed.

19 And the whole multitude sought to touch him: for there went virtue out of him, and healed *them* all.

The Marvelous Ministry of Jesus

Notice that from far and near they came to hear the Saviour — from the Mediterranean coast around Tyre and Sidon, from Jerusalem all the way up to Galilee, and we suppose to Capernaum. Healing was a great part of His ministry. Devils were cast out. People came for blessing and got it. The fame of Jesus went everywhere. We can see that the carnal, natural man takes more to the healing ministry and material blessing than to spiritual preaching. But there ought to be a lesson for us in that the Spirit-filled man of God should have power for whatever is needed in the will of God.

VERSES 20—26:

20 And he lifted up his eyes on his disciples, and said, Blessed *be ye* poor: for your's is the kingdom of God.

21 Blessed *are ye* that hunger now: for ye shall be filled. Blessed *are ye* that weep now: for ye shall laugh.

22 Blessed are ye, when men shall hate you, and when they shall separate you *from their company*, and shall reproach *you*, and cast out your name as evil, for the Son of man's sake.

23 Rejoice ye in that day, and leap for joy: for, behold, your reward *is* great in heaven: for in the like manner did their fathers unto the prophets.

24 But woe unto you that are rich! for ye have received your consolation.

25 Woe unto you that are full! for ye shall hunger. Woe unto you that laugh now! for ye shall mourn and weep.

26 Woe unto you, when all men shall speak well of you! for so did their fathers to the false prophets.

The Beatitudes

Compare these with the beatitudes in Matthew 5:3-12. There nine of these blessings are named; here there are four. The meek, they that hunger and thirst after righteousness, the merciful, the pure in heart, the peacemakers are specifically named there. The merciful are brought in later in the discussion here in verse 36. They that mourn and they that weep are the same. Wherever He went, no doubt Jesus spoke these truths in different words again and again.

Notice the division of the thought here. There are three states of blessedness which are purely conditions and not virtues. They that are poor, they that hunger, they that weep, are blessed. You will note that these words are given to "*his disciples*" (vs. 20), so they would not always be true to the unsaved. The man who

weeps and goes on in his sin has no promise of future
laughter and blessing. Those who are lazy or drunken
or gamble away their means and so are hungry now,
have no promise that they will later be filled. But to
the disciple of Christ there is the blessed promise that
there will be an end of weeping, there will be an end of
hunger, there will be an end of poverty. And that is
to come simply because God is so good and He loves us.

One blessing here, the blessing of persecution, is earned.
The persecution and separation and reproach are to
be *"for the Son of man's sake."* People are not hated
because they are nominal Christians or because they
are lukewarm. They are hated because they are fervent,
outspoken, witnessing Christians. There is a sense in
which *"all that will live godly in Christ Jesus shall suffer
persecution"* (II Tim. 3:12). Christians who do not live
godly lives, who are some way a reproach and rebuke
to those about them, are not persecuted. The world
hated Jesus and if we are enough like Jesus, the world
will hate us. God does not make us an unwilling sacrifice, but we are besought to *"present your bodies a
living sacrifice"* (Rom. 12:1) and to be *"not conformed
to this world."* Thus a Christian will earn his persecution and he will be greatly blessed and rewarded for it.

Why rejoice? and even leap for joy? Because there is
great reward in Heaven. The Lord has promised, *"If
we suffer, we shall also reign with him"* (II Tim. 2:12).
We should rejoice because in some way we have so
earned and proved a kinship with the prophets who have
gone on before who suffered persecution. Yes, and we
have proved ourselves in some sense like Jesus if for
His namesake we are persecuted. So we are to rejoice
in that.

But there are three woes here also as a matter of
condition and not simply of virtue. There is woe to the
rich, woe to the full, woe to those who laugh. Those

who are rich now do not have the reward of those who give their riches away. Those who laugh now instead of weeping over sinners will weep later for lack of fruit and rewards. Those who are full now will not know the blessing of God's provision.

But here is a woe that is opposite the blessing for persecution, "*Woe unto you, when all men shall speak well of you.*" So men always have spoken of false prophets. It is strange that this world hated and cruci-fied Jesus Christ, and stoned Stephen and beheaded Paul and burned Savonarola, Latimer, and Ridley at the stake, and so has martyred many thousands and reproached and persecuted millions more, and then here is someone who has all the favor of this world!

Woe be to the Christian who does not offend the newspapers and they praise him; who does not offend the rich and powerful and they seek his company. He never condemns the modernist or the heretic, never chastens the skeptic nor the Pharisee, never thunders against the gross sins about him. Such an one has earned this woe when all men speak well of him.

Every Christian ought to make sure he does not get persecuted because of flaws in his character and daily life, but he ought to make sure that he is such a fervent Christian that his life and witnessing will be a reproach to those who do not live godly and that there will be the reproach there ought to be on a fervent child of God.

VERSES 27—31:

27 But I say unto you which hear, Love your enemies, do good to them which hate you,

28 Bless them that curse you, and pray for them which despite-fully use you.

29 And unto him that smiteth thee on the *one* cheek offer also the other; and him that taketh away thy cloke forbid not *to take thy* coat also.

30 Give to every man that asketh

of thee; and of him that taketh away thy goods ask *them* not again.
31 And as ye would that men should do to you, do ye also to them likewise.

Blessing Others for Jesus' Sake

The Christian is not to be like the world. We are to love our enemies, do good to those who hate us, bless them who curse us. We are to be patient and conciliatory to those who demand of us more than is right.

Verses 29 to 31 should be understood in the light of the fuller discussion in Matthew, chapter 5. In verses 23 to 26, and then again in verses 38 to 42, the Saviour speaks of making restitution, making right the things where we have wronged others. Everyone is to be reconciled to the brother before he offers a gift (Matt. 5:24). In verse 39 we are told not to resist evil, that is, not to resist those who would demand we make more restitution than is perhaps deserved. Matthew 5:40 says, "*If any man will sue thee at the law, and take away thy coat, let him have thy cloke also.*" So if a man sues you and says you owe him a certain amount, pay it and agree to pay more if necessary. If he claims that you owe him to go a mile or carry his burden for a mile, then offer to go two.

Since the command is that you are to make good an eye for an eye, or a tooth for a tooth (See Exod. 21:24; Lev. 24:20; Deut. 19:21.), you are not only to pay what you really owe but more if it is demanded. If you smote a man on the cheek, you must allow him to smite you back, in restitution, and then you should offer the other cheek. The idea is that the Christian must be so insistent on paying every debt and making good every wrong that he is willing to go further than simple justice demands, in order to prove his love and honesty.

So Zacchaeus, the new convert at Jericho, said, "*If I have taken any thing from any man by false accusation,*

I restore him fourfold." This spirit of restitution of wrong is indicated in the Mosaic law in Exodus 22:1, "*If a man shall steal an ox, or a sheep, and kill it, or sell it; he shall restore five oxen for an ox, and four sheep for a sheep.*" And if an ox, or ass, or sheep be found alive in his hand, "*he shall restore ·double*" (Exod. 22:4).

Thus the Christian is not only to be honest, but he is to "*provide things honest IN THE SIGHT OF ALL MEN*" (Rom. 12:17).

Here in Luke 6:31 is the golden rule: "*And as ye would that men should do to you, do ye also to them likewise.*" It is taken for granted that you, a disciple, want to do right, and thus that you would not want to take what you do not earn or to cause another loss. So with the understanding that what you would want from others is right, you must be sure to do for them.

If you have a sin or failure, you know a good reason that seems to excuse the sin or failure. Oh, then, make sure that you think the best of others for they, too, probably feel that some condition mitigates their sin or excuses their failure. Be as charitable to others as you are to yourself!

VERSES 32—38:

32 For if ye love them which love you, what thank have ye? for sinners also love those that love them.
33 And if ye do good to them which do good to you, what thank have ye? for sinners also do even the same.
34 And if ye lend *to them* of whom ye hope to receive, what thank have ye? for sinners also lend to sinners, to receive as much again.
35 But love ye your enemies, and do good, and lend, hoping for nothing again; and your reward shall be great, and ye shall be the children of the Highest: for he is kind unto the unthankful and *to* the evil.

36 Be ye therefore merciful, as your Father also is merciful.
37 Judge not, and ye shall not be judged: condemn not, and ye shall not be condemned: forgive, and ye shall be forgiven:
38 Give, and it shall be given unto you; good measure, pressed down, and shaken together, and running over, shall men give into your bosom. For with the same measure that ye mete withal it shall be measured to you again.

We Are to Love Those Who Do Not Earn Our Love, Give to the Unworthy

The worldling may say, "I want what is coming to me." The Christian may not insist on that. He is to love those who hate him. He is to pray for good things for them who despitefully use him and persecute him. He is to give to those who will not give back. He is to lend when there is not much prospect of having the borrowed money or thing restored.

All of us send Christmas cards to those who send us cards. We send gifts to those who give us gifts. We invite to our homes those who invite us to their homes. But do not even worldlings the same? Ought not a Christian to have some other standard?

Yes, the Christian ought to do everything he does to the glory of God, whether he eats or drinks or whatever he does (I Cor. 10:31). So if he is to be like God, he must love those who do not love him, he must give to those who do not give back. He must look to God for the reward, as verse 35 promises, and not depend too much on rewards from men. He is to be merciful as God the Father is merciful. He is not to judge the heart of men, since he does not want men to judge his heart. Besides, "*Man looketh on the outward appearance, but the Lord looketh on the heart*" (I Sam. 16:7). God has not given to us the privilege of passing judgment on others.

It is true that concerning false prophets Jesus said in

Matthew 7:15,16, *"Beware of false prophets, which come to you in sheep's clothing, but inwardly they are ravening wolves. Ye shall know them by their fruits."* I may judge a prophet by his fruit: a man who openly denies the deity of Christ, His virgin birth, the inspiration and authority of the Bible, the atoning death and resurrection of the Saviour, has thus by his fruit proven that he is a false prophet. But no Christian has the right to decide by outward appearance who is saved and who is not.

Consider the adultery and murder by David: then would you say that he was not saved? Hear Peter cursing and swearing, denying Christ and quitting the ministry: would you think that he is not saved? If you think David and Peter unsaved, you would be mistaken. So you are not to judge the hearts and motives of men. In this matter we are to be like our Father and be *"children of the Highest."*

Verse 38 is one of the great promises of Scripture. Oh, we beg you to memorize it, praise God for it, put it in practice, claim all its rich blessings! By giving money and expecting God to repay one can very quickly prove that it pays to take the Bible at face value, that God meets His promises. But we ought to prove it also in a thousand other ways besides giving money.

VERSES 39—46:

39 And he spake a parable unto them, Can the blind lead the blind? shall they not both fall into the ditch?

40 The disciple is not above his master: but every one that is perfect shall be as his master.

41 And why beholdest thou the mote that is in thy brother's eye, but perceivest not the beam that is in thine own eye?

42 Either how canst thou say to thy brother, Brother, let me pull out the mote that is in thine eye, when thou thyself beholdest not the beam that is in thine own eye? Thou hypocrite, cast out first the beam out of thine own eye, and then shalt thou see clearly to pull out the mote that is in thy brother's eye.

43 For a good tree bringeth not forth corrupt fruit; neither doth a

corrupt tree bring forth good fruit.
44 For every tree is known by his own fruit. For of thorns men do not gather figs, nor of a bramble bush gather they grapes.
45 A good man out of the good treasure of his heart bringeth forth that which is good; and an evil man out of the evil treasure of his heart bringeth forth that which is evil: for of the abundance of the heart his mouth speaketh.
46 And why call ye me, Lord, Lord, and do not the things which I say?

Forgiving, Compassion, Not Judging

We are to be like our Saviour. "*The disciple is not above his master,*" but we should be like Him. We should be merciful as He is (vs. 36). We should forgive (vs. 37) as Jesus on the cross prayed, "*Father, forgive them; for they know not what they do*" (Luke 23:34). How can we lead the unsaved world to the light if we are as blind as they are, if we love only those who love us, if we give only to those who give to us, if we lend only when we hope for repayment with interest? And how can we, judging others with no compassion for men's sins and failures, and no humble consciousness of our own sinfulness, lead others? So let us be more concerned about the beam in our own eyes than the mote in other's eyes.

A good Christian ought to bring forth the fruits of a Christian, as we see from verses 43 to 45.

And God expects us to follow His patient, unselfish, loving and forgiving example, if we are to call Him Lord (vs. 46).

VERSES 47 — 49:

47 Whosoever cometh to me, and heareth my sayings, and doeth them, I will shew you to whom he is like:
48 He is like a man which built an house, and digged deep, and laid the foundation on a rock: and when the flood arose, the stream

beat vehemently upon that house, and could not shake it: for it was founded upon a rock.

49 But he that heareth, and doeth not, is like a man that without a foundation built an house upon the earth; against which the stream did beat vehemently, and immediately it fell; and the ruin of that house was great.

The House Built on the Rock

Here the Lord speaks about Christian character. One can have the kind of character that will stand the storms and temptations of life. It will take love, forgiveness, and humility, looking to God for reward and not to men, giving to those who do not give to us, loving those who hate us, being merciful because God is merciful. God give us that kind of character. Then when the storms of temptation, poverty or sickness or persecution come, the house of our character and service will stand.

Oh, there are storms ahead for Christians. Paul and Barnabas went back to cities they had visited before and taught the new converts that *"we must through much tribulation enter into the kingdom of God"* (Acts 14:22). The trial of faith is precious, says I Peter 1:7. And we are to *"think it not strange concerning the fiery trial which is to try you, as though some strange thing happened unto you"* (I Pet. 4:12). And the character that is Christ-like in its love for others, in its forgiving, in its humility, compassion and witnessing, will stand the storms.

LUKE 7

VERSES 1 — 10:

NOW when he had ended all his sayings in the audience of the people, he entered into Capernaum.

2 And a certain centurion's servant, who was dear unto him, was sick, and ready to die.

3 And when he heard of Jesus, he sent unto him the elders of the Jews, beseeching him that he would come and heal his servant.

4 And when they came to Jesus, they besought him instantly, saying, That he was worthy for whom he should do this:

5 For he loveth our nation, and he hath built us a synagogue.

6 Then Jesus went with them. And when he was now not far from the house, the centurion sent friends to him, saying unto him, Lord, trouble not thyself: for I am not worthy that thou shouldest enter under my roof:

7 Wherefore neither thought I myself worthy to come unto thee: but say in a word, and my servant shall be healed.

8 For I also am a man set under authority, having under me soldiers, and I say unto one, Go, and he goeth; and to another, Come, and he cometh; and to my servant, Do this, and he doeth *it*.

9 When Jesus heard these things, he marvelled at him, and turned him about, and said unto the people that followed him, I say unto you, I have not found so great faith, no, not in Israel.

10 And they that were sent, returning to the house, found the servant whole that had been sick.

The Centurion's Servant Healed

The same story is told in Matthew 8:5-13.

In the preceding chapter we find that Jesus has gone up into a mountain to pray (vs. 12), called the disciples to Him and chose twelve apostles. Then in verse 17, *"He came down with them, and stood in the plain"* and there dealt with a great multitude of people. Now, He has entered into the city of Capernaum (vs. 1), His home during nearly all of His ministry. The *centurion* here was a captain in the Roman army, normally over a company of a hundred men. He was a striking character.

Compare the account of this centurion's approach to Jesus with that given of the same story in Matthew 8:5-13. That Scripture says, "...*there came unto him a centurion.*" But here in Luke we are told he came through the mediation of some Jewish elders. Doubtless he came to the great group of people who surrounded Jesus and asked some of the Jewish elders whom he well knew to speak for him instead of speaking directly to Jesus. And here in Luke 7:6 we read that Jesus went on His way toward the house, "*And when he was not now far from the house, the centurion sent friends to him, saying unto him, Lord, trouble not thyself: for I am not worthy that thou shouldest enter under my roof.*" In Matthew, the fact that Jesus approached the house is not told us. We suppose that this humble and godly centurion did not speak personally to Jesus but felt unworthy to do so. The shorter account in Matthew does not tell all the details, of course, but the fact that in Matthew 8:10 Jesus "*said to them that followed, Verily I say unto you, I have not found so great faith, no, not in Israel,*" indicates that the man was not present. Throughout the Scriptures a plan often followed is that each particular passage tells only the part needed for that passage and does not attempt to explain matters that are told more fully elsewhere. That is often true in the four Gospels, and in parallel accounts in I and II Samuel, I and II Kings, and I and II Chronicles.

Note these things about the centurion:

1. His compassion for his servant.

2. He loved the Jews and was loved by them and had built them a synagogue. That was possibly the synagogue on the same site as the ruins of a second century synagogue have now been uncovered, where Capernaum once was.

3. Instead of thinking of him as a foreign oppressor, the Jewish elders say that *"he was a worthy man."* And they interceded with Christ for him.

4. His humility. Although he had a place of honor, and centurions were likely to be arrogant and proud, he felt unworthy for Christ to come under his roof in order that he should come to Christ personally.

5. Most amazing was his faith. Ian Maclaren says that Jesus marvelled twice, once in Mark 6:6 at the unbelief, and here in Luke 7:9 at the Gentile's amazing faith, greater than any He had found in Israel. We have found a number of people whose hearts were prepared, just waiting to love and trust the Saviour when He should appear. No doubt that was true about Zacharias and Elisabeth in Luke 1, about Simeon and Anna the prophetess in Luke 2. It was certainly true of Joseph and Mary. Beyond any doubt Cornelius, another Roman centurion, most earnestly sought the Lord and was open to the Gospel in Acts 10. Here, we think, was another such case. It seems obvious that the centurion loved the Lord Jesus, believed everything Jesus said, and accepted Him at face value. There was a loving faith that was heart faith. Although the Scripture does not expressly say that the man was saved, it is clearly inferred. Romans 2:6 and 7 tells us about God, *"Who will render to every man according to his deeds: To them who by patient continuance in well doing seek for glory and honour and immortality, eternal life."* And again in verse 10, *"But glory, honour, and peace, to every man that worketh good, to the Jew first, and also to the Gentile."*

These verses do not mean that anybody is saved by his good deeds, by his virtuous life. They surely do mean that anybody who honestly seeks the Lord will have a way open to find Him, that even as in the case of Cornelius, God would even send an angel to get

Peter to preach to him, so God will, at any cost, make sure that the earnest, seeking heart can find God, and one who repents of his sins will be converted. So on reading the story of this centurion, one feels some of the tender sentiment that seems to come from a Christian's heart in his compassion, love, his humility, his faith.

Notice how simple and direct was the centurion's faith. He himself was an officer, having authority. He could tell a soldier to come or go, or could say to his servant, *"Do this, and he doeth it."* And he immediately thought of Jesus as One who was Creator and Controller of all things. Diseases would be gone at His word! So it is really true, and how blessed that the man saw it by faith.

VERSES 11—17:

11 And it came to pass the day after, that he went into a city called Nain; and many of his disciples went with him, and much people.

12 Now when he came nigh to the gate of the city, behold, there was a dead man carried out, the only son of his mother, and she was a widow: and much people of the city was with her.

13 And when the Lord saw her, he had compassion on her, and said unto her, Weep not.

14 And he came and touched the bier: and they that bare *him* stood still. And he said, Young man, I say unto thee, Arise.

15 And he that was dead sat up, and began to speak. And he delivered him to his mother.

16 And there came a fear on all: and they glorified God, saying, That a great prophet is risen up among us; and, That God hath visited his people.

17 And this rumour of him went forth throughout all Judæa, and throughout all the region round about.

The Raising of the Widow's Son at Nain

Nain was perhaps six miles south of Nazareth, and so twenty miles or more southwest of Capernaum. It was now *"the day after"* so we suppose that Jesus walked that twenty miles or more. Since *"many of his disciples went with him, and much people,"* it would have taken most of a day to walk that far with a crowd. Coming near to the city they met a funeral procession. The body of a young man, the only son of his mother, was, we suppose, wrapped in linen with spices *"as the manner of the Jews is to bury"* (John 19:40) and, like Lazarus, *"bound hand and foot with graveclothes: and his face was bound about with a napkin"* (John 11:44). There was no coffin, so we suppose the body was carried by men on something like a stretcher.

The heart of the Lord Jesus was moved with compassion at the weeping woman who had lost her only son. He bade her to cease weeping, then He touched the bier on which the corpse lay, and said, *"Young man, I say unto thee, Arise."* Immediately, in response to that voice which shall one day awaken all the dead, *"he that was dead sat up, and began to speak."* Then Jesus *"delivered him to his mother."* Who can dry tears like Jesus!

The motivation for most of the healings, most of the miracles that Jesus did on earth was compassion! His miracles were not, as some would suppose, either to prove His deity or to authenticate a new dispensation. Jesus expressly denied that any kind of miracle would be given to prove His deity but the sign of the Prophet Jonah, that is, He would be three days and nights in the grave as Jonah was three days in the belly of the whale (Matt. 12:40,41). And for the other, there is this favorite theme of people who must some way excuse the fact that no miracles seem to appear today by saying that such things happen only at the beginning of a new dispensation. Such an idea is not even mentioned in the Bible. We are not to suppose that the dear Saviour has less compassion for people in trouble now than He had when He walked in the flesh among men.

How scoffers hate the idea of miracles! But if Christ be God in the flesh, Creator of all things, then miracles to Him would be a normal and inevitable part of His life. If the resurrection of the widow's son and that of Lazarus seem unbelievable, then how can you believe that one day all that are in the grave shall hear Christ's voice and come forth? If God could make a whale or great fish, why could not that fish swallow Jonah and keep him alive three days and then have him come forth? If God made this earth and the whole planetary system, the universe, by the Word of Christ, then why would it be so difficult for Him to have the sun stand still in its relation to the earth for a day, as happened at the command of Joshua?

Some would say that when the children of Israel crossed the Red Sea, it was not the Red Sea at all but just some marshes and was not miraculous. When Israel crossed the Jordan River and the water was held back so that they crossed on dry land at floodtime, they say a landslide had blocked the river temporarily. When Sodom and Gomorrah were destroyed, some would say a volcanic eruption had covered the cities. But the Bible believer must believe that Jesus Christ could and did raise the dead and that He Himself was raised from the dead. Else as Paul said in I Corinthians 15:14, our faith is vain and we are still in our sins.

The people, amazed and impressed, *"glorified God, saying, That a great prophet is risen up among us; and, That God hath visited his people"* (vs. 16). And so His fame went abroad through all Galilee and Judaea.

O, dear Lord Jesus, they wanted You to heal their sick, raise their dead, to feed them on loaves and fishes, but they will not heed Your demand for repentance and a new heart, Your warnings of Hell and judgment for the impenitent!

VERSES 18—23:

18 And the disciples of John shewed him of all these things.

19 And John calling *unto him* two of his disciples sent *them* to Jesus, saying, Art thou he that should come? or look we for another?

20 When the men were come unto him, they said, John Baptist hath sent us unto thee, saying, Art thou he that should come? or look we for another?

21 And in that same hour he cured many of *their* infirmities and plagues, and of evil spirits; and unto many *that were* blind he gave sight.

22 Then Jesus answering said unto them, Go your way, and tell John what things ye have seen and heard; how that the blind see, the lame walk, the lepers are cleansed, the deaf hear, the dead are raised, to the poor the gospel is preached.

23 And blessed is *he*, whosoever shall not be offended in me.

John the Baptist's Question, "Is Jesus the Christ?"

We suppose John the Baptist was in prison at Herod's winter palace at Machaerus, east of the Dead Sea, arrested by order of King Herod because John told that wicked king of his sin with his brother's wife, Herodias. There had been such crowds who had attended the ministry of Jesus from Tyre and Sidon, over on the Mediterranean, from Jerusalem on the south, and all Decapolis, that John in prison would hear of the marvelous ministry of Jesus and the great miracles which He did. So John sent two disciples to ask, *"Art thou he that should come? or look we for another?"*

There are two themes of prophecy about the coming Messiah in the Old Testament. In Isaiah 51 and 53, and in Psalm 22, He is clearly depicted as the suffering Saviour, dying for the sins of others, hated, despised, and bearing reproach. But in II Samuel 7:10-14, in Isaiah 9:6, in Isaiah 11, in Psalm 2, in the interpretation of the dream of Nebuchadnezzar in Daniel 2, and in many, many other places, the Messiah is promised to be a great King who shall rule with glory. And so

people thought of two great persons *"that should come."*
John the Baptist may have had this in mind. He may
have been asking: "Are You the One and only Messiah,
or should we look for another?"

Or possibly he knows that the Messiah is to be hated,
despised, and killed. Ah, John the Baptist knows the
price that a prophet should pay, for he, too, had enormous crowds, baptized multitudes of converts, but his
plain preaching against Herod and Herodias and others
got him first in jail, and later he would be beheaded.
John would not have been ignorant to the truth Jesus
so clearly preached in Luke 6:22 and 23, and in Matthew 5:10-12, that it is blessed to be persecuted, for so
were all the prophets persecuted, and sure is their reward in Heaven. If Jesus is received with glad acclaim
and His fame goes everywhere, with no objection, is
Jesus really the promised Messiah? If so, why does He
not suffer persecution? Why, if He is to be a King, does
He not seize power?

Many have thought that John the Baptist, in prison,
perhaps discouraged, had begun to entertain doubts and
was, perhaps, backslidden. We do not think so. The
Lord Jesus had not a word of rebuke for his question.
Rather, Jesus knew that John the Baptist would be
familiar with the passage about the coming Saviour in
Isaiah 61:1, *"The Spirit of the Lord God is upon me;*
because the Lord hath anointed me to preach good tid-
ings unto the meek; he hath sent me to bind up the
brokenhearted, to proclaim liberty to the captives, and
the opening of the prison to them that are bound."
Jesus Himself has quoted this passage, and down to the
comma in the next verse, about Himself, in the synagogue
in Nazareth (Luke 4:18,19). Now, instead of giving a
direct "yes" or "no" answer, He shows His marvelous
power. *"And in that same hour he cured many of their*
infirmities and plagues, and of evil spirits; and unto

many that were blind he gave sight" (Luke 7:21). *"Go your way, and tell John what things ye have seen and heard,"* Jesus said. To a Bible believer like John the evidence would be enough.

Here is a Bible principle, that to the wicked and unbelieving heart God always gives some leeway to continue in unbelief, if he insists. The Lord Jesus often spoke in parables so that only those who had a heart to hear would hear and believe (Matt. 13:13-15).

Then Jesus pronounced that blessed truth, *"Blessed is he, whosoever shall not be offended in me"* (Matt. 11:6). One who would have a loving and believing heart about Jesus would not find it difficult to believe that He is the very Messiah. Although Jesus had not yet publicly announced Himself as the Messiah, let the earnest, seeking heart believe. Others would hear His claim soon enough. He even forbade devils to openly proclaim that He was the Messiah (Luke 4:41). But John would know by this evidence!

VERSES 24 — 28:

24 And when the messengers of John were departed, he began to speak unto the people concerning John, What went ye out into the wilderness for to see? A reed shaken with the wind?

25 But what went ye out for to see? A man clothed in soft raiment? Behold, they which are gorgeously apparelled, and live delicately, are in kings' courts.

26 But what went ye out for to see? A prophet? Yea, I say unto you, and much more than a prophet.

27 This is *he*, of whom it is written, Behold, I send my messenger before thy face, which shall prepare thy way before thee.

28 For I say unto you, Among those that are born of women there is not a greater prophet than John the Baptist: but he that is least in the kingdom of God is greater than he.

The Praise of Jesus for John the Baptist

The affection and deep approval of the Saviour for John the Baptist is very touching. Their mothers were cousins (Luke 1:36), but there is no account of their being together in boyhood. John the Baptist was *"in the deserts till the day of his shewing unto Israel"* (Luke 1:80). John did not know that Jesus was the Messiah until he baptized Him. He knew that Jesus was wonderfully good, and felt unworthy to baptize Him (Matt. 3:14). But God had given him one sign by which he should know the Saviour: *"And John bare record, saying, I saw the Spirit descending from heaven like a dove, and it abode upon him, And I knew him not: but he that sent me to baptize with water, the same said unto me, Upon whom thou shalt see the Spirit descending, and remaining on him, the same is he which baptizeth with the Holy Ghost. And I saw, and bare record that this is the Son of God"* (John 1:32-34).

Not only was John unashamed that the Saviour should supersede him, but he openly said he was not worthy to unloose the Messiah's shoe latchets (John 1:27). When people came to John and said, *"Rabbi, he that was with thee beyond Jordan, to whom thou barest witness, behold, the same baptizeth, and all men come to him,"* John answered and said, *"A man can receive nothing, except it be given him from heaven. Ye yourselves bear me witness, that I said, I am not the Christ, but that I am sent before him. He that hath the bride is the bridegroom: but the friend of the bridegroom, which standeth and heareth him, rejoiceth greatly because of the bridegroom's voice: this my joy therefore is fulfilled. He must increase, but I must decrease"* (John 3:27-30).

Jesus loved John and felt concern that the dear, faithful prophet should not be forlorn; so in John 4:1-3 we read how Jesus slipped away to avoid the praises of the people and not to seem to compete with John: *"When therefore the Lord knew how the Pharisees had heard that Jesus made and baptized more disciples than John, (Though Jesus himself baptized not, but his disciples,) He left Judaea, and departed again into Galilee."* And now he praises John the Baptist:

First, He praises John's steadfastness: John was not a *"reed shaken with the wind"* (Luke 7:24); he was not guilty of that fear of man which bringeth a snare (Prov. 29:25); he obeyed the command that Paul was inspired to write later, in Romans 12:2, *"Be not conformed to this world: but be ye transformed by the renewing of your mind..."*; he did not shun facing Herod with his sin (Luke 3:19,20) or calling the religious leaders a *"generation of vipers"* (Matt. 3:7); he was not like Obadiah who had a job feeding 450 prophets of Baal at Jezebel's table, but like Elijah (I Kings 18). God give us preachers who are not like reeds shaken with the wind!

Second, Jesus praised John for living an austere life of self-sacrifice and poverty. John was not *"clothed in soft raiment"* but with a leathern girdle about his loins; and his meat was locusts and wild honey (Matt. 3:4). He lived in the desert, or wilderness, till *"the day of his shewing unto Israel"* (Luke 1:80). John had the character and the blessedness which Jesus praised when He said, *"Blessed be ye poor"* and *"Blessed are ye that hunger now"* (Luke 6:20,21).

The Apostle Paul rejoiced in his poverty and struggles and sufferings for Christ. He said we may approve *"ourselves as the ministers of God"* by patience, afflictions, necessities, distresses, stripes, imprisonments, tumults, labors, watchings, fastings (II Cor. 6:4,5). It is not bad for a minister of God to be poor, sometimes to go hungry, to sleep on hard beds, and not to live with all the comforts some other people have. God's prophet ought to be more concerned with another world. Sometimes he ought to feast, but sometimes he ought to fast. Sometimes he ought to ride in a good car, but sometimes he ought to walk.

Jesus praised John the Baptist for his self-denial, that he was not *"gorgeously apparelled"* and did not *"live delicately"* and was not *"in kings' courts"* (Luke 7:25).

Third, Jesus praised John the Baptist as a prophet: *"Yea, I say unto you, and much more than a prophet"* (Luke 7:26). John was a prophet but above all the prophets before him in that he was the forerunner, the announcer of the Saviour Himself. Morally, there was none greater born of woman than John, but positionally he was even more above other men. Other women probably had been as good, as spiritual, and as devoted as the virgin Mary, but she was *"Blessed...among women"* because she was given the privilege of bearing the Saviour. Positionally, she was greater than some others, though, like all human beings, she was a sinner and needed a Saviour herself. So, positionally, John the Baptist was greater.

And perhaps that gives a key to the rest of the statement: *"but he that is least in the kingdom of God is greater than he"* (Luke 7:28). I do not think that here the Lord Jesus meant those who live in the New Testament age are better than John, for John himself lived in the New Testament age; rather, we think that when Christ's kingdom on earth is set up, the lowliest Christian, in a glorified body, in perfect communion with Christ, with the frailties and the sins and disappointments and frustrations of the flesh all gone, will be in greater blessedness than John the Baptist was in his earthly life. Of course, John, too, will be in that kingdom.

Charles K. Williams' translation of the New Testament gives a note on the same statement as recorded in Mat-

thew 11:11. It says, "Greatness here is measured by his
exalted mission in heralding the Messiah." The Scofield
Bible note on that passage reads: "Positionally greater,
not morally. John Baptist was as great, morally, as
any man 'born of woman,' but as to the *kingdom* he
had but announced it at hand.... The least in the kingdom when it is set up in glory...will be in the fullness
of power and glory. It is not heaven which is in question, but Messiah's kingdom." And so we agree.

Knowing that John the Baptist would recognize the
evidence of Isaiah 61:1 which his messengers had seen
fulfilled, Jesus said, *"Blessed is he, whosoever shall not
be offended in me"* (Matt. 11:6). In Jesus' tender love
and praise for John the Baptist, we are reminded of the
kindness of God and His angels to the troubled Elijah,
who ran from Jezebel (I Kings 19).

VERSES 29—35:

29 And all the people that heard *him*, and the publicans, justified God, being baptized with the baptism of John.

30 But the Pharisees and lawyers rejected the counsel of God against themselves, being not baptized of him.

31 And the Lord said, Whereunto then shall I liken the men of this generation? and to what are they like?

32 They are like unto children sitting in the marketplace, and calling one to another, and saying, We have piped unto you, and ye have not danced; we have mourned to you, and ye have not wept.

33 For John the Baptist came neither eating bread nor drinking wine; and ye say, He hath a devil.

34 The Son of man is come eating and drinking; and ye say, Behold a gluttonous man, and a winebibber, a friend of publicans and sinners!

35 But wisdom is justified of all her children.

Insincere and Inconsistent Complaints
of Worldly People About Christ
and the Gospel

Thousands of people had heard John preach, had believed him and were baptized in repentance. The term *"justified God"* (vs. 29) doubtless means that they took God's side, admitted their sinfulness, saw the need of an atoning Saviour which John preached. Not so, the Pharisees and lawyers; they did not repent. They did not admit their wickedness, and so they refused the charges John the Baptist brought against them and they were not baptized. Note carefully that the baptism of John involved repentance, and those proud, haughty legalists refused to take the place of lost, needy sinners, and so would not be baptized since it meant repenting of their sins.

Baptism was not a Jewish ceremony; it was *"the answer of a good conscience toward God"* (I Pet. 3:21), a public profession of repentance and of faith in Christ.

Note the complaints against the ascetic, sacrificial John, living in poverty. They said, *"He hath a devil"* (Luke 7:33). But of Jesus, who went out to meals and dinners with the people, they said, *"Behold a gluttonous man, and a winebibber, a friend of publicans and sinners!"* (Luke 7:34). They are like foolish children, irresponsible, unreasonable, Jesus said (vs. 32). And these missed the wisdom of God which was revealed in both John the Baptist and Jesus.

VERSES 36 — 40:

36 And one of the Pharisees desired him that he would eat with him. And he went into the Pharisee's house, and sat down to meat.

37 And, behold, a woman in the city, which was a sinner, when she knew that *Jesus* sat at meat in the Pharisee's house, brought an

alabaster box of ointment,
38 And stood at his feet behind
him weeping, and began to wash
his feet with tears, and did wipe
them with the hairs of her head,
and kissed his feet, and anointed
them with the ointment.
39 Now when the Pharisee which
had bidden him saw *it*, he spake

within himself, saying, This man,
if he were a prophet, would have
known who and what manner of
woman *this is* that toucheth him:
for she is a sinner.
40 And Jesus answering said unto
him, Simon, I have somewhat to
say unto thee. And he saith, Master, say on.

Jesus in a Pharisee's House,
Saves a Fallen Woman

Jesus was invited to the house of a Pharisee for dinner.
Doubtless He was so famous that both the saved and
the lost wanted the distinction of having Him in their
homes; so the Pharisee had Jesus. (In verse 36 the
term "*sat down to meat*" really should be "reclined" for
the meal. They lay on couches around a low table,
usually U-shaped, we suppose, and were served from
within the horseshoe.) Verse 49 says "*they that sat at
meat with him,*" so evidently others were invited to hear
the Galilean prophet. The Pharisee himself seemed not
to have been a disciple nor a believer in Christ.

The woman in verse 37 "*which was a sinner*" was
evidently a prostitute, a harlot. The term, as used here,
had a very definite meaning. We can suppose that in
the warm climate the meal was served in the patio, an
open courtyard, and with a number of guests. It was
somewhat a public affair. And the poor, fallen woman
came purposely to see Jesus. Doubtless there were other
interested spectators who had gathered, but she brought
"*an alabaster box of ointment,*" that is, the box for perfume was carved out of the translucent alabaster stone.
No doubt this expensive perfume was purchased with
gains from her wicked trade, or it may have been the

gift of some admirer in sin; but she brought it with loving hands as a gift for Jesus.

Some have thought this woman was Mary Magdalene, out of whom Jesus cast seven devils (Mark 16:9), but there is no evidence of that. This woman was a sinner, but there is no evidence she was devil-possessed. The Bible never identifies her with Mary Magdalene.

Others have thought this was the same event as the supper at Bethany, told about in John 12:1-11, Matthew 26:6-13, and Mark 14:3-9, and that this harlot is Mary, the sister of Martha and Lazarus. That hardly seems possible. This supper and this woman are up in Galilee. In verses 11-18 Jesus was at Nain. That supper at Bethany was in a suburb of Jerusalem in Judea, far away. Jesus was so pleased with the love and devotion of this woman and was so glad to forgive her sins, He may have told the story to others. And Mary of Bethany may have had the holy desire to bring some ointment for Jesus also and may have followed this example; we do not know. But that Mary who sat at the feet of Jesus and who had *"chosen that good part"* (Luke 10: 42) is not, we are sure, the harlot of Luke 7:37.

This was no form or ritual but a loving approach of a penitent sinner to the Saviour. The tears that fell on the feet of Jesus were tears over her sins, and it was a tender expression of her love that she took down her hair and wiped the feet of Jesus and kissed them as she anointed His feet with the ointment. And Jesus was pleased with that devotion.

The unconverted Pharisee could not see the penitent heart of the woman. He thought Jesus would shrink from having her touch Him, if He were a prophet. Oh, but he didn't know the tender heart of Jesus! And here he had the same complaint that Pharisees always tend to have against Jesus. So it was when Levi, after he was converted, made a feast for publicans and sinner friends and invited Jesus (Luke 5:30-32). So it would be later in Luke 15:1,2; so it would be when Jesus forgives and saves Zacchaeus and goes to his house (Luke 19:7-10).

VERSES 41 — 50:

41 There was a certain creditor which had two debtors: the one owed five hundred pence, and the other fifty.

42 And when they had nothing to pay, he frankly forgave them both. Tell me therefore, which of them will love him most?

43 Simon answered and said, I suppose that *he*, to whom he forgave most. And he said unto him, Thou hast rightly judged.

44 And he turned to the woman, and said unto Simon, Seest thou this woman? I entered into thine house, thou gavest me no water for my feet: but she hath washed my feet with tears, and wiped *them* with the hairs of her head.

45 Thou gavest me no kiss: but this woman since the time I came in hath not ceased to kiss my feet.

46 My head with oil thou didst not anoint: but this woman hath anointed my feet with ointment.

47 Wherefore I say unto thee, Her sins, which are many, are forgiven; for she loved much: but to whom little is forgiven, *the same* loveth little.

48 And he said unto her, Thy sins are forgiven.

49 And they that sat at meat with him began to say within themselves, Who is this that forgiveth sins also?

50 And he said to the woman, Thy faith hath saved thee; go in' peace.

The Parable of the Creditor and Two Debtors
Which Shows the Forgiven Harlot's Love

How sweetly Jesus illustrated the difference in the attitude of the Pharisee in whose house He ate, and this woman who wept over His feet and kissed them and anointed them! A man had two debtors, and he forgave both—the man who owed five hundred pence and the one who owed fifty. The *pence* is the denary, named as a day's wages in Matthew 20:2. Who would love him best? The Pharisee answered, "*He, to whom he forgave most.*" Then Jesus, with kindly but burning words, reminded the Pharisee that he had not shown Jesus the ordinary courtesy due a guest, had given Him no water to wash His feet, dusty from His walk on the unpaved paths in sandals. (In every house it was customary to remove the sandals and wash the feet.)

In the East it was and still is customary to greet a guest or an honored person with a kiss on each cheek. So did an Arab guide and I greet each other when we, old friends, met again. And so did some godly saints in India, who gave me a dinner after a campaign in Madras, kiss me on each cheek, in loving fellowship. But Simon the Pharisee had not so greeted Jesus.

It was customary to give a bit of olive oil to a guest as he smoothed down his hair and combed it after a journey, but Jesus had not been so treated. Oh, but the love of a forgiven woman, who kissed His feet and anointed them with ointment, pictured a greater love than the Pharisee had.

And so another woman was saved. Jesus said plainly, "*Thy sins are forgiven.*" And again He said, "*Thy faith hath saved thee; go in peace*" (Luke 7:50). So we know that she had trusted Christ and was saved.

Note the question in verse 49, "*Who is this that forgiveth sins also?*" So it was when Jesus healed a palsied man let down through the roof (Luke 5:21). For if Jesus can forgive sins, He is not only a prophet but is God the Son, the Saviour.

LUKE 8

AND it came to pass afterward, that he went throughout every city and village, preaching and shewing the glad tidings of the kingdom of God: and the twelve *were* with him,

2 And certain women, which had been healed of evil spirits and infirmities, Mary called Magdalene, out of whom went seven devils,

3 And Joanna the wife of Chuza Herod's steward, and Susanna, and many others, which ministered unto him of their substance.

The Crowd That Followed Jesus

Notice that Jesus went *"throughout every city and village"* in the province of Galilee, and perhaps beyond, preaching the Gospel. With Him were the twelve apostles, and a number of women who had been wonderfully healed or blessed followed also. *"Mary called Magdalene, out of whom went seven devils,"* was the Mary of the town of Magdala, on the west coast of the little Sea of Galilee. Joanna was *"the wife of Chuza Herod's steward."* The Herod here is *"the tetrarch of Galilee"* (Luke 3:1), son of Herod the Great, who ruled all of Judea when Christ was born. This Herod, who took his brother Philip's wife, had John the Baptist arrested and then beheaded, visited in Jerusalem when Christ was tried before Pilate (Luke 23:6-12). We suppose that Joanna had been wonderfully healed of some affliction, and very likely, Chuza, Herod's steward, had been converted and was willing for his wife to go with Jesus, as did others *"which ministered unto him of their substance."* So Jesus and the apostles lived on the beneficence of good women and others.

VERSES 4—15:

4 And when much people were gathered together, and were come to him out of every city, he spake by a parable:

5 A sower went out to sow his seed: and as he sowed, some fell by the way side; and it was trodden down, and the fowls of the air devoured it.

6 And some fell upon a rock; and as soon as it was sprung up, it withered away, because it lacked moisture.

7 And some fell among thorns; and the thorns sprang up with it, and choked it.

8 And other fell on good ground, and sprang up, and bare fruit an hundredfold. And when he had said these things, he cried, He that hath ears to hear, let him hear.

9 And his disciples asked him, saying, What might this parable be?

10 And he said, Unto you it is given to know the mysteries of the kingdom of God: but to others in parables; that seeing they might not see, and hearing they might not understand.

11 Now the parable is this: The seed is the word of God.

12 Those by the way side are they that hear; then cometh the devil, and taketh away the word out of their hearts, lest they should believe and be saved.

13 They on the rock *are they*, which, when they hear, receive the word with joy; and these have no root, which for a while believe, and in time of temptation fall away.

14 And that which fell among thorns are they, which, when they have heard, go forth, and are choked with cares and riches and pleasures of *this* life, and bring no fruit to perfection.

15 But that on the good ground are they, which in an honest and good heart, having heard the word, keep *it*, and bring forth fruit with patience.

Sowing the Gospel Seed

Parallel passage is in Matthew 13. Notice: "*The seed is the word of God*" (vs. 11). Preaching and witnessing the Gospel is thus sowing the seed. This figure is often used in the Scriptures about soul-winning effort, as in Psalm 126:5,6: "*They that sow in tears shall reap in joy. He that goeth forth and weepeth, bearing precious seed, shall doubtless come again with rejoicing, bringing his sheaves with him.*" And Isaiah 32:20 says, "*Blessed are ye that sow beside all waters, that send forth thither the feet of the ox and the ass.*" And Ecclesiastes 11:1: "*Cast thy bread upon the waters: for thou shalt find it after many days.*" And verses 4-6, following, say: "*He that observeth the wind shall not sow; and he that regardeth the clouds shall not reap. As thou knowest not what is the way of the spirit, nor how the bones do grow in the womb of her that is with child: even so thou knowest not the works of God who maketh all.   In the morning sow thy seed, and in the evening withhold not thine hand: for thou knowest not whether shall prosper, either this or that, or whether they both shall be alike good.*" This is also emphasized in Galatians 6:8,9: "*He that soweth to his flesh shall of the flesh reap corruption; but he that soweth to the Spirit shall of the Spirit reap life everlasting. And let us not be weary in well doing: for in due season we shall reap, if we faint not.*"

There is a Bible law that "*he which soweth sparingly shall reap also sparingly; and he which soweth bountifully shall reap also bountifully*" (II Cor. 9:6).   They who sow more seed reap a bigger crop. The fisherman who puts more hooks in the water catches more fish. The Christian who earnestly witnesses to more people wins more souls.

One cannot win everyone, but everyone can win someone.

Why a Parable?

First, because "*. . . unto you it is given to know the mysteries of the kingdom of God: but to others in parables; that seeing they might not see, and hearing they might not understand*" (vs. 10).   Only to the seeking, believing heart will a parable tell its message.

Then parables have the charm of a story, colorful, easily remembered, making spiritual truth obvious and impressive to the spiritual mind. See what Jesus said about parables in Matthew 13:10-14, and pray that you may have *"ears to hear."*

Four Classes Who Hear the Gospel

Some seed fell *"by the way side,"* on the turn row and path at the border of the field. The ground was hard. The people walked on it, and the birds ate it up. So it is that the Gospel sometimes falls on the hearts of people who are preoccupied, not interested; they have no *"ears to hear"*; and so Satan takes the Word out of their hearts ere it could sprout and bring forth gospel fruit.

But we are to *"sow beside all waters."* In hilly, barren Palestine they were to sow the seed in the bit of good soil by every little creek, as well as in the Jordan valley. So we are to sow the gospel seed *"to every creature,"* and who knows *"whether shall prosper, either this or that, or whether they both shall be alike good"* (Eccles. 11:6). Those who will not give much attention and who may never get saved, at least ought to hear the Gospel before they go to Hell!

Some seed *"fell upon a rock"* (vs. 6). When the seed got wet, it would sprout but soon dry up, could not take root, and would die under the sun. These are those who, *"when they hear, receive the word with joy,"* that is, they think favorably about the Christian life. They may believe the truth that is preached and give mental acceptance to it, but there is no repentance, no heart turning to Jesus in saving faith. And in time of trial, with no repentance and no miraculous new birth, they fall away from their convictions and principles; they do not fall away from Christ, whom they never did know in their hearts.

We must remember that mental assent to the truth is
not salvation. *"Thou believest that there is one God;
thou doest well: the devils also believe, and tremble"*
(James 2:19). As long as the seed is all on the surface,
with no root in the soul, one is not saved.

Some seed *"fell among thorns; and the thorns sprang
up with it, and choked it"* (vs. 7), although the seed
sprouted and had roots. Then these must represent
those who have trusted Christ and been converted, but
then *"are choked with cares and riches and pleasures
of this life, and bring no fruit to perfection"* (vs. 14).
They are saved people, born again, who are baby
Christians. They are carnal, not spiritual, so must be
fed with milk and not with meat (I Cor. 3:1-3). These
are the Christians whose works are to be found *"wood,
hay and stubble"* at the judgment seat of Christ, and so
their works will be burned up, although they are *"saved;
yet so as by fire"* (I Cor. 3:12-15). And even more
mature Christians, if they do not beware, may find
themselves *"choked with cares and riches and pleasures
of this life, and bring no fruit to perfection."*

So a David may fall into adultery and murder, and a
Jehoshaphat into compromise, and a Solomon into the
temptations of luxury and many wives and idolatry; so
a Peter may curse and deny Christ and quit the ministry,
or a Mark may leave Barnabas and Paul on a missionary journey, or a Demas may forsake Paul in prison.

One may be *"choked with cares."* That does not seem
to be wicked; but one may so fret and be absorbed with
burdens that he does not pray, does not feed upon the
Word, does not delight in the Lord, does not have Holy
Spirit power. Worry is a sin. Martha was wrong to
be *"cumbered about much serving"* (Luke 10:40), and
did not, like Mary, sit at the feet of Jesus to learn.

Beware about being overburdened by the cares of this
world.

And one may be *"choked with. . . riches"* or with, as Jesus said in the parallel passage in Matthew 13:22, *"the deceitfulness of riches."* And so the Christian is warned to beware of *"coveteousness, which is idolatry"* (Col. 3:5), and that *"the love of money is the root of all evil"* (or, all kinds of evil) (I Tim. 6:10). And God's minister who would bring forth fruit must not be *"greedy of filthy lucre"* (I Tim. 3:3).

And one may find his Christian life choked with the *"pleasures of this life,"* and so *"bring no fruit to perfection."* God meant for His people to be happy but not to be absorbed in happiness or pleasure. With sinners about us lost and undone, surely all our pleasures should be tempered with deep concern for souls. God provides food for His own, but food should never be a main thing. God gives happy families and loving affection to Christians, and *"crowneth thee with lovingkindness and tender mercies"* (Ps. 103:4). We should enjoy pleasures as they come, but no one should give his life over to pleasure. *"She that liveth in pleasure is dead while she liveth"* (I Tim. 5:6). So to be absorbed with pleasure, or to be burdened about making money, or to have cares and fret about job or clothes or provisions or debts, may all hinder the fruit-bearing of a Christian. And so there are Christians who never have family devotions, Christians who smoke cigarettes, Christians who company with the lewd and the profane and attend the movies, and Christians who never win souls. They *"bring no fruit to perfection."*

But the best is the last! Thank God, some seed *"fell on good ground, and sprang up, and bare fruit an hundredfold"* (vs. 8). The companion passage in Matthew 13:23 says, *". . . some an hundredfold, some sixty, some thirty."* The proportions are not always the same. We may be

> "Going forth with weeping, sowing for the Master,
> Though the loss sustained our spirit often grieves;"

but it is still true that those who sow in tears shall reap in joy, it is still true that everybody can win some. We are to sow the seed *"beside all waters,"* we are to take the Gospel *"to every creature."* We may weep over those who reject it, and may grieve that some who are saved are not full-blown, fruitful Christians; but, thank God, with some others who hear the Gospel there will be an abundant harvest. Kimball, the teacher of a class of boys, may have given his earnest testimony to many a lad without spectacular results, but when he won D. L. Moody the seed bore fruit *"an hundredfold."* Hundreds and hundreds of people had heard the little band from the Pacific Garden Mission in Chicago, who had been singing and witnessing on Chicago streets, but when the big league ballplayer Billy Sunday sat on the curb and heard them, the seed brought forth *"an hundredfold."*

So keep on sowing, and do not be discouraged, you Christians who would win souls.

VERSES 16 — 18:

16 No man, when he hath lighted a candle, covereth it with a vessel, or putteth *it* under a bed; but setteth *it* on a candlestick, that they which enter in may see the light.
17 For nothing is secret, that shall not be made manifest; neither any *thing* hid, that shall not be known and come abroad.
18 Take heed therefore how ye hear: for whosoever hath, to him shall be given; and whosoever hath not, from him shall be taken even that which he seemeth to have.

The Christian Is the Light of the World

Check carefully the parallel passages in Matthew 5:13-16, Mark 4:21-24. Here are truths that Jesus often spoke. 1. The Christian's saving influence: light, salt, witness.   2. Secrets are made manifest, things come to light.   3. One should have ears to hear, a heart tuned to hear and do God's will.   4. Judgment and reaping coming for what we sow.

"Let your light so shine before men." The Christian is a light to shine in this benighted, dark world. Every Christian has the Holy Spirit abiding in his body. He is the temple of God. In John 8:12 Jesus said, *"I am the light of the world."* In John 9:5 he amplified, *"As long as I am in the world, I am the light of the world."* Oh, there is no doubt about the unique Sonship and Saviourhood of the atoning Saviour, yet in Matthew 5:14 Jesus said, *"YE are the light of the world."* Christ has no temple on earth but the body of a Christian, has no hands but ours. So, very truly, Christians are the light of the world.

A great Bible teacher once said that Christ is the True Light like the sun, and we are, like the moon, only reflectors of that Light with no light of our own. But that is not quite true. No, it is not that *"you reflect the light of the world,"* but *"Ye ARE the light of the world."* We have the light inside, *"Christ in you, the hope of glory."* It is true that Christ is the Water of Life and the lost are invited, *"Whosoever will, let him take the water of life freely"* (Rev. 22:17). But Jesus promised, *"If any man thirst, let him come unto me, and drink. He that believeth on me, as the scripture hath said, out of his belly shall flow rivers of living water"* (John 7:37,38). Oh, the water of life, carried out by the Holy Spirit from the innermost being of a Christian, is to flow out to all about us!

But men do not light a candle and put it under a bushel or under a bed. The candle is for the candlestick, to give light. Oh, Christian, then, rise and shine! What shame that we are silent when we ought to witness! What shame when we conform when we ought to be transformed! (Rom. 12:1,2). Here in different words is the Great Commission that we are to go to all the world and give the Gospel to every creature. What shame to have the artesian well inside and never turn the faucets! What shame to never *"with joy. . . draw water out of the wells of salvation"* (Isa. 12:3). The daily walk and the daily talk (both are needed) are the shining light of a Christian.

VERSES 19—21:

19 Then came to him *his* mother and his brethren, and could not come at him for the press.
20 And it was told him *by certain* which said, Thy mother and thy brethren stand without, de-siring to see thee.
21 And he answered and said unto them, My mother and my brethren are these which hear the word of God, and do it.

The Mother and Brothers of Jesus

The same account is given in Matthew 12:46-50 and Mark 3:31-35. These brothers of Jesus were born to Mary and Joseph after Jesus. Mary was a virgin till after the birth of Jesus. The other brothers are named James, Joses, Simon, and Judas (Matt. 13:55). This James, *"the Lord's brother,"* was called an apostle (Gal. 1:19). This is the James who seems to have presided at the council in Jerusalem (Acts 15:13). The James who wrote the book of James, there simply called himself *"James, a servant of God and of the Lord Jesus Christ. . ."* (James 1:1). The Judas here wrote the book of Jude. The sisters are not named.

It is important here to note that Mary was put on exactly the same basis as other Christians. She had no special influence with Jesus as His mother and neither did the half brothers. Jesus said, *"My mother and my brethren are these which hear the word of God, and do it*" (Luke 8:21). And in Luke 11:27 we read that "*a certain woman of the company lifted up her voice, and said unto him, Blessed is the womb that bare thee, and the paps which thou hast sucked.*" Jesus said, "*Yea rather, blessed are they that hear the word of God, and keep it.*" Mary was saved by grace, was a good Christian woman, but was in exactly the same relationship to Christ as every Christian who hears the Word of God and does it.

It is impressive that Mary is simply mentioned once after the ascension of Christ. She was mentioned as being in the prayer meeting before Pentecost (Acts 1:14). After that she was never mentioned. The whole idolatrous matter of prayers to Mary, calling her a "mediatrix," calling her the "queen of Heaven" and the "mother of God," arose as a wicked heresy in the Roman church far later. New Testament Christians gave Mary no more place than other good women had, and Jesus Christ does the same.

Dear Christian, you are a brother of Jesus Christ, and so am I. And with all Christians, we rejoice that "*he is not ashamed to call them brethren*" (Heb. 2:11).

VERSES 22—25:

22 Now it came to pass on a certain day, that he went into a ship with his disciples: and he said unto them, Let us go over unto the other side of the lake. And they launched forth.

23 But as they sailed he fell asleep: and there came down a storm of wind on the lake; and they were filled *with water*, and were in jeopardy.

24 And they came to him, and awoke him, saying, Master, master, we perish. Then he arose, and rebuked the wind and the raging of the water: and they ceased, and there was a calm.

25 And he said unto them, Where is your faith? And they being afraid wondered, saying one to another. What manner of man is this! for he commandeth even the winds and water, and they obey him.

The Storm Quieted by Christ's Word!

The parallel passages are in Matthew 8:23-27 and in Mark 4:36-41. Although the little Sea of Galilee is only eight miles across and fifteen miles long, a windstorm can bring great danger to a small ship.

As they launched to go across that lake we are not surprised that Jesus *"fell asleep."* In Mark we learn that He was asleep *"on a pillow."* Oh, how good that somebody who loved Him provided a pillow! But the storm was so great that *"they were filled with water, and were in jeopardy"* (vs. 23). And Matthew 8:24 says, *". . . There arose a great tempest in the sea, insomuch that the ship was covered with the waves. . . ."* The frightened disciples awoke Jesus saying, *"Master, master, we perish."* And they seemed a little indignant that Jesus slept and did not share their concern, for in Mark 4:38 we read, *". . . They awake him, and say unto him, Master, carest thou not that we perish?"* Oh, troubled disciples! As the song so sweetly says:

**"No water can swallow the ship where lies
The Master of ocean and earth and skies."**

And so He rebuked them saying, *"Where is your faith?"* (vs. 25).

Oh, no Christian is in danger who is in the will of God, and in the presence of the Saviour! One is safer with Him in the night than being alone in the daytime. One is safer with Him in the storm than being alone in a peaceful, quiet place. One is safer with Him in war than without Him in peace.

Lack of faith is a great sin. Jesus rebuked it here. He rebuked Peter for faltering faith when he walked on the water (Matt. 14:31). He rebuked the disciples for lack of faith about food after Jesus had fed the five thousand and the four thousand (Matt. 16:8-11). He rebuked them for lack of faith and power to heal the devil-possessed boy in Luke 9:41. The best thing one can do to please the Lord Jesus is to believe Him, rely upon Him. Leave things in His hand with loving trust and happy hearts. *"In the world ye shall have tribulation,"* Jesus said, *"but be of good cheer; I have overcome the world"* (John 16:33).

VERSES 26—33:

26 And they arrived at the country of the Gadarenes, which is over against Galilee.

27 And when he went forth to land, there met him out of the city a certain man, which had devils long time, and ware no clothes, neither abode in *any* house, but in the tombs.

28 When he saw Jesus, he cried out, and fell down before him, and with a loud voice said, What have I to do with thee, Jesus, *thou* Son of God most high? I beseech thee, torment me not.

29 (For he had commanded the unclean spirit to come out of the man. For oftentimes it had caught him: and he was kept bound with chains and in fetters; and he brake the bands, and was driven of the devil into the wilderness.)

30 And Jesus asked him, saying, What is thy name? And he said, Legion: because many devils were entered into him.

31 And they besought him that he would not command them to go out into the deep.

32 And there was there an herd of many swine feeding on the mountain: and they besought him that he would suffer them to enter into them. And he suffered them.

33 Then went the devils out of the man, and entered into the swine: and the herd ran violently down a steep place into the lake, and were choked.

Legions of Devils in the Maniac of Gadara

Now after the storm they have crossed the little Sea of Galilee and on the southeastern side is the country of the Gadarenes *"over against Galilee,"* that is, on the opposite side of the Sea of Galilee and of the Jordan River from Galilee.

What a pitiful creature was this devil-possessed man. He had *"devils long time, and ware no clothes, neither abode in any house, but in the tombs."* He was *"ex-ceeding fierce, so that no man might pass by that way"* (Matt. 8:28). *"He had been often bound with fetters and chains, and the chains had been plucked asunder by him, and the fetters broken in pieces: neither could any man tame him. And always, night and day, he was in the mountains, and in the tombs, crying, and cutting himself with stones"* (Mark 5:4,5). What was his name? He replied, *"Legion."* He had a whole legion or army of devils in him.

Oh, poor, frail, unbelieving men with darkened minds and rebellious hearts may not know that Jesus is God in the flesh, but all the devils know it! And devils here cried out, *"What have I to do with thee, Jesus, thou Son of God most high? I beseech thee, torment me not."* Torment them? Luke tells us of only one of these men, but Matthew lets us know that there were two and they said, *"What have we to do with thee, Jesus, thou Son of God? art thou come hither to torment us before the time?"* (Matt. 8:29). So demons know that they must be subject to Christ. At one time even in Hell they will bow their knee to Him (Phil. 2:10). We are even told that Satan *"knoweth that he hath but a short time"* (Rev. 12:12).

And now these demons asked to be sent into a herd of swine feeding there. There were *"many swine"* and Mark 5:13 tells us, *"They were about two thousand."* And when the devils entered these hogs, *"The herd ran violently down a steep place into the lake, and were choked,"* were drowned (vs. 33).

Why did the demons wish to enter the swine? Partly, we suppose, because demons want a home, they want some creature they can influence, some way to do harm. Probably they hoped to arouse enmity among the people against Jesus and that did happen. And why did Jesus grant their request? Perhaps because Jews were forbidden to eat pork, and if these were Jews they ought not to have been raising the unclean beasts they would doubtless use for food. And those who bred them were guilty of helping those who broke the ceremonial law by eating them. And so, we believe Jesus was willing to take the reproach of bringing financial loss to the owners, to let the contrast be made clear to them and to us how much more important it was to have a man without devils than to have the hogs.

VERSES 34—39:

34 When they that fed *them* saw what was done, they fled, and went and told *it* in the city and in the country.

35 Then they went out to see what was done; and came to Jesus, and found the man, out of whom the devils were departed, sitting at the feet of Jesus, clothed, and in his right mind: and they were afraid.

36 They also which saw *it* told them by what means he that was possessed of the devils was healed.

37 Then the whole multitude of the country of the Gadarenes round about besought him to depart from them; for they were taken with great fear: and he went up into the ship, and returned back again.

38 Now the man out of whom the devils were departed besought him that he might be with him: but Jesus sent him away, saying,

39 Return to thine own house, and shew how great things God hath done unto thee. And he went his way, and published throughout the whole city how great things Jesus had done unto him.

They Preferred Pigs to the Lord Jesus!

What a stir in the whole area! Those who had fed the hogs ran and *"told it in the city and in the country."* The crowd assembled to see the marvel. And there was a man who had been so fearful that people could not pass that way, a man who screamed and cried in the night and cut himself with stones and slept in the caves where they buried the dead, a man who could not be bound with chains nor kept behind steel bars, and now he is "*sitting at the feet of Jesus, clothed, and in his right mind!*" They ought to have been glad, but they were afraid. Those who do not love the Lord Jesus are afraid of His power. Those who prefer their worldly possessions and ill-gotten gains, seeing devils cast out, and souls saved will be afraid of Jesus and of the people who have His power. So then "*the whole multitude . . . besought him to depart from them; for they were taken with great fear.*" And Jesus did leave them. Doubtless He was sad. They drove away life and salvation and blessing. How often covetousness is idolatry, and people prefer the hams and bacon, or the business and salaries, to the rich blessings the Lord Jesus gives.

And note the poor devil-possessed man. What a change had come on this maniac, this fearsome creature with demoniac strength! But now he is clothed instead of naked. When people get right with God they have a proper modesty and dress decently. A genuine revival in the heart of a woman will fix the miniskirts and the skimpy bathing suits, and it will fix shorts and nakedness. Now instead of being insane he is "*in his right mind.*" He sits quietly and at the feet of Jesus. What peace is in his heart! Oh, thank God for the transforming power of Christ and the Gospel.

The poor man knows these fellow-countrymen do not rejoice in his good fortune. They are thinking about the loss of the pigs! They are begging the Saviour to depart and He will. Oh, then, if He could only go with Jesus!

But no, Jesus tells him, "*Return to thine own house, and shew how great things God hath done unto thee*" (vs. 39), and he did!

Jesus told the disciples that repentance and remission of sin should be preached in all nations, "*beginning at Jerusalem"* (Luke 24:47). Since they were Jews they went *"to the Jew first."* So Andrew first got his brother Peter (John 1:40-42). So every Christian ought to most earnestly seek to win his own household, his immediate neighbors and friends.

VERSES 40 — 42:

40 And it came to pass, that, when Jesus was returned, the people *gladly* received him: for they were all waiting for him.

41 And, behold, there came a man named Jairus, and he was a ruler of the synagogue: and he fell down at Jesus' feet, and besought him that he would come into his house:

42 For he had one only daughter, about twelve years of age, and she lay a dying. But as he went the people thronged him.

The Wayside Ministry of Jesus

Jesus had been across the little Sea of Galilee to the east bank, where He had delivered the Gadarene from a legion of devils; and now, returning, He finds a crowd waiting. Ever since Jesus was filled with the Spirit after His baptism and started His preaching tours over the province of Galilee, crowds had thronged to see Him, often day and night.

Luke 4:14 tells us *"there went out a fame of him through all the region round about."* And verse 37 says, *"The fame of him went out into every place of the country round about."* Luke 4:40 says, *"Now when the sun was setting, all they that had any sick with divers diseases brought them unto him; and he laid his hands on every one of them, and healed them."* In the same chapter, verse 42 tells how the people followed Jesus *"into a desert place"* and *"sought him, and came unto him, and stayed him, that he should not depart from them."* Luke 5:15 tells us, *"But so much the more went there a fame abroad of him: and great multitudes came together to hear.*"

When Jesus preached in a home in Capernaum, Mark 2:1 and 2 tells us, "*it was noised that he was in the house. And straightway many were gathered together, insomuch that there was no room to receive them, no, not so much as about the door.*" And those who brought the man "*sick of the palsy*" had to break up the tile roof and let him down through the roof to Jesus, for salvation and healing.

After the twelve were chosen, Luke 6:17 tells us, He "*came down with them, and stood in the plain, and the company of his disciples, and a great multitude of people out of all Judaea and Jerusalem, and from the sea coast of Tyre and Sidon, which came to hear him, and to be healed of their diseases.*"

Even when He took the twenty-mile walk down to Nain of Galilee, then, we are told, "*many of his disciples went with him, and much people*" (Luke 7:11).

Then Luke 8:4 tells us that on His preaching tour of Galilee, "*Much people were gathered together, and were come to him out of every city.*"

Thus we can understand that Jesus preached on the streets, by the wayside, by the seaside, or wherever He happened to be; and the crowds, greatly moved and blessed, with sinners saved and devils cast out and the sick healed, came to hear the wonderful words of Jesus.

So now Jesus came back by boat across the Sea of Galilee and "*the people gladly received him: for they were all waiting for him*" (Luke 8:40).

It is important to remember, then, that the ministry of Jesus was not primarily a set, stated ministry of preaching in a church house on the Sabbath day. He preached in many synagogues, but He preached much more and to much larger crowds by the wayside.

We are reminded of the field preaching of Whitefield

and John Wesley. And let us say that the great tent campaigns and tabernacle revival campaigns of evangelists in the old days are more like the ministry of Jesus than the regular routine preaching in church buildings on Sunday by official pastors.

The burning heart of the Saviour, then, was always aflame with a burden to help and to save, so the amazing results simply followed His ministry everywhere He went. And those who were saved and blessed under the ministry of Jesus were won in their ordinary times and places by the wayside.

Nicodemus came to Jesus at night for the message that he must be born again. The startled woman at the well at Sychar in Samaria was won there by the well. Blind Bartimaeus was won by the roadside near Samaria. And Zacchaeus, as he left the same city, was called down from the tree he had climbed in order to see Jesus, and there was saved. Jesus broke up a funeral to raise the son of the widow of Nain. At a wedding in Cana, He turned the water to wine. They brought to Him in public the woman taken in adultery, and there Jesus forgave her. When He was in the house of Simon at Bethany, the woman which was a sinner slipped in to weep over His feet, at the dinner table, and she was saved. When Jesus went up to Tyre and Sidon in the country of Lebanon, a Canaanite woman came to plead with Him there, and the devil was cast out of her daughter.

So here the people "*were all waiting for him*" and were glad to see Him. And bustling through the crowd comes Jairus, ruler of the synagogue, to plead for Jesus to heal his dying daughter.

We need not be surprised that Jesus, thronged and crowded by the multitude as He went toward the house of Jairus, was followed by the afflicted woman who felt that she must touch Him and then she would be healed!

Let us learn, first, that the dear Lord Jesus is always available. He illustrated that Himself in Luke 11:5 when He said, "*Which of you shall have a friend, and shall go unto him at midnight, and say unto him, Friend, lend me three loaves...?*" And He has invited the weary, the heavy laden to come, for He is "*meek and lowly in heart* [always available]" (Matt. 11:28-30).

The other lesson is that we ought to be, like Jesus, day and night about the Father's business of saving souls and helping the troubled. Our hearts ought, at every human contact, to go out in holy compassion. If Jesus were here today, would He ever ride in a taxi without talking to the driver? Would He ever visit a hospital without His heart going out to every sufferer and witnessing to all who would hear? If He walked the crowded streets in a city, would He stop to comfort this one, to heal that one, to save another? O God, help us to always be about the one big business of saving souls, as was the Lord Jesus!

VERSES 43 — 48:

43 And a woman having an issue of blood twelve years, which had spent all her living upon physicians, neither could be healed of any,

44 Came behind *him*, and touched the border of his garment: and immediately her issue of blood stanched.

45 And Jesus said, Who touched me? When all denied, Peter and they that were with him said, Master, the multitude throng thee and press *thee*, and sayest thou, Who touched me?

46 And Jesus said, Somebody hath touched me: for I perceive that virtue is gone out of me.

47 And when the woman saw that she was not hid, she came trembling, and falling down before him, she declared unto him before all the people for what cause she had touched him, and how she was healed immediately.

48 And he said unto her, Daughter, be of good comfort: thy faith hath made thee whole; go in peace.

Only a Touch, and a Miracle Takes Place

The woman was a pitiful case. With an issue of blood for twelve years, she had doubtless grown thin and pale. In Mark 5:26 we find that not only had she spent all of her money on physicians and was no better, "*but rather grew worse.*" So her case was desperate indeed, in her sickness and poverty, and the prospect of an early death if Jesus did not heal her. Humanly speaking, her case was incurable. How like the state of every lost sinner! All the reformation, all the good influences, all the pleasant environment, all the moral teaching, all the sincere vows, all the rites of the church, cannot fix the awful disease that is in the heart and body of every sinner. Only Jesus can do that!

Notice that she only "*touched the border of his garment*" (vs. 44). But what faith she had! "*For she said within herself, If I may but touch his garment, I shall be whole*" (Matt. 9:21). And so when she "*touched the hem of his garment*" (Matt. 9:20), she was instantly made whole.

Note how simple it is to come to Christ! The answer came not by her toiling, not by her virtues, not by her faithfulness — simply a touch and she was instantly healed.

It is significant that she did not even touch the body of Jesus, but only His garment. Oh, there is a sense in which the power of Jesus is in His garment, as it is in all of us who are His body and who touch Him. So when the lame man at the Beautiful Gate of the Temple, in Acts 3, took the right hand of Peter, his feet and ankle bones received strength and he was instantly healed. So the hands of Paul, laid on Timothy in ordination, gave the gift of Holy Spirit power to Timothy (II Tim. 1:6; I Tim. 4:14). For the power of the Lord Jesus can be exercised through His garment as well as through His body, and can be exercised through us who are His, for He said, "*He that believeth on me, the works that I do shall he do also; and greater works than these shall he do; because I go unto my Father*" (John 14:12) and "*as my Father hath sent me, even so send I you. And when he had said this, he breathed on them, and saith unto them, Receive ye the Holy Ghost*" (John 20:21,22).

Just a touch! There is no long process in salvation. So, of the passover lamb Jews were to eat only one meal, and any of the feast that remained was to be burned (Exod. 12:10). The passover lamb, with the blood on the door, pictured salvation, and so they were to eat only one meal of that, as the sinner comes with saving faith only one time. Then they could eat the unleavened bread through the seven days as a Christian partakes of Christ for daily strength and joy and righteousness. But only one touch even of the hem of Christ's garment and the woman was wonderfully healed.

Let no one think, then, that long mourning or rites and ceremonies are required for salvation.

But she must tell it! Jesus knew that, aside from the throngs that jostled Him from time to time as He walked down the way, saving faith had touched Him, too. So when He asked, "*Who touched me?*" He asked not for Himself, surely, but for the sake of the woman. She needs to claim the Lord Jesus openly and give Him the praise for the miraculous healing.

Jesus said to the woman, "*Daughter, be of good comfort: thy faith hath made thee whole; go in peace*" (Luke 8:48). Certainly her faith had made her well physically and she was done with the plague; but it seems sure also that she was saved either at this moment or before. She most certainly believed that Jesus is the Son of God. Jesus called her "*Daughter,*" indicating kinship or sweet personal relationship. And it is unthinkable that she should trust Jesus for healing as she did without loving Him and trusting Him as Saviour.

In the case of the man "*sick of the palsy*" in Luke 5: 17-26, Jesus first forgave him, then the healing was given as evidence. Blind Bartimaeus was healed and then "*followed Jesus in the way*" (Mark 10:52). We should not miss the point that the one main thing people need is forgiveness and salvation, and the one main thing Jesus came for was to save sinners (I Tim. 1:15). So the woman here healed not only illustrates the matter of salvation but is probably a good example of it.

VERSES 49 — 56:

49 While he yet spake, there cometh one from the ruler of the synagogue's *house*, saying to him, Thy daughter is dead; trouble not the Master.

50 But when Jesus heard *it*, he answered him, saying, Fear not: believe only, and she shall be made whole.

51 And when he came into the house, he suffered no man to go in, save Peter, and James, and John, and the father and the mother of the maiden.

52 And all wept, and bewailed her: but he said, Weep not; she is not dead, but sleepeth.

53 And they laughed him to scorn, knowing that she was dead.

54 And he put them all out, and took her by the hand, and called, saying, Maid, arise.

55 And her spirit came again, and she arose straightway: and he commanded to give her meat.

56 And her parents were astonished: but he charged them that they should tell no man what was done.

A Delayed Blessing

While Jesus tarried in healing and demanding the public profession of the woman who was healed, one comes running from the house of Jairus saying, "*Thy daughter is dead; trouble not the Master.*" Was the ruler of the synagogue resentful? Did he feel that the delay had allowed his daughter to die who might have been healed? We are not told. But Jesus said, "*Fear not: believe only, and she shall be made whole.*"

God often has a good reason for delay in some answer
to prayer. It was good that the disciples *"continued...in
prayer and supplication"* (Acts 1:14) ten days before the
power of God came at Pentecost. The power of the Holy
Spirit does not come cheaply and ought not so to come.
It does not come to the mildly interested and lackadaisi-
cal Christian.

When Jacob prayed all night and wrestled with the
angel of God, in Genesis 32, he not only got deliverance
from the wrath of his brother Esau, but he got changed
from Jacob to Israel and could say, *"I have seen God
face to face."*

In John 11:3, when Jesus heard the plea that He
should come quickly for Lazarus was sick, He tarried
until Lazarus should die.   And when He arrived at
Bethany, Lazarus had been four days dead! But He
had said, *"This sickness is not unto death, but for the
glory of God."* God's delay in answering prayer may
mean that we should seek God all the more.   It never
means that God is indifferent or powerless.

And so the parents had greater joy in having a child
restored from the dead instead of simply healed of sickness, and Jesus had a greater testimony to the power of
God that was upon Him.

There is a great promise of God on this matter in
Hebrews 10:35-37: *"Cast not away therefore your confidence, which hath great recompence of reward. For ye
have need of patience, that, after ye have done the will
of God, ye might receive the promise. For yet a little
while, and he that shall come will come, and will not
tarry."*

God is always on time.

King Saul sinned and ran ahead of God because he
was not willing to wait for God to come to his help (I
Sam. 13:8-14).

The great crowd did not see the marvel of the girl

raised from the dead. Jesus *"suffered no man to go in, save Peter, and James, and John, and the father and the mother of the maiden."* So only these three apostles went with Jesus on the Mount of Transfiguration, and only these three were asked to pray with Jesus in the hour of extremity in the Garden of Gethsemane. And when Peter was called to pray about Tabitha, and to see her raised from the dead, then Peter *"put them all forth, and kneeled down, and prayed"* (Acts 9:40). The miracles of God are not for the casual onlookers, generally. Some people say that God works no miracles in this generation, but it is probable that if these same unbelieving people had been present in Galilee, they would not have seen that twelve-year-old girl raised from the dead or other miracles. And even now, after the girl is alive, Jesus *"charged them that they should tell no man what was done."* God saves the marvelous displays principally for those who trust Him and believe Him.

So, when God spoke to Paul on the road to Damascus and saved him, he heard a voice saying unto him, *"Saul, Saul, why persecutest thou me?"* (Acts 9:4). *"And the men which journeyed with him stood speechless, hearing a voice, but seeing no man."* Dr. Scofield says, "Cf. Acts 22.9; 26.14. A contradiction has been imagined. The three statements should be taken together. The men heard the 'voice' as a sound (Gr. *phone*), but did not hear the 'voice' as articulating the *words*, 'Saul, Saul,' etc."

"She is not dead, but sleepeth," Jesus said. Death for a Christian is only a sleep. A Christian will awake. So Jesus said to the disciples when Lazarus was dead, *"Our friend Lazarus sleepeth; but I go, that I may awake him out of sleep"* (John 11:11). And the word "sleep" is all the more pertinent when the period of death was as short as with this little girl and with Lazarus. Besides, Jesus may have wanted to let any

doubters continue believing that the girl had not really died and only got well, and He may have used the term "sleep" just as He used parables to tell a truth but veiled to the unbelieving.

The resurrection of the little girl was a miracle. But one day all that are in the graves will hear Christ's voice and come forth. It would be foolish to believe in a future resurrection of all men and not to believe that Jesus sometimes raised the dead in His ministry.

LUKE 9

VERSES 1 — 6:

THEN he called his twelve disciples together, and gave them power and authority over all devils, and to cure diseases.

2 And he sent them to preach the kingdom of God, and to heal the sick.

3 And he said unto them, Take nothing for *your* journey, neither staves, nor scrip, neither bread. neither money; neither have two coats apiece.

4 And whatsoever house ye enter into, there abide, and thence depart.

5 And whosoever will not receive you, when ye go out of that city, shake off the very dust from your feet for a testimony against them.

6 And they departed, and went through the towns, preaching the gospel, and healing every where.

The Twelve Sent Forth to Preach and Cast Out Devils

The call and the authority and the gifts were given to all twelve of the apostles and, therefore, to Judas; so unsaved Judas was for a time given the power to cast out devils and cure diseases. He and others like him may say at the judgment, as Jesus tells us in Matthew 7:22, "*Lord, Lord, have we not prophesied in thy name? and in thy name have cast out devils? and in thy name done many wonderful works?*" But Jesus will tell them, "*I never knew you.*"

They were to preach "*the kingdom of God,*" and that means not only the plan of salvation but the whole matter of being right with God and serving God. And they were to heal the sick. Healing is never the most important thing, but the tender heart of the Saviour was moved, and is moved now, with all the heartaches and troubles and pains of the people. There is no way to serve the Lord Jesus without a compassionate heart that will pray for the sick and will sometimes see them healed in answer to believing prayer, as James 5:13-16 has promised.

The unusual instructions given here were more particularly for this limited time and journey. It is not always wrong to have money or to have a suitcase or handbag (scrip), or to have an extra coat. They were to have a hurried journey through certain cities and towns. As they were walking, they could return walking. As they would be entertained in the homes, they did not need money. And they needed to learn to trust the Lord. These instructions remind us that God's man should often be poor and should not shrink from poverty.

The Lord Jesus Himself had not *"where to lay his head"* (Matt. 8:20). The bishop, or pastor, is to be *"not greedy of filthy lucre"* (I Tim. 3:3). In II Corinthians 6:4-10 we have instructions on *"approving ourselves as the ministers of God,"* and that includes *"in necessities, in distresses"* and *"as poor, yet making many rich; as having nothing, and yet possessing all things."*

The minister should be like Jesus who was anointed *"to preach the gospel to the poor"* (Luke 4:18). He is to seek especially *"the poor, and the maimed, and the halt, and the blind"* (Luke 14:21), so the man of God should remember the beatitude, *"Blessed be ye poor: for your's is the kingdom of God"* (Luke 6:20). That means that one who would serve the Lord Jesus must learn to trust Him. And he can ask for *"this day our daily bread,"* and be content. That does not mean that the man of God should not be supported, provided for. In the companion passage in Matthew 10:9,10 the Lord says that these apostles should *"provide neither gold, nor silver, nor brass in your purses, Nor scrip for your journey, neither two coats, neither shoes, nor yet staves: for the workman is worthy of his meat."*

If you compare the orders given these twelve with the orders given the seventy later sent on the same mission, you will see they are much alike (Luke 10:1-12). Verse 7 says, *"And in the same house remain, eating and drinking such things as they give: for the labourer is worthy of his hire."* And we have very, very clear instructions in I Corinthians 9:10-14, *"The Lord ordained that they which preach the gospel should live of the gospel."* In whatever home they were received, they were told, *"there abide till ye go thence,"* or as in Luke 10:7, *"Go not from house to house."* They were not to expect elaborate entertainment, with big dinners. They were on serious business, and it is always a mistake for the preacher to spend too much time in eating and fellowship when there is urgent work to do.

And if a city would not receive them, they were to *"shake off the dust of your feet...for a testimony against them."* God would hold people to account for whether or not they were willing to hear the Gospel.

In 1936 the writer had a tremendous revival campaign, sponsored by six or eight churches, in Binghamton, New York, in the 2,000-seat Binghamton theater building. Although hundreds were saved and the city tremendously moved, some liberal and worldly preachers combined against the campaign, criticised it in the public press, passed resolutions against the plain preaching on sin; and so I announced on the closing day that when I should leave the city, I would stand beside my car and shake the dust off my feet and call on God to hold the city accountable for the Gospel they had heard and that many had rejected. So we drove away; but that day a great thaw set in to melt the 19 inches of packed snow that was on the ground, and in two days a great flood had done a million dollars' worth of damage and taken one or two lives.

The Lord Jesus Himself pronounced a woe on Chorazin and Bethsaida and Capernaum, in Matthew 11:20-23, *"The cities wherein most of his mighty works were done, because they repented not."* And those cities have disappeared, although other cities like Nazareth and Tiberias in the same area have remained unto this day.

One who preaches in God's power and lives by the Saviour's rules may expect God to back up his preaching.

VERSES 7 — 9:

7 Now Herod the tetrarch heard of all that was done by him: and he was perplexed, because that it was said of some, that John was risen from the dead;

8 And of some, that Elias had appeared; and of others, that one of the old prophets was risen again.

9 And Herod said, John have I beheaded: but who is this, of whom I hear such things? And he desired to see him.

Herod's Guilty Conscience

The rest of the story is told in more detail in Matthew 14:1-14 and in Mark 6:14-29. There we are told how Herod put John the Baptist to death, on the plea of Herodias, who had left her husband, Philip, to live with Herod.

Verse 9 here says, *"Herod said, John have I beheaded: but who is this, of whom I hear such things?"* But in Mark 6:14 we find that King Herod actually thought Christ was John the Baptist risen from the dead. *"And king Herod heard of him; (for his name was spread abroad:) and he said, That John the Baptist was risen from the dead, and therefore mighty works do shew forth themselves in him."* He says the same thing as reported in Matthew 14:2. It is a striking fact that such a wicked man as Herod must still deal with the conscience he has violated.

So Joseph's brethren, when perhaps a score of years had passed, remembered their sin against Joseph. *"And they said one to another, We are verily guilty concerning our brother, in that we saw the anguish of his soul, when he besought us, and we would not hear; therefore is this distress come upon us. And Reuben answered them, saying, Spake I not unto you, saying, Do not sin against the child; and ye would not hear? therefore, behold, also his blood is required"* (Gen. 42:21,22).

And Judas Iscariot found that the thirty pieces of traitor's money he got for betraying Jesus burned like fire in his hands, and he wanted to rue back the trade. He said, *"I have sinned in that I have betrayed the innocent blood. And they said, What is that to us? see thou to that. And he cast down the pieces of silver in the temple, and departed, and went and hanged himself"* (Matt. 27:4,5).

Must we not believe, then, that the conscience, though temporarily deadened and seared by sin, reawakes to torment the lost even in Hell?

The conscience takes part in the divine law of sowing and reaping and the warnings, *"be sure your sin will find you out"* (Num 32:23) and *"whatsoever a man soweth, that shall he also reap"* (Gal. 6:7).

VERSES 10—12:

10 And the apostles, when they were returned, told him all that they had done. And he took them, and went aside privately into a desert place belonging to the city called Bethsaida.

11 And the people, when they knew *it*, followed him: and he received them, and spake unto them of the kingdom of God, and healed them that had need of healing.

12 And when the day began to wear away, then came the twelve, and said unto him, Send the multitude away, that they may go into the towns and country round about, and lodge, and get victuals: for we are here in a desert place.

Interrupted Rest

Jesus and the disciples needed a time of rest and quiet after the crowds and heavy duties and the whirlwind preaching tour of the cities of Galilee. Speaking of the same time, Mark 6:31 tells us: *"He said unto them, Come ye yourselves apart into a desert place, and rest a while: for there were many coming and going, and they had no leisure so much as to eat."* Those who work strenuously for the Lord Jesus need also times of quietness, meditation, prayer, rest, and waiting upon God.

But their rest was interrupted again. They again crowded around Jesus to hear Him; *"and he received them, and spake unto them of the kingdom of God, and healed them that had need of healing."* But when the day was about done and the multitudes who took no thought for food or rest for themselves or for Jesus would need to eat, the disciples said, *"Send the multitude away, that they may go into the towns and country round about, and lodge, and get victuals: for we are here in a desert place."* (The term *"a desert place"* does not mean a sandy wasteland but simply an open, uninhabited space. In a companion passage in Mark 6:32-44, we find that the people sat *"by companies upon the green grass"* [vs. 39]. The place was in the area near Bethsaida, thought to have been north of the Sea of Galilee.) We think that the disciples were not only weary and needing rest themselves but they had compassion on the people, and they asked Jesus to send them away so that they could buy food.

VERSES 13—17:

13 But he said unto them, Give ye | them to eat. And they said, We

have no more but five loaves and two fishes; except we should go and buy meat for all this people.

14 For they were about five thousand men. And he said to his disciples, Make them sit down by fifties in a company.

15 And they did so, and made them all sit down.

16 Then he took the five loaves and the two fishes, and looking up to heaven, he blessed them, and brake, and gave to the disciples to set before the multitude.

17 And they did eat, and were all filled: and there was taken up of fragments that remained to them twelve baskets.

The Feeding of the Five Thousand

This miracle is of special importance, being told in all four of the Gospels.

Jesus said to the disciples, "*Give ye them to eat*" (vs. 13). In the parallel passage in John 6:1-14, a conversation Jesus had with Philip is recorded: "*When Jesus then lifted up his eyes, and saw a great company come unto him, he saith unto Philip, Whence shall we buy bread, that these may eat? And this he said to prove him: for he himself knew what he would do. Philip answered him, Two hundred pennyworth of bread is not sufficient for them, that every one of them may take a little.*" There we are told also that Andrew "*saith unto him, There is a lad here, which hath five barley loaves, and two small fishes: but what are they among so many?*"

In Luke is the briefest account of the four   Note that the people were to be seated in very orderly fashion, "*by fifties in a company.*" Then Jesus began to break the bread and fishes. They were multiplied in His divine fingers, so each one of the apostles, with a basket, took the bread and fish sandwiches to the people. The "*five loaves*" were probably small flat cakes, about the size of a pancake, such as would bake easily in the earthen or stone ovens they used, and the bread common in all Arab countries today. And how wonderfully the miracle of actual creation took place in the presence of the multitude for Jesus is the Creator who made the heavens and the earth, and He could create again, and did!

If that seems a marvelous miracle—and it was!—we should remember that every time a child is conceived, an immortal soul comes into being. And that which seems to us so common is actually a new creation, even as Adam was formed from the dust of the earth, and God *"breathed into his nostrils the breath of life; and man became a living soul"* (Gen. 2:7). And God will make anew the bodies of all those who are resurrected from the graves, including those whose bodies are burned or eaten by wild beasts or devoured in the seas.

There were twelve baskets left over, not of scraps and garbage but bread and fish sandwiches—twelve baskets because, we suppose, each one of the twelve men had a basket full when all were satisfied. All the wonder of the food Jesus had created, which they ate, was for them; but the twelve basketsful surely are for the rest of us! That means that the Lord Jesus was saying He could provide for the needs of His own always, without any limit.

Jesus had commanded the disciples, *"Give ye them to eat."* Does that mean that the disciples themselves could have wrought that miracle? I think, certainly, yes; what Jesus commanded, they could have done. We will find the same lesson in the healing of the devil-possessed lad (vss. 37-43). The Lord Jesus used the lunch of one boy—five loaves and two fishes; and so we would learn that "little is much if God is in it." Whatever we have, wholly given to Christ, is enough.

So, a sling in the hand of the shepherd boy can kill! the giant Goliath. So, a shepherd's rod in the hand of Moses can lead a nation to freedom, can open the Red Sea, can bring water out of a rock for the millions. So, a widow's pot of oil can be multiplied to pay her debts and support her family (II Kings 4:1-7). So the widow at Zarephath could find when she fed the prophet of God that *"the barrel of meal wasted not, neither did the cruse of oil fail, according to the word of the Lord, which he spake by Elijah"* (I Kings 17:16).

VERSES 18—21:

18 And it came to pass, as he was alone praying, his disciples were with him: and he asked them, saying, Whom say the people that I am?

19 They answering said, John the Baptist; but some say, Elias; and others say, that one of the old prophets is risen again.

20 He said unto them. But whom say ye that I am? Peter answering said, The Christ of God.

21 And he straitly charged them, and commanded *them* to tell no man that thing;

Peter's Confession of Christ

The parallel passages are Matthew 16:13-20 and Mark 8:27-30. We know that many people were looking forward to the coming of the Saviour. Anna and Simeon are examples (Luke 2:25-38). We read: *"The Jews sent priests and Levites from Jerusalem to ask him* [John the Baptist], *Who art thou? And he confessed, and denied not; but confessed, I am not the Christ"* (John 1:19,20). There are so many prophecies in the Old Testament about the coming of the Saviour that spiritually-minded people and those with even a casual acquaintance with the Old Testament would expect the coming Messiah. So the Jews had asked John, *"Art thou Elias?"* (John 1:21) thinking of Malachi 4:5 where the forerunner Elijah is promised. *"Art thou that prophet?"* (John 1:21) refers to the promise in Deuteronomy 18:15 of a prophet like unto Moses. And John announced to the eager multitude, *"Behold the Lamb of God, which taketh away the sin of the world"* (John 1:

29). Any thoughtful person must have known that all
the animal sacrifices pointed to a coming Sacrifice.

Now some people, like Herod, thought that John the
Baptist had risen from the dead. Some thought Jesus
was the prophet Elijah returned. But Peter answered
plainly, "*The Christ of God.*"

Jesus was greatly pleased with this answer of Peter in
the parallel passage in Matthew 16:17, and said, "*Blessed art thou, Simon Bar-jona: for flesh and blood hath
not revealed it unto thee, but my Father which is in
heaven.*"

Then follows the great promise in Matthew 16:18, so
perverted by Catholicism, "*I say also unto thee, That
thou art Peter, and upon this rock I will build my
church; and the gates of hell shall not prevail against
it.*" The Lord did not say He would build His church
upon Peter. He said, "*...thou art Peter* [the Greek word
for Peter means a small stone], *and upon this rock* [the
word used here for "rock" means a heavy foundation] *I
will build my church.*" Christ Himself is the Rock on
which His church is built. So, clearly, I Corinthians 3:
11 tells us: "*Other foundation can no man lay than that
is laid, which is Jesus Christ.*" And Jesus is the Foundation Stone prophesied in Isaiah 28:16, "*Therefore thus
saith the Lord God, Behold, I lay in Zion for a foundation a stone, a tried stone, a precious corner stone, a
sure foundation: he that believeth shall not make haste.*"
So, then, they are wrong who think that it is upon this
confession that Christ would build the church. No, it is
upon Christ Himself. He is the Foundation Stone,
Cornerstone, Capstone, Smiting Stone so often mentioned
in the Bible.

So, for the time being, these disciples are not to tell
people that Jesus is the Christ. Spiritually-minded ones
who look for Him will know it. The evidence is abun-

dant. Give Jesus time to prove Himself to honest hearts.

VERSES 22 — 26:

22 Saying, The Son of man must suffer many things, and be rejected of the elders and chief priests and scribes, and be slain, and be raised the third day.

23 And he said to *them* all, If any *man* will come after me, let him deny himself, and take up his cross daily, and follow me.

24 For whosoever will save his life shall lose it: but whosoever will lose his life for my sake, the same shall save it.

25 For what is a man advantaged, if he gain the whole world, and lose himself, or be cast away?

26 For whosoever shall be ashamed of me and of my words, of him shall the Son of man be ashamed, when he shall come in his own glory, and *in his* Father's, and of the holy angels.

Christian Participation in Christ's Crucifixion

Verse 22 is saying that the Lord Jesus came into this world to die on the cross. He is the *"Lamb slain from the foundation of the world"* (Rev. 13:8). Every bleeding sacrifice from that of Abel down to Christ pictured a Saviour who would die for the sins of the world. His atoning death was explicitly taught in Isaiah 53. That is the saving Gospel of John 3:16 and of I Corinthians 15:3 and 4. And His resurrection was as clearly foretold as His crucifixion. Psalm 16:10 was used by Peter at Pentecost to show that the resurrection of Christ was foretold in the plan of God, just as the second Psalm showed that the uniting of the rulers and people against Him was foretold. There follows, then, a test of discipleship. For one to *"take up his cross daily, and follow"* Christ is not the plan of salvation; it is a daily plan of consecrated discipleship. So Paul says in Galatians 2: 20, *"I am crucified with Christ: nevertheless I live; yet not I, but Christ liveth in me: and the life which I now live in the flesh I live by the faith of the Son of God, who loved me, and gave himself for me."*

Christ died literally in our place, but the Christian should day after day be a partaker of the crucified life. In Hebrews 13:12-14 we are taught to be partakers with Christ: *"Wherefore Jesus also, that he might sanctify the people with his own blood, suffered without the gate. Let us go forth therefore unto him without the camp, bearing his reproach. For here have we no continuing city, but we seek one to come."*

Just before His death Jesus told the disciples: *"If the world hate you, ye know that it hated me before it hated you. If ye were of the world, the world would love his own: but because ye are not of the world, but I have chosen you out of the world, therefore the world hateth you. Remember the word that I said unto you, The servant is not greater than his lord. If they have persecuted me, they will also persecute you; if they have kept my saying, they will keep your's also"* (John 15: 18-20).

The Lord's Supper is always to remind us of the death of Christ in our stead. And in baptism, one solemnly pictures that now he counts the old self dead and buried, and that he is risen to walk in newness of life (Rom. 6:3-6).

Here is the blessed truth that *"whosoever will lose his life for my sake, the same shall save it"* (Luke 9:24). The Lord speaks not primarily of physically dying for Christ but of day by day giving up one's own way to have Christ's way, so that *"to me to live is Christ"* (Phil. 1:21). And if one had his own way and gained the whole world, he would lose himself, that is, his life and his usefulness and his future rewards. And so, at the judgment seat of Christ, his work and life would be as wood, hay, and stubble, as taught in I Corinthians 3:10-15.

Oh, then, the Christian should not be ashamed of the

Lord Jesus and of His words.   Christ and the Bible
stand or fall together. The person who is ashamed of
the Scriptures, ashamed to claim their inspiration,
ashamed to keep them and live by them and defend
them, is thus ashamed of Christ and will bear the reproach of that when Christ comes and when Christians
have their judgment seat before Christ for rewards.

Ashamed of Jesus

Jesus, and shall it ever be
A mortal man ashamed of Thee?
Ashamed of Thee, whom angels praise,
Whose glories shine through endless days.

Ashamed of Jesus! sooner far
Let evening blush to own a star;
He sheds the beams of light divine
O'er this benighted soul of mine.

Ashamed of Jesus! that dear Friend
On whom my hopes of Heav'n depend!
No! when I blush, be this my shame,
That I no more revere His name.

Ashamed of Jesus! yes, I may,
When I've no guilt to wash away;
No tear to wipe, no good to crave,
No fears to quell, no soul to save.

— Joseph Griggs

VERSES 27 — 36:

27 But I tell you of a truth, there be some standing here, which shall not taste of death, till they see the kingdom of God.

28 And it came to pass about an eight days after these sayings, he took Peter and John and James, and went up into a mountain to pray.

29 And as he prayed, the fash-

ion of his countenance was altered, and his raiment *was* white *and* glistering.

30 And, behold, there talked with him two men, which were Moses and Elias:

31 Who appeared in glory, and spake of his decease which he should accomplish at Jerusalem.

32 But Peter and they that were with him were heavy with sleep: and when they were awake, they saw his glory, and the two men that stood with him.

33 And it came to pass, as they departed from him, Peter said unto Jesus, Master, it is good for us to be here: and let us make three tabernacles; one for thee, and one for Moses, and one for Elias: not knowing what he said.

34 While he thus spake, there came a cloud, and overshadowed them: and they feared as they entered into the cloud.

35 And there came a voice out of the cloud, saying, This is my beloved Son: hear him.

36 And when the voice was past, Jesus was found alone. And they kept *it* close, and told no man in those days any of those things which they had seen.

The Transfiguration of Christ

The transfiguration here is said to be a foretaste of the kingdom of God, that is, of Christ's coming in glory (vs. 27). That is the inspired explanation the Apostle Peter gives of it in II Peter 1:16-18: *"For we have not followed cunningly devised fables, when we made known unto you the power and coming of our Lord Jesus Christ, but were eyewitnesses of his majesty. For he received from God the Father honour and glory, when there came such a voice to him from the excellent glory, This is my beloved Son, in whom I am well pleased. And this voice which came from heaven we heard, when we were with him in the holy mount."*

It is unfortunate that in the parallel account, in the last verse in Matthew 16 and then in the 17th chapter of Matthew, the promise and the transfiguration are separated by the chapter heading men inserted. It tends to obscure the fact that the apostles will *"see the Son of man coming in his kingdom,"* in figure, on the Mount of Transfiguration.

I can believe that the dear Saviour Himself was greatly comforted in looking forward to the blessing of the future. We know that *"for the joy that was set before him"* He *"endured the cross, despising the shame..."* (Heb. 12:2). So the transfiguration must have been a happy and blessed encouragement to Him, as it was surely a revelation of the future glory, briefly, to the apostles who saw it.

Notice again that only three, Peter, James, and John, went with Jesus. Perhaps one reason is that they *"went up into a mountain to pray."* Not as many people go to a prayer meeting as would go to a spectacular event, and others thus miss the blessing.

It is impressive that Moses and Elijah met the Lord Jesus there. Elijah had gone bodily to Heaven in a whirlwind and a chariot of fire (II Kings 2:11). Moses had been buried by the hand of God alone, in a valley by Mount Nebo, and no man ever knew where he was buried (Deut. 34:5 and 6). In Jude, verse 9, we find that Michael the archangel contended with the Devil about the body of Moses. But he was buried. What kind of a body had Moses when he appeared on the Mount of Transfiguration? Or was it simply an appearance of Moses, visible in form but without physical substance? We do not know. The body was buried. These two, Moses and Elijah, were the greatest in the Law and the Prophets. Some think that they are the two witnesses of Revelation 11:3 and 4, and prophesied also in Zechariah 4:2 and 3, since they are the most important as lawgiver and prophet. Others think that the two witnesses will be Elijah (since he is promised to come, in the last two verses in Malachi) and Enoch, because neither of these two died physically before, and these two witnesses will die, according to Revelation 11:7. Since it is not revealed, we do not need to know.

Notice that people in Heaven carefully observe things

on earth. Moses and Elijah knew exactly when to come
to the Mount of Transfiguration (we think probably it
was Mount Tabor) to meet the Lord Jesus. And their
discussion was not of things in Heaven but of things on
earth, *"his decease which he should accomplish at Jerusalem."* Since in Heaven they rejoice over souls saved
(Luke 15:7,10), and since we are surrounded with such
a great cloud of heavenly witnesses (Heb. 12:1,2), we
think that people in Heaven watch us earnestly and
know what goes on here, rejoice over souls that are
saved, and maybe even weep with us over those who
are not saved. Guardian angels watch over men and
report in Heaven (Gen. 28:12; Ps. 34:7; specially Matt.
18:10). Abraham in Heaven had contact with earth and
Hell (Luke 16:22-31). In Heaven the souls of martyrs
cry out for judgment on sinners yet on earth (Rev. 6:
9-11).

The appearance of Jesus was glorious. The parallel
passage in Mark 9:3 says, *"his raiment became shining,
exceeding white as snow; so as no fuller on earth can
white them."* And the description in Matthew 17:2 tells
us that *"his face did shine as the sun, and his raiment
was white as the light."* That compares with the Lord
Jesus as John saw Him: *"And in the midst of the
seven candlesticks one like unto the Son of man, clothed
with a garment down to the foot, and girt about the
paps with a golden girdle. His head and his hairs were
white like wool, as white as snow; and his eyes were as
a flame of fire; And his feet like unto fine brass, as if
they burned in a furnace; and his voice as the sound of
many waters. And he had in his right hand seven stars:
and out of his mouth went a sharp twoedged sword:
and his countenance was as the sun shineth in his
strength"* (Rev. 1:13-16). In such glory will Jesus
come with His own when He returns with us to reign on
the earth. And the vision was necessary for the apostles

and necessary for us to have some inkling of the marvel
and glory that awaits and, oh, the shining, glorious
power of our Saviour!

Peter would like to stay there on the Mount of Transfiguration. Confused and somewhat beside himself, he
suggested that they set up three tents for Moses and
Elijah and Jesus, and stay there. But that was a mistake in more ways than one. First, Jesus has work to
do on earth, and so have they; they cannot stay. And,
second, Jesus is not on an equal with Moses and Elijah.
So the cloud of God overshadowed them, and God said,
"*This is my beloved Son: hear him.*" Hear Jesus,
as the final Authority — not Moses, though the Scriptures
he wrote are the words of Christ, too — not Elijah,
though as a prophet of God he often preached the Word.
But, personally, Jesus is not on an equal with these frail
men; He is Lord of all. No bishop nor pope nor apostle
nor prophet is on a level with the unique, infinite, sinless, eternal Son of God! Moses and Elijah were gone.
The apostles cherished the marvels they had seen but
were commanded not to tell it "*till the Son of man were
risen from the dead*" (Mark 9:9). And the Lord explained that John the Baptist was a type of Elijah
(Mark 9:11-13), though Elijah may come literally again
as one of the two witnesses of Revelation 11.

VERSES 37 — 41:

37 And it came to pass, that on the next day, when they were come down from the hill, much people met him.

38 And, behold, a man of the company cried out, saying, Master, I beseech thee, look upon my son: for he is mine only child.

39 And, lo, a spirit taketh him, and he suddenly crieth out; and it teareth him that he foameth again, and bruising him hardly departeth from him.

40 And I besought thy disciples to cast him out; and they could not.

41 And Jesus answering said, O faithless and perverse generation, how long shall I be with you, and suffer you? Bring thy son hither.

The Powerless Disciples

This story is given in Matthew 17:14-21 and Mark 9:14-29 in more detail. Matthew tells how the father came *"kneeling down to Jesus"* and Matthew 17:15 says the man said, *"Lord, have mercy on my son: for he is lunatick, and sore vexed: for ofttimes he falleth into the fire, and oft into the water."* Mark 9:17 and 18 says, *"...I have brought unto thee my son, which hath a dumb spirit; And wheresoever he taketh him, he teareth him: and he foameth, and gnasheth with his teeth, and pineth away...."* The father was in deep concern. He came to Jesus *"kneeling down to him."* The affliction had been *"of a child"* (Mark 9:21). Perhaps the father meant throughout childhood or from infancy. The lad is only a child still, as verse 42 here tells us. The father pleads, *"...If thou canst do any thing, have compassion on us, and help us"* (Mark 9:22), and then *"said with tears, Lord, I believe; help thou mine unbelief"* (vs. 24).

Note in Luke that this boy is an *"only child"* (vs. 38). The daughter of Jairus was *"one only daughter"* (Luke 8:42). And at Nain it was the widow's *"only son of his mother,"* which Jesus raised from the dead (Luke 7:12).

How the heart of Jesus goes out in compassion to all the troubled and burdened, the weeping! We should remember that *"the Lord is nigh unto them that are of a broken heart; and saveth such as be of a contrite spirit"* (Ps. 34:18). The Lord invites us to *"call upon me in the day of trouble: I will deliver thee, and thou shalt glorify me"* (Ps. 50:15). How often we are invited to, *"Cast thy burden upon the Lord, and he shall sustain thee..."* and to cast *"all your care upon him; for he careth for you"* (Ps. 55:22; I Pet. 5:7)! And so *"is any among you afflicted? let him pray...Is any sick among you? let him call for the elders of the church; and let them pray over him, anointing him with oil in the name of the Lord: And the prayer of faith shall save the sick, and the Lord shall raise him up...*" (Jas. 5:13-15).

The troubled father had come to plead that his child be healed and that the devil be cast out. With Jesus away on the mountain, the father appealed to the disciples; they tried but failed!

It is not surprising that the man expected the disciples to cast out the devil and that the disciples tried. They had been given "*power over all devils, and to cure diseases*" (Luke 9:1). They had before cast out devils. Even the seventy, sent later ahead of Jesus into every city and town of Galilee, had returned with joy, "*saying, Lord, even the devils are subject unto us through thy name*" (Luke 10:17). Oh, the disciples had sometimes cast out devils and should have been able to do it now, but they failed! Then the brokenhearted, frustrated father appealed to Jesus.

Now there was some doubt in the father's mind, we suppose, that even Jesus could meet his need. The demon possession was so terrible. Mark 9:22 quotes the father, "*...if thou canst do any thing, have compassion on us, and help us.*" When God's men fail to help people with God's power, it tends to cast doubt on Christ Himself and on the Bible, or whether God still works His wonders, whether God still has the heart compassion for people in trouble, whether Jesus is really "*the same yesterday, and to day, and for ever*" in His heart of love and compassion for troubled, sinful people.

Oh, then, we should expect that where Christians go, drunkards should be made sober, harlots made pure, infidels made into saints of God. We should expect prayers to be marvelously answered and God to show His power. And if we fail to have the power of God, to have answers to prayer, to win souls, our unbelief will limit God and dampen the faith of others in God's power and love.

The Saviour's Grief at the Disciples' Failure

"*O faithless and perverse generation,*" Jesus said, "*how long shall I be with you, and suffer you? Bring thy son hither.*" It was lack of faith that they could not cast out the devil. As Jesus had commanded them to feed the hungry five thousand, they had no faith to do it or even that Jesus would; so now when they had been commanded to cast out devils, they could not and it grieved the heart of Jesus. His words indicate grief, not simply over one failure but over repeated failure to have faith to do the marvels that were needed.

More than that is the whole "*generation*" which is faithless, and there is a perverseness back of the powerlessness. As the Lord Jesus grieved then over their powerlessness, so He grieves now, we believe, over the unbelief, the perverseness of a whole generation that does not expect and does not seek God's miraculous power, when needed, to cast out devils and do marvels.

In John 14:12 Jesus said, "*He that believeth on me, the works that I do shall he do also; and greater works than these shall he do; because I go unto my Father.*" We are to do the same work as Jesus did. That strange, marvelous promise says that one may do the very work of Jesus, and this promise is for him "*that believeth.*" So it is for us to claim by believing.

And the two following verses, John 14:13 and 14, surely say "*whatsoever,*" putting no limit on the magnitude of the request and "*if ye shall ask ANY THING in my name. . . .*" We are not to believe that the name of Jesus, used in faith (and used legitimately and actually with His authority because He has made clear what He wants us to ask), has lost its power. When we find what Jesus would have us ask and what He wants to give, and we ask Him, then it is *"whatsoever"* and *"any thing."*

In Mark 9:23 Jesus told the father, *"If thou canst believe, all things are possible to him that believeth."* The promise, then, is not just to him alone but to us. No other interpretation is honestly possible, we think. So the attitude of our poor, needy hearts should be like that of the father who said with tears, *"Lord, I believe; help thou mine unbelief."*

In this case we are sure that the disciples could have had power to cast out the devil and heal the lad. Why were they not able to do it? They asked Jesus the same question, recorded in Matthew 17:19 and in Mark 9:28.

Why did not the disciples have faith for this healing? Jesus was away. Peter, James and John, the most spiritual, we suppose, and certainly the leaders, were away, too. It may be they felt if the boy was brought first for Jesus to heal, it was too great for them to do.

In any case, their failure was *"because of your unbelief,"* as Jesus said in Matthew 17:21 and Mark 9:29. Their failure was because of a lack of persistent prayer. These two verses in Matthew and Mark say, *"This kind goeth not out but by prayer and fasting."*

Dr. Scofield notes that in Matthew "The two best MSS. omit v. 21," and of Mark 9:29, "The two best MSS. omit 'and fasting.'"

But if the requirement of fasting was added by some copyist in those verses (it may not have been added), many Scriptures show that fasting is often a blessed part of prevailing prayer. Sometimes a burden of *"day and night"* praying (Luke 18:7) makes sleep or food undesired. Or one so burdened may deliberately concentrate on prayer and so set himself not to be distracted by food or sleep or work or pleasure. At any rate, prevailing, persistent prayer could have had the blessing these disciples did not have faith to claim.

And their lack of faith in them displeased Jesus, as surely lack of faith in us displeases Him.

Those of us who have seen God work wonders in response to faith need beware lest by lack of prayer and pleading and waiting on God we lose faith for His marvels.

VERSES 42—45:

42 And as he was yet a coming, the devil threw him down, and tare *him*. And Jesus rebuked the unclean spirit, and healed the child, and delivered him again to his father.
43 And they were all amazed at the mighty power of God. But while they wondered every one at all things which Jesus did, he said unto his disciples,
44 Let these sayings sink down into your ears: for the Son of man shall be delivered into the hands of men.
45 But they understood not this saying, and it was hid from them, that they perceived it not: and they feared to ask him of that saying.

Christ's Mighty Power Is Not to Avoid Crucifixion

To accent the power of Christ in the deliverance, we are told that the evil spirit in the boy "*threw him down, and tare him.*" So before those who may have doubts, Jesus rebuked the spirit and healed the child.

After the delay, the obvious power of Christ over the wicked spirit amazed all. But lest the disciples should think that Jesus would win approval of all by His great works, He must remind His disciples most earnestly He would "*be delivered into the hands of men.*" So the Lord Jesus reminds them again of His warning in verse 22; Jesus came to die. Any temporary or outward approval of unconverted men would not last. Jesus must be betrayed and crucified!

Did they not understand? *"It was hid from them."* The paradox of such a mighty Being, so hated, such a good One being killed, they did not understand. Who can really understand the awful wickedness of the carnal heart of men? Or the grace of God to give the Righteous One to die for sinners?

From this exalted experience, Jesus *"departed thence, and passed through Galilee; and he would not that any many should know it"* (Mark 9:30). He had compassion on troubled, afflicted people, but He did not want unconverted men to follow Him only for healing and for miracles.

VERSES 46—48:

46 Then there arose a reasoning among them, which of them should be greatest.
47 And Jesus, perceiving the thought of their heart, took a child, and set him by him,
48 And said unto them, Whoso-ever shall receive this child in my name receiveth me: and whosoever shall receive me receiveth him that sent me: for he that is least among you all, the same shall be great.

Who Would Be Greatest?

Akin to the lesson of verse 44 is the lesson here. Jesus is greater as an atoning Saviour than as a wonder-working Teacher. So the greatest among men is the one who serves most. A certain childlike dependence, reliance on God, not claiming pre-eminence, is to be really great. Jesus so *"humbled himself"* and *"took upon him the form of a servant"* (Phil. 2:5-8). He is our pattern. *"The Son of man came not to be ministered unto, but to minister..."* (Matt. 20:28).

In Matthew 18, ten verses are given telling of this incident. 1. Jesus taught that one must be converted as a little child. 2. One must humble himself as the

way to greatness.   3.   To offend or cause to stumble
one of these little ones brings awful responsibility and
judgment.   4.   The guardian angels of little children
find God always   available for help.   He who clothes
the wild flowers, who feeds the sparrows, who counts
the very hairs upon the heads of God's people, would
take special care of little children!   And to receive even
a little child in Jesus' name is to receive Jesus.

People Are to Be "Converted and Become as Little Children"

Little children can be converted.   In Matthew 18:6
Jesus speaks of the conversion of little children *"which
believe in me."*

There is no set age when children become accountable
sinners and need to be converted.   Probably it is earlier
with some than with others.   Surely, as soon as a child
learns to know that he sins against God, he needs to be
converted.   My own six daughters were all saved before
they were six years old.   But they had already learned
discipline, learned what sin is, had come to know that
Christ died for sinners.   They had sung gospel songs
and heard much Bible preaching.

This passage is no authority for infant *"baptism."*
No unaccountable babies are to be received in the
church, and nobody is to be baptized except on a public
profession of faith in Christ.

When I was saved at nine, my godly father doubted
if I understood and if I were saved.   He did wrong in
not encouraging me.   It was three years after his dis-
couragement that I found the assurance through the
Word of God, in John 3:36, that when I had trusted
Christ I then and there had *"everlasting life."*

Remember that God commands that little children
should be taught the Scriptures diligently (Deut. 6:6,7).

Paul reminded Timothy *"that from a child thou hast*

known the holy scriptures, which are able to make thee wise unto salvation through faith which is in Christ Jesus" (II Tim. 3:15). And the word *"child"* there is the Greek *brethos,* defined as "newly born or unborn" by Young.

Children who are taught the Word of God from babyhood can be won to love and trust Jesus Christ for salvation early.

VERSES 49, 50:

49 And John answered and said, Master, we saw one casting out devils in thy name; and we forbad him, because he followeth not with us.

50 And Jesus said unto him, Forbid *him* not: for he that is not against us is for us.

A Rebuke of Sectarianism

One who casts out devils in Jesus' name, one who loves and trusts and serves Him is to be loved and received by all who love and serve Jesus. Psalm 119:63 says, *"I am a companion of all them that fear thee, and of them that keep thy precepts."* We are to be for all people of God. Romans 14:1 says, *"Him that is weak in the faith receive ye, but not to doubtful disputations."* The real basis of Christian fellowship is *"the faith of the gospel"* (Phil. 1:27). So one who believes and teaches the sinfulness of man, Christ's atoning death, His resurrection, therefore His deity, His virgin birth and sinlessness — as the Gospel is stated in I Corinthians 15:3 and 4, is *"in the faith."* And even if one should, on lesser matters, be weak, but if he is *"in the faith"* he is to be loved and received, provided it is not *"to doubtful disputation."*

Another way of stating this *"faith of the Gospel"* is the *"doctrine of Christ,"* that is, what the Bible teaches about Christ. So II John, verses 9-11, says: *"Whosoever transgresseth, and abideth not in the doctrine of*

Christ, hath not God. He that abideth in the doctrine
of Christ, he hath both the Father and the Son. If
there come any unto you, and bring not this doctrine,
receive him not into your house, neither bid him God
speed: For he that biddeth him God speed is partaker
of his evil deeds." To deny that Jesus is the virgin-
born Son of God, is deity, dying to save all who trust
Him, means that one "hath not God," is not saved
and is not to be received as a Christian, nor to be aided
in his work.

One who casts out devils in Jesus' name believes in
and loves that dear name of Christ as Saviour and
Lord, "for he that is not against us is for us."

This Scripture does not say we are to receive all who
are in some kind of religious work. In Matthew 7:15
Jesus warned us, "Beware of false prophets, which come
to you in sheep's clothing, but inwardly they are ravening
wolves." And He said in Matthew 7:22 and 23: "Many
will say to me in that day, Lord, Lord, have we not
prophesied in thy name? and in thy name have cast out
devils? and in thy name done many wonderful works?
And then will I profess unto them, I never knew you:
depart from me, ye that work iniquity." So not everyone who says Jesus is Lord, but those who really
believe Him and trust Him and claim Him as the Christ
of the Bible, are to be received as Christians.

We cannot properly withhold Christian fellowship
from those who truly love the Lord Jesus and serve
Him, provided they do not cause division and strife
over lesser details.

The essential doctrines of the Gospel must be the basis
of salvation. But not all teaching in the Bible is as
important as these. Jesus said to the Pharisees in
Matthew 23:23, "Ye pay tithe of mint and anise and
cummin, and have omitted the weightier matters of the
law, judgment, mercy, and faith...." So some essential

doctrines of *"the faith"* are *"weightier matters."* The divisions at Corinth between those who would be followers of Apollos and Peter and Paul, were wrong (I Cor. 3:1-9). Peter, Apollos and Paul preached the same Gospel. But I am never to give Christian recognition and fellowship to the unconverted and the infidels. Yet I should have fellowship with good Christians who may not have been well taught on baptism or who differ on the interpretation of some prophecy. All the truth is good and we should preach it in love, but we should have fellowship with all of God's people where we can do so without division and strife, whether or not they bear our church name or do things our way.

VERSES 51 — 56:

51 And it came to pass, when the time was come that he should be received up, he stedfastly set his face to go to Jerusalem,

52 And sent messengers before his face: and they went, and entered into a village of the Samaritans, to make ready for him.

53 And they did not receive him, because his face was as though he would go to Jerusalem.

54 And when his disciples James and John saw *this*, they said, Lord, wilt thou that we command fire to come down from heaven, and consume them, even as Elias did?

55 But he turned, and rebuked them, and said, Ye know not what manner of spirit ye are of.

56 For the Son of man is not come to destroy men's lives, but to save *them*. And they went to another village.

Touring, Preaching: Destination Jerusalem

Dr. Scofield labels this passage, "final departure from Galilee." Rather, this is only the beginning of the departure. Jesus did go to Jerusalem for the feast of tabernacles (John 7:2-10). He spent some time there, stayed, we understand, for the *"feast of dedication"* in the winter (John 10:22). Perhaps on this journey to Jerusalem He passed through a Samaritan village

of verse 52 here. But after that time or just before
Jesus appointed the seventy (Luke, chapter 10), He
came to Bethany, a suburb of Jerusalem (Luke 10:38)
to the home of Mary and Martha and Lazarus.

The Lord Jesus did not immediately go on that last
and final trip to Jerusalem. In Luke 10:1,2, the seventy
were appointed, and they set out. In Luke 10:13-15,
the curse on Chorazin, Bethsaida, and Capernaum is
given. In Luke 10:38-42 He went as far as Bethany,
near Jerusalem. In Luke 13:22 He is still *"journeying
toward Jerusalem."* In Luke 13:31 they warned Jesus,
"Herod will kill thee." But Herod was king in Galilee,
not in Judaea, so we suppose He was still in Galilee.

Luke 17:11 tells us that *"as he went to Jerusalem,...
he passed through the midst of Samaria and Galilee."*
In Luke 18:31 He says, *"Behold, we go up to Jerusalem
...."* He was en route to Jerusalem (Luke 19:1) and His
triumphal entry is recorded in Luke 19:28. Before He
went to Jerusalem, in Matthew 19:1 we are told that
Jesus went from Galilee *"into the coasts of Judaea beyond Jordan."* So this is a period of rushing, climactic
tours through Galilee, Samaria, and Judaea, warning
and reaching all that He can through His disciples and
the seventy and through His own ministry before He is
to die at Jerusalem.

Dr. Scofield labels this passage, "The new spirit of
grace,..." But no, Jesus certainly did not suddenly
become merciful. It has always been true that *"the Son
of man is not come to destroy men's lives, but to save
them"* (vs. 56). It is too much dispensationalism to
think that the grace of God was now new.

And we probably should not say that this was Christ's
"final departure from Galilee." It is quite possible He
no longer has a home at Capernaum.

But do not leave this passage without taking much to
heart the message of verse 56. Jesus does not want to

kill but to save. On the cross He prayed for His murderers, "*Father, forgive them; for they know not what they do*" (Luke 23:34). Stephen prayed for his murderers, "*Lord, lay not this sin to their charge*" (Acts 7:60). We may be heartsick over the sins of lost people, but we should love them and wish them well. We should earnestly seek to save them.

VERSES 57 — 62:

57 And it came to pass, that, as they went in the way, a certain *man* said unto him, Lord, I will follow thee whithersoever thou goest.

58 And Jesus said unto him, Foxes have holes, and birds of the air *have* nests; but the Son of man hath not where to lay *his* head.

59 And he said unto another, Follow me. But he said, Lord, suffer me first to go and bury my father.

60 Jesus said unto him, Let the dead bury their dead: but go thou and preach the kingdom of God.

61 And another also said, Lord, I will follow thee; but let me first go bid them farewell, which are at home at my house.

62 And Jesus said unto him, No man, having put his hand to the plough, and looking back, is fit for the kingdom of God.

The Cost of Discipleship

Here three men have the urge to follow Jesus, but they must be warned it is not easy. As David said about the threshingfloor of Araunah, "*Nay; but I will surely buy it of thee at a price: neither will I offer burnt-offerings unto the Lord my God of that which doth cost me nothing*" (II Sam. 24:24). So Jesus reminds the first man that to follow Jesus means a life of poverty and hardship. How keenly Jesus felt the pressure—those long travels on foot, no home, no regular sleeping place—cared for in part by small gifts of good women who followed Him from town to town (Matt. 27:55)! Doubtless He often went hungry. The hungry disciples sometimes plucked the ripe grain, rubbed it out of the husks and ate it raw (Luke 6:1). In the last verse of John, chapter 7, we read, "*And every man went unto his own house,*" after a day at the feast of the tabernacles, but the next verse in John 8:1 says simply, "*Jesus went unto the mount of Olives.*" Other people went to their homes but Jesus went out to the mount of Olives where He probably slept on the ground in the Garden of Gethsemane that night. John 18:1 and 2 tells us, "*He went forth with his disciples over the brook Cedron, where was a garden, into the which he entered, and his disciples. And Judas also, which betrayed him, knew the place: for Jesus ofttimes resorted thither with his disciples.*" No doubt such experiences were in the mind of Jesus when He said, "*Foxes have holes, and birds of the air have nests; but the Son of man hath not where to lay his head*" (vs. 58).

Oh, if one would follow Jesus he must be willing to be poor, to lack some comforts. Do not seek to follow Jesus without counting the cost.

The man of God may have his college and university degree, may have great ability: must he therefore have as good pay as the physician or lawyer or business executive of similar training and ability? No, the servant is not to be above his lord. The bishop must be "*not greedy of filthy lucre*" (I Tim. 3:3). Let us not think it is unnatural or bad that God's man must often be poor. So were Jesus and the disciples and "*godliness with contentment is great gain*" (I Tim. 6:6).

Another man would follow Jesus, but only after his father died and after he should take part in the traditional burial and, we suppose, the settling of the estate. Jesus did not allow that. To serve Him supercedes all other ties and loyalties. To serve Jesus does not make for dishonor to parents but others can care for the old man and bury him. Keeping people out of Hell is more important than comforting the aged and infirm. So Elisha left his father and mother to follow Elijah (I King

19:19-21). And James and John "*immediately left the ship and their father, and followed him*" (Matt. 4:22). Christ demands first place. His work is greater than all other. As Peter and Andrew left their nets and as Levi left his profitable tax gathering (Luke 5:11, 28), so must men forsake all to follow Jesus.

Another man was almost ready to follow Jesus, but first he was to go home for a farewell period of feasting and entertainment. No! Don't put the hand to the plow and look back! In a few days Jesus is to die! If he will follow Him come at once! Among sad memories is a man fifty-six years old with a family of eight children who had resisted the call of God to preach and now it was too late. And the memory of a woman of thirty who for ten years had resisted the call to the mission field to stay with her father and mother; the mission board would not take her at that age.

LUKE 10

AFTER these things the Lord appointed other seventy also, and sent them two and two before his face into every city and place, whither he himself would come.

2 Therefore said he unto them, The harvest truly *is* great, but the labourers *are* few: pray ye therefore the Lord of the harvest, that he would send forth labourers into his harvest.

3 Go your ways: behold, I send you forth as lambs among wolves.

4 Carry neither purse, nor scrip, nor shoes: and salute no man by the way.

5 And into whatsoever house ye enter, first say, Peace *be* to this house.

6 And if the son of peace be there, your peace shall rest upon it: if not, it shall turn to you again.

7 And in the same house remain, eating and drinking such things as they give: for the labourer is worthy of his hire. Go not from house to house.

8 And into whatsoever city ye enter, and they receive you, eat such things as are set before you:

9 And heal the sick that are therein, and say unto them, The kingdom of God is come nigh unto you.

10 But into whatsoever city ye enter, and they receive you not, go your ways out into the streets of the same, and say,

11 Even the very dust of your city, which cleaveth on us, we do wipe off against you: notwithstanding be ye sure of this, that the kingdom of God is come nigh unto you.

12 But I say unto you, that it shall be more tolerable in that day for Sodom, than for that city.

The Seventy Sent Out to Witness

Jesus had sent the twelve out to the cities and towns where He Himself would come. But in this whirlwind tour to cover all of Palestine He must have others to go. The twelve are not enough, the time is so short. They were going two and two to save some time in each town (vs. 7) preaching, healing and telling that Jesus was to be there. The work of the twelve and of these seventy for days or weeks in a place preaching, winning, healing, casting out devils, helps explain the enormous crowds that attended Jesus' ministry everywhere. These workers were to be received into homes and fed and kept for Jesus' sake. They were to pronounce judgment on any town that would not receive them for Jesus' sake.

Who were these seventy? We do not know the name of one. They were, we suppose, not very mature Christians, but rather earnest, new converts. They were *"lambs,"* not sheep, sent *"among wolves."* So any convert should at once become a soul winner. And God would hold the hearers of such a witness to solemn accounting.

In the Great Commission in Matthew 28:19 and 20 we are commanded that the new converts should be baptised and then immediately teach *"them to observe all things whatsoever I have commanded you."* The soul-winning command of the Great Commission is to be given to every convert. And so the Lord Jesus sends these seventy lambs out to witness for Him.

The White Harvest

Jesus said in Luke 10:2, " *Therefore said he unto them, The harvest truly is great, but the labourers are few: pray ye therefore the Lord of the harvest, that he would send forth labourers into his harvest."* How Jesus yearned over the multitude of the lost! And they could be won—not all of them but many of them, if there were enough laborers! So, first, He sent the twelve and now seventy more, and then they were to pray then and we are to pray now *"the Lord of the harvest, that he would send forth labourers into his harvest."*

When Christ had first sent the twelve, He told them the same thing almost word for word in Matthew 9:35-38. The harvest was *"plenteous"* then. To the seventy

He said "*truly is great.*" In John 4:35, 36, at Sychar, speaking of another time and place He said the same thing, "*Say not ye, There are yet four months, and then cometh harvest? behold, I say unto you, Lift up your eyes, and look on the fields; for they are white already to harvest. And he that reapeth receiveth wages, and gathereth fruit unto life eternal: that both he that soweth and he that reapeth may rejoice together.*"

So we may be sure in all ages, in every country, God has a white harvest waiting. When He had only Elijah at Mount Carmel, a multitude could be brought to cry, "*The Lord, he is the God!*" (I Kings 18:39). When Nineveh, so wicked it cried for destruction, God could bring thousands to repentance if He had a preacher but God had a problem getting Jonah to go. In Samaria the fields are white and many could be won when a shabby woman claimed Christ and called her friends to meet Him (John 4:39-41). Even at wicked Jerusalem where the multitudes cried out to have Jesus crucified, where Judas betrayed Him, where Peter denied Him and cursed and quit the ministry and where the disciples all "*forsook him and fled,*" yet a white harvest waited. When a few disciples prayed down the power of God (Acts 1:14), there were three thousand at Pentecost to claim Christ and join with the Christians.

But the trouble is not with the harvest but with the laborers. It is not with the sinners but with the saints. The trouble is not with the world but with the church. The lack of soul-winning results is not to be blamed then on the times, on the conditions and circumstances, but on the lack of Spirit-filled witnesses. It is not the hard heart of drunkards, of worldlings, or infidels, but the unbelief, the coldness, the lack of obedience of God's men and women that let people go to Hell, that quench revivals, that waste the harvest. Not the modernist who is unsaved and could not have God's power, but the

Bible-believer who does not pay God's price for power could reap the harvest, if he would.

God has a harvest and *"the weapons of our warfare are not carnal, but mighty through God to the pulling down of strong holds"* (II Cor. 10:4). We have the Word of God, *"quick, and powerful, and sharper than any twoedged sword"* (Heb. 4:12). Jeremiah 23:29 says, *"Is not my word like as a fire? saith the Lord; and like a hammer that breaketh the rock in pieces?"* We have the grace of God, loving, seeking the lost, *"Not willing that any should perish, but that all should come to repentance"* (II Pet. 3:9). We have within us the Holy Spirit who *"when he is come, he will reprove the world of sin, and of righteousness, and of judgment"* (John 16:8). And we have recourse to prayer and a God who hears the prayer of faith, or the prayer in Jesus' name. Oh, the harvest is always plenteous, great, white, so that one can win some even if some we cannot win.

VERSES 13—16:

13 Woe unto thee, Chorazin! woe unto thee, Bethsaida! for if the mighty works had been done in Tyre and Sidon, which have been done in you, they had a great while ago repented, sitting in sackcloth and ashes.
14 But it shall be more tolerable for Tyre and Sidon at the judg-ment, than for you.
15 And thou, Capernaum, which art exalted to heaven, shalt be thrust down to hell.
16 He that heareth you heareth me; and he that despiseth you despiseth me; and he that despiseth me despiseth him that sent me.

Destruction Promised to Three Cities

In certain cities not far apart about the north end of the little Sea of Galilee, Jesus did *"most of his mighty works*" (Matt. 11:20). They were Chorazin, Bethsaida and Capernaum.

In Capernaum Jesus made His home, moving from Nazareth when He began His public ministry (Matt. 4:13). Bethsaida was nearby, we think, four or five miles from Capernaum further east on the shore of Galilee. It was *"the city of Andrew and Peter"* (John 1:4). In Capernaum Jesus did so many great works that even Tyre and Sidon, cities of the Gentiles destroyed for their wickedness (Ezek. chapters 26 and 28), and Sodom (so the parallel passage in Matt. 11:20 says) would have repented and been spared had they seen such mighty works, Jesus said! So judgment for Tyre and Sidon will be more tolerable than the judgment of these cities. Capernaum, Jesus said, *"which art exalted to heaven, shalt be thrust down to hell."* I suppose that means surely that many people in Capernaum would go to eternal torment. But the city itself will go *"down to hell,"* in the sense of to the realm of death. Capernaum would pass out of existence and so it did.

Where are these cities now? Disappeared! Even the site of Bethsaida is unknown. Chorazin, it is thought, was north of Capernaum five or six miles. The site of Capernaum was not certain until a few years ago when the ruins of a second century synagogue there were uncovered. Other towns of Jesus' time, Nazareth, Tiberias, Nain have continued, but these cities that Jesus cursed for their impenitent rejection of His Gospel have disappeared.

Let the ruin of these cities and the history of Nineveh, Babylon, Tyre, Sidon, Memphis, Greece and Rome be a lesson that the curse of God goes on the city or nation that continues in sin, unrepentant when it hears the Gospel. And the curse of God is plainly promised to any city that would not receive the seventy messengers, if they give this warning (vss. 11,16).

VERSES 17—24:

17 And the seventy returned again with joy, saying, Lord, even the devils are subject unto us through thy name.

18 And he said unto them, I beheld Satan as lightning fall from heaven.

19 Behold, I give unto you power to tread on serpents and scorpions, and over all the power of the enemy: and nothing shall by any means hurt you.

20 Notwithstanding in this rejoice not, that the spirits are subject unto you; but rather rejoice, because your names are written in heaven.

21 In that hour Jesus rejoiced in spirit, and said, I thank thee, O Father, Lord of heaven and earth, that thou hast hid these things from the wise and prudent, and hast revealed them unto babes: even so, Father; for so it seemed good in thy sight.

22 All things are delivered to me of my Father: and no man knoweth who the Son is, but the Father; and who the Father is, but the Son, and *he* to whom the Son will reveal *him*.

23 And he turned him unto *his* disciples, and said privately, Blessed *are* the eyes which see the things that ye see:

24 For I tell you, that many prophets and kings have desired to see those things which ye see, and have not seen *them;* and to hear those things which ye hear, and have not heard *them*.

The Return of the Seventy

Wonderful blessings followed the seventy in their witnessing. They returned to report gladly, "*Lord, even the devils are subject unto us through thy name.*"

Jesus rejoiced greatly in the blessing of God on these seventy. In verse 21 He said, "*I thank thee, O Father, Lord of heaven and earth, that thou hast hid these things from the wise and prudent, and hast revealed them unto babes. . . .*" The babes are these seventy, "*lambs,*" sent among "*wolves*" (vs. 3). How wonderful that God can use the soul winner who does not have all the wisdom of the schools, the prestige of experience and age! It was truly no accident that the twelve apostles were known as *"unlearned and ignorant men"* (Acts 4:13). We do not wonder that the Jewish leaders marveled at Peter and John. So have people marveled at D. L. Moody and Billy Sunday and at many a godly man of limited training and ability who preached the Gospel in the power of God. For these seventy, like Peter and John, *"had been with Jesus."* God does sometimes call a Moses or a Paul, men of great learning, but we should remember *"that not many wise men after the flesh, not many mighty, not many noble, are called. But God hath chosen the foolish things of the world to confound the wise; and God hath chosen the weak things of the world to confound the things which are mighty; And base things of the world, and things which are despised, hath God chosen, yea, and things which are not, to bring to nought things that are: That no flesh should glory in his presence"* (I Cor. 1:26-29).

Oh, let us rejoice that ordinarily God chooses to use poor people instead of rich people, weak people instead of strong people, and more ignorant people than learned people.

Jesus rejoiced that God blessed these young converts and said, *"Even so, Father; for so it seemed good in thy sight."*

But joy that God blesses our service should not crowd out the greater joy: *"but rather rejoice, because your names are written in heaven"* (vs. 20). The Lord Jesus said He could understand their joy. He Himself rejoiced because *"I beheld Satan as lightning fall from heaven."* And He it was that gave them *"power to tread on serpents and scorpions, and over all the power of the enemy: and nothing shall by any means hurt you."* The blessing of God's power is wonderful. But, oh, the grace of God in saving sinners and forgiving all our transgressions, and giving us everlasting life is a matter of greatest joy of all.

Notice verse 22 that *"all things are delivered to me of my Father,"* Jesus said. And nobody knows the Father *"but the Son, and he to whom the Son will reveal him."* There is no way to know God except by Christ. Not the Unitarian, not the Buddhist or Hindu, not the Christian Scientist nor any religious liberal can know the Father until he learns to come, in his penitent, believing heart, to Christ, the Son of God, the atoning Saviour who reveals the Father.

Jesus is saying here what He said in Matthew 28:18, *"All power* [or authority] *is given unto me in heaven and in earth."* He is saying the same here as in John 5:22 and 23, *"For the Father judgeth no man, but hath committed all judgment unto the Son: That all men should honour the Son, even as they honour the Father. He that honoureth not the Son honoureth not the Father which hath sent him."* First John 5:11 and 12 says a similar thing: *"And this is the record, that God hath given to us eternal life, and this life is in his Son. He that hath the Son hath life; and he that hath not the Son of God hath not life."* There is no coming to God, no salvation, no forgiveness, no everlasting life except as one comes to the Father by the Son. *"No man cometh unto the Father, but by me,"* Jesus said (John 14:6).

What great blessings have New Testament Christians! Jesus reminded the disciples in verse 24 that *"many prophets and kings have desired to see those things which ye see, and have not seen them; and to hear those things which ye hear, and have not heard them."* Even Old Testament prophets who wrote the Scriptures *"have inquired and searched diligently...Searching what, or what manner of time the Spirit of Christ which was in them did signify, when it testified beforehand the sufferings of Christ, and the glory that should follow. Unto whom it was revealed, that not unto themselves, but unto us they did minister the things, which are now reported unto you by them that have preached the gospel unto you with the Holy Ghost sent down from heaven; which things the angels desire to look into*" (I Pet. 1:10-12). The distinction between the truth given to Old Testament and New Testament saints is emphasized in Hebrews 1:1 and 2. God who "*at sundry times and in divers manners spake in time past unto the fathers by the prophets, Hath in these last days spoken unto us by his Son, whom he hath appointed heir of all things, by whom also he made the worlds.*" And much of the book of Hebrews is concerned with the thought that Christ is better than the angels, that He is better than Moses, and His covenant better than the Mosaic law, that Christ is better than the priest at Jerusalem, that He is the Son not the servant. We are not surprised that Jesus said of Himself, "*Behold, a greater than Solomon is here*" (Matt. 12:42). Oh, we who now have a Bible printed and widely distributed, with all the Word of God, and we who now know that Christ is come, has paid for sin, has arisen and is on the right hand of the Father, is our High Priest and is coming again — how we ought to glorify God that the Scriptures are all written down and printed, that revelation is complete, that the types have been fulfilled, and we have some way entered into the glorious liberty of the Gospel! How much better than to seek Christ only through the ceremonies and types of the Old Testament, or the half-remembered words of a prophet, or some words of Scripture read in the synagogue when others could not have printed Bibles! How we should rejoice and treasure the Word and the truth revealed!

VERSES 25—29:

25 And, behold, a certain lawyer stood up, and tempted him, saying, Master, what shall I do to inherit eternal life?

26 He said unto him, What is written in the law? how readest thou?

27 And he answering said, Thou shalt love the Lord thy God with all thy heart, and with all thy soul, and with all thy strength, and with all thy mind; and thy neighbour as thyself.

28 And he said unto him, Thou hast answered right: this do, and thou shalt live.

29 But he, willing to justify himself, said unto Jesus, And who is my neighbour?

Only Perfection Could Earn Eternal Life

The word *lawyer* refers not to a man who practiced civil law before the courts but a student and an authority on the Mosaic law, the Old Testament. And such a scholar asked Jesus a question, "*What shall I do to inherit eternal life?*" Note two things that colored Jesus' answer. One is that the man said this in some insincerity "*to tempt Jesus.*" The other is that he wanted some way to get eternal life by doing: "*What shall I do to inherit eternal life?*"

So since the man was a student of the Old Testament law, Jesus asked him to summarize duty according to the law.

The man was a good student of the law and he answered, quoting first Deuteronomy 6:5 and then Leviticus 19:18. And it was correct that these two summed up the law of God. And it is true that "*love is the fulfilling of the law*" (Rom. 13:10). And James 2:8 calls "*Thou shalt love thy neighbour as thyself*" the "*royal law.*" And I John 4:8 says "*God is love.*" And again I John 2:10 tells us, "*He that loveth his brother abideth in the light.*" So all righteousness is summed up in this command to love God with all your heart, mind, soul and strength and to love one's neighbor as himself.

But is this a plan of salvation? Jesus said to the man, *"Thou hast answered right: this do, and thou shalt live."* And we understand Christ to mean spiritual life, not spiritual death.

Yes, this is a plan of salvation, but it is only good for perfect people! And there are none perfect this side of the Garden of Eden but the Lord Jesus Himself! It is true that if one never sinned, he would never need forgiveness. If one were born right the first time, he would not need to be born again. If one had never been away from God, he would never need to come back to God. Paul was inspired to remind us that *"Moses describeth the righteousness which is of the law, That the man which doeth those things shall live by them"* (Rom. 10:5). And he there refers to Leviticus 18:5. But that righteousness is the righteousness of perfection which no man has in himself. That plan of everlasting life is for people who never sinned, and there are none who walk the earth now who never sinned.

Why did Jesus give him this answer? Because *"the law was our schoolmaster to bring us unto Christ."* To learn the perfection which the law demands is immediately to bring conviction to any honest heart who considers it.

So the lawyer immediately felt a need *"to justify himself,"* and he said, *"And who is my neighbour?"* And then follows the parable of the Samaritan.

VERSES 30—37:

30 And Jesus answering said, A certain man went down from Jerusalem to Jericho, and fell among thieves, which stripped him of his raiment, and wounded him, and departed, leaving him half dead.

31 And by chance there came down a certain priest that way: and when he saw him, he passed by on the other side.

32 And likewise a Levite, when he was at the place, came and looked on him, and passed by on the other side.

33 But a certain Samaritan, as he journeyed, came where he was: and when he saw him, he had compassion on him,

34 And went to him, and bound up his wounds, pouring in oil and wine, and set him on his own beast, and brought him to an inn, and took care of him.

35 And on the morrow when he departed, he took out two pence, and gave them to the host, and said unto him, Take care of him; and whatsoever thou spendest more, when I come again, I will repay thee.

36 Which now of these three, thinkest thou, was neighbour unto him that fell among the thieves?

37 And he said, He that shewed mercy on him. Then said Jesus unto him, Go, and do thou likewise.

The Good Samaritan

The parable of the good Samaritan is given only in Luke, not in the other Gospels. And it is given in answer to the question of the self-righteous lawyer who was "*willing to justify himself*" and said to Jesus, "*Who is my neighbour?*" (vs. 29). If one is to love his neighbor even as himself, surely then that would involve only a very small circle! No, Jesus said it would involve the stranger, the foreigner, even an enemy, even a despised person of another race through whom He had no human ties at all. And so He gave this charming parable of the good Samaritan.

"*A certain man went down from Jerusalem to Jericho,*" it was literally "down." In the 22 miles one goes from perhaps 2,400 feet above sea level down to 1,200 feet below sea level. He "*fell among thieves.*" And so it might well have happened because the country was largely barren, canyons, hills, and was long a hide-out for bandits and robbers.

To show contrast Jesus says that a priest came that way, "*and when he saw him, he passed by on the other side. And likewise a Levite, when he was at the place, came and looked on him, and passed by on the other*

side. " Surely the indication is that if you really want
to know "*what shall I do to inherit eternal life?*" as
the lawyer asked in verse 25, neither the priest nor the
Levite can give the answer. The ceremonial law will not
do it. The life of a good Jew does not earn eternal life
by any human standards. Note the Samaritan. The
Samaritans were hated of the Jews. A handful of them
still live around Mount Gerizim at Nablus and have a
synagogue there. There are only some three hundred
of them now. They are that mixed breed of Babylonians
brought in at the time of the captivity of the Jews. They
have the Pentateuch but no other books of the Old Testament. They claim that the real capital for God's people
should have been Mount Gerizim, not Jerusalem. The
Jews so hated them that a little before Christ's time,
John Hyrcanus, high priest at Jerusalem, led the Jews
to Mount Gerizim and destroyed the Samaritan temple.
The worse name that Jews could call anybody was
"Samaritan," as they called Jesus (John 8:48). Even
James and John suggested that they "*command fire
to come down from heaven, and consume*" a village of
the Samaritans (Luke 9:51-54). So, of all the people
that a Samaritan would not be expected to love would
be a Jew. So the deed of this good Samaritan was
beyond all human ties of a family, race or kinship or
friendship.

The Lord Jesus was using the righteousness of the law
to show it has a standard that no man can reach without Christ. The good Samaritan "*had compassion,*" so
it was not a ceremonial righteousness. He bound up
the wounds, pouring in oil and wine. He brought him
to an inn, paid the bill, offered to pay any future expense!

Actually, the righteousness pictured here is the perfect
righteousness following the standards set up in the
Sermon on the Mount. To really love God with all your
heart, mind and soul and love your neighbor as your-

self, to "*love your enemies, bless them that curse you, do good to them that hate you, and pray for them which despitefully use you, and persecute you,*" as commanded in Matthew 5:44, and "*be ye therefore perfect, even as your Father which is in heaven is perfect,*" in Matthew 5:48, is the perfect righteousness that no man has attained to but Jesus Christ.

I do not say the standard is wrong. I simply say nobody can reach it. The matter of gaining eternal life by keeping the law would mean absolute perfection. So the law is a "*schoolmaster to bring us unto Christ.*" And Jesus so intended it at this time.

And there is a sense in which surely that good Samaritan pictured Jesus. Like the Samaritans were alien to the Jews, so Christ is of another world, alien to this one. He is from above, all we are from beneath. Christ has compassion on poor, undone sinners, wounded by thieves and robbers of Satan and his devils. Christ binds up the wounds and pours in oil and wine. The oil must picture the Holy Spirit coming in as salvation. The wine must picture Christian rejoicing and happiness. And note the Samaritan put the wounded man "*on his own beast.*" Oh, the sinner does not have to walk to Heaven like the shepherd carries the sheep on his shoulder in Luke 15:1-7. And as the good Samaritan puts the wounded man on his own beast, so Christ furnishes the certainty of our getting to Heaven. The task is His, not ours.

Will you note that at the inn the bill is paid in advance. We are saved because Christ paid it, not because we paid it. And the saving work of Christ is continued as our High Priest ever interceding for us, just as the good Samaritan offered to pay any future bill. Oh, thank God, I am saved and kept saved. My sins of the past are all paid for, and if there is anything else that needs to be paid for, the Lord Jesus has obligated Himself to take care of that.

As Paul wrote to Philemon about the runaway slave, Onesimus, and said if he *"oweth thee ought, put that on mine account,"* so the dear Lord Jesus has charged to His account all our sins, all our burdens, all our weaknesses and failures. *"All we like sheep have gone astray; we have turned every one to his own way; and the Lord hath laid on him the iniquity of us all"* (Isa. 53: 6). And again, *"For he hath made him to be sin for us, who knew no sin; that we might be made the righteousness of God in him"* (II Cor. 5:21). So we can truly say that *"the chastisement of our peace was upon him; and with his stripes we are healed."* Oh, Jesus is the only one who ever met the standard of the good Samaritan.

And all the wonderful work of this good Samaritan is summed up in verse 37. He was *"he that shewed mercy on him."*

VERSES 38—42:

38 Now it came to pass, as they went, that he entered into a certain village: and a certain woman named Martha received him into her house.

39 And she had a sister called Mary, which also sat at Jesus' feet, and heard his word.

40 But Martha was cumbered about much serving, and came to him, and said, Lord, dost thou not care that my sister hath left me to serve alone? bid her therefore that she help me.

41 And Jesus answered and said unto her, Martha, Martha, thou art careful and troubled about many things:

42 But one thing is needful: and Mary hath chosen that good part, which shall not be taken away from her.

The Sisters Mary and Martha

Jesus *"entered into a certain village."* It was Bethany, as we are told in John 11:1. It was at the home of

Mary and Martha and their brother Lazarus at Bethany where Jesus often stayed (see Mark 11:1, and particularly verse 11). The context indicated that during His last week in Jerusalem, Jesus would go out in the evening to Bethany on the east side of the Mount of Olives, a mile and a half or two miles from Jerusalem, and stay with Mary and Martha and Lazarus. He was particularly close to Lazarus and the sisters. Lazarus was *"he whom thou lovest."* And John 11:5 says, *"Now Jesus loved Martha, and her sister, and Lazarus."* Verse 38 says, *"Martha received him into HER house."*

We judge then, that Martha was the older of the two sisters. Lazarus may have lived with them, as a younger brother. He may not have lived with them. John 11:1 says, *"Now a certain man was sick, named Lazarus, of Bethany, the town of Mary and her sister Martha."* No wife is mentioned. It has been assumed that the three lived together but that is only a supposition. We can understand that the relationship must have been very intimate and pleasant. When Jesus came, the eleven apostles came, too, and for them to spend the nights there day after day, when He went into Jerusalem to speak in the daytime, must have been somewhat of a burden for the home.

The indication here is that Martha ran the home, possibly owned it, and her younger sister Mary lived with her.

Martha surely loved Jesus, and gladly worked hard entertaining the Saviour and the apostles. But, like many good people today, she was *"cumbered about much serving."* Many a Christian works hard at church suppers, or keeping the nursery, or getting out the church bulletin, or selling something to make money for the church, without necessarily being a spiritual, happy Christian.

Martha was evidently a worrier. Jesus said, *"Martha,*

Martha, thou art careful and troubled about many things." She particularly needed to rest her heart and trust in Jesus instead of laboring and worrying about whether the house was clean or whether dinner would be ready and whether the food prepared was good enough for the Saviour and the apostles.

And worry is a sin forbidden in Philippines 4:6. *"Be careful for nothing,"* or, as the American Standard version has it, *"Be anxious for nothing."* And such carefulness was rebuked by the Saviour in Matthew 6:25-34. He who clothes the lilies and feeds the fowls of the air will care for His own who seek first the kingdom of God. So Jesus said, *"Take therefore no thought for the morrow"*—that is, no anxious, fretful thoughts, certainly.

It is possible to be so occupied with the work of the Lord that we do not enjoy the Lord. Some people work hard at church charities or church dinners who never win a soul and do not delight in the Word of God. Such people are like those at Ephesus, addressed in Revelation 2:1-4. They are praised for *"thy works, and thy labour, and thy patience, and how thou canst not bear them which are evil: and thou hast tried them which say they are apostles, and are not, and hast found them liars: And hast borne, and hast patience, and for my name's sake hast laboured, and hast not fainted."* Yet there is rebuke: *"Nevertheless I have somewhat against thee, because thou hast left thy first love."*

Good, earnest, hard-working, Bible-believing people sometimes lose the glow, the sweet sense of fellowship, the sweet warmth of consciously knowing the Saviour's presence. They are still married to Christ but the honeymoon seems over. They love the Lord, but they do not delight in Him. They do their duties as they see it, but that does not satisfy the heart of God.

So Mary, eagerly sitting at the feet of Jesus to hear all He would say, with a burning, glowing heart, pleased the Lord more than the honest, good service of Martha who was cumbered with much serving. Mary seems to have had a spiritual understanding that many Bible Christians did not have. Later when Simon of Bethany gave a big dinner to Jesus after Lazarus was risen from the dead, Martha served, as such a good soul would, but Mary took "*a pound of ointment of spikenard, very costly, and anointed the feet of Jesus, and wiped his feet with her hair: and the house was filled with the odour of the ointment.*" And although she was rebuked by Judas and others who said that expensive ointment should have been sold and the money given to the poor, Jesus said, "*Let her alone: against the day of my burying hath she kept this*" (John 12:7).

Perhaps Mary had understood that Jesus would die and be raised from the dead. At least that was the symbolism of the precious ointment, whether she understood it so or whether her heart was moved by the Holy Spirit to do what she did not quite understand. Dr. Scofield says, in his comments on Luke 11:13,

> It is evident that none of the disciples, with the possible exception of Mary of Bethany, asked for the Spirit in the faith of this promise... Save Mary, not one of the disciples but Peter, and he only in the great confession (Mt. 16.16), manifested a spark of spiritual intelligence till after the resurrection of Christ...."

Martha was a good woman but what Mary chose in sitting at the feet of Jesus and learning from Him and enjoying His company was far better. It was "*that good part,*" Jesus said.

LUKE 11

VERSE 1

A ND it came to pass, that, as he was praying in a certain place, when he ceased, one of his disciples said unto him, Lord, teach us to pray, as John also taught his disciples.

We Need to Learn to Pray Aright

The disciples asked, "*Lord, teach us to pray.*" John had taught his disciples to pray. It is true that prayer "is the soul's sincere desire, unuttered, or expressed," but it is not necessarily effective prayer, unless we learn to pray aright. We, too, should earnestly learn, from the Word of God, and led by the Holy Spirit, how to pray.

As they heard Jesus praying, the disciples realized how limited they were. Oh, may He teach us to pray as He did, in the will of God, and desiring what He desires!

VERSES 2—4:

2 And he said unto them, When ye pray, say, Our Father which art in heaven, Hallowed be thy name. Thy kingdom come. Thy will be done, as in heaven, so in earth. 3 Give us day by day our daily bread.

4 And forgive us our sins; for we also forgive every one that is indebted to us. And lead us not into temptation; but deliver us from evil.

The Model Prayer

It is likely that Jesus gave the model prayer, the Lord's Prayer, several times. It is recorded twice—here and in Matthew 6:9-15. But there is a slight difference in the wording, and the occasion in the midst of the

Sermon on the Mount does not seem to be the same as here in Luke when Jesus was found praying and the disciples, so deeply moved, pleaded that He teach them to pray, also, as John had taught his disciples.

Good preachers often preach some sermons in many different situations, and they should. Surely Jesus did the same. We know that He gave the Great Commission at least five times. The Ten Commandments are given twice (Exod. 20:2-17 and Deut. 5:7-21). It is in God's plan that I and II Chronicles would tell largely the same stories given in I and II Samuel and in I and II Kings. Anything as important as a brief comprehensive model for daily prayer would deserve being repeated more than once.

There is little difference in the two accounts of the Lord's Prayer. One says, *"Give us this day our daily bread,"* and the other says, *"Give us day by day our daily bread."* One pleads, *"Forgive us our debts"*; the other, *"Forgive us our sins."* And Matthew gives the ending: *"For thine is the kingdom, and the power, and the glory, for ever. Amen,"* not given here in Luke. One reason, perhaps, is that the lesson on prayer continues in Luke beyond the Lord's Prayer. Also, it may mean that the suggested close of the prayer is not necessarily always best and using these exact words is, of course, not the only way to pray. Some Bible scholars think that Matthew's ending is an interpolation. It is not included in all the manuscripts. The ASV of 1901 omits it.

"Our Father which art in heaven." So this is a prayer for saved people only, those born in the kingdom. Perhaps little children should be taught this prayer, but it also should be taught that God is Father only to those who are born in His kingdom, trusting Christ for salvation. It is a very tender and reverent prayer: *"Hallowed be thy name."* Oh, for the time when the name of Jesus, the name of God, will be holy and mentioned only reverently on the lips of anybody. So

it is now in Heaven; oh, for it to be so on earth, as
it will when Jesus returns to reign.

"*Thy kingdom come.*" There is a sense now in which
all of us Christians have been "*translated. . . into the
kingdom of his dear Son*" (Col. 1:13). Christ is King
to us, it is true, but His kingdom is not yet a literal
kingdom as it will be. The promise to Mary when the
Saviour's birth was announced was, "*The Lord God
shall give unto him the throne of his father David: And
he shall reign over the house of Jacob for ever*" (Luke
1:32,33). That promise was made to David in II
Samuel 7:10-17 when the throne of David's kingdom
should be established forever. The reign of Christ on
earth, the "Branch" from the stump of David, is foretold in Isaiah 11 and in many other places. And
Zechariah 14:9 tells us how after Christ's return in glory
to reign after the battle of Armageddon, after the regathering of Israel and their conversion, then "*the Lord
shall be king over all the earth: in that day. . . .*" So
those who pray with some spiritual understanding look
forward to the happy day when Christ shall reign, when
"*the eyes of the blind shall be opened, and the ears of
the deaf shall be unstopped. . . the tongue of the dumb
sing,*" the time when "*sorrow and sighing shall flee
away,*" and "*the desert shall. . . blossom as the rose,*"
and the lion and the lamb shall lie down together and
the "*child shall put his hand on the cockatrice' den.
They shall not hurt nor destroy in all my holy mountain*"! So it is promised in Isaiah 35 and elsewhere. So
we pray for Christ's kingdom to come. It has not
yet come.

There is a kingdom of God, referring to all the work
of God, but the personal kingdom of Christ on earth in
fulfillment of prophecy is in the future.

Of course there is a sense in which God, the Ruler of
the universe, is King always. But in the sense of the
spiritual kingdom it is for those who are born again

(John 3:3,5). In this sense, the Gospel is "*the gospel of the kingdom*" (Matt. 4:23; 9:35; 24:14; Mark 1:14 Luke 4:43; Acts 20:25; 28:31).

So we are to "*seek. . . first the kingdom of God*" (Matt. 6:33), that is, getting people saved, "*and his righteousness,*" that is, for saved people to live in Christ's righteousness, imputed (Rom. 4:5-8; 10:4) and imparted (Rom. 8:4). Then the prayer, "*Thy kingdom come. Thy will be done. . .*" is a prayer for souls to be saved, righteousness lived now, and a prayer for the final completion and manifestation of the kingdom in the personal return and reign of Christ.

So we are to live and pray now as citizens of Heaven. "*For our conversation* ["citizenship" is better] *is in heaven; from whence also we look for the Saviour. . .*" (Phil. 3:20). We have not attained to the perfection of the resurrection we will have then, but like Paul we should "*. . . press toward the mark for the prize of the high calling of God in Christ Jesus*" (Phil. 3:14). And the context clearly shows it is the resurrection and the kingdom of Christ after His return which the Holy Spirit had Paul refer to. Then let us sincerely pray, "*Thy kingdom come.*"

"*Give us day by day our daily bread*" — not our bread for a week or for a year but our bread for today. Several truths shine out in this inspired pattern for prayer about physical needs.

1. It is proper to ask God for all our needs. Dr. Harry Emerson Fosdick foolishly and wickedly said, 'God is not a Santa Claus who gives things in answer to prayer.' Millions of people know better by the unanswerable proof of experience. I have seen those who by all human medical wisdom were certain to die in a few hours, wonderfully, completely healed to live for many years. I have seen God send rain when it was asked for, and I have seen the rain stop when it was earnestly pleaded for, for His cause. I have asked for

and received cars, clothes, and thousands of dollars. I have seen great revivals in answer to prayer. For forty-four years I have lived, reared a family, sent six daughters through college and musical training, all with no salary, no promised income, no agreement of men to depend on. Ask for daily bread and all your needs, even your earnest desires. So says Mark 11:24, John 15:7, and many Scriptures!

2. We learn here also that we are to come regularly, daily, as if it is the normal way, to ask *"what things soever ye desire, when ye pray. . ."* (Mark 11:24), as the need and as the desire occurs. God is not far off. It does not require a long journey to talk to Him, nor long pleading to get what we ask. As a child at the table may ask for bread, then butter, then milk, then honey, so in this frequent, informal, direct, specific way we are to come for our daily needs.

3. We learn, then, to live one day at a time, ask for today's bread, but *"take therefore no thought for the morrow: for the morrow shall take thought for the things of itself. Sufficient unto the day is the evil thereof"* (Matt. 6:34). There is virtue in thrift and hard work (Prov. 6:6-11;13:4;20:4). The wastrel is wrong. Paul says, *". . . for the children ought not to lay up for the parents, but the parents for the children"* (II Cor. 12:14). But to fret about the future is wrong. God who feeds the sparrows and clothes the beautiful wild flowers will surely care for His own who *"seek. . . first the kingdom of God, and his righteousness"* (Matt. 6:33). And *"lay not up for yourselves treasures upon earth . . . ,"* said Jesus (Matt. 6:19). And a Christian is not here encouraged to pray for provisions far ahead. No, we shall pray, *"Give us day by day. . ."* — as we need daily bread. God was much nearer Israel, giving manna daily, than if he had given a year's supply of grain ahead of time, with no daily gathering of His loving provision necessary. Then, in this prayer God is nearer

to the poor who need and ask daily provision, than to the rich who feel no need to pray for daily bread.

"And forgive us our sins; for we also forgive every one that is indebted to us." — Luke 11:4.

1. A daily prayer — we ask for *"daily bread"* (as the model prayer in Matthew 6:11 states it) and so for daily forgiveness.

2. The term "forgive" is used in two senses in the Scripture.   There is forgiveness in the sense of God's daily approval and fellowship of people already saved. That is the meaning here.   The term is also used of salvation, in the sense that all our sins were laid on the Lord Jesus — all our sins of past, present, and future — and paid for on the cross; so as Ephesians 1:7 and Colossians 1:14 state: *". . . we have redemption through his blood, even the forgiveness of sins,"* we need not daily pray for forgiveness in this sense, that our sins be laid on Jesus, that we thus escape the doom sin deserves.   So; *"Blessed are they whose iniquities are forgiven, and whose sins are covered. Blessed is the man to whom the Lord will not impute sin"* (Rom. 4:7,8).   One who has trusted Christ for salvation has his sins already forgiven, as far as his eternal destiny is concerned. He is already *"now justified by his blood"* (the blood of Christ).   We are not only reconciled to God, but *"not only so, but we also joy in God through our Lord Jesus Christ, by whom we have now received the atonement"* (Rom. 5:11).   And the blessedness includes the fact that now, as far as our eternal destiny is concerned, saved are those *"to whom the Lord will not impute sin."* So the believer has eternal life, *"shall not come into condemnation"* (John 5:24), *"shall never perish"* (John 10:28), are born of God, *"partakers of the divine nature"* (II Pet. 1:4).

"For we also forgive. . . ," we are to say.   And the model prayer as given in Matthew, chapter 6, is followed, in verses 14 and 15, by this one comment: *"For*

if ye forgive men their trespasses, your heavenly Father will also forgive you: But if ye forgive not men their trespasses, neither will your Father forgive your trespasses. "

3. Here the term *forgive* obviously does not refer to salvation of the soul, but refers to the daily fellowship of a Christian with his heavenly Father. First John 1:6 and 7 says, *"If we say that we have fellowship with him, and walk in darkness, we lie, and do not the truth: But if we walk in the light, as he is in the light, we have fellowship one with another, and the blood of Jesus Christ his Son cleanseth us from all sin."* So to have fellowship, we are to walk in the light. And verse 9, following, says, *"If we confess our sins, he is faithful and just to forgive us our sins, and to cleanse us from all unrighteousness."* So in the Lord's prayer we are to pray daily for forgiveness and cleansing so we may have fellowship and all the sweet rewards of walking in His light.

But if we do not forgive those who wrong us, we have sin, unlamented and unforgiven, piling up between us and God. So prayers will go unanswered (Isa. 59:1,2; Ps. 66:18; I Pet. 3:7). How God hates grudges, the sin of Christians who will not forgive others. Jesus tells us in the parable in Matthew 18:21-35 of the king who would have forgiven a servant who owed him ten thousand talents (millions of dollars) but that creditor would not forgive a fellow servant a hundred pence. The unforgiving servant was *"delivered. . . to the torment-ors, "* and the amazing comment of Jesus was: *"So likewise shall my heavenly Father do also unto you, if ye from your hearts forgive not every one his brother their trespasses."* The torment of split churches, broken friendship, divorce, bitter hearts, and ruined testimonies follow when Christians do not forgive. So Ephesians 4:32 commands us: *"Be ye kind one to another, tender-*

hearted, forgiving one another, even as God for Christ's sake hath forgiven you. "

4. Dr. Scofield here, in the older Scofield Bible notes on this passage, is mistaken when he says (pages 1089 and 1090), "Used as a *form*, the Lord's prayer is, dispensationally, upon legal, not church ground; it is not a prayer in the name of Christ. . . ; and it makes human forgiveness, as under the law it must, the condition of divine forgiveness; an order which grace exactly reverses."

Errors in that statement are: (a) Forgiveness and salvation were always by grace. Works never earned salvation; the blood of bulls and goats never did take away sin. The one plan of salvation as given by all the prophets, we are plainly told in Acts 10:43, was the same—faith in Christ. Romans 4 tells us the same, and Abraham is held up as our example of how both Jews and Gentiles must be saved by believing God, in both Old and New Testament times. (b) To pray in the name of Christ means that one knows what Christ wants and has His authority to ask it. That is not always the case when we pray, so the form is not always sincere, often only a form that cannot claim and does not get what John 14:13,14, and 16:24 promise. (c) The plan is *not reversed* now. Still, we are forgiven, saved by grace, undeserving. On that basis we should forgive others. But to have the daily cleansing and fellowship meant by the forgiveness we ask for in the Lord, we must forgive others, just as we must forsake other known and cherished sins.

The teaching that we are to forgive others if we are to have the daily cleansing and fellowship is repeated also in Mark 11:25,26, in another connotation. And making right any wrong against others before our sacrifice or service or prayers are acceptable is insisted on in Matthew 5:23,24.

"*And lead us not into temptation; but deliver us from evil.*" — Luke 11:4.

Temptation may mean trials, persecution, tribulations. So it is proper to pray that the Lord protect us and lead us away from them.

Temptation may mean, as we usually use the word, an urge to sin. James 1:13,14 says: *"Let no man say when he is tempted, I am tempted of God: for God cannot be tempted with evil, neither tempteth he any man: But every man is tempted, when he is drawn away of his own lust, and enticed."* So we know God does not tempt people to sin. Satan does. Jesus was *"forty days tempted of the devil"* (Luke 4:2). He tempts Christians, too, and Paul was troubled about the Thessalonians, *"lest by some means the tempter have tempted you..."* (I Thess. 3:5). Satan desired to have Peter *"that he may sift you as wheat,"* Jesus said (Luke 22:31). Jesus did not tempt Peter but He allowed Satan to tempt him, even as God allowed Satan to tempt Job. And when Jesus was tempted He was *"led by the Spirit into the wilderness"* to be tempted, as both Luke 4:1 and Matthew 4:1 tell us. God has the power to set a hedge about a Christian, as He did about Job (Job 1:10-12; 2:3-6). Satan can go only as far as God allows. So it is proper to pray, *"Lead us not into temptation; but deliver us from evil."* Perhaps part of the sense is, *"Lead me OUT OF temptation, and a way not where I will be tempted"* and, *"Deliver me from the evil one when I am tempted."*

Jesus told Peter, *"Watch and pray, that ye enter not into temptation"* (Matt. 26:41). So it is evident that Peter could have escaped the temptation had he prayed as he should have. And Ephesians 6:11 commands us, *"Put on the whole armour of God, that ye may be able to stand against the wiles of the devil,"* and then in verse 18, to pray *"always with all prayer and supplication...."*

VERSES 5—8:

5 And he said unto them, Which of you shall have a friend, and shall go unto him at midnight, and say unto him, Friend, lend me three loaves;
6 For a friend of mine in his journey is come to me, and I have nothing to set before him?
7 And he from within shall answer and say, Trouble me not: the door is now shut, and my children are with me in bed; I cannot rise and give thee.
8 I say unto you, Though he will not rise and give him, because he is his friend, yet because of his importunity he will rise and give him as many as he needeth.

Begging for the Bread of Life for Sinners

Jesus has given one lesson on prayer. It is a young Christian's prayer. It is simple. It is rather general, asking for all the world to hallow God's name, for His will to be done in all the earth. It is self-centered —I ask for my daily bread, forgiveness for my sins, deliverance from my temptations. But the Lord Jesus now has another lesson, about another kind of prayer. It is intercessory prayer, for others. It is about spiritual bread, not daily food for our bodies. It is a prayer for power to take the bread of life to sinners. Here is prayer like that of the 120 before Pentecost (Acts 1:14) as Jesus had commanded in Luke 24:49.

Note the Heavenly Friend who has the bread of life. We may plead with Him at midnight without appointment, for *"three loaves"* — we suppose for all the power of Father, Son, and Holy Spirit, since all have part in saving sinners. God loved and gave, Jesus died, the Holy Spirit convicts and regenerates.

Another friend: *"For a friend of mine in his journey is come to me."* Every Christian should stand as the go-between, reaching both God and sinners. Without the Bread of Heaven, we can win no one, and God has no way to save sinners unless someone gives them the Gospel. *"The gospel. . . is the power of God unto salva-*

tion" (Rom. 1:16). "... It pleased God by the foolishness of preaching to save them that believe" (I Cor.
1:21). "*How then shall they call on him in whom
they have not believed? and how shall they believe in
him of whom they have not heard? and how shall they
hear without a preacher?*" (Rom. 10:14). Cornelius
could not be told how to be saved by an angel (Acts
10). The Ethiopian eunuch could not be saved by
reading Isaiah 53, as he said, "...*except some man
should guide me?*" (Acts 8:31).

So God intends for the Christian to take the Gospel
bread to sinners. "*We are ambassadors for Christ, as
though God did beseech you by us: we pray you in
Christ's stead, be ye reconciled to God*" (II Cor. 5:20).
God "*hath given to us the ministry of reconciliation*"
(II Cor. 5:18).

"*A friend of mine...IS COME TO ME.*" Every
Christian has some who in their journey of life have
come to us, in the sense that God has put us in touch
with them, made it so we can win them when many
others could not, made it so we must account for their
souls. Lot was accountable for the souls of Sodom. If
he had won nine others, the wicked city could have been
spared (Gen. 18:23-32). Every Christian has loved
ones, friends, associates, neighbors, who would listen
to him. God has sent them his way, made that contact.
As Mordecai suggested to Esther, God had brought her
to the place she had to save the Jews from destruction
(Esther 4:14). God planned the circumstances. It is no
accident that each Christian has the contact with some
he could win.

I have often found I could win someone when many
other earnest souls had tried and failed. But I have
found that many whom I could not win, despite my
earnest prayer and pleading, someone else did win, and
seemingly with ease. Every Spirit-filled preacher who
preaches the Gospel will be the best preacher someone

ever heard. And every Christian man and woman has the key to someone's heart if they really have the Bread of Heaven, as meant here, the power of the Holy Spirit as they witness. Someone has come to *you* for bread! *". . . and I have nothing to set before him. . . ."* This is part of Jesus' lesson on prayer. Did you, like the twelve, ask Jesus to teach you to pray? By all means ask Him now, if you have not asked Him most earnestly before. But remember here is part of this advanced course on prayer. *Confess your powerlessness!* Away with excuses! You say, "Sinners are so hard!" You may blame your lack of soul winning on modernism, or TV influence, or on *"the last days."* Your community, you think, is more barren, more difficult than others. But your excuses are wrong. Confess it! You do not have the bread! You do not have the power of God you could have.

In Spurgeon's Tabernacle, London, with attendance of one hundred or so where, on the same site, there were, in Spurgeon's time, usually five thousand on a Lord's Day, and standing room only, an attendant said, "The times are different now. If Mr. Spurgeon were here now he couldn't do any better than we are doing." But some in the same church, in the same city, had failed miserably before Spurgeon took the pulpit. When Moody won thousands in Chicago, many others were failing. *"The harvest truly is plenteous, but the labourers are few,"* Jesus said (Matt. 9:37; Luke 10:2). The trouble is not with sinners but with saints. The problem is not with the world but with the church. The failure is not because there are some modernists who, of course, cannot bring revival nor win souls; it is because so many fundamentalists have no power!

In Glasgow, Scotland, I spoke to some six hundred ministers in whose churches, they said, not more than 8 per cent of the people ever came, and conversions were few indeed. I called these erudite and scholarly

men's attention to "a classic poem" which described
their problem:

> Old Mother Hubbard
> Went to the cupboard
> To get her poor dog a bone;
> But when she got there,
> The cupboard was bare,
> And so the poor dog had none!
>
> — (Mother Goose rhyme.)

Or, I reminded them, Tennyson wrote, on the death of
his preacher-friend Arthur Hallam, in the poem "In
Memoriam,"

> "The hungry sheep look up and are not fed."

Oh, let us each confess it; if it be true, confess it with
tears, with the earnest entreaty,

"... *friend, lend me three loaves; For a friend of
mine... is come to me, AND I HAVE NOTHING TO
SET BEFORE HIM? And he from within shall answer
and say, Trouble me not: the door is now shut, and
my children are with me in bed; I cannot rise and
give thee.*"

Who is the Friend who has bread for sinners? He
represents God. Does God not want to give soul-winning
power to Christians who ask it? No, not too easily — not
without serious burden! Not without heart searching,
counting the cost. God does not want the careless giving
of a few coins, like a tip for a waitress or porter, with
no sacrifice, no holy surrender of your best. God does
not want preaching with no passion, no tears, no holy
zeal. So God does not give soul-winning power to one
to whom it is incidental, to one who has no burden
for souls.

Soul winning cost the Lord Jesus over thirty years of
lonely absence from Heaven, when He was despised and

rejected. It cost Him the traitor's kiss, the bloody sweat in Gethsemane, the being forsaken by His disciples, the scourge, the crown of thorns, the *Via Dolorosa*, that sad way of sorrows up to Calvary; the shame of nakedness and mockery while He thirsted; and God turned His face away from the Forsaken One nailed between two thieves. If you want to join with Stephen and Paul and Jesus, yea, and with Spurgeon and Truett and Moody and Torrey and Sunday, then you must come to insist, to plead, to wait, to put souls for Christ first.

"I say unto you, Though he will not rise and give him, because he is his friend, yet because of his importunity he will rise and give him as many as he needeth."

Are you a friend of Christ? Are you saved? Have you obeyed Him in baptism? Do you read the Word, and love it? Do you give your money, your testimony, to the Lord? Do you love the honor and service of God? Do you gather your family to read the Bible and pray? Do you seek to live a clean and obedient life? Do you believe the great essentials of our historic faith? Is your heart surrendered to God's will as you know it? Then you are a good Christian: *a friend of Christ!*

But *THAT DOES NOT GET SOUL-WINNING POWER!* Only importunity, begging, waiting on God, gets that. Not because he is his friend but *"because of his importunity he will rise and give him as many as he needeth."*

So the disciples, as far as we know, were devoted, obedient, loving, and clean when Christ had been with them forty days and then ascended to Heaven. Their doubts were gone; they now had their hearts opened to understand all the Scriptures about Christ (Luke 24:25-27,45). They had been given repeatedly the Great Commission. Why, then, must they *"wait for the promise"* of the Holy Spirit's fullness (Acts 1:4,5; Luke

24:49)? Because they will receive power only *"because of his* [their] *importunity."*

So we need to learn again the Bible commands to *"Seek my face,"* to *"Wait upon the Lord,"* to be *"Praying always with all prayer and supplication"* (Eph. 6:18).

VERSES 9—13:

9 And I say unto you, Ask, and it shall be given you; seek, and ye shall find; knock, and it shall be opened unto you.

10 For every one that asketh receiveth; and he that seeketh findeth; and to him that knocketh it shall be opened.

11 If a son shall ask bread of any of you that is a father, will he give him a stone? or if *he ask* a fish, will he for a fish give him a serpent?

12 Or if he shall ask an egg, will he offer him a scorpion?

13 If ye then, being evil, know how to give good gifts unto your children: how much more shall *your* heavenly Father give the Holy Spirit to them that ask him?

Praying for the Holy Spirit

It is a mistake to separate these verses from the parable of the importunate friend just preceding them. These verses expound the lesson of the parable. They are a part of Jesus' second lesson on prayer: pleading for bread for sinners.

"Ask, and it shall be given you; seek, and ye shall find; knock, and it SHALL BE OPENED UNTO YOU." The word *ask* here is intended to emphasize the word *importunity* in verse 8. So of course we find it, in the Greek New Testament in the present tense, meaning continued action. A more detailed translation would be: "Keep on asking, and ye shall receive; keep on seeking, and ye shall find; keep on knocking, and it shall be opened unto you." So also with the verbs in verse 10. Not everyone who asks one time, but every-

one who persistently asks, receives, says the Lord Jesus. And the same meaning is clearly intended in verse 13: "... *how much more shall your heavenly Father give the Holy Spirit to them that keep on asking,*" or "them that plead with importunity." The *asking* in verses 9, 10, and 13 expound the *importunity* in verse 8.

Note that in a similar passage in Matthew 7:7-11, Jesus said, "... *how much more shall your Father which is in heaven give good things to them that ask him?*"

But someone says, "I do not believe in praying for the Holy Spirit." Well, we are not to pray for the indwelling of the Spirit, which every Christian has, since in John 20:19-22 the resurrected Saviour had the disciples to "*Receive ye the Holy Ghost.*" Nor do we believe we should pray for tongues (languages), unless as at Pentecost there are souls who could not otherwise hear the Gospel in a language they could understand. No one is commanded to "talk in tongues." Nor should we pray for the carnal nature to be burned out, a "second work of grace," which is really promised only at the resurrection. But, clearly, Luke 11:13 says we should pray for the Holy Spirit, persistently. And Ephesians 5:18 plainly commands all to be filled with the Spirit. Acts 2:38,39 offers the "*gift of the Holy Ghost*" to all that God shall call.

Pray for the Holy Ghost? Yes, for His power to win souls. Did you not ever pray for sinners to be convicted? Who, then, convicts sinners? The Holy Spirit. Did you pray for yourself or some other preacher or witness to have special help in getting the Gospel to sinners? Who, then, helps preachers and witnesses to have such blessing and success as we properly seek? The Holy Spirit, of course!

So II Chronicles 7:14 promises God's healing and revival on the land, "*If my people. . . shall humble themselves, and pray, and seek my face, and turn*

from their wicked ways.... " Note: "*seek my face*" —
importunity.

And Isaiah 40:29-31 promises us:

"*He giveth power to the faint; and to them that have
no might he increaseth strength. Even the youths shall
faint and be weary, and the young men shall utterly
fall: But they that wait upon the Lord shall renew their
strength; they shall mount up with wings as eagles; they
shall run, and not be weary; and they shall walk, and
not faint.*"

There is the promise again of "power," renewal of
strength, wonderful walking, running, flying for God, if
we "*wait upon the Lord.*"

So the disciples continued in prayer for power before
Pentecost (Acts 1:14).

Again, needing boldness and power, they prayed
(Acts 4:31), "*and they were all filled with the Holy
Ghost*"—exactly the same nine words recording exactly
the same enduement as at Pentecost (Acts 2:4)..

Paul fasted and prayed three days before being filled
with the Holy Ghost (Acts 9:9,11,17).

The way to Holy Spirit power for soul winning is by
persistent prayer!

VERSES 14—23:

14 And he was casting out a
devil, and it was dumb. And it
came to pass, when the devil was
gone out, the dumb spake; and the
people wondered.

15 But some of them said, He
casteth out devils through Beelzebub the chief of the devils.

16 And others, tempting *him*,

sought of him a sign from heaven.

17 But he, knowing their
thoughts, said unto them, Every
kingdom divided against itself is
brought to desolation; and a house
divided against a house falleth.

18 If Satan also be divided
against himself, how shall his kingdom stand? because ye say that I

cast out devils through Beelzebub.

19 And if I by Beelzebub cast out devils, by whom do your sons cast them out? therefore shall they be your judges.

20 But if I with the finger of God cast out devils, no doubt the kingdom of God is come upon you.

21 When a strong man armed keepeth his palace, his goods are in peace:

22 But when a stronger than he shall come upon him, and overcome him, he taketh from him all his armour wherein he trusted, and divideth his spoils.

23 He that is not with me is against me: and he that gathereth not with me scattereth.

Demon Cast Out: Pharisees Blaspheme

Jesus cast out a devil, "*and it was dumb.*" But Matthew 12:22 adds that he was also blind. Now wonderfully delivered "*the blind and dumb both spake and saw.*"

It was an obvious and remarkable miracle, but "*some of them said, He casteth out devils through Beelzebub the chief of devils.*" In the parallel passage of Matthew 12:24 we are told that they were Pharisees. Pharisees believed in miracles, while the Sadducees did not (Acts 23:8). But they did not want to admit that Jesus was what He claimed to be, the Son of God, the Christ or Messiah foretold in the Old Testament.

They were insincere in their protestations of unbelief. They claimed that Jesus cast out devils by Satan the prince of devils himself. What a sensible answer Jesus gave: "*Every kingdom divided against itself is brought to desolation; and a house divided against a house falleth.*" If Satan, then, were casting out his own devils, how could his kingdom stand?

These Pharisees themselves could not cast out devils; none of their disciples or children could. If Jesus is casting out devils by Beelzebub, "*By whom do your sons cast them out?*" He said. Your fruitless children and representatives are evidence against you, Jesus said. If they were against Jesus, and Jesus cast out devils by Beelzebub, were they then of God and did they have God's power to cast out devils? They did not. It was a foolish and insincere complaint they made.

But Jesus was not answering only their insincere words. *"But he, knowing their thoughts, said unto them...."* What were their thoughts? In the parallel passage in Matthew, Jesus adds the warning against the unpardonable sin. Speaking against the Son of man could be forgiven. People have opposed Him and then repented and have been saved. But if they should so blaspheme the Holy Spirit, who urged upon them that this was the Saviour, that they should love Him and trust Him, and if they should come to permanent decision of rejection, so that the Holy Spirit of God offended should not press upon them any more the matter of salvation, then their sin would be unpardonable.

Dr. Scofield is wrong when he labels that passage in Matthew 12:31,32, as "The unpardonable sin: ascribing to Satan the works of the Spirit." The sin of these Pharisees was not in their words but in their hearts. And the unpardonable sin has to be on the question of accepting or rejecting Christ and has to be as one deals with the Holy Spirit who convicts him to come. One who so wishes and blasphemes that same Holy Spirit until He leaves them alone, cannot be saved. The unpardonable sin is not of the mouth or the hands, it is of the heart. And all sin is pardonable except that which results in permanent rejection of Christ as Saviour. Thus a saved person whose sins are already pardoned could not commit the unpardonable sin.

The key here is that Jesus *"knowing their thoughts"* gave His answer.

And verse 16 says, *"And others, tempting him, sought of him a sign from heaven."* That is, they tried Him, tested Him, tried to incite Him. He answers that in verses 29-32.

Here note the strong, plain division which Jesus insisted upon in verse 23: "*He that is not with me is against me: and he that gathereth not with me scattereth.*" These Pharisees had strict moral codes. As with the Pharisee in Luke 18:10-12, they fasted, they did not commit adultery, they gave tithes, they were very religious. As in the case of Saul of Tarsus, "*of the strictest sect, a Pharisee,*" Paul was, "*as touching the law, a Pharisee; Concerning zeal, persecuting the church; touching the righteousness which is in the law, blameless*" (Phil. 3:5,6). Paul, then Saul of Tarsus, was unsaved at that time as were these Pharisees here with their morality, rejecting Christ. So, those who were not with Christ were against Him and against God. He that did not gather with Jesus gathers for Satan.

A wife said to me about her husband, "He is such a good man. All he needs is to join the church." But she was wrong. He was unconverted, and though outwardly moral was like the Pharisees whom Jesus likened to "*whited sepulchres*" while inwardly they were like the decay and stench of dead men's bones (Matt. 23:27).

Once I, as a young Christian, said about a fellow schoolteacher, "I want him to be a Christian, he has such a good heart." But a pastor wisely rebuked me, saying, "No, his heart is what is wrong with him." And so it always is. The unconverted man or woman is not good. One who has not turned to Christ has rejected Him. One who is not for Him is against Him. According to the words of Jesus in Matthew 6:24, one who does not love Him hates Him and one who does not hold to Him despises Him. One who wickedly rejects Christ does evil, intentionally, about the greatest moral issue in this world, that is, about Christ Himself and His Lordship and Saviourhood.

All the "do good" social programs by ungodly men are not for Christ and the Bible. There is no real goodness that leads men to try morality without Christ, or preach a social righteousness, which leaves the heart wicked.

VERSES 24—26:

24 When the unclean spirit is gone out of a man, he walketh through dry places, seeking rest; and finding none, he saith, I will return unto my house whence I came out.
25 And when he cometh, he find-eth *it* swept and garnished.
26 Then goeth he, and taketh *to him* seven other spirits more wicked than himself; and they enter in, and dwell there: and the last *state* of that man is worse than the first.

The Failure and End of Self-Reformation
Without Christ

Here is the story, not of one who is converted and turns to God and later falls into sin. No, this is the case where the unclean spirit, a devil, leaves a man of his own choice. He is not cast out, he *"is gone out."* I think we may say that Satan sometimes is in morality, that is, the surface morality, without Christ, just as he is often in the outrageous coarsest sins. The unconverted Pharisee rejecting Christ and hating Him is as much in the power of the Devil as the drunkard, the whoremonger, the harlot, so sometimes an evil spirit may leave a man at his own pleasure or the pleasure of the master Devil, Satan.

But here also we see the failure of any morality or righteousness which is the product of the unconverted heart, his own resolutions. No alcoholic or drunkard is ever safe from the curse of drink until a heart-change within him gives him the motivation and the spiritual help to be good. How many men have told me that they made vows to leave liquor alone but could not! One man told me how he had sworn to his mother a solemn oath, had written out the vow, then had opened a vein and dipped a pen in the blood and signed the vow in his own blood, that he would never taste liquor again. And in a few hours he was drunk again.

People do not grow better of themselves. The course of depraved human nature is always downward, unless it is arrested supernaturally. Judas Iscariot was evidently a trusted, morally clean man, when all the apostles consented for him to be treasurer of the group, but he turned out to be a thief and then a betrayer of Jesus and eventually, having unpardonably sinned, he took his own life. Here, the Scriptures give us the taking of the evil spirit. He resolves, "*I will return unto MY HOUSE whence I came out.*" He speaks not of a child of God, the dwelling place of the Spirit of God.

Verse 25 says, "*And when he cometh, he findeth it swept and garnished.*" But the parallel passage in Matthew 12:44 says, "*. . . he findeth it EMPTY, swept, and garnished.*"

Note how one sin, harbored or allowed to stay in the heart, gathers to it other sins. The man who is profane, taking God's name in vain, is likely also to be lewd, without respect for the virtue of a woman. The man who lies is likely to steal. And so one who turns down Christ and decides to do wrong in this great matter has some way given consent of his heart to sin, and so the evil spirit in the picturesque language of Jesus "*taketh to him seven other spirits more wicked than himself; and they enter in, and dwell there: and the last state of that man is worse than the first.*" The man who takes dope probably took alcohol before he took dope. The criminal who robbed a bank probably stole hub caps or radios or other small things first. The man who murders first hated in his heart. There is a progress of evil that is inescapable when one harbors some sin, allows some wickedness without rebuke and without repentance. Self-reformation and self-morality fail without Christ.

VERSES 27, 28:

27 And it came to pass, as he | spake these things, a certain woman

of the company lifted up her voice, and said unto him, Blessed is the womb that bare thee, and the paps which thou hast sucked.

28 But he said, Yea rather, blessed are they that hear the word of God, and keep it.

A Good Woman, Like All Others Who Hear the Word of God and Do It, Keeps It

Some woman, greatly blessed by the preaching of the Lord Jesus and possibly knowing that He is the Messiah, thought, how blessed was His mother to have to be born of her the Saviour and to have nursed Him at her breast.

But Jesus reminds her that the claim Mary had to blessedness was not in that she bore the Saviour but in that she heard the Word of God and followed it. There is some spectacular element of unique blessing in that Mary was chosen to be the mother of the Saviour and so the angel could say to her, "*Blessed art thou among women*" (Luke 1:28). But blessedness in that sense is not that Mary is any greater in God's sight than any other person who does the will of God. We are reminded in Luke 8:19-21 of the same truth. His mother and brothers stood without the great crowd wanting to see Him and Jesus said, "*My mother and brethren are these which hear the word of God, and do it.*" It is significant that James, a younger son of Mary, fathered by Joseph, and thus the brother of Jesus, through his mother, in introducing his epistle was inspired simply to say, "*James, a servant of God and of the Lord Jesus Christ. . .,*" while Jude, another brother, signed his epistle, "*Jude, the servant of Jesus Christ, and brother of James. . .*" Their honor was to be a servant of Jesus Christ, not that they were born from the same womb.

So, then, Mary is very strictly put down as simply a good Christian woman, not to be especially honored more than other good women. The New Testament knows none of those Romish idolatrous words about

Mary like, "Queen of Heaven," "Mother of God," and "Mediatrix." After the death of Jesus, Mary is mentioned only once and that is in Acts 1:14 where she, with other women, attended a prayer meeting. It is never hinted that she had any position of honor in New Testament churches, that she ever was looked to for counsel. So prayers to Mary are idolatry and those who exalt Mary thus take from the honor and glory that properly belongs to Jesus Christ Himself.

VERSES 29—32:

29 And when the people were gathered thick together, he began to say, This is an evil generation: they seek a sign; and there shall no sign be given it, but the sign of Jonas the prophet.

30 For as Jonas was a sign unto the Ninevites, so shall also the Son of man be to this generation.

31 The queen of the south shall rise up in the judgment with the men of this generation, and condemn them: for she came from the utmost parts of the earth to hear the wisdom of Solomon; and, behold, a greater than Solomon is here.

32 The men of Nineve shall rise up in the judgment with this generation, and shall condemn it: for they repented at the preaching of Jonas; and, behold, a greater than Jonas is here.

Jonah, a Type of the Resurrection of Christ

The Lord Jesus is still answering those Pharisees who accuse Him of casting out devils by the prince of devils, those who "*tempting him, sought of him a sign from heaven*" (vs. 16).

So, here He says, "*This is an evil generation: they seek a sign.*" Why was it evil for them to seek a sign, that is, some miraculous manifestation? Because, in the first place, Jesus already had performed many wonderful miracles day after day. Even Nicodemus, a Pharisee and ruler of the Jews, was compelled to say, "*No man*

*can do these miracles that thou doest, except God be
with him"* (John 3:2). Miracles did not prove the deity
of Christ, for He plainly says that no sign or miraculous manifestation would be given of His deity except
His resurrection. Other men before and since have been
used of God to work miracles, including Moses, Elijah,
Elisha, Peter, John, the Apostle Paul, and many others.
The miracles did not prove they were deity: it did prove
they were from God and they could be trusted in what
they were saying. And so the miracles that Jesus worked
authenticated Him as One sent from God, and all the
Jewish leaders plainly acknowledged that He claimed to
be the unique Son of God (John 5:18), and there was
no honest way to avoid the conclusion that Jesus is God,
the Christ or Messiah promised in the Old Testament.

Why, then, should Jesus work other miracles at the
whim of the Pharisees? Or, did they hope to ask something that He *could* not fulfill? Their request was insincere quibbling of wicked hearts who had rejected
Him. So it was *"an evil generation."*

And here we are plainly told, as Jesus did in Matthew
12:39-41, that Jonah, being three days in the belly of
the whale and then miraculously coming out alive,
pictures Jesus who would be three days and three nights
in the grave and then rise from the dead.

So those commentators, those theological infidels, who
say that the book of Jonah is only a myth with a spiritual lesson, that it is not historical and factual, actually
are striking at the deity of Christ. When you do away
with the miraculous you do away with the incarnation,
of course, and just so you do away with the miraculous
new birth, the virgin birth of Christ, His miraculous
resurrection from the dead, His second coming, and
Bible Christianity as a whole. Jesus Himself accepted at
face value the historical account of the Prophet Jonah
and God Himself worked that miraculous deliverance
of Jonah, because He would raise Christ from the dead

and thus pictured it, prophesied it ahead of time. So, these Jewish leaders were inexcusable in rejecting the Saviour. Judgment will come to them, and witnesses would prove their folly. The Queen of Sheba who came *"from the utmost parts of the earth to hear the wisdom of Solomon,"* will stand and say how wicked were these who on such overwhelming evidence still rejected the Saviour. The inference is here that the Queen of Sheba learned of the Saviour and trusted Him through the wisdom of Solomon.

And the people of Nineveh who were converted under Jonah's preaching will stand up in the judgment, also, who repented at the preaching of Jonah, yet they never saw such wonders as did these Pharisees and others in the time of Christ.

We know then that at the Great White Throne Judgment of the unsaved dead pictured in Revelation 20: 11-15, saved people will be there to witness standing beside Jesus Christ as He judges the unconverted and we will give our witness against those who rejected Him. They are now and will be then without excuse.

VERSES 33—36:

33 No man, when he hath lighted a candle, putteth *it* in a secret place, neither under a bushel, but on a candlestick, that they which come in may see the light.

34 The light of the body is the eye: therefore when thine eye is single, thy whole body also is full of light; but when *thine eye* is evil, thy body also *is* full of darkness.

35 Take heed therefore that the light which is in thee be not darkness.

36 If thy whole body therefore *be* full of light, having no part dark, the whole shall be full of light, as when the bright shining of a candle doth give thee light.

"Let Your Light Shine"

Jesus has repeated here the lesson He gave in another

context in Luke 8:16,17. The parallel passages are in
Matthew 5:14-16 and in Mark 4:21,22.

Light is used throughout the Bible as a picture of the
presence of God or of Christ. God revealed Himself to
Moses in a burning bush. He led Israel by a pillar of
fire by night and a cloud by day. In the holy of holies
was the Shekinah Glory in the Tabernacle. After Moses
had been on the mountain with God, his face shone. In
the transfiguration, Jesus was revealed with His face
shining as the sun and His raiment as white as the light!
Christ is pictured by the golden lampstand of the Tabernacle, burning with oil, so Christ carried on His ministry
on earth in the power of the Holy Spirit. In John the
first chapter, Jesus is repeatedly called "*the light.*" He is
the "*Light, which lighteth every man that cometh into
the world.*" James 1:17 says, "*Every good gift and every perfect gift is from above, and cometh down from the
Father of lights.*" In John 8:12 Jesus said, "*I am the
light of the world.*" In John 9:5 He says, "*As long as
I am in the world, I am the light of the world.*" And
John 12:46 says, "*I am come a light into the world. . . .*"

A Christian having fellowship with God is to "*walk in
the light*" (I John 1:7). We are the "*children of light*"
(I Thess. 5:5).

But a born-again Christian has the indwelling Christ
through the constant presence of the Holy Spirit within.
In Matthew 5:14 Jesus said, "*Ye are the light of the
world.*" As long as Jesus was in the world physically,
literally, He was the Light of the world, as He said in
John 9:5. But we Christians are still the light of the
world. Just as Jesus was sent by the Father, so we are
sent to do His work (John 17:18; John 20:19-21). A
godly scholar, careful lest he should take an honor for
man that detracted from the honor to Christ, said that
Christ is the real light, like the sun, and we are only
like the moon, dead in ourselves but reflecting that light.
But that is not the picture here. I do not merely reflect

the light; I have Christ within. A Christian does not only reflect the light; he is the light of the world.

It is in this context, then, that Jesus commands us in verses 35 and 36 that we must take heed *"that the light which is in thee be not darkness."* Christ is to dominate all of our lives. We are to represent Christ in every relationship. It is in the same context that in Matthew 5:16 Jesus commanded us, *"Let your light so shine before men, that they may see your good works, and glorify your Father which is in heaven."*

How May Christians Let Their Light Shine?

The emphasis here is that our love for Christ and the presence of the Holy Spirit representing Christ within us, are not to be hidden, not to be covered over in some secret place in our lives. So, as Jesus said in the parallel passages a candle is not lighted to be put under a bushel or under a bed but on a candlestick to give light to all who are in the house. God wants us to so shine representing Jesus Christ.

That would obviously mean a Christian must make public profession of his faith in Christ. Jesus said in Matthew 10:32 and 33, *"Whosoever therefore shall confess me before men, him will I confess also before my Father which is in heaven. But whosoever shall deny me before men, him will I also deny before my Father which is in heaven."* There is a hint of shame in that the Bible three times mentions Nicodemus as one who came to Jesus by night, and that Joseph of Arimathaea was a good man, a disciple of Jesus, *"but secretly for fear of the Jews."* He said the same in Luke 12:8,9.

The plain command of Christ that every convert should be baptized certainly means an open, public profession of faith in Christ. Thus the confessing Christ openly before others is such a natural manifestation of saving faith that Romans 10:9,10 says, *"That if thou shalt confess with thy mouth the Lord Jesus, and shalt believe in thine heart that God hath raised him from the dead, thou shalt be saved. For with the heart man believeth unto righteousness; and with the mouth confession is made unto salvation.* " And surely the Lord's Supper, too, not only reminds us but should remind all who see that we are relying on the shed blood of Jesus Christ who paid for our sins!

And each Christian should take heed lest part of his inward life be in darkness. We should have *"a single eye."* Some men applying for a public office are charged with having "conflicting interests," that is, they have some business enterprise or own some property or are officially connected with some organization as would influence their vote in Congress or their decision on the judge's bench. So the Christian must beware, lest he have conflict of interest, lest the ties of this world or *"the care of this world, and the deceitfulness of riches,"* and other things choke the Word of God within us so it does not bring fruit to perfection as with the seed sown among thorns.

VERSES 37—44:

37 And as he spake, a certain Pharisee besought him to dine with him: and he went in, and sat down to meat.

38 And when the Pharisee saw *it,* he marvelled that he had not first washed before dinner.

39 And the Lord said unto him, Now do ye Pharisees make clean the outside of the cup and the platter; but your inward part is full of ravening and wickedness.

40 *Ye* fools, did not he that made that which is without make that which is within also?

41 But rather give alms of such things as ye have; and, behold, all things are clean unto you.

42 But woe unto you, Pharisees! for ye tithe mint and rue and all manner of herbs, and pass over judgment and the love of God: these ought ye to have done, and not to leave the other undone.

43 Woe unto you, Pharisees! for ye love the uppermost seats in the synagogues, and greetings in the markets.

44 Woe unto you, scribes and Pharisees, hypocrites! for ye are as graves which appear not, and the men that walk over *them* are not aware *of them.*

The Futility of Outward Righteousness

The Pharisees had many little ceremonial rules not required by the ceremonial law of Moses. Yet they criticised Jesus because He *"had not first washed before dinner."* Their trouble was they made clean the outward side of the cup and platter, that is, they were outwardly righteous, but their hearts were *"full of ravening and wickedness,"* Jesus said. A parallel passage is Matthew 23:13-35, and verse 42 here says the same as Matthew 23:23. It is shocking that anybody could be religious outwardly but inwardly a poor, unconverted, lost sinner. No wonder Jesus calls these Pharisees hypocrites. The solemn warning Jesus gave them and others like them in Matthew 7:21-23 and in the seven woes mentioned in Matthew 23 should teach us to beware of the outward forms of righteousness, which never satisfy a God who demands inward righteousness wrought by Jesus Christ.

VERSES 45—54:

45 Then answered one of the lawyers, and said unto him, Master, thus saying thou reproachest us also.

46 And he said, Woe unto you also, ye lawyers! for ye lade men with burdens grievous to be borne, and ye yourselves touch not the burdens with one of your fingers.

47 Woe unto you! for ye build the sepulchres of the prophets, and your fathers killed them.

48 Truly ye bear witness that ye allow the deeds of your fathers: for they indeed killed them, and ye build their sepulchres.

49 Therefore also said the wisdom of God, I will send them prophets and apostles, and some of them they shall slay and persecute:

50 That the blood of all the prophets, which was shed from the foundation of the world, may be required of this generation;

51 From the blood of Abel unto the blood of Zacharias which perished between the altar and the temple: verily I say unto you, It shall be required of this generation.

52 Woe unto you, lawyers! for ye have taken away the key of knowledge: ye entered not in yourselves, and them that were entering in ye hindered.

53 And as he said these things
unto them, the scribes and the
Pharisees began to urge *him* vehemently, and to provoke him to
speak of many things:

54 Laying wait for him, and seeking to catch something out of his
mouth, that they might accuse him.

Jesus Pronounces Woes Upon Lawyers Also

The lawyers were students, copyists and teachers of
the law. Usually the term means the same as scribes.
You will notice it was these same scribes, along with the
Pharisees, who murmured against Jesus in receiving
sinners (Luke 15:1,2) and the *"chief priests and scribes"*
who sought how they might kill Jesus (Luke 22:2). So
the scribes had the general viewpoint of the Pharisees,
but the term "scribe" means one of an occupation; the
term "Pharisee" means one of a religious sect, a believer
in certain doctrines.

So when Jesus rebuked the Pharisees, the scribes knew
that they were also included (vs. 45). They meticulously
studied out details of the law and of the traditions to lay
burdens on men but they offered no salvation, brought
no compassion. Such people had put to death prophets
in the past and they would have part in the crucifixion
of Jesus.

It is of note that in verse 51 Abel is counted with the
prophets. So Abel died, then, not over some ordinary
personal quarrel but as a witness for God, hated because
he was righteous; so he is listed among the martyrs.

As Jesus is the culmination of all the prophets and
preachers and messengers of God, so His murder, insti-
gated by Jewish leaders, is the culmination of generations
of sin, rejecting the prophets of God.

Is it not strange that those who set out to know and
copy the Old Testament Scriptures *"have taken away the
key of knowledge: Ye entered not in yourselves, and
them that were entering in ye hindered"* Jesus said in

verse 52! How angry they were! They would have no peace till they saw Jesus crucified!

LUKE 12

IN the mean time, when there were gathered together an innumerable multitude of people, insomuch that they trode one upon another, he began to say unto his disciples first of all, Beware ye of the leaven of the Pharisees, which is hypocrisy.

2 For there is nothing covered, that shall not be revealed; neither hid, that shall not be known.

3 Therefore whatsoever ye have spoken in darkness shall be heard in the light; and that which ye have spoken in the ear in closets shall be proclaimed upon the housetops.

4 And I say unto you my friends, Be not afraid of them that kill the body, and after that have no more that they can do.

5 But I will forewarn you whom ye shall fear: Fear him, which after he hath killed hath power to cast into hell; yea, I say unto you, Fear him.

The Leaven of the Pharisees

In the parallel passage in Mark 8:14-21 the command is, "*Take heed, beware of the leaven of the Pharisees, and of the leaven of Herod;*" while in Matthew 16:6 the word is, "*Beware of the leaven of the Pharisees and of the Sadducees.*" In the case of the Pharisees particularly, leaven is called hypocrisy.

The word *leaven* in the Bible, when used symbolically, always has a bad meaning. The passover supper began the seven days' feast of unleavened bread among Israel in Exodus 12. The bread there pictured the Christian daily partaking of Christ and so to picture Christ, the bread must be without leaven. Leaven had a bad meaning. Remember, Lot provided unleavened bread for the angels who visited him in Sodom (Gen. 19:3).

In I Corinthians 5:4-13 the church was instructed to withdraw fellowship from a man living in gross sin who would not repent. The Lord gave them the warning, "*Know ye not that a little leaven leaveneth the whole lump?"* So sin, tolerated in a group, has the infiltrating effect that leaven has in dough. So they were commanded, *"Purge out therefore the old leaven, that ye may be a new lump, as ye are unleavened. For even Christ our passover is sacrificed for us: Therefore let us keep the feast, not with old leaven, neither with the, leaven of malice and wickedness; but with the unleavened bread of sincerity and truth"* (I Cor. 5:7,8). Leaven there means malice and wickedness — it may be things wrong in life or in doctrine.

Then the parable of the leaven in Matthew 13:33 is not a picture of the Gospel slowly, constantly winning out and infiltrating and taking the whole world. The Gospel is spread by sowing seed; it does not spread automatically. And leaven means bad things, not good things. This is the picture of how worldliness, sin and unbelief creep into the church and spread. One rotten apple brings decay to a barrel of apples. So sin or unbelief tolerated or excused leads to ruin of those affected.

But here with the Pharisees the Lord Jesus is particularly speaking of the leaven of hypocrisy. The Pharisees carried on religious performances *"to be seen of men"* (Matt. 6:1, 6, 16), that is, to have the approval of men. So Jesus warns here that that which appears outwardly to men is not the only part on which people will be judged but the judging is on the secrets of the heart as well: *"Man looketh on the outward appearance, but the Lord looketh on the heart"* (I Sam. 16:7). How important it is then that our almsgiving, our praying, our fasting, be from the heart; that our religious services be *"in spirit and in truth"* instead of simply forms, ceremonies and approved religious exercises. Oh, the secret things will come to light.

Jesus goes further here in verse 4. Christians may shrink from the persecution and even from martyrdom for not pleasing men, so these disciples must be warned. Oh, they should not fear simply losing their lives; they should be afraid of God instead of men — God who sends poor impenitent sinners to Hell. Oh, to please God without too much regard for pleasing men!

VERSES 6 — 9:

6 Are not five sparrows sold for two farthings, and not one of them is forgotten before God?

7 But even the very hairs of your head are all numbered. Fear not therefore: ye are of more value than many sparrows.

8 Also I say unto you, Whosoever shall confess me before men, him shall the Son of man also confess before the angels of God:

9 But he that denieth me before men shall be denied before the angels of God.

Our Protecting Heavenly Father Watches Us Much Closer Than Men Watch!

In the passage above the Lord Jesus had warned the disciples to beware of the leaven of the Pharisees: hypocrisy, pleasing men, and seeking their approval.   He warned that all the secret things would come to light and they should not be afraid of those who had power only to harm or kill in this world.   They must give an account to God, which is much more serious.

And now we are told of the tender care of our Heavenly Father.   The infinite care of God gives attention even to a sparrow.   Five sparrows were sold for two farthings (about one cent).   In a kindred passage, Matthew 10:28-31 reminds us that two sparrows were sold for a farthing.   Evidently, if one took four, the seller would give him a fifth one! How little the value!   Yet *"one of them shall not fall to the ground without your Father"* (Matt. 10:29).   And we are reminded: *"Fear ye not therefore, ye are of more value than many sparrows"* (Matt. 10:31).   What a wonderfully sweet passage of assurance from Christ in Matthew 6:25-34! We are reminded that the fowls of the air do not sow nor reap, yet God feeds them, and we are better than they! And the very hairs of every Christian's head are numbered. And when a few hairs come out as we comb, the Lord has the heavenly record changed. Oh, with what infinite care He watches over us!

So Jesus in Matthew 6 urged Christians not to take anxious thought for what they should eat or drink, nor to fret as do the heathen. In verse 33 He said, "*But seek ye first the kingdom of God, and his righteousness; and all these things shall be added unto you.*"

With this in mind, let us not be afraid to claim Christ openly. A special joy and sense of assurance and blessing come from claiming Christ before men. When one calls Christ's name in loving acceptance here, all the angels in Heaven hear the Son of man claim him in Heaven; "*but he that denieth me before men shall be denied before the angels of God*" (vs. 9). I do not think that in either case the primary thought is in the words but in the heart attitude. One can be saved trusting Christ in the heart and before he makes any public profession of that faith. And when one does confess with the mouth the Lord Jesus—"*with the heart man believeth unto righteousness; and with the mouth confession is made unto salvation*" (Rom. 10:10). And in whatever sense a born-again Christian might deny Christ, as Peter denied that he knew Him, in that sense there would come the sense of grief, shame and broken fellowship. But it would not mean that one lost his salvation. Rather, we think here the idea is primarily that one who openly, boldly turns his heart away from Christ and will not accept Him is so denied before the angels of God. That kind of heart attitude on the part of sinners is indicated by verse 10 following.

VERSE 10:

10 And whosoever shall speak a word against the Son of man, it shall be forgiven him: but unto him that blasphemeth against the Holy Ghost it shall not be forgiven.

The Unpardonable Sin

There has been much confusion about this statement of the Lord Jesus and about what the unpardonable sin is. Here we think are important facts:

1. The sin of blaspheming against the Holy Ghost is a heart sin, not a sin of words. Jesus dealt with it much more in detail in Matthew 12:22-32. When He cast out a devil, the Pharisees said, "*This fellow doth not cast out devils, but by Beelzebub the prince of devils.*" Then the Scripture says, "*And Jesus knew their thoughts, and said unto them. . . .*" And then in verses 31 and 32 is the statement that "*blasphemy against the Holy Ghost shall not be forgiven unto men.*" It was not that they said He cast out devils by Beelzebub, but it was that in their hearts they thought, "Well, He must be the Son of God which He claims to be; but we still hate Him; we still will not have Him as Saviour!" And so Jesus had in mind the wicked, fully decided rejection in their hearts.

So the unpardonable sin is not murder, not adultery, not profanity, and not "ascribing to Satan the work of the Holy Spirit" as the Scofield Bible comment says, but it is a complete and final rejection of the plea of the Holy Spirit for a sinner to turn to Christ. The Holy Spirit will not return to bring conviction again, and the sinner is so hardened in sin that he is not now susceptible to the Gospel. Hebrews 6:4-6 carefully warns that if one who has been greatly enlightened and the Holy Spirit has gone along with him convicting and teaching so that he has "*tasted the good word of God, and the powers of the world to come*" — if such people shall fall away from this conviction, this enlightenment, it will be impossible "*to renew them again unto repentance; seeing they crucify to themselves the Son of God afresh, and put him to an open shame.*" It is not simply to reject Christ but it is when that rejection becomes so insistent and after so much enlightenment that one may know he is rejecting Christ and his decision is so hardened and settled that he cannot be renewed to repentance.

Jesus prayed for those who crucified Him, saying, "*Father, forgive them; for they know not what they do.*" Evidently, if they had known fully just what they were doing and understood all the implications of it, their sin would have been unpardonable because the decision would have been irrevocable.

According to Genesis 6:3 God's Spirit does cease to strive with men. There is much evidence that the Pharaoh of the Exodus and that Judas Iscariot and some of these chief priests who had part in the crucifixion probably committed the unpardonable sin. But it was a heart sin of an unsaved person, greatly enlightened, who deliberately turned down permanently the Saviour. And hence it is a blasphemous act or attitude toward the Holy Spirit who presses the conviction.

2. A saved person then cannot commit the unpardonable sin because his sins are already forgiven. All the sins of the past, present and future are laid on Christ. And so, "*Blessed are they whose iniquities are forgiven, and whose sins are covered. Blessed is the man to whom the Lord will not impute sin*" (Rom. 4:7,8). Though Peter sinned, Jesus had prayed for him and Satan could not have him. Neither can he have any one of God's children. "*I give unto them eternal life; and they shall never perish*" (John 10:28).

First John 5:16,17 says, "*If any man see his brother sin a sin which is not unto death, he shall ask, and he shall give him life for them that sin not unto death.*

There is a sin unto death: I do not say that he shall pray for it. All unrighteousness is sin: and there is a sin not unto death." Evidently this is a sin of a Christian, a *"brother,"* and the sin is not the unpardonable sin and it does not mean that it is unforgivable.

Sometimes Christians sin and as punishment they are taken out of this world. See the case of those Christians at Corinth who took the Lord's Supper unworthily (I Cor. 11:30). Ananias and Sapphira may have been examples (Acts 5:1-10). One who is saved and going to Heaven might be sick because of sin or he might die because of sin but, of course, that one must appear at the judgment seat of Christ.

3. One who wants to be saved has not committed the unpardonable sin and can be saved. All God's promises are still true. The unpardonable sin does not change God; it changes the sinner.

VERSES 11,12:

11 And when they bring you unto the synagogues, and *unto* magistrates, and powers, take ye no thought how or what thing ye shall answer, or what ye shall say: 12 For the Holy Ghost shall teach you in the same hour what ye ought to say.

Good Christians Should Expect Persecution

In connection with the Great Commission in Matthew 28:19,20 Jesus said, *". . . and, lo, I am with you alway, even unto the end of the world."* These same apostles to whom Jesus speaks would be brought before the Sanhedrin and *"unto the synagogues, and unto magistrates"* because of their urgently preaching the Gospel, as we see reading through the book of Acts. So it was with Paul and Barnabas and Silas. James was beheaded in

Acts 12, and Peter was imprisoned for the same purpose, though delivered in answer to prayer.

We remember that Daniel was put into the lions' den for his faithfulness, and the three Hebrew children were cast into the fiery furnace. And good Christians who are active and Spirit-filled in soul winning may expect opposition and persecution. Jesus said, "*If the world hate you, ye know that it hated me before it hated you . . . . The servant is not greater than his lord*" (John 15:18,20).

But God gives His children a holy boldness when they trust Him and when they are willing to suffer for Him. God has the answer and He will tell us what to do in such a case. The Christian is not to be afraid of the scholars, he is not to be afraid of the rich, he is not to be afraid of officials, he is not to be afraid of denominational leadership. The blessed Holy Spirit will teach one in an emergency what to say and uphold him in the hour of trial. God does not promise to always deliver us. John the Baptist was beheaded and so eventually was Paul, but whether we live or die, if we glorify the Lord, it is enough.

VERSES 13—15:

13 And one of the company said unto him, Master, speak to my brother, that he divide the inheritance with me.

14 And he said unto him, Man, who made me a judge or a divider over you?

15 And he said unto them, Take heed, and beware of covetousness: for a man's life consisteth not in the abundance of the things which he possesseth.

"Beware of Covetousness"

We are not told whether the plea of the man was justified who wanted Jesus to intercede for him. It may be that the brother was the eldest son and that according to Mosaic law he had some rights of inheritance as the eldest son that others would not have. Thus it was intended that plots of ground should be handed down from elder son to elder son so there would be a stability and permanence in the boundary lines and in the traditions and national life. Possibly one son had seized more than his share of the inheritance; we do not know. The important point is that whenever possible God's people should settle such matters by kind and loving agreement, not by laws and judges. And the Saviour says not to take sides one against another in an incidental matter. It is far more important, He tells them, that they should *"beware of covetousness."* For if the man should get all the inheritance that he desired, he might be worse off because of the sin of covetousness. A man's life, his happiness, his influence, his welfare, does not depend on *"the abundance of the things which he possesseth."* How often we learn that *"riches. . . make themselves wings"* (Prov. 23:5). And Christians are counseled, *". . . having food and raiment let us be therewith content"* (I Tim. 6:8).

VERSES 16—21:

16 And he spake a parable unto them, saying, The ground of a certain rich man brought forth plentifully:

17 And he thought within himself, saying, What shall I do, because I have no room where to bestow my fruits?

18 And he said, This will I do: I will pull down my barns, and build greater; and there will I bestow all my fruits and my goods.

19 And I will say to my soul, Soul, thou hast much goods laid up for many years; take thine ease, eat, drink, *and* be merry.

20 But God said unto him, *Thou* fool, this night thy soul shall be required of thee: then whose shall those things be, which thou hast provided?

21 So *is* he that layeth up treasure for himself, and is not rich toward God.

The Parable of the Rich Fool

In verse 15 the Lord Jesus warned of covetousness; now He gives an example.

There are many commendable things about the rich man mentioned here. The truth is that ordinarily wealth is a sign of industry. The farmer who makes better crops than another farmer usually works harder, and keeps up his fences better, and plows the field earlier, and spends more time and effort than the other. The Bible law of sowing and reaping and the commendation of thrift and diligence make it so that generally the man who has gained wealth honestly is worthy of great respect. The cases of Job, Abraham, Jacob, David, Solomon, and Joseph of Arimathaea, come to mind — all godly people who were rich. We take for granted that here was a man who worked hard, who saved things carefully.

It is to his credit that he was very careful to preserve what his field produced. He built barns to preserve the fruit of his fields. The Bible never approves the spendthrift, the improvident, the sluggard.

We would suppose that this man attained what the covetous man would hope to attain. Ah, but what a mistake he made! He supposed he would have many years to enjoy what he had earned. I suppose it is to his credit that he felt that now he could retire after a life of labor. But, alas, he was thinking about food for his belly and clothes for his back and a house for his body — without thinking about the eternal welfare of his soul. So God said he was a fool — a fool simply in that he died unprepared. And he was a fool to have spent so much time and thought and labor, in laying by money and property for the future. Oh, how much better would have been his diligence had he made sure of his salvation and had he made use of his goods so as to have treasure in Heaven. He did not.

And the lesson is this: "*So is he that layeth up treasure for himself, and is not rich toward God.*" Oh, Christian, do not set your heart on the things of this world but lay up for yourselves treasure in Heaven.

VERSES 22—34:

22 And he said unto his disciples, Therefore, I say unto you, Take no thought for your life, what ye shall eat; neither for the body, what ye shall put on.

23 The life is more than meat, and the body *is more* than raiment.

24 Consider the ravens: for they neither sow nor reap; which neither have storehouse nor barn; and God feedeth them: how much more are ye better than the fowls?

25 And which of you with taking thought can add to his stature one cubit?

26 If ye then be not able to do that thing which is least, why take ye thought for the rest?

27 Consider the lilies how they grow: they toil not, they spin not; and yet I say unto you, that Solomon in all his glory was not arrayed like one of these.

28 If then God so clothe the grass, which is to day in the field, and to morrow is cast into the oven; how much more *will he clothe* you, O ye of little faith?

29 And seek not ye what ye shall eat, or what ye shall drink, neither be ye of doubtful mind.

30 For all these things do the nations of the world seek after: and your Father knoweth that ye have need of these things.

31 But rather seek ye the kingdom of God; and all these things shall be added unto you.

32 Fear not, little flock; for it is your Father's good pleasure to give you the kingdom.

33 Sell that ye have, and give alms; provide yourselves bags which wax not old, a treasure in the heavens that faileth not, where no thief approacheth, neither moth corrupteth.

34 For where your treasure is, there will your heart be also.

Seek First the Kingdom of God

See the parallel passage in Matthew 6:25-34.

Jesus here continues this sweet theme that God cares for His own, that covetousness is not necessary, that fretting and anxiety do not fit with Christians who have such a loving and provident Heavenly Father!

"*Take no thought for your life, what ye shall eat, or what ye shall drink; nor yet for your body, what ye shall put on*"—what does He mean? Certainly He means take no *anxious* thought, give no long attention to it. It is not wrong to enjoy the good food that God gives, for the psalmist said, *"Bless the Lord, O my soul, and forget not all his benefits. . . Who satisfieth thy mouth with good things; so that thy youth is renewed like the eagle's"* (Ps. 103:2,5). Here is the lesson again in Philippians 4:6,7: *"Be careful for nothing; but in every thing by prayer and supplication with thanksgiving let your requests be made known unto God. And the peace of God, which passeth all understanding, shall keep your hearts and minds through Christ Jesus."* To be full of care, to be anxious, to worry and fret is a sin. John Wesley said, "I would no more fret than curse or swear." Fretting, worrying is the opposite of faith, and how it shames and dishonors and grieves God!

As Jesus before mentioned the sparrows, He now mentions the ravens. Do they have farms like the rich man above had and do they build barns and put money in the bank? No, yet God feeds them, and we are better than the fowls.

And how helpless we are! One cannot make himself tall or short. There are a thousand things ahead of us that we cannot control. Why not leave it all in the hands of a loving Heavenly Father and be content?

"Consider the lilies," Jesus said (vs. 27) — the little scarlet flowers that grow wild in Palestine. *". . . lilies of the field,"* says Matthew 6:28. They are a kind of anemone and more beautiful than King Solomon in his robes and jewels sitting in state! And every single wild flower is personally colored and personally enjoyed by the Saviour and by our Heavenly Father.

Full many a gem of purest ray serene,
The dark, unfathomed caves of ocean bear:

Full many a flower is born to blush unseen,
And waste its sweetness on the desert air.

So says Gray in his "Elegy Written in a Country Churchyard."

So the Christian is not to be "*of doubtful mind.*" That is what the inspired apostle meant, no doubt, in II Timothy 1:7, "*For God hath not given us the spirit of fear; but of power, and of love, and of a sound mind,*" that is, of an established, settled, peaceful mind.

The unsaved people of the world seek after food, clothes, housing, security, and treasure laid by on earth (vs. 30); and we read in Matthew 6:32, "(*For after all these things do the Gentiles seek:*)," that is, heathen people. A Christian ought to be better than a heathen and ought to have peace in heart about daily provision for their future.

But what is the Christian's attitude? "*Rather seek ye the kingdom of God; and all these things shall be added unto you.*" The same thing is stated in Matthew 6:33. God knows our needs. He loves us. In Romans 8:32 we are told, "*He that spared not his own Son, but delivered him up for us all, how shall he not with him also freely give us all things?*" So it is the good will of the Father to take care of His own. And we are commanded, "*Let your conversation be without covetousness; and be content with such things as ye have; for he hath said, I will never leave thee, nor forsake thee. So that we may boldly say, The Lord is my helper, and I will not fear what man shall do unto me*" (Heb. 13:5,6).

How much better to have treasure in Heaven where wealth never takes wings, where property does not decay nor lose its value, where thieves do not steal nor prodigal children waste! And where our treasure is, there will be our heart's devotion, too.

VERSES 35—48:

35 Let your loins be girded about, and *your* lights burning;

36 And ye yourselves like unto men that wait for their lord, when he will return from the wedding; that when he cometh and knocketh, they may open unto him immediately.

37 Blessed *are* those servants, whom the lord when he cometh shall find watching: verily I say unto you, that he shall gird himself, and make them to sit down to meat, and will come forth and serve them.

38 And if he shall come in the second watch, or come in the third watch, and find *them* so, blessed are those servants.

39 And this know, that if the goodman of the house had known what hour the thief would come, he would have watched, and not have suffered his house to be broken through.

40 Be ye therefore ready also: for the Son of man cometh at an hour when ye think not.

41 Then Peter said unto him, Lord, speakest thou this parable unto us, or even to all?

42 And the Lord said, Who then is that faithful and wise steward, whom *his* lord shall make ruler over his household, to give *them their* portion of meat in due season?

43 Blessed *is* that servant, whom his lord when he cometh shall find so doing.

44 Of a truth I say unto you, that he will make him ruler over all that he hath.

45 But and if that servant say in his heart, My lord delayeth his coming; and shall begin to beat the menservants and maidens, and to eat and drink, and to be drunken;

46 The lord of that servant will come in a day when he looketh not for *him*, and at an hour when he is not aware, and will cut him in sunder, and will appoint him his portion with the unbelievers.

47 And that servant, which knew his lord's will, and prepared not *himself*, neither did according to his will, shall be beaten with many *stripes*.

48 But he that knew not, and did commit things worthy of stripes, shall be beaten with few *stripes*. For unto whomsoever much is given, of him shall be much required: and to whom men have committed much, of him they will ask the more.

Warning of the Second Coming and Parables Connected

The discourse of the Saviour continues. Since a Christian's treasure is to be in Heaven, and since he is not to be too much concerned about the daily needs and future security on earth, he should look forward to Christ's return. Compare this passage with Matthew 24, Mark 13 and with Luke 17:22-27. Oh, a great heavenly wedding is planned, and Christ is the Bridegroom. How anxiously we should wait for His return! That illustration is given in the parable of the ten virgins also in Matthew, chapter 25. And here we are admonished to be like servants sitting awake at night, keeping the lights burning, clothes on, ready to meet the Master and serve Him when He comes. And we are to watch whether it be in the second watch of the night, from 9:00 to 12:00, or whether in the third watch, from midnight to 3:00 in the morning.

The nighttime is pictured as the possible time for Christ's coming because people are more likely to be asleep then, they less expect visitors then, and the coming of Christ for His own is to be so sudden and unexpected. And just as a thief might break into a house at night and one would not know what hour to expect his coming, so Christ will come *"at an hour when ye think not,"* says verse 40.

It is clear, very clear that no one can foretell or predict when Christ will come for His own — not even approximately. He may come as this author writes these words; He may not come for hundreds of years — I do not know. No one knows. That is expressed so clearly in Matthew 24:36 and in Mark 13:32. Matthew says, *"But of that day and hour knoweth no man, no, not the angels of heaven, but my Father only."* And Mark adds, *". . . not the angels which are in heaven, neither the Son."*

It is natural for men to want to know when Jesus will return, so people have tried in so many ways to figure out when Christ will come. Dates have been set again and again when teachers confidently affirmed the Saviour would return. All have failed. No one knows. No one is supposed to know. When the disciples said, *"Lord, wilt thou at this time restore again the kingdom to Israel?"* He answered them plainly, *"It is not for you to know the times or the seasons, which the Father hath put in his own power"* (Acts 1:6,7). They were rather commanded to wait for the power of the Holy Spirit for soul winning and to get the Gospel to every creature.

Those who set dates for Christ's coming do great harm to the cause of Christ. First, some are disillusioned and disheartened and quit watching for Christ to come because He did not come at some time imagined by some teacher. Others make the hope of Christ's sudden coming an excuse for not winning souls. They say the great *"falling away"* is on, that men are blinded with sin, that one cannot have revival now. That is foolish talk and they are wrong. In truth, if the Lord Jesus should come within the next day after you read this (as He may, or even before), still every promise in the Bible is true; the power of the Holy Spirit is available; the Gospel is still the power of God unto salvation to everyone that believeth. It is still true that he that goes forth weeping, bearing precious seed, shall come again rejoicing, bringing his sheaves with him (Ps. 126:6). Rather, God wants us to happily expect the Saviour to return, which He may do at any moment and we should be ready. That is the normal attitude for a Christian in this age.

But Peter said, *"Lord, speakest thou this parable unto us, or even to all?"* So Jesus fitted the parable more particularly to Christian workers, to the apostles and to us who preach the Word. He told of a faithful, wise steward whom his lord sets over all his business while the master is away. If he is faithful when his master returns, *"He will make him ruler over all that he hath."* This is like the parable of the pounds in Luke 19:11-27. There the man whose pound had gained ten was made ruler over ten cities. Then he whose pound had gained five was made ruler over five cities.

Surely the Lord here speaks of rewards for Christians who serve Him, proportionate rewards according to our works. Surely this is what Paul the apostle meant also when he was inspired to write, *"Wherefore we labour,*

*that, whether present or absent, we may be accepted of
him.   For we must all appear before the judgment seat
of Christ; that every one may receive the things done in
his body, according to that he hath done, whether it be
good or bad.   Knowing therefore the terror of the Lord,
we persuade men. . .*" (II Cor. 5:9-11). And that judgment time is particularly discussed in I Corinthians
3:10-15.   One whose work abides will receive a reward.
One whose work is burned and worthless "*shall be
saved; yet so as by fire,*" though he suffers loss.

Verse 46 must mean that the Lord intended part of
this message also for the Jewish leaders of His day and
for denominational leaders, popes, priests and bishops
of this age who must give an account for spiritual
leadership even if they are unsaved.   Surely such a
religious leader will be "*cut. . . in sunder*" and be appointed "*his portion with the unbelievers.*"   And Jesus
must mean also Judas Iscariot who was present with
Him when this parable was given.

But verses 47 and 48 teach us Christians that one
who knew the Lord's will and did it not would be beaten
with many stripes, and one who had more opportunity,
had more responsibility, would suffer more when he
meets Christ if he is not faithful.   And one who had less
information, had less place of opportunity, would be
punished less if he fails.

Oh, how seriously we should take every open door of
service!

VERSES 49 — 53:

49 I am come to send fire on the earth; and what will I, if it be already kindled?

50 But I have a baptism to be baptized with; and how am I straitened till it be accomplished!

51 Suppose ye that I am come to give peace on earth? I tell you, Nay; but rather division:

52 For from henceforth there shall be five in one house divided, three against two, and two against three.

53 The father shall be divided against the son, and the son against the father; the mother against the daughter, and the daughter against the mother; the mother in law against her daughter in law, and the daughter in law against her mother in law.

Christ, the Great Divider

Jesus came into the world "*to send fire on the earth,*" and He had in mind primarily the future and eventual punishment of the wicked and the future division in Heaven and Hell.

But in His own body He has "*a baptism to be baptized with.*" He must be overwhelmed in sorrows and suffering. He must bear the sin of the world. He must have God's face turned away. He must be slain as a transgressor. So in some sense Jesus took on Himself all the fire of God's judgment.

But when Jesus came into the world, He had in mind not only the first coming but also the second coming. Those who study the life of Christ remember that we have seen up to this time only the first act. Christ will return. His plans will be completed. Jesus is the Lord who has gone into a far country to receive a kingdom and to return. And all during His ministry on earth He had the eventual end in His mind.

That means that Jesus came not only as a Saviour of the world but also as the Judge of the world. He came not only to bring salvation but to bring damnation.

So when we read in John 3:16 that "*God so loved the world, that he gave his only begotten Son,*" we should note also that there is the solemn warning that one who does not believe in Him "*should perish*" and only those who believe in Him "*should not perish.*" One who believes has everlasting life, but one who does not believe has the wrath of God abiding on him (John 3:36).

The fire that Jesus had come to start on the earth is indicated in that prophetic passage in Isaiah 61:1 and 2. It tells how Jesus would come and would be anointed to preach the Gospel. And He quoted these two verses down to the middle of verse 2 when He came into the synagogue at Galilee in Luke 4:18,19. But He stopped at a comma in the midst of a sentence when He had read the part that had immediate application. He had just been filled with the Holy Spirit and now they could see the fulfillment of this Scripture as He went about in the power of the Holy Spirit. We may be sure He had in mind the rest of the verse which was there before His eyes — He came not only "*to proclaim the acceptable year of the Lord*" but also to proclaim "*the day of vengeance of our God,*" as Isaiah 61:2 says.

So in Matthew 3:11 and 12 John the Baptist said, "*I indeed baptize you with water unto repentance: but he that cometh after me is mightier than I, whose shoes I am not worthy to bear: he shall baptize you with the Holy Ghost, and with fire: Whose fan is in his hand, and he will throughly purge his floor, and gather his wheat into the garner; but he will burn up the chaff with unquenchable fire.*" Jesus is the One who will baptize His people with the Holy Ghost, but He is also the One who will baptize the unsaved with fire and He will "*burn up the chaff with unquenchable fire.*"

So there is to be a great division between saved and lost, pictured so clearly in the term, "*one shall be taken, and the other left,*" in Matthew 24:40 and 41 and in Luke 17:34-36. Separation is pictured again when Christ returns to sit upon His throne in Jerusalem and when unsaved Gentiles will come before Him for judgment after the tribulation time: "*And he shall separate them one from another, as a shepherd divideth his sheep from the goats*" — the sheep for the heavenly kingdom, the goats to go to Hell. And that is the meaning in the parable of the tares which Jesus explained in Matthew 13:40-42: "*As therefore the tares are gathered and burned in the fire; so shall it be in the end of this world. The Son of man shall send forth his angels, and they shall gather out of his kingdom all things that offend, and them which do iniquity; And shall cast them into a furnace of fire: there shall be wailing and gnashing of teeth."*

And that is so, too, about the good fish and bad fish in the net: *"So shall it be at the end of the world: the angels shall come forth, and sever the wicked from among the just, And shall cast them into the furnace of fire: there shall be wailing and gnashing of teeth"* (Matt. 13:49,50).

And that great separation climaxes in that *"great gulf fixed"* between the saved and the lost, between Heaven and Hell, which Jesus mentioned in Luke 16:26.

So there is a vast difference now between the child of God and the child of Satan. What a contrast!

"What fellowship hath righteousness with unrighteousness? and what communion hath light with darkness? And what concord hath Christ with Belial? or what part hath he that believeth with an infidel? And what agreement hath the temple of God with idols? for ye are the temple of the living God; as God hath said, I will dwell in them, and walk in them; and I will be their God, and they shall be my people." — II Cor. 6:14-16.

No wonder then that God commands, *"Be ye not unequally yoked together with unbelievers"* in this context and that He says, *"Wherefore come out from among them, and be ye separate, saith the Lord."* Saved people and lost people are not alike. They are not alike in their inmost nature even if they do sometimes appear alike outwardly. They are certainly not akin at all in their destiny.

So there will be division on earth between the saved and lost. A Christian is to have a home in Heaven and he is to be *"not conformed to this world"* but to be *"transformed"* (Rom. 12:2). Oh, then, we can expect division in the same family with three against two or two against three; between the father and the son, the

mother and the daughter; between the mother-in-law and
daughter-in-law — if one be saved and the other be lost.

Oh, we must maintain all the tender ties of family and
love.   We dare not disavow responsibility for those
whom God has put near us. We must love them, must
try to win them, must do them good. But we must face
it that a Christian is divided from an unsaved person.
And if he lives as he ought, he may often appear queer
and foolish to this world.

VERSES 54 — 59:

54 And he said also to the people,
When ye see a cloud rise out of
the west, straightway ye say, There
cometh a shower; and so it is.

55 And when ye see the south
wind blow, ye say, There will be
heat; and it cometh to pass.

56 Ye hypocrites, ye can discern
the face of the sky and of the earth;
but how is it that ye do not discern this time?

57 Yea, and why even of yourselves judge ye not what is right?

58 When thou goest with thine
adversary to the magistrate, as
thou art in the way, give diligence
that thou mayest be delivered from
him; lest he hale thee to the judge,
and the judge deliver thee to the
officer, and the officer cast thee into
prison.

59 I tell thee, thou shalt not depart thence, till thou hast paid the
very last mite.

A Blinded Generation Did Not
Recognize the Saviour

Jesus says that His hearers who did not recognize that
God had sent Him, that He was the Son of God, that
He was the fulfillment of prophecy, were hypocrites.
That means their rejection of Christ was dishonest rejection.   They pretended to want more signs of His
deity (Matt. 12:38-42). He told them, *"An evil and
adulterous generation seeketh after a sign; and there
shall no sign be given to it, but the sign of the prophet
Jonas."* Because of darkened minds and hearts and
deliberate blindness, Jesus spoke in parables often so
that those who did not want to believe would not be

compelled to believe (Matt. 13:10-17). No doubt for the same reason He often told those whom He healed not to tell it but to go quietly. Oh, any honest heart could know that Jesus was the Saviour. So did Simeon and aged Anna the prophetess in the Temple know, when Jesus was brought there as a Baby. So did Nathanael, when he first came face to face with Jesus, know Him as the Christ (John 1:46-49). The dying thief recognized Jesus as Lord and believed the prophecies about His coming kingdom and asked for mercy (Luke 23:39-43). Even the centurion who had charge of the crucifixion, when he saw the things that were done at the crucifixion, said, "*Truly this was the Son of God*" (Matt. 27:54).

And after His resurrection, Jesus said even to His disciples, "*O fools, and slow of heart to believe all that the prophets have spoken*" (Luke 24:25).

The lawyers, scribes, those who copied and wrote and taught the Scriptures, not only refused to enter the kingdom, not only refused to accept the Saviour but they taught others so; they were insincere hypocrites (Luke 11:52).

Then Jesus gives an illustration for them and for us: One is arrested and brought before the court. He should hastily try to get the matter settled peaceably. If one person persisted in his wrongdoing, the judge would fine him heavily.

And all who hear the Gospel and turn down the Saviour are as foolish as the criminal who argues with the policeman or one who does not immediately try to rectify his wrong and make peace before he comes to final judgment. Judgment will come to every poor, unsaved sinner and he had better heed the Word of God and turn to Christ while he can. Those who do not accept the deity of Christ and the authority of the Bible are unbelievers, not because they are cultured and educated, not because they think they know science or history that gives them reason for their unbelief—no;

unbelief is a matter of a wicked heart, not a matter of an intellectual mind. It is sin and not science that turns people away from God and the Bible. Anyone who wants to find Jesus Christ may find Him and may know He is all He claims to be.

LUKE 13

VERSES 1—5:

THERE were present at that season some that told him of the Galilæans, whose blood Pilate had mingled with their sacrifices.

2 And Jesus answering said unto them, Suppose ye that these Galilæans were sinners above all the Galilæans, because they suffered such things?

3 I tell you, Nay: but, except ye repent, ye shall all likewise perish.

4 Or those eighteen, upon whom the tower in Siloam fell, and slew them, think ye that they were sinners above all men that dwelt in Jerusalem?

5 I tell you, Nay: but, except ye repent, ye shall all likewise perish.

Jesus and the Death Penalty

Here are two cases brought to our attention. They told Jesus of *"the Galileans, whose blood Pilate had mingled with their sacrifices."* These were probably followers of the rebel Judas of Galilee, mentioned in Acts 5:37. In a conspiracy at Jerusalem, when they came pretending to worship and offered sacrifices but intending to seize the government, Pilate had them slain; so the Scripture says, *"whose blood Pilate had mingled with their sacrifices."* Here Jesus obviously regards it that those who were slain by the government for crime, were slain rightly and He warns, *"except ye repent, ye shall all likewise perish."*

The other case we would call an accident. The law would call it "an act of God," when the tower in Siloam fell on eighteen people. Again, Jesus takes it as an act of God, takes it as the punishment of God on sin and warns that *"except ye repent, ye shall all likewise perish."*

God commanded Noah in Genesis 9:5 and 6: *"And surely your blood of your lives will I require; at the hand of every beast will I require it, and at the hand of*

*man; at the hand of every man's brother will I require
the life of man. Whoso sheddeth man's blood, by man
shall his blood be shed: for in the image of God made
he man."*

The death penalty, then, was given of God before the
Mosaic Law, then incorporated in the law.   Exodus
21:12 commands, *"He that smiteth a man, so that he die,
shall be surely put to death."*   The death penalty was
also ordered for one who should smite his father or
mother or kidnap a man for sale, even one who cursed
his father or mother.   A distinction was made between
first degree murder and second degree murder.   The
death penalty was also commanded for adultery (See
Lev. 20:10-12), also for sodomy (vs. 13) and for per-
version with a beast (vss. 15,16). And the death penalty
was also commanded for worshiping certain heathen
gods.

In the New Testament the command about the death
penalty is repeated in Romans 13:1-7, although the
Roman government was not then a theocracy, as Israel
had under the Mosaic Law, and so it was left to the
government to decide which crimes deserved death.   Yet
we are told, *"For there is no power but of God: the
powers that be are ordained of God,"* and we are told
that the ruler *"is the minister of God to thee for good,"*
and that *"he beareth not the sword in vain: for he
is the minister of God, a revenger to execute wrath upon
him that doeth evil."*   It is significant that Jesus approved the death penalty under Pilate, knowing that
Pilate would deliver Him to be scourged and crucified;
and that the Apostle Paul approved the death penalty by
the Roman emperor when the Emperor Nero, then in
power, would have Paul beheaded.

The obvious truth is twofold: First, human government is of God.   Just as God had told Nebuchadnezzar,
*". . . that the most High ruleth in the kingdom of men,
and giveth it to whomsoever he will"* (Dan. 4:25); and

to Belteshazzar, "... *God ruled in the kingdom of men, and that he appointeth over it whomsoever he will*" (Dan. 5:21). Second, God authorizes governments to execute criminals. So governments act for God, execute the laws for God, put criminals to death for God. So good Christians are patriots, honoring the government which has God's authority even to prosecute war when necessary.

But Jesus here clearly approves of the death penalty, which Pilate executed on Judas of Galilee and other rebels.

This truth is borne out in all the Scriptures again and again. God Himself struck men, individuals or groups, and killed them in punishment for their sin. Pharaoh and his army were destroyed by the act of God. God had Moses to lift his rod and the Red Sea suddenly returned into the walled channel it had made for Israel's crossing. Priests Nadab and Abihu were killed by fire from God for bringing "*strange fire*" (Lev. 10:1). Many were slain at the rebellion of Korah (Num. 26:9,10), and many, many when Israel worshiped the golden calf Aaron had made (Exod. 32:28).

And God had men to act for Him in putting others to death. King Saul was commanded to go and exterminate the Amalekites (I Sam. 14:48). God commanded the man to be stoned who picked up sticks on the Sabbath day (Num. 15:32-36). He commanded that Achan and his family be stoned and burned (Josh. 7:25). Phinehas, the priest, the son of Eleazar, saw a man bring a Midianite harlot into the camp and Phinehas went into the tent and killed them both, and was commended for it (Num. 25:6-8). And then God commanded a war upon the Midianites, as recorded in Numbers 31.

But God used men directly to bring others to death in the New Testament, too. Ananias and Sapphira were struck dead at the words of Peter for lying to the Holy Ghost (Acts 5:1-11).

Surely we can say that the life of every man is in the hands of the Lord and God numbers every person's days. He could warn King Hezekiah he would die, then in answer to tears and prayer could add fifteen years to his life. The date for death for every man is surely decided by the will of God.

So that was the act of God when that tower in Siloam fell upon eighteen (vs. 4) and killed them.

Also it is important to note that God does not regard punishment simply as a way to rehabilitate men. People die because they ought to die. People are punished because a holy God requires that sin be punished. God sends people to Hell who die impenitent, not in order that they may be rehabilitated or one day restored to favor with God but as the eternal punishment for their eternal, unforgiven sin. Punishment, then, is not simply to rehabilitate the sinner but as a warning to others and to discourage sin and to bring sinners to repentance. The natural and proper *"wages of sin is death"* and no human government ought try to do away with God's plain law. Sin ought to be punished.

A Solemn Warning to Repent

To all those present, Jesus said that they were sinners like those Galilean rebels Pilate had put to death, that they were sinners like those eighteen upon whom the tower in Siloam fell; and that they, too, except they repented, should likewise perish. The whole human race, then, is sinful and God *"now commandeth all men every where to repent"* (Acts 17:30). That bears out the clear teaching of Romans 3:9-23; I John 1:8,10; Romans 5:12 and many other Scriptures.

There are those who foolishly believe that the doctrine of John the Baptist was different from that of Jesus because John came preaching repentance. But a penitent heart was always required for saving faith and so repentance is preached here, as in Acts 16:30,31 and II Peter 3:9, etc.

Then the preacher ought never preach love without preaching wrath, ought never preach Heaven without preaching Hell, ought never preach forgiveness without preaching repentance.

VERSES 6—9:

6 He spake also this parable; A certain *man* had a fig tree planted in his vineyard; and he came and sought fruit thereon, and found none.

7 Then said he unto the dresser of his vineyard, Behold, these three years I come seeking fruit on this fig tree, and find none: cut it down; why cumbereth it the ground?

8 And he answering said unto him, Lord, let it alone this year also, till I shall dig about it, and dung *it:*

9 And if it bear fruit, *well:* and if not, *then* after that thou shalt cut it down.

The Barren Fig Tree to Be Cut Down

The lesson here is akin to that in Isaiah 5:1-7 where the planted vineyard "*is the house of Israel.*" The vineyard brought forth wild grapes and brought no good fruit for the owner and so Israel was to be carried away in judgment. It is akin also to the parable of the householder demanding fruit from his vineyard, given in Matthew 21:33-43. That parable is spoken for the chief priests and Pharisees (Matt. 21:45) and it prophesied that the promised kingdom would be taken from the Jews who rejected Christ, and the Gospel given to the Gentiles.

There is surely an individual application intended also. One fig tree in the vineyard did not bear fruit year after year. So many a man hears the Gospel and does not repent. At long last the patience of God is exhausted but the loving Saviour still pleads for sinners to have another chance, then if they do not repent, they will be destroyed.

Jesus did destroy one fig tree which had no fruit, as told in Mark 11:12-14 and in Matthew 21:18-22. The parable of the talents (Matt. 25:14-30) and of the pounds (Luke 19:11-27) teach also that men must give an account for the opportunities and blessings God showers upon them, and that men must use or be punished for failure to use the opportunities and gifts which God freely gives to His servants.

How tender is the Lord toward those who fail Him! That mercy and longsuffering is illustrated in the words of the vine dresser who said to the Master, "*Lord, let it alone this year also, till I shall dig about it, and dung it: And if it bear fruit, well: and if not, then after that thou shalt cut it down.*"

A prominent man kept company with the scoffers and unbelievers and modified his plans and his message to keep their cooperation. Vexed, someone said, "Why does not God slap him down for his compromise?" We replied, "Would you want God to slap you down the first time you did wrong? Would you not rather God's loving patience and mercy would deal with you and call you again and again before bringing judgment?" None of us could long continue unpunished if God were not merciful and longsuffering. He called Jonah a second time to serve Him. He forgave David and blessed him after great sin. After the Apostle Peter had cursed and sworn and denied Jesus and quit the ministry, Jesus personally went looking for him and called him back into His service. Thank God for His mercy, often long extended before He brings judgment on an unfaithful servant.

VERSES 10—17:

10 And he was teaching in one of the synagogues on the sabbath.
11 And, behold, there was a woman which had a spirit of infirmity eighteen years, and was bowed together, and could in no wise lift up *herself*.
12 And when Jesus saw her, he called *her to him*, and said unto her, Woman, thou art loosed from thine infirmity.
13 And he laid *his* hands on her:

and immediately she was made straight, and glorified God.

14 And the ruler of the synagogue answered with indignation, because that Jesus had healed on the sabbath day, and said unto the people, There are six days in which men ought to work: in them therefore come and be healed, and not on the sabbath day.

15 The Lord then answered him, and said, *Thou* hypocrite, doth not each one of you on the sabbath loose his ox or *his* ass from the stall, and lead *him* away to watering?

16 And ought not this woman, being a daughter of Abraham, whom Satan hath bound, lo, these eighteen years, be loosed from this bond on the sabbath day?

17 And when he had said these things, all his adversaries were ashamed: and all the people rejoiced for all the glorious things that were done by him.

Woman Afflicted Eighteen Years Is Healed

How sweet is the story of this woman who was so bowed down that she could not even straighten her back for eighteen years! And the Saviour's healing touch released her from her infirmities. How suggestive that Jesus could cure and did cure every kind of sickness or disease and trouble in mind and body.

Luke 4:18 quoted the prophecy of Isaiah 61:1 that Jesus would heal the mind and the spirit and the body; He would *"preach the gospel to the poor. . . heal the brokenhearted. . . preach deliverance to the captives. . . recovering of sight to the blind. . . set at liberty them that are bruised."* We read in Matthew 9:35 that Jesus went about teaching and preaching *"and healing every sickness and every disease among the people."* And then He gave the apostles power to cast out devils and *"to heal all manner of sickness and all manner of disease"* (Matt. 10:1): the lepers, the blind, the deadly fever of Peter's mother-in-law, the paralytic, the withered hand, the woman with an issue of blood, the deaf—oh, Jesus could heal them all.

More than that, He even raised the dead! And when John the Baptist inquired if He was the Saviour, Jesus sent him word, *"Tell John what things ye have seen and heard; how that the blind see, the lame walk, the lepers are cleansed, the deaf hear, the dead are raised, to the*

poor the gospel is preached" (Luke 7:22). Oh, Jesus,
the Master of all infirmities and diseases! When loaves
and fishes were created for the multitude out of one boy's
lunch; when at His word the storm could be stilled by a
command; He who walked on waters and went through
closed doors — surely He meant for every open-hearted
one to see that He was God in human form. He did not
do the miracles as a sign to prove His deity, yet they did
prove His deity in that they did prove surely that God
was with Him without limit, and if He claimed to be the
Son of God, all He said must be received without question.

And surely here, too, is a picture of how salvation will
eventuate for all of us one time, with all the weakness
and frailties of the body gone; all the curse of sin removed. Perfect in mind and body and soul, we will rise
to be with Jesus and to be like Jesus, for all healing
now is relative and temporary until the resurrection or
rapture.

And we must not think that we are excluded from the
power of Christ. The apostles, too, went forth with the
same power. In Acts 5:16 we read, "*There came also
a multitude out of the cities round about unto Jerusalem, bringing sick folks, and them which were vexed
with unclean spirits: and they were healed every one.*"
And the lame man was healed at the Beautiful gate of
the Temple (Acts 3). The young man who fell from the
third story window and was taken up dead was brought
to life (Acts 26:9-12). Dorcas was raised from the dead,
and Paul was able to heal the father of Publius on the
island of Melita (Malta). Whether you think the ending
of the Gospel of Mark in Mark 16:17,18 ought to have
been included in that Gospel or not, those signs did
follow those who had faith for them and doubtless do
today in the rare cases when God gives faith for them.
And all these joyful healings at the hand of Christ and
at the word of the apostles, and those whom God gra-
ciously heals today, point only to the more perfect full-

ness and health and happiness when our bodies arise like His body and all tears are wiped away.

Great Controversy Arises Over the Sabbath

Jesus healed the poor infirm woman at the synagogue on the Sabbath (vss. 12,13). The ruler of the synagogue was indignant and publicly announced, *"There are six days in which men ought to work: in them therefore come and be healed, and not on the sabbath day."* The issue of the Sabbath will arise again and again in the ministry of Jesus and it soon becomes clear that He deliberately forces the issue. Here He plainly calls the ruler of the synagogue, *"Thou hypocrite."* He would lead an ox or ass to watering and would be properly concerned about the comfort of his beast, yet he did not want relieved and healed this woman, who was bound by Satan eighteen years. No wonder the adversaries of Jesus *"were ashamed,"* but they would not end their opposition to Christ's healing work on the Sabbath nor His treatment of the Sabbath. The question comes up again in Luke 14:1-6 when Jesus heals the man with the dropsy at the house of a chief Pharisee. When the disciples, passing through ripe grain and, being hungry, rubbed some of the grain out to eat on the Sabbath day, the Pharisees objected that they did unlawful labor and blamed Jesus (Matt. 12:1-8). Jesus healed the man born blind at the pool of Siloam and so was accused by the Pharisees (John 9:1-16). At the pool of Bethesda, Jesus healed a man infirm for thirty-eight years, and the Jews objected because *"it was not lawful for him to carry his bed on the Sabbath day"* (John 5:1-10)!

This was one of the great issues over which the Jewish leaders planned to have Jesus killed. John 5:16-18 says:

"And therefore did the Jews persecute Jesus, and sought to slay him, because he had done these things on the

*sabbath day. But Jesus answered them, My Father
worketh hitherto, and I work. Therefore the Jews sought
the more to kill him, because he not only had broken
the sabbath, but said also that God was his Father,
making himself equal with God."*

Why Did Jesus Make the Sabbath a Particular Issue?

At first it seems surprising that the greatest point of
contention between Christ and the Pharisees and Jewish
leaders was that He healed people on the Sabbath and
did not Himself keep the Sabbath day (as John 5:18
says) and particularly did not observe the Pharisees'
interpretation of the Sabbath commandment. There is
surely a very serious reason why Jesus made the Sabbath such an issue. Note carefully.

The Sabbath is the only part of the Ten Commandments which is ceremonial law, not moral law. All the
other commands of the ten are repeated in the New Testament, but the command about the Sabbath is not. The
moral law was in force before the Ten Commandments
were given, but Nehemiah 9:14 tells us that the Sabbath
was made known at Mount Sinai, not before. Neither
Adam, Abel, Noah, Abraham, Isaac, Jacob nor Joseph
ever heard of the Sabbath. God set it apart when He
created the earth, but He did not reveal it until it was
made known in the sixteenth chapter of Exodus to the
children of Israel camped near Sinai and then soon it
was incorporated in the Ten Commandments.

The Sabbath was ceremonial law, as we are told in
Colossians 2:16,17. The Levitical laws about food and
drink and holy days, new moons and sabbath days were
all *"a shadow of things to come,"* we are told.

The Sabbath pictures salvation. It commanded, *"Six
days shalt thou labour, and do all thy work"* (Exod.
20:9). Man's life is pictured by six. A man who did

everything he ought to do all his life, would enter into the heavenly sabbath pictured by the weekly day of rest. This was incorporated in the law because *"the law was our schoolmaster to bring us unto Christ"* (Gal. 3:24).

And since man, so sinful and utterly ruined, did not and could not perfectly keep the moral law of God, He gave another picture of the way to Heaven by grace in the passover supper (Exod. 12:3-16). On the basis of a slain lamb with blood on the door a Jew could enter into a Sabbath the very first day. And that pictures Christ our Passover, so that I enter into heavenly rest at the very beginning of a life for Christ and I can feast on Christ, the Bread of Life, throughout the six days, then the seventh day pictures the heavenly rest.

That blessed truth of the Sabbath is told in Hebrews 4:9,10: *"There remaineth therefore a rest to the people of God. For he that is entered into his rest, he also hath ceased from his own works, as God did from his."* The Christian immediately has rest or Sabbath in his heart when he ceases from his own works to trust in Christ, but there still remains a heavenly rest for the Christian. And Hebrews 4:11 urges us to *labor* (or more literally to *give diligence*) *"to enter into that rest."*

So when the rich young ruler shall come to Jesus and Jesus will name certain commandments and he will claim to have kept so many of them about adultery, murder, stealing, lying, and honoring father and mother — the Sabbath will not be mentioned because that young ruler will be seeking some way to earn salvation by the law, by doing good things (Luke 18:18-24).

It becomes clear that the Pharisees were hypocrites because they missed the entire point of salvation, and, of course, they refused the Saviour, wanting to rely on their own good deeds.

VERSES 18, 19:

18 Then said he, Unto what is the kingdom of God like? and whereunto shall I resemble it?

19 It is like a grain of mustard seed, which a man took, and cast into his garden; and it grew, and waxed a great tree; and the fowls of the air lodged in the branches of it.

The Parable of the Mustard Seed

This parable is also given in Matthew 13:31,32, and in Mark 4:30-32. In Matthew Jesus uses the term *"kingdom of heaven."* Here He says *"the kingdom of God,"* meaning the same thing, that is, this parable tells, we think, of the progress of the kingdom of professed Christendom, that kingdom which will eventually be God's perfect heavenly kingdom.

Surely the picture here is that Christian activity starts out as a business of sowing the blessed seed of the Gospel and getting people saved, but degenerates into building institutions and denominations.

That going forth to preach the Gospel to every creature is pictured in the parable of the sower in Luke 8:4-15. And taking the Gospel to lost sinners is called sowing seed also, in Psalm 126:5,6: *"They that sow in tears shall reap in joy. He that goeth forth and weepeth, bearing precious seed, shall doubtless come again with rejoicing, bringing his sheaves with him."* Isaiah, chapter 32, starts out with a wonderful prophecy about Christ the King who shall come to reign, the Man who will be *"a hiding place from the wind, a covert from the tempest,"* etc., and then verse 20 closes the chapter saying, *"Blessed are ye that sow beside all waters, that send forth thither the feet of the ox and the ass."* Surely the meaning is, Blessed are those who go to tell the Good News that Christ died for sinners and wants to forgive and save them.

And Isaiah 52:7, quoted in Romans 10:15, says, *"How beautiful are the feet of them that preach the gospel of peace, and bring glad tidings of good things!"*

However, as most of the parables of the kingdom teach, there is a tendency to drift into false doctrine and to lose the message and the methods and zeal of New Testament Christianity. We find tares sown among the wheat. We find bad fish in the net along with the good. We find foolish virgins without oil along with the wise virgins who have the oil of salvation, waiting for the Bridegroom to come. In the messages to the seven churches of Asia we find God's Christians growing lukewarm and losing their first love and taking up with false teachers. So here in the parable of the mustard seed is a prophecy: the disciples who started out under the command to preach the Gospel in all the world to every creature will have a tendency to grow trees instead of planting gospel seed!

In the dream of Nebuchadnezzar in Daniel 4, a great tree pictured his realm, his organization and kingship and institution of government. So where there were once simply local congregations of Christians preaching the Gospel everywhere, now there have grown up denominational organizations, institutions all occupied with maintaining themselves instead of keeping in mind the primary business of preaching the Gospel. In such an organization, false teachers crowd in; they want the position; with feigned words they make merchandise of common people; they are denominational secretaries and bishops and cardinals and popes among those *"fowls of the air lodged in the branches"* of the tree.

This picture is carried on in Revelation 18, in that great superchurch which is to be the official state church of the coming Antichrist. Revelation 18:2 says, *"And he cried mightily with a strong voice, saying, Babylon the great is fallen, is fallen, and is become the habitation of devils, and the hold of every foul spirit, and a cage of*

every unclean and hateful bird." So the spiritual Babylon, the world church which is coming in the tribulation
time, will be the *"habitation of devils, the hold of every
foul spirit, and a cage of every unclean and hateful
bird."* Let us beware of the fateful tendency to turn to
organization and institutions instead of to the one great
central work of New Testament Christianity — spreading
the gospel message everywhere.

VERSES 20, 21:

20 And again he said, Whereunto shall I liken the kingdom of God? 21 It is like leaven, which a woman took and hid in three measures of meal, till the whole was leavened.

The Parable of the Leaven

Many commentators think that this parable pictures
the slow and natural growth of the kingdom of Heaven,
the spread of the Gospel to the whole world so that
eventually all would be converted. That is far from the
truth. It is quite clear from many Scriptures that the
whole world will not be converted. And leaven has a
bad meaning, not a good meaning. Lot fed the angels
unleavened bread (Gen. 19:3). In the feast of unleavened
bread following the Passover feast, Jews were not allowed
to eat any leaven, not even to have it in their houses
(Exod. 12:15-20). The offering to consecrate the priest
must have unleavened bread (Exod. 29:2). The food
offering must be with unleavened cakes or in a pan of
"fine flour unleavened" (Lev. 2:4,5). And Israel was
plainly commanded, *"Ye shall burn no leaven, nor any
honey, in any offering of the Lord made by fire"* (Lev.
2:11). The peace offering was to be offered with *"unleavened cakes"* (Lev. 7:12).

In the New Testament the meaning is equally clear. Jesus said, "*Beware of the leaven of the Pharisees and of the Sadducees*" (Matt. 16:6), and He referred to "*the doctrine of the Pharisees and of the Sadducees*" (vs. 12). In Mark 8:15 His warning is, "*Beware of the leaven of the Pharisees and. . . of Herod.*" In commanding the church at Corinth to refuse fellowship to the man living in sin, Paul said, "*Know ye not that a little leaven leaveneth the whole lump? Purge out therefore the old leaven, that ye may be a new lump, as ye are unleavened. For even Christ our passover is sacrificed for us: Therefore let us keep the feast, not with old leaven, neither with the leaven of malice and wickedness; but with the unleavened bread of sincerity and truth*" (I Cor. 5:6-8). Leaven means evil in life and doctrine.

So here is a solemn warning that we should beware of a constant tendency in the churches for false doctrine and worldliness to come in. It is the natural spread and decay of evil among the churches which is pictured here and it goes with all the Scripture warnings to beware of false prophets and to beware of the "*care of the world, and the deceitfulness of riches,*" and other things which "*choke the word*" and make Christians unfruitful (Matt. 13:22).

VERSES 22—30:

22 And he went through the cities and villages, teaching, and journeying toward Jerusalem.

23 Then said one unto him, Lord, are there few that be saved? And he said unto them,

24 Strive to enter in at the strait gate: for many, I say unto you, will seek to enter in, and shall not be able.

25 When once the master of the house is risen up, and hath shut to the door, and ye begin to stand without, and to knock at the door, saying, Lord, Lord, open unto us; and he shall answer and say unto you, I know you not whence ye are:

26 Then shall ye begin to say, We have eaten and drunk in thy presence, and thou hast taught in our streets.

27 But he shall say, I tell you, I know you not whence ye are; de-

part from me, all ye workers of iniquity.

28 There shall be weeping and gnashing of teeth, when ye shall see Abraham, and Isaac, and Jacob, and all the prophets, in the kingdom of God, and you *yourselves* thrust out.

29 And they shall come from the east, and *from* the west, and from the north, and *from* the south, and shall sit down in the kingdom of God.

30 And, behold, there are last which shall be first, and there are first which shall be last.

Will Many or Few Be Saved?

Jesus is journeying toward Jerusalem and teaching and preaching in many villages en route. So in Luke 17:11 again we read, "*And it came to pass, as he went to Jerusalem, that he passed through the midst of Samaria and Galilee.*" In chapter 19 He will come to Jericho and then on up to Jerusalem for the last time.

Verse 23 gives a vital question that has to do with the parables of the mustard seed and the leaven. Did Jesus mean to say that relatively only a few would be saved and that the mass of people would reject Him and go to Hell? Did He mean that the leaven would go into the gospel message and pervert it? and into the churches, making them into self-serving, worldly institutions instead of simply having everybody press out to win souls?

Here Jesus does not strictly say that only a few will be saved, but He does say that "many" would not enter into the kingdom, would not come through the door of salvation. In verse 24 the way to Heaven is a strait gate, that is, a narrow gate. Here is the same teaching of Matthew 7:13,14: "*Enter ye in at the strait gate: for wide is the gate, and broad is the way, that leadeth to destruction, and many there be which go in thereat: Because strait is the gate, and narrow is the way, which leadeth unto life, and few there be that find it.*" It is a broad way that leads to Hell, a narrow way that leads to Heaven. And Christ Himself is the only door (John 14:6). Jesus said, "*I am the door of the sheep*" (John 10:7).

And here in verse 25 but in different words is the same

teaching as Jesus gave in Matthew 7:21-23. Many people will claim that they prophesied in Jesus' name, cast out devils and did wonderful works, but He will profess unto them, "*I never knew you: depart from me, ye that work iniquity.*" So here Jesus tells how people will remind Him that He taught in their streets and they ate and drank at the same table with Him, but they are not saved.

How many people are in the churches or live moral lives or have some claim to religion or morality or lodge membership or rites of the church, but who have never personally repented and trusted Christ and so have never been born again! In answering the question, "*Are there few that be saved?*" Jesus says that many, many who claim to be saved or who think they are saved because of good works or church membership or morality, are not saved.

Verses 28 to 30 have special reference to the religious leaders among the Jews — chief priests and Pharisees. They would be the logical heirs of Abraham, Isaac and Jacob, should be the spiritual heirs of the prophets, but they will be thrust out (vs. 28), and people will come into the kingdom from the east and west and north and south. But many of the Jews who were first to hear the Gospel will be left out. This is the same teaching as Romans, chapter 11. Some of the branches of the tree of the true Israel are broken off; many Jews do not come to Abraham's God and Saviour and are not saved and believing Gentiles are grafted into the tree and become spiritual seed of Abraham. Gentiles, wild olive branches, are grafted in, for "*blindness in part is happened to Israel, until the fulness of the Gentiles be come in*" (Rom. 11:25). We read in Romans 4:13, "*For the promise, that he should be the heir of the world, was not to Abraham, or to his seed, through the law, but through the righteousness of faith.*" And Romans 2:28,29 tells us, "*For he is not a Jew, which is one outwardly; neither is that circumcision, which is outward in the flesh: But he is a Jew, which is one inwardly; and circumcision is that of the heart, in the spirit, and not in the letter; whose praise is not of men, but of God."*

So Jesus tells us that *"there are last which shall be first, and there are first which shall be last."* The Gospel came *"to the Jew first"* but now is accepted by more Gentiles than Jews. And the very Pharisees and chief priests who ought to have followed in the steps of believing Abraham did not and, no doubt, were cast out.

VERSES 31—33:

31 The same day there came certain of the Pharisees, saying unto him, Get thee out, and depart hence: for Herod will kill thee.
32 And he said unto them, Go ye, and tell that fox, Behold, I cast out devils, and I do cures to day and to morrow, and the third *day* I shall be perfected.
33 Nevertheless I must walk to day, and to morrow, and the *day* following: for it cannot be that a prophet perish out of Jerusalem.

Jesus' Atoning Work to Be Finished on the Cross

We do not suppose that the Pharisees were anxious to protect Jesus. Note that He was still in Galilee, in Herod's territory, not in Pilate's territory, Judaea.

I am sure that Jesus did not expect the Pharisees to approach Herod. Whatever sharpness was in His words was for these same wicked Pharisees, not for King Herod. And it is to them that He is saying that He will cast out devils for the immediate future, before He is to perish. I do not take the days to mean literal days but an indefinite short time. Eventually, *"and the third day,"* He would be perfected. We do not think the third day here refers to His resurrection and to the finished atonement.

Does He mean the same as in John 19:30 when on the cross He cried out, "*It is finished*"? Later in the high priestly prayer He will say to the Father, "*I have finished the work which thou gavest me to do*" (John 17:4). There remained only His crucifixion, I suppose, after He finished His work. And Hebrews 2:10 tells us that He was made "*perfect through suffering.*" Perhaps a little clearer would be that He was made complete in His life and atoning death through the sufferings and the cross. Yet He knew that His death would be in Jerusalem. No doubt He knew it would be at the time the Passover lambs were being slain, in the fulfillment of prophecy.

VERSES 34, 35:

34 O Jerusalem, Jerusalem, which killest the prophets, and stonest them that are sent unto thee; how often would I have gathered thy children together, as a hen *doth gather* her brood under *her* wings, and ye would not!

35 Behold, your house is left unto you desolate: and verily I say unto you, Ye shall not see me, until *the time* come when ye shall say, Blessed *is* he that cometh in the name of the Lord.

Jesus' Lament Over Jerusalem

Compare this with Matthew 23:37-39. There Jesus will lament over Jerusalem when He is in the city and the next verse, in chapter 24, tells us "*and Jesus went out, and departed from the temple. . . .*" Here Jesus is in Galilee but His heart aches for beloved Jerusalem, where He knows He will die, so He speaks as if to Jerusalem, with the same lament.

The companion passage to that in Matthew 23 is, we think, Luke 19:41-44, where Jesus beheld the city and wept over it. Doubtless neither case gives all the words which Jesus spoke at that time.

Verse 34 shows clearly that Christ wants people saved who will not be saved. He is "*not willing that any should*

perish, but that all should come to repentance" (II Pet.
3:9). *"He is the propitiation for our sins: and not for
our's only, but also for the sins of the whole world"*
(I John 2:2). Romans 5:20 says, *"Where sin abounded,
grace did much more abound."* The infinite, unlimited
grace of God provided for salvation for all men, so He
is, potentially, *"the Saviour of the world"* but especially
and actually of them that believe.

Verse 35 speaks of the Temple, left desolate of the
Presence of God. When Jesus died on the cross, the veil
of the Temple was torn from top to bottom (Matt. 27:
51). Whether just then, while Jesus was on the cross,
or before, we understand that the Shekinah Glory left the
Temple and it is no longer in that particular sense the
house of God. *"Ye shall not see me, until the time
come when ye shall say, Blessed is he that cometh in the
name of the Lord,"* may refer to the cries at His triumphal entry (Luke 19:37-40) as foretold in Zechariah
9:9. But we may be sure it refers not only to those
particular Jews but to other Jews who will inhabit Jerusalem at the blessed time when He returns to reign and
set up His kingdom on David's throne, as foretold in
Zechariah 14:1-9.

LUKE 14

VERSES 1 — 6:

AND it came to pass, as he went into the house of one of the chief Pharisees to eat bread on the sabbath day, that they watched him.

2 And, behold, there was a certain man before him which had the dropsy.

3 And Jesus answering spake unto the lawyers and Pharisees, saying, Is it lawful to heal on the sabbath day?

4 And they held their peace. And he took *him*, and ʳhealed him, and let him go;

5 And answered them, saying, Which of you shall have an ass or an ox fallen into a pit, and will not straightway pull him out on the sabbath day?

6 And they could not answer him again to these things.

Another Healing on the Sabbath

Jesus was a guest in the house of one of the chief Pharisees on this sabbath day and many other guests were there, principal lawyers (authorities on the Mosaic Law) and Pharisees. It seems that Jesus took special interest in healing on the Sabbath day. Perhaps He healed many others on other days but the Sabbath-day healings raised great controversy with the Pharisees. And Jesus presses the point here as He had in Luke 13:10-17. He uses a similar argument: before He said they would lead the ox or ass to watering on a Sabbath day, here He says if an ox or an ass had fallen into a pit, would he not pull him out on the Sabbath day? Sadly they did not have the compassion Jesus had for people in heartbreak and trouble and sickness.

There was no honest answer as to why on the Sabbath day they would prefer the comfort of a beast to that of a man. So in Luke 13:17 the adversaries were ashamed and here they could not answer. Jesus surely is emphasizing here what He said in Luke 6:5, "*The Son of man is Lord also of the sabbath.*" See the discussion on the Sabbath in Luke 13:10-17.

VERSES 7—11:

7 And he put forth a parable to those which were bidden, when he marked how they chose out the chief rooms; saying unto them,

8 When thou art bidden of any *man* to a wedding, sit not down in the highest room; lest a more honourable man than thou be bidden of him;

9 And he that bade thee and him come and say to thee, Give this man place; and thou begin with shame to take the lowest room.

10 But when thou art bidden, go and sit down in the lowest room; that when he that bade thee cometh, he may say unto thee, Friend, go up higher: then shalt thou have worship in the presence of them that sit at meat with thee.

11 For whosoever exalteth himself shall be abased; and he that humbleth himself shall be exalted.

The Guests Seeking a Place of Honor

A wedding would be a rather formal assembly, and at the feast would be relatives and prominent friends. Those closest to the family, best loved and most to be honored, would sit near the head of the table. It is only natural that all should covet that honor. Selfishness is the very heart of sin and self-seeking is a most prominent part of the carnal, human nature. It is not natural for men to love their neighbors as themselves, as Jesus commanded in summing up the law (Luke 10:27); to do unto others as ye would that they should do unto you (Matt. 7:12; Luke 6:31), is a very difficult thing. Within proper bounds, it is good to seek to succeed, to do much good, to make progress, to earn promotion. But it is not good for people to seek honors for themselves which they have not earned.

Christians have trouble about that. Paul commended Timothy to the Philippians, "*For I have no man like-minded, who will naturally care for your state. For all seek their own, not the things which are Jesus Christ's*"

(Phil. 2:20,21). There are many church officials and preachers who, like Diotrephes, "*loveth to have the pre-eminence*" (III John 9). And even James and John had their mother intercede with Jesus, seeking to have for them the first place, on the right hand and the left, in Christ's kingdom!

How much better to depend on God for honor and for promotion, than to seek them for one's self.

How often we are warned in the Scriptures: "*Pride goeth before destruction, and an haughty spirit before a fall*" (Prov. 16:18); and "*before honour is humility*" (Prov. 15:33); "*Every one that is proud in heart is an abomination to the Lord*" (Prov. 16:5); "*God resisteth the proud, but giveth grace unto the humble*" (Jas. 4:6); and "*Humble yourselves in the sight of the Lord, and he shall lift you up*" (Jas. 4:10).

At a time of crisis, a Christian leader of great prestige and nationwide influence threatened that one would get no recognition or wide usefulness without his approval. God led this poor Christian to answer him with the Scripture of Psalm 75:6 and 7, "*For promotion cometh neither from the east, nor from the west, nor from the south. But God is the judge: he putteth down one, and setteth up another.*" The influence and slanders of that man who wanted to control others failed and God proved faithful.

We are exhorted in I Peter 5:6, "*Humble yourselves therefore under the mighty hand of God, that he may exalt you in due time.*" Psalm 37 is rich comfort for all who rely on God to care for the prosperity and honor of all who love and trust Him.

VERSES 12—15:

12 Then said he also to him that bade him, When thou makest a din-ner or a supper, call not thy friends, nor thy brethren, neither thy kins-

men, nor *thy* rich neighbours; lest they also bid thee again, and a recompence be made thee.

13 But when thou makest a feast, call the poor, the maimed, the lame, the blind:

14 And thou shalt be blessed; for they cannot recompense thee: for thou shalt be recompensed at the resurrection of the just.

15 And when one of them that sat at meat with him heard these things, he said unto him, Blessed *is* he that shall eat bread in the kingdom of God.

How to Have a Banquet in Heaven

We think Jesus does not here mean we should never entertain in our homes our loved ones, our prosperous neighbors. Rather, He is saying that such normal fellowship has its own reward here and now. We invite them, they invite us. But there is no reward in Heaven for what we do expecting a reward here. We give Christmas presents to those who send us like gifts, and greetings to those who send us greetings. We remember the anniversaries of people who remember ours. Those who are good friends here have good friends here.

But we are taught here that the greater blessing comes when we do good to those who cannot repay. Even when we make a dinner for the poor, the maimed, the lame, the blind, beggars and bums and unfortunate, God will see that we are repaid by feasting in Heaven! There is no special virtue in loving those who love us, but Jesus said,

"*Love your enemies, bless them that curse you, do good to them that hate you, and pray for them which despitefully use you, and persecute you; That ye may be the children of your Father which is in heaven: for he maketh his sun to rise on the evil and on the good, and sendeth rain on the just and on the unjust. For if ye love them which love you, what reward have ye? do not even the publicans the same? And if ye salute your brethren only, what do ye more than others? do not even the publicans so? Be ye therefore perfect, even as your Father which is in heaven is perfect.*"— Matt. 5: 44-48.

Then there will be a reward in Heaven and we are promised that "*He that hath pity upon the poor lendeth unto the Lord; and that which he hath given will he pay him again*" (Prov. 19:17). When we "*lend, hoping for nothing again*" we are promised, "*your reward shall be great*" (Luke 6:35). So we are to do good to those who hate us and bless those who curse us, trusting in a heavenly reward.

Feasting in Heaven

Yes, as the man in verse 15 said, "*Blessed is he that shall eat bread in the kingdom of God.*" He understood Jesus to mean there would be literal feasting in Heaven. And surely we will feast there! Remember, in Heaven we will have literal, physical bodies that eat and drink. Jesus ate fish and honeycomb before the disciples in His resurrection body (Luke 24:42,43). Jesus will drink grape juice with the disciples "*in my Father's kingdom*" (Matt. 26:29).

In the millennial reign of Christ, every man will have his own vine and fig tree (Micah 4:4); will he not eat grapes and figs? The mountains of Israel will yield their fruit to converted Israel (Ezek. 36:8). The Dead Sea shall be healed of its excess salt and will furnish an abundance of fish for the people (Ezek. 47:9). And in the heavenly Jerusalem, "*in the midst of the street of it, and on either side of the river, was there the tree of life, which bare twelve manner of fruits, and yielded her fruit every month: and the leaves of the tree were for the healing of the nations*" (Rev. 22:2). Yes, we will eat and drink in Heaven.

Some people have supposed that we will not have real bodies of flesh and blood in the resurrection but these misinterpret Scriptures. First Corinthians 15:50 says that "*flesh and blood cannot inherit the kingdom of God; neither doth corruption inherit incorruption.*" But that simply means that people do not inherit Heaven by natural human descent. That is another way of saying that one must be born again. So they think these bodies will have no blood, but the same Scripture then would say that they would have no flesh if they have no blood! And that is wrong. Commentators say that the blood of Jesus was poured out at Calvary. So it was, but His life was poured out also, and His life was restored as His flesh was restored. They could feel the flesh and bones of His resurrected body (Luke 24:39). That did not mean that the body did not have blood which they could not feel. There are those who think that the body of Jesus was not now necessarily physical after His resurrection because, they say, He could come into the room where the doors were shut (John 20:19). But that does not forbid a real body. Couldn't the Lord Jesus, before His crucifixion, walk on water? or fade out of their hands when the Galileans would cast Him headlong down the hill? (Luke 4:29,30).

Adam and Eve were created perfectly the first time. Before they sinned they were perfectly fitted to live forever, to have perfect fellowship with God. If this earth is to be restored like the Garden of Eden, why should not our resurrection bodies be restored like the perfect bodies of Adam and Eve? Yes, we will eat and drink in Heaven!

VERSES 16—24:

16 Then said he unto him, A certain man made a great supper, and bade many:

17 And sent his servant at supper time to say to them that were bidden, Come; for all things are now ready.

18 And they all with one consent began to make excuse. The first said unto him, I have bought a

piece of ground, and I must needs go and see it: I pray thee have me excused.

19 And another said, I have bought five yoke of oxen, and I go to prove them: I pray thee have me excused.

20 And another said, I have married a wife, and therefore I cannot come.

21 So that servant came, and shewed his lord these things. Then the master of the house being angry said to his servant, Go out quickly into the streets and lanes of the city, and bring in hither the poor, and the maimed, and the halt, and the blind.

22 And the servant said, Lord, it is done as thou hast commanded, and yet there is room.

23 And the lord said unto the servant, Go out into the highways and hedges, and compel *them* to come in, that my house may be filled.

24 For I say unto you, That none of those men which were bidden shall taste of my supper.

The Parable of the Great Supper

In Matthew 22:1-14 is a similar parable, but since the emphasis in Matthew is of Jesus as the coming King of the Jews, He gave the parable in that case of a king who made a marriage supper for his son. The parables are similar. Here Jesus uses the occasion of the supper, where He is a guest, to stress that the great purpose of Christ's coming into the world was to save sinners (I Tim. 1:15), and the one main duty of His servants is to go invite people to the supper.

Note that the only servant mentioned here is the one going out to invite people to the great supper. He is to invite those who have been invited before. He is to invite "*the poor, and the maimed, and the halt, and the blind.*" He is to go to every house in town, then out in the highways and hedges. Oh, the heavenly supper shall be crowded with guests. The servant is to go with such urgency, such persuasion, such love, such persistence; he is to "*compel them to come in,*" Jesus said, "*that my house may be filled.*"

We are reminded that this way of personal soul winning — person to person, house to house — is a pattern to be followed by New Testament Christians. And so in Jerusalem we read, "*And daily in the temple, and in every house, they ceased not to teach and preach Jesus*

Christ" (Acts 5:42). And Paul reminded the elders at Ephesus that in his three years there, he had cleared his soul of guilt for any sinner who went to Hell from Ephesus. He said, *"I. . . have taught you publickly, and from house to house"* (Acts 20:20). He said, *"Therefore watch, and remember, that by the space of three years I ceased not to warn every one night and day with tears"* (Acts 20:31).

It is clearly implied in this parable, as in the parable of the lost sheep and the lost coin, that there is no limited atonement, that the Lord is *"not willing that any should perish, but that all should come to repentance"* (II Pet. 3:9). Also it is indicated that we should go again and again to those who have already been invited.

The Insincere Excuses of Those Who Reject Christ

How foolish are the excuses Jesus lists here! A man must go at suppertime to see land he has already bought. Did he not see it before he bought it? Surely he had. And, would it not be there tomorrow? And is the eveningtime, suppertime, the best time to see property? Obviously the excuse is insincere.

So it is with the man who had five yoke of oxen and he will hitch them up as night draws on, all ten of them, to prove them! And the man who had married a wife would ordinarily want to take her out to celebrate and would want friends to see his beautiful bride. The excuses are obviously insincere, as Jesus meant them to appear, because the excuses people make for not turning to Christ and trusting Him are always insincere. They are excuses, not reasons. He told us in John 3:19-21 the real reason people do not come to Christ:

"And this is the condemnation, that light is come into the world, and men loved darkness rather than light,

because their deeds were evil. For every one that doeth evil hateth the light, neither cometh to the light, lest his deeds should be reproved. But he that doeth truth cometh to the light, that his deeds may be made manifest, that they are wrought in God."

So we should not necessarily set out to answer all the excuses men would offer for living in sin and rejecting Christict. They should be boldly told that their excuses are insincere and ineffective.

Note the solemn warning in verse 24: *"For I say unto you, That none of those men which were bidden shall taste of my supper."* The wickedness of those who reject Christ and His sweet invitation to salvation is shown in the companion parable, Matthew 22:5-7. These verses tell us, *"But they made light of it, and went their ways, one to his farm, another to his merchandise: And the remnant took his servants, and entreated them spitefully, and slew them. But when the king heard thereof, he was wroth: and he sent forth his armies, and destroyed those murderers, and burned up their city."*

So there is a moral wickedness in rejecting Christ and the insincere excuses come from wicked hearts.

* * *

VERSES 25, 26:

25 And there went great multitudes with him: and he turned, and said unto them,
26 If any *man* come to me, and hate not his father, and mother, and wife, and children, and brethren, and sisters, yea, and his own life also, he cannot be my disciple.

All Human Ties Should Be Secondary

The rest of this chapter, verses 25 to 35, is about the cost of discipleship. These are not telling the plan of salvation: that is simple and easy. One who honestly

turns his heart from sin and trusts Jesus Christ is saved
at once, without any merit or without any good works.
These Scriptures tell how the born-again Christian may
become a disciple, that is, an honest follower and helper
for Christ. So the word "disciples" is used in verses
25, 27, and 33.

And here is a rather shocking statement: One is to
hate father, mother, wife, children, brethren, sisters, and
his own life also, in order to become a disciple!

But hyperbole is a legitimate form of expression. Of
course the meaning is that love for Christ and loyalty to
Him should so far exceed all other loves and loyalties
that they can hardly be expressed in the same terms.   If
you say that you love your father and mother and love
God, that puts God and parents in about the same relationship, and that is not what Jesus requires. So here,
to hate father and mother and wife and children and
brothers and your own life also does not mean malice.
It does not mean one should dishonor his parents.   This
Scripture does not here contradict the plain statement of
Ephesians 5:25, that a husband is to love his wife as
Christ loved the church and gave Himself for it. As a
car at sixty miles an hour passes a car at twenty miles
an hour "as if it were standing still," so the love for
Christ and loyalty for Christ so should supersede all
other relationships of life as to not even be labeled with
the same terms. It is true this is a figurative use of the
term "hate," but it is drastic and is intended to be to
make a shocking and drastic impression. If people are
to have the love and loyalty that will let them burn at
the stake for Christ or be torn by wild beasts, or be
tortured on the rack, or eaten by cannibals—as many
have been—then they must have a drastic love and
loyalty for Christ not measurable by human comparisons.

A man cannot love his wife too much since he is commanded to love her "*as Christ also loved the church,*"
but a man might make his wife an idol, coming between

him and God, and that would be a sin. And to put the welfare or the pleasure of any loved ones or one's own welfare and pleasure before pleasing Christ would be unworthy of a disciple.

In Matthew 19:27-30 this same subject is brought up by the Apostle Peter. He asked the Saviour, *"Behold, we have forsaken all, and followed thee; what shall we have therefore?"* They will reign with Christ when He returns to the earth in glory, Jesus told him. *"And every one that hath forsaken houses, or brethren, or sisters, or father, or mother, or wife, or children, or lands, for my name's sake, shall receive an hundredfold, and shall inherit everlasting life"* (Matt. 19:29).

The relationship of a husband and wife is only for time, not for eternity, for in Heaven *"they neither marry, nor are given in marriage; but are as the angels which are in heaven"* (Mark 12:25; Matt. 22:30), Jesus said. And I suppose that while in Heaven we will love our brothers and sisters, those who loved and served the Lord Jesus best here will be dearest to us there, too. So a man's wife or his circumstances or his acquaintance is limited and temporary, but the love and loyalty to Christ are eternal things and important far above any human ties.

VERSE 27:

27 And whosoever doth not bear his cross, and come after me, can- not be my disciple.

Self Crucifixion: the Price of Discipleship

Jesus more than once admonished His disciples to *"take up the cross."* In Matthew 16, verses 21 to 27, we find that in detail Jesus told His disciples that He

must go up to Jerusalem and suffer many things of the
scribes and elders and be killed. Then He said, *"If any
man will come after me, let him deny himself, and take
up his cross, and follow me."* And then He gave the
famous promise that one who saves his life shall lose it,
that whoever will lose his life for Christ will thus save it,
that is, its fruit and blessing and eternal rewards. And
one who saves his life now by failing to suffer for Jesus,
will lose it. And what profit *"if he shall gain the whole
world, and lose his own soul?"* that is, his own life in
the sense of its usefulness and impact and its rewards in
Heaven. And then Jesus promised that when they return
in glory, his reward will be with him for every saved
man *"according to his works."*

With slight modification, this same passage is given in
Mark 8:34-38, with the added word that *"whosoever
therefore shall be ashamed of me and of my words in
this adulterous and sinful generation; of him also shall
the Son of man be ashamed, when he cometh in the glory
of his Father with the holy angels."* The love and loyalty which Jesus requires is an unpopular attitude and
many saved people will shrink from paying this price of
discipleship.

In Luke 9:22-26 this call of Jesus to discipleship is
recorded again, and there it is not only that one should
take up his cross but *"take up his cross daily,"* Jesus
said. So, just as one is to come daily to God for forgiveness and cleansing and come for daily bread and
deliverance from evil, so one should daily make his un-
conditional surrender to the will of God, daily deny himself and to walk the crucifixion road!

Consecration is part of the same teaching connected
with baptism. Those who are saved should count themselves dead to sin and *"so many of us as were baptized
into Jesus Christ were baptized into his death"* (Rom.
6:3), that is, Christ died in our place and so we count
ourselves dead with Christ. We are planted in the like-

ness of His death and raised in the likeness of His resurrection, and so we are to "*walk in newness of life*" (Rom. 6:3-6). We count the old man buried and the new man is to live the Christ-life!

And the inspired apostle could write, "*I am crucified with Christ: nevertheless I live; yet not I, but Christ liveth in me: and the life which I now live in the flesh I live by the faith of the Son of God, who loved me, and gave himself for me*" (Gal. 2:20).

How often we find that though we made holy vows and a total surrender of our lives and our wills and our families and all we have to Christ, we thought, yet we find that old self climbs down from the cross and takes possession again and we have a tendency to live for self instead of for God. So the crucifixion must be a daily committal if we are to be good servants, disciples of Christ.

When Paul went to Corinth, he "*determined not to know any thing among you, save Jesus Christ, and him crucified*" (I Cor. 2:2). I am sure he meant to preach Christ and Him crucified, but, oh, he surely must have meant also that he must remember that Christ was crucified for us and he must count himself crucified with Christ day by day.

The Crucifixion Road is full of sorrows;
    The jeering voices added to the pain;
But take thy cross, O child of God, and follow,
    And shun not the reproach in Jesus' name.

Reproach there is defending, bold, the Bible.
    Reproach, with zeal and tears to seek the lost,
And shame to preach of sin and Hell and judgment;
    Reproach to seek God's pow'r at any cost.

I'm called unloving if I turn in sorrow
    From "learned" churchmen who reject the Word.
I'm mocked and shunned because I call not "brother"

Those famed false friends of Christ who mock His blood.

The servant is not better than His master;
   The world that so hates Him should hate me too!
Outside the gate is now the place for Christians.
   Not crowns, but crosses fit disciples true.

I'll suffer, then, with all the saints and prophets.
   I'll walk the Calv'ry road, smile at the pain.
Then, when He reigns, O glory! What a prospect!
   His own who suffer with Him, too, shall reign.

"Take up thy cross," said Jesus, and I will!
   Although discipleship be rugged still.
     But if He give me grace,
     I'll run this patient race,
Be crucified with Jesus as He wills.

Let us remember that Jesus is still *"despised and rejected of men; a man of sorrows, and acquainted with grief"* (Isa. 53:3). It is time now for crosses. After the resurrection, and when Christ comes back to reign on the earth, it will be time for crowns and we who suffer for Him, we who are faithful to Him, may reign with Him. But now *"let us go forth therefore unto him without the camp, bearing his reproach. For here we have no continuing city, but we seek one to come"* (Heb. 13:13,14).

VERSES 28—33:

28 For which of you, intending to build a tower, sitteth not down first, and counteth the cost, whether he have *sufficient* to finish *it?*
29 Lest haply, after he hath laid the foundation, and is not able to finish *it*, all that behold *it* begin to mock him,
30 Saying, This man began to build, and was not able to finish.

31 Or what king, going to make war against another king, sitteth not down first, and consulteth whether he be able with ten thousand to meet him that cometh against him with twenty thousand?
32 Or else, while the other is yet a great way off, he sendeth an ambassage, and desireth conditions of peace.

33 So likewise, whosoever he be of you that forsaketh not all that | he hath, he cannot be my disciple.

Workers for Jesus Short in Money and Support

The Christian should count the cost if he is going to be a disciple of Jesus. Again, Christ is not talking about what it costs to be saved. Salvation is free. One who turns penitently to trust in Christ has everlasting life immediately, and without any merit or labor to earn it. But one who will be a good disciple of Jesus must seriously count the cost.

These two parables show a truth. The Christian worker may seek to build a tower but often will not have the funds to build it, or to grow a church, or to have a revival, or to win an infidel, or support a mission program! Christian, you who are going to preach the Gospel, you who would win souls, can you make a drunkard sober? make a harlot pure? make an infidel into a believing saint? Human resources are never enough for spiritual tasks. That means that one must have it settled ahead of time that he must have and can have and will have the power of God, supernatural intervention to provide his needs and provide the power for service and to bring results that must be had!

No wonder many preachers quit the ministry, some have nervous breakdowns or commit suicide. They try to build a tower and have not money to finish it. They go to meet a king coming against them with 20,000 when they have only half as many helpers. This business of discipleship takes supernatural power, and no one need set out to be used of God unless he be willing to wait on God, seek His face, and have supernatural power. One must openly confess that human talent and human means are not enough for the holy business of winning souls and proclaiming abroad the Gospel with power.

Must good Christians always be in the minority? It seems so! Must the best Christians be misunderstood, often persecuted, misrepresented? Yes, Jesus said, "*If the world hate you, ye know that it hated me before it hated you.... The servant is not greater than his lord*" (John 15:18,20).

We can see that we are not only to forsake or to give up what other men hold dear, but we must give up reliance on our own wisdom and human resources. And to have the power of God, there needs to be a daily forsaking of our own things.

VERSES 34, 35:

34 Salt *is* good: but if the salt have lost his savour, wherewith shall it be seasoned?
35 It is neither fit for the land, nor yet for the dunghill; *but* men cast it out. He that hath ears to hear, let him hear.

Christians Should Be Saving Salt

This is a repetition of the figure of speech used in the Sermon on the Mount given in Matthew 5:13-16 and in Mark 4:21-23; and in Luke 8:16-18. In Matthew the Christian is mentioned as saving salt and the light of the world. In Mark 2 and Luke 8, only the figure of the lighted candle is used. In Mark 9:49 and 50 Christians are commanded to "*have salt in yourselves.*" Salt is a saving instrument. In some sense we are the light of the world (Matt. 5:14), yet Jesus is the Light of the world (John 8:12; John 9:5). We have Christ in us and join with Jesus in being the light of the world. Even so, we join with Him in being the saving salt.

If Lot had won ten souls, God would have spared Sodom. Moses could intercede for Israel and save the nation from destruction. Oh, Christian, do not lose your salt, your saving influence, your separated position, your protest against sin. Do not fail to have the saving influence in proclaiming the Gospel and winning souls.

LUKE 15

THEN drew near unto him all the publicans and sinners for to hear him.

2 And the Pharisees and scribes murmured, saying, This man receiveth sinners, and eateth with them.

The Lord Jesus Receives Sinners

What a charge is brought against Jesus! Not that He sins, not that He wrongs anyone, not that He violates the Scriptures, but He loves and forgives and saves sinners and takes them into intimate, sweet fellowship with Himself and the Heavenly Father!

Be sure you understand it is penitent sinners whom Jesus receives. He did not receive the most accepted religious leaders of His time who remained impenitent. To Nicodemus, *"a ruler of the Jews,"* Jesus insisted: *"Ye must be born again"* (John 3:7). He warned the disciples plainly to *"beware of the leaven of the Pharisees and of the Sadducees"* (Matt. 16:6), and He meant the insidious doctrine of the Pharisees and Sadducees. In the parable of the housholder demanding fruit from his vineyard, the Lord Jesus intended the wicked tenant to picture the Pharisees as He knew them (Matt. 21:45). And in the twenty-third chapter of Matthew again and again Jesus cried out, *"Woe unto you, scribes and Pharisees, hypocrites!"* Nor did Jesus receive the rich young ruler who wanted to earn Heaven by doing some good thing, although Jesus loved him.

But, oh, how gladly Jesus received the sinful woman who wept at His feet in the Pharisee's house and washed His feet with tears and kissed His feet and anointed them! (Luke 7:36-48). And as Jesus went preaching *"throughout every city and village . . . the twelve were with him, And certain women, which had been healed of evil spirits and infirmities, Mary called Magdalene, out of whom went seven devils"* (Luke 8:1,2).

Nor did Jesus ever condone sin. To the impotent man whom Jesus healed and saved, He said, *". . . sin no more, lest a worse thing come unto thee"* (John 5:14). When the guilty accusers crept away from the poor woman taken in the very act of adultery, whom the Pharisees demanded He should stone, Jesus said to the penitent woman who alone remained, *"Neither do I condemn thee: go, and sin no more"* (John 8:11).

But Getting Sinners Saved Is the Dearest Thing to the Heart of God and to the Heart of Christ

It is strange that the Pharisees could see the main intent of Jesus Christ — to receive sinners, to forgive them, to get them ready for eternal happiness; and so many religionists today miss the point!

First Timothy 1:15 properly says, *"This is a faithful saying, and worthy of all acceptation, that Christ Jesus came into the world to save sinners. . . ."* Oh, it was a faithful proverb, no doubt widely spread in Paul's day: the one thing Jesus came for was to save sinners.

The enormous impact of Christ and the Bible on civilization is beyond any measurement. Most of all the good things in laws, in literature, in art, in benevolence, in morals, can be traced back to the blessed influence of Christ and the Bible. But all these are incidental by-products — not the main thing; Christ came to save sinners! These are the garments that go with salvation, but salvation is the aim and burden of the Lord Jesus, the matter for which He came, for which He died.

How often He said it!

When Matthew (called Levi in Luke 5:27) was converted, he made a great supper, and "*there was a great company of publicans and of others that sat down with them*" (Luke 5:29). What a stir among the scribes and Pharisees! They asked, "*Why do ye eat and drink with publicans and sinners? And Jesus answering said unto them, They that are whole need not a physician; but they that are sick. I came not to call the righteous, but sinners to repentance*" (Luke 5:30-32). In a similar account in Matthew 9:10-13, Jesus added to the statement: "*But go ye and learn what that meaneth, I will have mercy, and not sacrifice: for I am not come to call the righteous, but sinners to repentance.*" And that same blessed statement is repeated in Mark 2:17. What did Jesus come for? To save sinners!

Again in Matthew 18:11 Jesus said, "*The Son of man is come to save that which was lost.*" In Luke 9:56 He said He did "*not come to destroy men's lives, but to save them.*" In Luke 19:10, when Zacchaeus, converted, came down from the tree and Jesus would go home with him, Jesus said, "*The Son of man is come to seek and to save that which was lost.*" Let us repeat it: winning souls is the one thing dearest to the heart of God, the one thing for which Jesus died. In fact, that is the very heart and substance of the Great Commission as given in Matthew 28:19,20; in Mark 16:15,16; in Luke 24:46-49; in John 20:19-21; and in Acts 1:8.

Ah, in fact, that is the very heart and substance of the whole Bible, for Acts 10:43 says, "To him give all the prophets witness, that through his name whosoever believeth in him shall receive remission of sins." That is the meaning of all the Scriptures and of the preaching of all the prophets.

Here, then, in this chapter we have three wonderful parables which Jesus gave to enforce and accent this wonderful concern He had for sinners and His purpose to save them.

VERSES 3 — 7:

3 And he spake this parable unto them, saying,

4 What man of you, having an hundred sheep, if he lose one of them, doth not leave the ninety and nine in the wilderness, and go after that which is lost, until he find it?

5 And when he hath found *it*, he layeth *it* on his shoulders, rejoicing.

6 And when he cometh home, he calleth together *his* friends and neighbours, saying unto them, Rejoice with me; for I have found my sheep which was lost.

7 I say unto you, that likewise joy shall be in heaven over one sinner that repenteth, more than over ninety and nine just persons, which need no repentance.

Parable of the Lost Sheep

In Matthew 18:12 and 13 Jesus briefly, in two verses, gives a restatement of this parable of the lost sheep. It was evidently a repetition and at a different time, and in connection with the little children who came to Him. But as the Gospel of Luke puts more emphasis on Christ as the Son of man, the model Man, our Pattern, so there is more stress on soul winning as our principal business as Christians. And here the parable of the lost sheep is given with more charm and with more detail and application.

As a shepherd would give more attention to bringing in one sheep that was lost than to caring for ninety-nine others that were in the wilderness but safe, so surely He means that Christian workers should spend more time in winning one lost soul than in looking after ninety-nine church people. The famous gospel song says, "There were ninety and nine that safely lay/In the shelter of the fold," but this Scripture does not say that those ninety-nine were "in the shelter of the fold." No, the shepherd would leave "*the ninety and nine in the wilderness, and go after that which is lost. . . .*" Some would say, "Let's get all in the church revived and taught, and then we can have a revival and win souls." No; when you get

everybody in the church right, it will not be a revival;
it will be the millennium!

Some pastor will remonstrate that his salary comes
from the members and they expect his time and attention
to be given to them. That pastor should begin to work
for the Lord and expect the Lord to pay him, and then
do what the Lord Jesus wants, and that is, first of all,
to save sinners! God's plan, in the Great Commission
Jesus gave in Matthew 28:19,20, is that people should
be won, made disciples, then baptized immediately, and
then taught *"to observe all things whatsoever I have
commanded you."* Notice, we are not commanded to
teach young converts *doctrine* immediately but *duty,*
that is, to observe the Great Commission command
themselves. The first duty of every new convert, after
confessing Christ and following Him in baptism as a
public committal, is to set out to get others saved and
baptized and winning souls.

This commentator is editor of the Christian weekly,
THE SWORD OF THE LORD. But, in the latter emphasis Jesus gives here, is it right to edit a Christian paper?
Yes, if it strives always to win souls and to teach others
to win souls. As of October 1, 1969, we had received
14,113 letters from those who claimed to have trusted
Christ through sermons in THE SWORD OF THE LORD
and through the editor's books and pamphlets in the
English language editions distributed through THE
SWORD. Thousands more had claimed Christ publicly
in response to his messages printed in thirty-seven foreign languages. A Christian magazine is justified if it
wins souls and makes soul winners. So a Christian
college is justified if it wins souls and particularly if it
trains and motivates Christians to win souls.

Some ministers claim they feel called to "feed the
sheep," but remember that with the Lord Jesus a lost
sheep should get more attention than ninety-nine *"just
persons, which need no repentance."* And when Jesus

told Peter, "*Feed my sheep,*" He evidently meant Peter's witnessing and preaching with others at Pentecost when three thousand were saved.

This parable of the lost sheep pictures soul winning as a person-to-person business, a house-to-house effort. There is a place for public preaching of the Gospel, and it is important; but it can never take the place of the person-to-person warning and pleading and invitation by Christians.

Remember that when Jesus said in the Great Commission that one should go and "*preach the gospel,*" in Mark 16:15, He is speaking not about the public sermon to a congregation but about the appeal to an individual, that is, "*to every creature.*" And Paul could remind the Ephesian elders that "*I . . . have taught you publickly, and from house to house*" (Acts 20:20). And most of those who were saved under the ministry of Christ, about whom we read in the Gospels, were won person to person.

Think of Nicodemus, of the woman at Sychar in John 4, of the woman taken in adultery, in the very act, of the sinful woman who wept over His feet in the house of the Pharisee, of blind Bartimaeus by the roadside, and of Zacchaeus the publican. Think of Philip (John 1:43) whom Jesus "*found,*" of "*Levi, sitting at the receipt of custom*"; think of the leper, of the Syrophenician woman, of the Gadarene demoniac, of the thief on the cross! The main way to win souls is person to person. So it was illustrated in the parable of the great supper, and so it is here. Soul winning is for every Christian, and the principal way people are won is person to person.

"Until He Find It"

Persistent and urgent effort is required to win the lost. The church in Jerusalem was persistent in house-to-house calling, going again and again. "*And daily in the temple, and in every house, they ceased not to teach and preach Jesus Christ"* (Acts 5:42). In the parable of the marriage feast Jesus told about a king who *"sent forth his servants to call them that were bidden to the wedding: and they would not come. Again, he sent forth other servants, saying, Tell them which are bidden, Behold, I have prepared my dinner: my oxen and my fatlings are killed, and all things are ready: come unto the marriage"* (Matt. 22:3,4).

Someone has said, "Why should anyone hear the Gospel twice when some have never heard it once?" That sounds wise but it is not. Hardly anybody ever gets saved the first time they hear the Gospel, and God's plan is that we should go persistently, again and again. To warn and to plead and to invite lost people we should have such persistence and such concern as would *"compel them to come in"* (Luke 14:23).

Dr. Tom Malone of the tremendous Emmanuel Baptist Church in Pontiac, Michigan, tells how he and others of his church had persistently visited a home and could not even get anyone there to attend the services. Then in an emergency he was called, he and his superintendent went to the home, and on the fiftieth visit made to that home by the workers, three—a mother and her grown son and daughter—were saved. They all came then to claim Christ and follow Him in baptism.

Before a child is born into this world, the mother has times of morning sickness, then months of some occasional distress and inconvenience; clothes do not fit; she feels unsightly; she may have strange taste in food; she may be irritable or nervous and upset. Often the complexion suffers and there is the long waiting before the labor and pain and distress when the child is born. Should we expect to win souls for Heaven without any care or tears or deep compassion? Should anyone expect to win souls without some of the rebuffs and insincere excuses and active opposition that the Lord Jesus foretold in the parables of the great supper and the king's wedding feast? When the sower sows the seed, some falls by the wayside and the birds get it, and so Satan takes the Gospel out of the hearts of some who hear. Then there are hearts so hard they cannot be won. And some who are won *"bring no fruit to perfection"* (Luke 8:14). But what rejoicing when the shepherd finds his sheep and brings it home!

It is important to see with this parable Jesus teaches that He wants every lost sinner in the world. In connection with the parable of the lost sheep, in Matthew 18:14, Jesus said, *"Even so it is not the will of your Father which is in heaven, that one of these little ones should perish."* So although there were ninety and nine safe, He wanted the one lost sheep.

And so in II Peter 3:9 we are told that He is *"not willing that any should perish, but that all should come to repentance."* We see here that Jesus has infinite compassion for the farthest lost sinner, and He wants that one, too.

A young mother had a miscarriage, and she sobbed in great grief. We said to her, "You have two children; you are young; you will have other children. Do not weep." But, sobbing, she said, "Oh, I know, but I wanted that one, too!" So Jesus feels, we are sure, about every lost sinner in the world. And so should we feel also.

On the Shepherd's Shoulder

What a sweet picture of salvation! All of grace and not of human merit nor works! The sheep is put safely on the Shepherd's shoulder. He does not have to know the way Home. He does not have to outrun wolves. He does not have to be faithful in effort. He simply rests on the Shepherd's shoulder and is carried Home.

Some "sheep" have stood up in prayer meeting and

have left the wrong impression; they have said, "I'm determined to make Heaven my home!" and "I want all
to pray for me that I may hold out faithful." People
do not go to Heaven because of persistent determination
nor because they hold out faithful. And as far as meeting God's standard for righteousness, none of us were
faithful to start with, and none of us have ever been
righteous for even ten minutes in the pure and absolute
sense that would deserve Heaven. No, our righteousness
is Christ's righteousness! *"For by grace are ye saved
through faith; and that not of yourselves: it is the gift
of God: Not of works, lest any man should boast"*
(Eph. 2:8,9).

So Jesus can say, *"My sheep hear my voice, and I
know them, and they follow me: And I give unto them
eternal life; and they shall never perish. . ."* (John
10:27,28). And He continues and says that no one
can take one of His own out of Christ's hand or take
one out of the hand of the Father! The security of a
child of God is not in his own merit or righteousness
but in the secure safety of being carried on the Shepherd's
shoulder.

Oh, sheep, if you want to get Home safely, do not
trust your wisdom to take the right path. You missed
the path before. Do not trust your own strength; there
are wolves about, stronger than you. Heaven is not
earned by deserving it; it is earned because Jesus bought
it for His own. I suggest you read the chapter, "Can a
Saved Person Ever Be Lost?" in the author's book,
Twelve Tremendous Themes, or get the pamphlet entitled *Can a Saved Person Ever Be Lost?* from the
same publisher.

Is it not an intimate picture of the Saviour's love for
His own, that He carries us on His shoulders? He did
not mind when John the beloved, at the Last Supper,
moved his couch nearer and laid his head on the breast
of Jesus! (John 13:23). Jesus was not offended that the

woman who was a sinner wept over His feet in the house
of the Pharisee and then washed His feet with tears,
wiped them with the hairs of her head, kissed His feet
and anointed them with ointment. The resurrected Saviour invited Thomas to put his hands into Jesus' side to
feel the wound and to put his fingers in the nail prints,
and know that He was really alive from the dead. Oh,
how dear to the heart of Christ are all of us whom He
has purchased with His blood!

The Shepherd's Rejoicing

We read that the Shepherd *"layeth it on his shoulders
rejoicing."* And he *"calleth together his friends and
neighbours, saying unto them, Rejoice with me."* As the
winning of souls is the one main purpose of Christ's incarnation and death on the cross, so of course that must
be His principal joy. Hebrews 12:2 tells us that Jesus
*"for the joy that was set before him endured the cross,
despising the shame...."* And in John 4:32, when the
disciples urged Him to eat, after He had won the
Samaritan woman, Jesus said to them, *"I have meat to
eat that ye know not of"!* Winning a soul was better
than food for the Lord Jesus.

And who are the *"friends and neighbours"* of the
shepherd who rejoice with him? Oh, that surely pictures
the saints in Heaven, for verse 7 says, *"I say unto you,
that likewise joy shall be in heaven over one sinner that
repenteth, more than over ninety and nine just persons,
which need no repentance."* D. L. Moody, Sam Jones,
Billy Sunday, R. A. Torrey, J. Wilbur Chapman, and
Truett and Spurgeon and Talmage and all the others
who loved to see sinners saved on earth, up in Heaven
rejoice when they hear the glad tidings. And so the
song says,

Ring the bells of heaven!

> there is joy today
> For a soul returning from the wild;
> See the Father meets him
> out upon the way,
> Welcoming His weary, wand'ring child.

Remember that Paul looked forward greatly to the joy of seeing in Heaven those he had won. In I Thessalonians 2:19,20 he said, "*For what is our hope, or joy, or crown of rejoicing? Are not even ye in the presence of our Lord Jesus Christ at his coming? For ye are our glory and joy.*"

And so we remember that Daniel 12:3 promises: "*They that be wise shall shine as the brightness of the firmament; and they that turn many to righteousness as the stars for ever and ever.*" Oh, the principal joy in Heaven now and for eternity is that souls are saved!

VERSES 8 — 10:

8 Either what woman having ten pieces of silver, if she lose one piece, doth not light a candle, and sweep the house, and seek diligently till she find *it?*

9 And when she hath found *it*, she calleth *her* friends and *her* neighbours together, saying, Rejoice with me; for I have found the piece which I had lost.

10 Likewise, I say unto you, there is joy in the presence of the angels of God over one sinner that repenteth.

The Parable of the Lost Coin

A woman had ten pieces of silver. The piece might have been called a *drachma*, a *denarius*, or a penny. It is worth perhaps eight pence, English money; by the gold standard, perhaps 15 cents American money; but its value was far greater in that day. It was the price of a full day's work, as seen in Matthew 20:2 and Revelation 6:6. Some think it may have been dowry money,

greatly treasured, and may have been strung like beads
on a cord and worn as a necklace or on the forehead.
Or, Gordet thinks, "The woman has laboriously earned
a small sum and saved it only at the cost of many priva-
tions and for some urgent necessity." At any rate, to
this woman it was far more valuable than we might
suppose. Thirty such pieces were worth the price of a
slave (Zech. 11:12). Thirty pieces of silver were paid
the traitor Judas, and that money was sufficient to buy
the potter's field. At any rate, the coin was very precious
to this woman, and with great concern she sought it.

Doth she not *"light a candle, and sweep the house,
and seek diligently till she find it?"*—*"light a candle,"*
because in the stone houses with no windows but only
the door for light, it would be dark. *"Sweep the house"*?
Yes, because in a corner or perhaps in a crack between
the stones in the floor she might find it. So urgently
does Jesus seek sinners, and so urgently should we go
to seek them, too.

Then is repeated the blessed statement: *"Likewise, I
say unto you, there is joy in the presence of the angels
of God over one sinner that repenteth."*

VERSES 11—16:

11 And he said, A certain man had two sons:

12 And the younger of them said to *his* father, Father, give me the portion of goods that falleth *to me.* And he divided unto them *his* living.

13 And not many days after the younger son gathered all together, and took his journey into a far country, and there wasted his substance with riotous living.

14 And when he had spent all, there arose a mighty famine in that land; and he began to be in want.

15 And he went and joined himself to a citizen of that country; and he sent him into his fields to feed swine.

16 And he would fain have filled his belly with the husks that the swine did eat: and no man gave unto him.

A Beloved Son Gone Astray

This parable is a part of the exposition Jesus gives of why and how He receives sinners, loves them, forgives them, takes them as God's children. As the lost sheep pictures a sinner, as the lost coin pictures a sinner, so here the prodigal son pictures a lost sinner. The elder son pictures these critical Pharisees and scribes whose religion was simply to maintain standards of human merit and righteousness, with no mercy for sinners, no atonement, no forgiveness, no reconciliation.

Note how clearly the Lord Jesus pictures the heart attitude and state of a lost sinner. If this were simply the narrative of a boy who became rebellious, disobedient, hating his father's principles and his way of life and determined to have his own way at any cost, then we could properly blame the father. The Scripture teaches: *"Train up a child in the way he should go and when he is old, he will not depart from it"* (Prov. 22:6). One can bring children up in *"nurture"* (that is, discipline) and *"admonition of the Lord"* (Eph. 6:4). It is true, *"The blueness of a wound cleanseth away evil: so do stripes the inward parts of the belly"* (Prov. 20:30). Old Eli's wicked sons went wrong because, as God's prophet told Eli that God said, *". . . honourest thy sons above me. . ."* (I Sam. 2:29), and an agelong curse was put on his family *"for the iniquity which he knoweth; because his sons made themselves vile, and he restrained them not"* (I Sam. 3:13). And Adonijah, son of David, went wrong, as did another son, Absalom, because *". . . his father had not displeased him at any time in saying, Why hast thou done so?. . ."* (I Kings 1:6). The father who obeys God in discipline, in example, in teaching consistently, can have God's help in rearing children and can have them turn out well.

But the righteousness of a man's sons, taught by their father and mother, is only relative righteousness. And here the parable pictures a sinner going away from God. For the righteousness that God requires is perfect righteousness, and no human being meets that requirement. And God has not failed, and God is not blamable because men are sinners. And so in the parable the father is not blamed.

And the Saviour does not mean to teach that the Pharisees and scribes are already Christians because they are moral, law-abiding, religious. He deals elsewhere most plainly with them on their sins. But here the parable is about how Christ loves sinners, receives them, forgives them, and about those who object to His receiving sinners.

The wayward son took without even a word of thanks all that the father provided and all that he would have later inherited. But is not that the way with sinners everywhere? The goodness of God is meant to lead men to repentance (Rom. 2:4). Is it not strange and wicked, and does it not show the awful alienation and blindness and selfishness of the unregenerate heart, that men breathe God's air and eat God's food and accept the bounties of wife and children, loved ones, health, and jobs, comforts, even luxuries, and never thank God and feel no obligation to seek God or serve Him?

And the son must get away from the father. You see, sinful men do not want the fellowship of God. As Jesus said in John 3:19-21, "*This is the condemnation, that light is come into the world, and men loved darkness rather than light, because their deeds were evil. For every one that doeth evil hateth the light, neither cometh to the light, lest his deeds should be reproved. But he that doeth truth cometh to the light, that his deeds may be made manifest, that they are wrought in God.*"

So all lost sinners are "*the children of disobedience*" (Eph. 2:2). When Adam had become a sinner, he wanted to hide from God. So unconverted men do not love the Bible, do not love the songs of praise, do not

seek especially the society of devoted Christians. No,
just as do the wild, undisciplined youth of today, leaving
home to get away from the restraints, the discipline, the
admonishing of father and mother, so sinners themselves go away from God intentionally. All mankind is
in that *"far country,"* man who was made in the image
of God and intended to be His constant companion and
enjoyment, has become an alien, a stranger, a foreigner, an enemy!

Does it seem a fool's folly that the lad wasted his
substance in riotous living? Oh, but do not men do so
every day? It is true that *"a fool and his money are
soon parted,"* but it is also true that the wicked man is
likely to lose his happy marriage, lose the fellowship of
his children, and even to lose his business and nearly
all things dear. How often in a rescue mission is found
among the bums and drunks and wrecks of society one
who was a famous lawyer, or a member of Congress, or
a judge of a court, or a former business executive or a
man once wealthy. This is a true picture of the influence
and way of sin.

Then *"there arose a mighty famine in that land"* — there
always does come a famine! Sooner or later the Scripture will be proved true: *"the way of transgressors is
hard"* (Prov. 13:15). And the warning, *". . . be sure
your sin will find you out"* (Num. 32:23), must be
proved valid. Oh, sinners find that *"the wages of sin is
death"* (Rom. 6:23) and that *"sin, when it is finished,
bringeth forth death"* (Jas. 1:15).

It turns out so, first, because that is the way sin works.
The gambler who would get rich without working does
not get rich. The man who drinks and drinks to make
friends and increase his business may lose his business.
The man who lives for pleasure ends up in misery. Sin
is like a fire that, uncontrolled, burns down buildings
and cities. It is like a cancer which, if not killed or removed by surgery, will spread and bring inevitable death.

But the righteousness of God is at stake, too; and God Himself seems to see to it that one who deliberately continues on the wayward road of sin must be punished, must find that sin doesn't pay; he must find that sooner or later there is a judgment day. And one who does not learn all that in this life is certain to learn it in the next.

Where now are the friends who helped him in his folly and spent his money? They are gone; *"no man gave unto him."* The bartender and the drinking buddies are eager friends while one spends his money for their evil pleasure. When the man becomes a drunkard and a bum, when his money is gone and his respectability and even his self-respect, then do his drinking buddies help him to get rehabilitated, gain back his business, gain back his broken home? Where, then, are the bartender, the brewer, the distiller, the politician who caters to the liquor crowd? No, now the fallen sinner who has come to disaster at the end of the road must go to a preacher, to a rescue mission, to godly people for help to get right with God, to regain his character, his usefulness, his happiness. When Judas came back to the chief priests with the thirty pieces of silver burning like fire in his heart and conscience and said, *"I have betrayed the innocent blood!"* and wanted to rue back on his betrayal of Jesus, the heartless chief priests said, *"What is that to us? see thou to that"* (Matt. 27:4).

VERSES 17—24:

17 And when he came to himself, he said, How many hired servants of my father's have bread enough and to spare, and I perish with hunger!

18 I will arise and go to my father, and will say unto him, Father, I have sinned against heaven, and before thee,

19 And am no more worthy to be called thy son: make me as one of thy hired servants.

20 And he arose, and came to his father. But when he was yet a

great way off, his father saw him, and had compassion, and ran, and fell on his neck, and kissed him.

21 And the son said unto him, Father, I have sinned against heaven, and in thy sight, and am no more worthy to be called thy son.

22 But the father said to his servants, Bring forth the best robe, and put *it* on him; and put a ring on his hand, and shoes on *his* feet:

23 And bring hither the fatted calf, and kill *it;* and let us eat, and be merry:

24 For this my son was dead, and is alive again; he was lost, and is found. And they began to be merry.

Repenting

In the hogpen, hungry, disillusioned, heartsick, the prodigal *"came to himself."* No man is quite in his right mind when he goes on in sin to heartbreak and ruin. Now he sees things as they are: sin does not bring happiness; revelry does not make true friends. The pleasures of sin do not last. Now he recognizes the goodness, the benevolent kindness, the devoted love of his father, and grieves that he has offended and wronged him. Now he sees that the friends in sin are false friends. Now the old home place seems so safe a haven, and the surroundings so happy, that he envies even the hired servants there who have plenty while he perishes with hunger! Thoughtless sinners should heed the admonition of Isaiah 1:18, *"Come now, and let us reason together."* One who comes to himself will see the folly of his sins.

Blessed be God, who many times brings men to their senses by sharp judgment. It was easy once to lead a brokenhearted father to trust in Jesus as he knelt by the grave of his baby son. Young people bruised and in tears of penitence after an automobile wreck were easy to win to the Lord. A doctor's report that a grayheaded sinner, bootlegger and convict, had heart trouble and might not live six months caused him to send for this preacher, and with tears the ex-convict sought the Lord.

And how blessed it is that God's preachers can preach on sin and Hell and judgment and give God's warnings and tell of God's examples so that men in sin can be like the prodigal, who *"came to himself."* Convicted, a man can repent. And this young man must learn first the wages of sin and then he can appreciate the love and forgiveness of his father! It would be no complete story, no adequate Gospel, if a preacher preaches about the happy return of the prodigal but leaves out all the story of wasted years, prodigal living, harlots and drunkards and the hogpen and famine. The Gospel is not only that Christ saves, but that He saves sinners. And the Gospel is not only that they will have everlasting life but that they *"shall not perish."* It is good to preach that he that *"believeth on the Son hath everlasting life,"* but it is only honest to preach the rest of the same verse: *"he that believeth not the Son shall not see life; but the wrath of God abideth on him"* (John 3:36).

Now comes the holy resolution, *"I will arise and go to my father, and will say unto him, Father, I have sinned against heaven, and before thee, And am no more worthy to be called thy son: make me as one of thy hired servants."* And so he did, at once.

I once pictured in my mind the long road home, the deep concern, the tired steps. Would the father receive him and forgive him, or would the father scorn him? But as I meditated further, I noted that it was not a long way home. That boy might have been a thousand miles from home, but as far as this parable is concerned it was only a step. If one, in deepest sin, turns heart and face toward God, He is there!

The Happy Homecoming

Remember that the theme of this chapter is *"This man receiveth sinners."* So the father, faithfully waiting, loving, praying, and watching for the lost boy's return, saw him *"when he was yet a great way off. . . and had compassion, and ran, and fell on his neck, and kissed him."*

The prodigal confessed his sin, his unworthiness; he said, "*I have sinned against heaven, and in thy sight, and am no more worthy to be called thy son.*" But the father interrupted him before he could propose, as he had solemnly vowed to do, that he would be only a servant.

Thus a sinner must come to Jesus for salvation and forgiveness, as unworthy, as penitent. Christ died to save sinners (I Tim. 1:15) and no one else. Only *penitent* sinners get saved, like the publican of Luke 18: 9-14, like the thief in Luke 23:39-43. Those do not get saved who come like the self-righteous Pharisee in the Temple nor like the rich, young ruler asking, ". . . *what good thing shall I do, that I may have eternal life?*" (Matt. 19:16). Christ receives sinners but only self-confessed, penitent sinners, who cannot rely on merit.

What did the returning prodigal receive?

1. The father said, "*Bring forth the best robe, and put it on him.*" So everyone who trusts Christ for salvation has Christ's robe of righteousness put around him. Isaiah 61:10 speaks of it thus: "*I will greatly rejoice in the Lord, my soul shall be joyful in my God; for he hath clothed me with the garments of salvation, he hath covered me with the robe of righteousness, as a bridegroom decketh himself with ornaments, and as a bride adorneth herself with her jewels.*" Of all of us who have relied on Christ for salvation it is said, "*Blessed are they whose iniquities are forgiven, and whose sins are covered. Blessed is the man to whom the Lord will not impute sin*" (Rom. 4:7,8).

That righteous robe is pictured in the parable of the king who made a marriage for his son, in Matthew 22. One man who would have attended "*had not on a wedding garment*" and he was cast out (Matt. 22:11-13). There is no getting to Heaven without being clothed in the garment of Christ's righteousness.

Did not blind Bartimaeus picture this, when Jesus called him and he, "*casting away his garment, rose, and came to Jesus"* (Mark 10:50)? He threw away his beggar's rags; now with his sight he could dress better than a beggar.

2. *"Put a ring on his hand,"* said the father. As the robe was put upon him without his lifting a finger, since it was received righteousness pictured, not his own works, so even the ring is put upon his hand; it is the sign of sonship. He is in the family. So we are *"heirs of God, and joint-heirs with Christ"* (Rom. 8:17). Jesus is not ashamed to call us brethren (Heb. 2:11). How sweet it is to read, *"Behold, what manner of love the Father hath bestowed upon us, that we should be called the sons of God: therefore the world knoweth us not, because it knew him not. Beloved, now are we the sons of God, and it doth not yet appear what we shall be: but we know that, when he shall appear, we shall be like him; for we shall see him as he is"* (I John 3:1,2). And we come as unworthy as the prodigal, to be received by God's mercy and grace into the very family of God.

Some translations of the Bible, as the *Revised Standard Version,* the *N. E. B.,* and the *Good News for Modern Man,* are not only presumptuous to change John 3:16 to say that *"God gave his only Son,"* leaving out the word *"begotten";* it was irreverent presumption to conjecture about the text but it is also fatally wrong in doctrine: Jesus is not the only Son of God. He is simply the only one physically begotten of God without a human father. In our second birth, Christians are *"born of the Spirit"* and so we became *"partakers of the divine nature"* (II Pet. 1:4).

3. And *"put. . . shoes on his feet,"* said the father. As a prince might be dressed by his attendants, they put shoes on the tired feet of the prodigal. So the sinner not only receives the imputed righteousness of Christ and the position of a son but his walk is changed. When he turns to Christ, God gives him new shoes! The prodigal surely intended now to live at home to please his

father, to walk in the father's will. So the penitent sinner who comes to Christ has a change of mind and attitude that should show in newness of life. Now the Christian should *"work out your own salvation with fear and trembling. For it is God which worketh in you both to will and to do of his good pleasure"* (Phil. 2:12,13). He should *"work out"* now the salvation which God has put in him.

After one is saved he will still find a conflict within. He will find that *"the flesh lusteth against the Spirit."* He will find, like Paul, that *"when I would do good, evil is present with me"* (Rom. 7:21), and he cannot do the things he would; but, like Paul, he may long to be delivered. Like David's penitent prayer in Psalm 51, he may show how sin grieves and offends him. He may, like Peter, go out and weep bitterly, after sin (Luke 22: 62). But salvation should radically affect the walk.

The shoes on the prodigal's feet—what for? They speak here, surely, of soul winning. Along with the whole armor of God, the Christian is admonished to have *"your feet shod with the preparation of the gospel of peace"* (Eph. 6:15). As the Great Commission teaches that every new convert should be taught at once *"to observe all things whatsoever"* Jesus had commanded the apostles about soul winning (Matt. 28:20), so the returned, forgiven prodigal is given these shoes of gospel going. *"Let him that heareth say, Come"* (Rev. 22:17). The *"first love"* (Rev. 2:4) which the church at Ephesus had lost is a certain warmth and evangelistic zeal and concern for poor lost sinners that we ought to so carefully nourish and retain. The obligation and the joy of soul winning comes immediately to the new convert. And so the Gadarene demoniac out of whom Jesus had cast a legion of devils, when he wanted to go with Jesus away from the heartless people who preferred their hogs to healing, was refused. Jesus told him, *"Return to thine own house, and shew how great things God hath done unto thee.''* And the Scripture says *"he went his way, and published throughout the whole city how great things Jesus had done unto him"* (Luke 8:39).

4. The returned prodigal now shares the feasting at the father's house. The father said, *"And bring hither the fatted calf, and kill it; and let us eat, and be merry: For this my son was dead, and is alive again; he was lost, and is found.''* And we read that *"they began to be merry.''* The famine is over! The perishing with hunger is past. For salvation means not only forgiveness of sins and redemption from eternal torment, it means entering into a rich and blessed life. The shepherd rejoiced when he found his sheep. The woman who lost one piece of silver rejoiced when she found it, and had her neighbors rejoice with her. There is great joy in Heaven when a sinner repents, and so we should be happy here, too. When one comes to Christ, he should confess Christ openly and should have the greetings, the congratulations, the good wishes, the handshakes and caresses of those who love him. Salvation is a time of rejoicing.

When this author had been saved and was baptized, he stood then with others at the edge of the water, and people came by to shake hands. And, oh, how gladly we sang,

> O happy day that fixed my choice
> On Thee, my Saviour and my God!
> Well may this glowing heart rejoice,
> And tell its raptures all abroad.
>
> Happy day, happy day
> When Jesus washed my sins away!

As the shepherd and the woman, in this chapter, rejoiced when the lost was found, so the father and others at the prodigal's return, and he rejoiced with them.

And he ate of *"the fatted calf.''* You see, in the passover lamb Jesus is pictured as the Saviour; one meal of the passover lamb pictures salvation. But following that, the Jewish ceremony required a seven-days feast of unleavened bread, picturing all of a Christian's life. The Christian has a sabbath to begin with when he partakes of the Passover Lamb, and he has a sabbath in Heaven waiting, because he may feast on Christ, the Unleavened Bread, all his life!

So in the Tabernacle and in the Temple, on the right in the Holy Place, was a table of showbread, and there twelve new loaves of bread were placed every Sabbath (Lev. 24:5-9). Christ is thus the Bread of life, and the Christian may feed on Him continually. There is rich meaning in the fact that baptism, which is the burial of the old sinner symbolically and of a rising to walk in newness of life — and baptism is only once; but the Lord's Supper is to be repeated again and again, for we are partakers of the Lord Jesus all of our lives, and Christians should feast on Him.

Oh, the happy days had only begun for the prodigal son, and the feasting that day of his return would continue all the years in the father's house.

VERSES 25 — 32:

25 Now his elder son was in the field: and as he came and drew nigh to the house, he heard musick and dancing.

26 And he called one of the servants, and asked what these things meant.

27 And he said unto him, Thy brother is come; and thy father hath killed the fatted calf, because he hath received him safe and sound.

28 And he was angry, and would not go in: therefore came his father out, and intreated him.

29 And he answering said to *his* father, Lo, these many years do I serve thee, neither transgressed I at any time thy commandment: and yet thou never gavest me a kid, that I might make merry with my friends:

30 But as soon as this thy son was come, which hath devoured thy living with harlots, thou hast killed for him the fatted calf.

31 And he said unto him, Son, thou art ever with me, and all that I have is thine.

32 It was meet that we should make merry, and be glad: for this thy brother was dead, and is alive again; and was lost, and is found.

The Older Brother Pictured the Pharisees Who Did Not Want Sinners Forgiven and Saved

Here Jesus is still answering the complaint of the scribes and Pharisees that *"This man receiveth sinners, and eateth with them"* (vs. 2). The elder brother represents those same Pharisees. The first of the eight woes Jesus pronounced on the Pharisees, in Matthew 23, was this one: *"But woe unto you, scribes and Pharisees, hypocrites! for ye shut up the kingdom of heaven against men: for ye neither go in yourselves, neither suffer ye them that are entering to go in"* (Matt. 23:13). The Pharisees would not themselves get saved. They did not want others to be saved. He could have said the same things about the Sadducees that He said about the scribes and Pharisees. Later, as Peter and John preached to the people, *"the priests, and the captain of the temple, and the Sadducees, came upon them, Being grieved that they taught the people, and preached through Jesus the resurrection from the dead"* (Acts 4:1,2). They put the apostles in jail and then later *"they called them, and commanded them not to speak at all nor teach in the name of Jesus"* (Acts 4:18). This same kind of Jewish leaders hindered Paul, forbidding *"us to speak to the Gentiles that they might be saved, to fill up their sins alway..."* (I Thess. 2:16).

The Lord Jesus lets the elder brother speak as the Pharisees and scribes would have spoken. He complained to his father, *"Lo, these many years do I serve thee, neither transgressed I at any time thy commandment: and yet thou never gavest me a kid, that I might make merry with my friends."* So these Jewish leaders said of themselves. They were like the Pharisee in the Temple, which Jesus described in Luke 18:9-14. They were like the rich young ruler who claimed he had kept all the commandments from his youth (Luke 18:18-22;

Matt. 19:16-30; Mark 10:17-31). But, like Nicodemus, for all the outward ceremonial correctness, they had wicked hearts. As Jesus told one of them, Nicodemus, *"Ye must be born again,"* so these rejected the Saviour, had wicked hearts, and would eventually have the Saviour killed. It was to such Pharisees and Sadducees that John the Baptist said, *"O generation of vipers, who hath warned you to flee from the wrath to come? Bring forth therefore fruits meet for repentance"* (Matt. 3:7,8; Luke 3:7). They were claiming: *"We have Abraham to our father."* They did not seek and did not want to be born again, to have a personal Saviour.

We can be sure that that older brother was not really as good as he claimed, nor were the Pharisees he represented. It was not true: *"neither transgressed I at any time thy commandment."* Instead of being glad for his father's happiness and the answer to his father's prayers, the elder brother was angry. Instead of having compassion for his own blood brother and rejoicing that he returned, the older brother wanted the younger son disowned and cast out. Even Esau, concerning his brother Jacob, who had wronged him so seriously, did better than that (Gen. 33:4). The righteousness of these scribes and Pharisees was an outer righteousness, not heart righteousness. He did not care for the happiness of his father nor the welfare of his brother, and so Jesus pictured the Pharisees and scribes who complained that Jesus *"receiveth sinners, and eateth with them."*

We fear that many church people are scribes and Pharisees on this matter. They want only formal, elite church services, classic music, with little intellectual essays from the pulpit. They do not want the services made to fit the needs and tastes of the poor and the worldling. They do not want an extended public invitation with tender pleading for sinners to come to Christ. They do not want the deep emotions which are often expressed when there is plain, sharp, Bible preaching and when sinners repent and come to Christ and godly people rejoice.

A certain large church put out buses to bring in from far and near all the underprivileged children and young people, families without cars, and all they could get to come and hear the Gospel. The children had a tendency to make some noise in the sedate Sunday morning services. They were not all well dressed. The preaching was fitted to *"the poor, and the maimed, and the halt and the blind"* that were brought in from everywhere, and many were saved. A haughty millionaire, seeing the throng about him after the service, said to the pastor, "What are we going to do with all these dirty kids?"

The pastor answered, "I am going to love them with all my heart!"

The Pharisee answered, "If they stay, I go!" And go he did, and the church continued to win multitudes in a record-breaking fashion.

Some modern Pharisees and scribes want the pastor to spend all his time visiting and catering to the church members, and they resent what time he takes to seek out the lost and win them and counsel with them, get them saved. And some fashionable singers resent it when into the choir come some of these not well trained, not very well dressed but earnest and believing souls who have found Christ. Some Pharisees and scribes criticize revivals and evangelists. How all must grieve the heart of the Saviour who do not want those to be loved and sought and won and taught, for whom Christ died, the publicans and sinners, who are so dear to Christ's heart.

LUKE 16

AND he said also unto his disciples, There was a certain rich man, which had a steward; and the same was accused unto him that he had wasted his goods.

2 And he called him, and said unto him, How is it that I hear this of thee? give an account of thy stewardship; for thou mayest be no longer steward.

3 Then the steward said within himself, What shall I do? for my lord taketh away from me the stewardship: I cannot dig; to beg I am ashamed.

4 I am resolved what to do, that, when I am put out of the stewardship, they may receive me into their houses.

5 So he called every one of his lord's debtors unto him, and said unto the first, How much owest thou unto my lord?

6 And he said, An hundred measures of oil. And he said unto him, Take thy bill, and sit down quickly, and write fifty.

7 Then said he to another, And how much owest thou? And he said, An hundred measures of wheat. And he said unto him, Take thy bill, and write fourscore.

8 And the lord commended the unjust steward, because he had done wisely: for the children of this world are in their generation wiser than the children of light.

9 And I say unto you, Make to yourselves friends of the mammon of unrighteousness; that, when ye fail, they may receive you into everlasting habitations.

The Parable of the Unjust Steward

A steward of a wealthy man was like a superintendent of a plant or the treasurer of a company. This steward was about to be fired on the indefinite charge that he had wasted his master's goods. And what would the steward do? He must use what time he had left of his stewardship to make friends who would receive him into their houses when he was discharged. He was too old, we suppose, to dig ditches. He does not want to be a beggar. He felt he must use opportunities now to make friends so he would have a home.

The Lord does not here discuss the rightness of the steward's action. It may be that the steward had been given such authority that he had a perfect right to decide what rent he would require, what payment for bills. Abraham's chief servant had disposal of all of Abraham's goods (Gen. 24:10), so he could decide how many camels he should take on his journey, what jewels he should give to Rebekah and to Laban and to her mother (Gen. 24:53). But if the steward was thus dishonest in so disposing of the goods of his master, that is not the point here. The Lord Jesus is saying that just as that man took all the opportunity he could to make himself friends for the future, using money or things for that purpose, just so the Christian ought to use his money to *"make to yourselves friends of the mammon of unrighteousness; that, when ye fail, they may receive you into everlasting habitations"* (vs. 9). The unjust steward, from the point of self-interest, had done wisely, *"for the children of this world are in their generation wiser than the children of light,"* Jesus said (vs. 8).

This writer pleaded most earnestly with a young man to turn to Christ and be saved. He was deeply concerned. He had attended a Catholic church only one time, had never even seen a Bible before. He was entranced with the heavenly message, and yet it was all so new I could not persuade him to settle the matter now for Christ; rather, he said, "Buddy, I'll have to think about it. I never heard of this before."

Where would he sleep tonight? It was a cold winter night. He had on a shabby suit, had no overcoat, had no money for a bed. Oh, he thought he and his buddy could walk or wrestle or perhaps sleep in a doorway until tomorrow. In pity I took him upstairs to a flophouse, and for fifty cents bought a cot for him for the night, and a friend paid for a cot for his buddy. I was at that time in seminary, and was very poor, working day by day between classes and struggling to make ends meet, but I could not think of the boy sleeping in the cold. I again made him promise to read the New Testament I had given him and I turned to leave, but he held onto my sleeve. I looked, and he was weeping. "I believe I will just settle that right now," he said. Oh, when I get to Heaven I may find that fifty cents was the best money I ever spent!

Earnestly I raised money to print a million copies of my gospel message, "*What Must I Do to Be Saved?*" in Japan. In Japan, some years later, I found myself in services with a young Japanese man who interpreted for me. A habitual criminal had been converted in a penitentiary by reading the little booklet we had raised money for at such cost. His changed life was so amazing that the warden and the guards united to beg the judge to release the prisoner, and he did. This prisoner then found a young man, a sot, a drunkard, who had tried to commit suicide, desolate and alone in a park, wishing he were dead, and he won him to Christ. And now, as I heard this story, that young Japanese preacher, my spiritual grandchild perhaps, raised his hands high and, weeping, chattered in Japanese over and over, "Hallelujah! Hallelujah!"

I say, money spent to win souls will guarantee heavenly friendships and glad greetings there! Daniel 12:3 says, "*They that be wise shall shine as the brightness of the firmament; and they that turn many to righteousness as the stars for ever and ever.*"

Oh, we should use money and things and time and talents to make for us friends who will receive us "*into everlasting habitations*"! Five minutes after one dies it will not matter whether he had a crust of bread or a T-bone steak to eat, whether he rode in a limousine or a jalopy. What will matter in the next world is whether or not you use your money, talents, efforts, time to get people saved, so they will greet you in the heavenly kingdom!

VERSES 10 — 13:

10 He that is faithful in that which is least is faithful also in much: and he that is unjust in the least is unjust also in much.

11 If therefore ye have not been faithful in the unrighteous mammon, who will commit to your trust the true *riches?*

12 And if ye have not been faith-ful in that which is another man's, who shall give you that which is your own?

13 No servant can serve two masters: for either he will hate the one, and love the other; or else he will hold to the one, and despise the other.　Ye cannot serve God and mammon.

The Choice Between God and Mammon

The term *"mammon"* here simply means money and things, and money is so much less important than right-eousness and happiness and eternal blessedness.　But if you are not faithful in the way you use money and things to get out the Gospel, you would not be faithful in preaching the Gospel itself or in doing some great deed of mercy.　If you are not faithful in little, you will not be faithful in much.

If one is not faithful in the matter of money, why would God permit a Christian the true riches of spiritual truth, the joy of the Lord, the power of the Holy Spirit, and spiritual leadership?

Money is in our hands only temporarily.　*"The earth is the Lord's, and the fulness thereof"* (Ps. 24:1).　*"Thou shalt remember the Lord thy God: for it is he that giveth thee power to get wealth"* (Deut. 8:18).　That truth is pictured in the parable of the pounds (Luke 19:11-27) and in the parable of the talents (Matt. 25:14-30).　Oh, if the borrowed money which God allows you to use for a few days is not used faithfully, why would God give you the eternal possessions and riches which a Christian may gain for himself and have at the judgment seat of Christ?　The Lord is not here talking about gaining

salvation but about gaining blessed rewards in Heaven
by the way we use money and things here.

It is shocking that money becomes a master. It is a
good servant but a bad master. Verse 13 is often taken
to mean that one cannot serve God and Satan.   That is
true, of course, but that is not what this verse means.
This verse says that in this life you cannot put money
first, things first, prosperity first, your business first, and
at the same time put God first. You will love the one
and hate the other, or you will hold to the one and
despise the other.

Oh, Christian, beware of being absorbed in things, in
money, in jobs, in possessions.   You see, covetousness
is idolatry (Col. 3:5) and *they that will be rich fall into
temptation and a snare, and into many foolish and
hurtful lusts*" (I Tim. 6:9).

VERSES 14, 15:

14 And the Pharisees also, who were covetous, heard all these things: and they derided him.
15 And he said unto them, Ye are they which justify yourselves before men; but God knoweth your hearts: for that which is highly esteemed among men is abomination in the sight of God.

Covetous Pharisees Answered

The parable of the unjust steward was "*said also unto
his disciples,*" but obviously it was still answering those
Pharisees and scribes who did not want Jesus preaching
to sinners and receiving them.   Obviously Jesus was
further exposing the faults He had indicated in the elder
brother who did not want the prodigal son to come back
and share the blessings of home.   The Pharisees were
covetous, so they derided Jesus when He said, "*Ye
cannot serve God and mammon* [money].*"

So they scoffed at Jesus. But the Pharisees, whose principal righteousness was an outward righteousness to be seen of men, to be heard of men, and that they might *"appear unto men to fast"* (Matt. 6:1,2,5,16), were principally concerned as Jesus told them to *"justify yourselves before men"* (Luke 16:15). But while men esteem riches and the approval of the world, often that is an *"abomination in the sight of God."*

VERSES 16, 17:

16 The law and the prophets *were* until John: since that time the kingdom of God is preached, and every man presseth into it.

17 And it is easier for heaven and earth to pass, than one tittle of the law to fail.

The Kingdom of God Now Preached

Verse 16 is strange. A similar passage is in Matthew 11:12,13, which says, *"And from the days of John the Baptist until now the kingdom of heaven suffereth violence, and the violent take it by force. For all the prophets and the law prophesied until John."*

Dr. Scofield's note there says:

> It has been much disputed whether the "violence" here is external, as against the kingdom in the persons of John the Baptist and Jesus; or that, considering the opposition of the scribes and Pharisees, only the violently resolute would press into it. Both things are true. The King and His herald suffered violence, and this is the primary and greater meaning, but also, some were resolutely becoming disciples. (Cf. Lk. 16.16.)

This verse does not mean that the law (strictly the Pentateuch) and the prophets (the rest of the Old Testament) are out of date since John the Baptist and Jesus came. That is not true and verse 17 plainly indicates that. Matthew 5:17,18 is even clearer, where Jesus says, *"Think not that I am come to destroy the law, or the prophets: I am not come to destroy, but to fulfil. For verily I say unto you, Till heaven and earth pass, one jot or one tittle shall in no wise pass from the law, till all be fulfilled."*

I think it surely means that as the forerunner of Christ, John the Baptist was the first who began to preach that *"the kingdom of heaven is at hand"* (Matt. 3:2). Jesus preached the same message (Matt. 4:17).

What does Jesus mean by *"every man presseth into it"*? Probably He means that no man, because he is a Jew, will automatically be in the kingdom of God, as Jesus made clear to Nicodemus in John 3, and as John the Baptist made clear to the Pharisees and Sadducees in Matthew 3:9. Only those who personally repent and make the decision to turn to Christ, to love Him and trust Him for salvation, are saved. No one gets into the kingdom of God except those who themselves decide to get in.

Some hyper-dispensationalists would say that John the Baptist was an Old Testament preacher and that the repentance and baptism which he preached were simply Jewish ceremonials. But this Scripture shows that they are wrong. Jesus and John were in the same dispensation; they preached the same Gospel. John baptized Jesus and all the twelve disciples. John preached exactly the same Gospel as Jesus preached, as you see from Acts 10:43 and John 3:36, the latter, we think, a statement by John the Baptist.

We will not discuss in detail here, but verse 17 mentions again the theme the Lord Jesus so often stressed, that the Bible, the Word of God, is settled forever in Heaven and will never pass away (Matt. 4:4; Luke 4:4; Ps. 119:89; Matt. 5:17,18). Isaiah 40:8 says, *"The grass withereth, the flower fadeth: but the word of our God shall stand for ever."* And this is quoted in I

Peter 1:23: The Christian is *"born again, not of corruptible seed, but of incorruptible, by the word of God, which liveth and abideth for ever,"* and in verse 25, *"But the word of the Lord endureth for ever."* So Jesus Himself knew and plainly said.

―――――――

VERSE 18:

18 Whosoever putteth away his wife, and marrieth another, committeth adultery: and whosoever marrieth her that is put away from *her* husband committeth adultery.

Jesus' Teaching on Divorce

Read similar statements from Jesus in Matthew 5:31, 32; Matthew 19:3-11; Mark 10:2-12. The two passages in Matthew both name the one exception: *"except it be for fornication."* Here in verse 18 and in Mark 10:11 the general rule is stated. In Old Testament times, because of the hardness of men's hearts, men were allowed to put away their wives for various causes (Deut. 24: 1-4), but that was not God's intention when He made man and woman in the Garden of Eden. Marriage was intended for life and was intended one man for one woman. Divorce, then, is always sad, and a marriage ought never be broken except by death.

But does the statement of Jesus in Matthew 5:31,32 and in Matthew 19:9 contradict this verse 18 or Mark 10:11? No. It simply means, it seems, that in the case of fornication (persistent adultery, like the sin of a harlot or whoremonger) the marriage is already broken in fact. If a man or woman lives the life of a harlot or a whoremonger (and this Scripture particularly refers to the wife), the marriage is already broken in spirit and happiness, and a divorce is permitted.

Notice that the Scripture does not permit a divorce for

one act of adultery. The term "fornication" refers to a
life of adultery. It is a form of the same word translated
"harlot" and "whoremonger" in the New Testament.
And a divorce is not commanded even in such a case.
Surely when there is a fall, if possible it ought to be forgiven and the home restored. Do not be deceived by the
dictionary definition of fornication—the sin of the unmarried. A harlot may be unmarried or she may not
be, but that is not the point of the word in the Greek
New Testament.

In I Corinthians 7:10-15 the wife is commanded not to
depart from her husband and the husband is not to put
away his wife. And if, in distress, they separate temporarily, let them remain unmarried or be reconciled. A
Christian man was not to divorce even an unconverted
wife if she was willing to live with him.

However, I Corinthians 7:15 says, "*But if the unbelieving depart, let him depart. A brother or a sister is
not under bondage in such cases: but God hath called
us to peace.*" Sometimes an unsaved mate may break
the marriage. It ought not to be broken but the Christian
mate sometimes cannot prevent the departure of the
unsaved one.

Fornication, that is, continued adultery, is a reason
that allows a divorce. But an unsaved mate may break
the marriage and the Christian cannot prevent it.

What about the remarriage of divorced people?

Some preachers make a great to-do about whether
only the "innocent party" in a divorce can remarry or
whether the "guilty party" can remarry also. The simple truth is that in the Bible, as in our regular English
usage, the word "divorce" means simply that one is
not married. One might like to punish someone who
broke a marriage by forbidding him to remarry, but
the Bible does not do so, as you see in Deuteronomy
24:2. The divorced woman, "*when she is departed out
of his house* [her husband's house], *may go and be*

another man's wife." Note also that the Bible never speaks of a man, married again after a divorce, as "having two living wives," as some men speak. Rather, the Scripture speaks of the woman's *"latter husband"* and her *"former husband."* A divorced person is not married. Marriage ought not be broken but if it is broken for the legitimate cause which Jesus named, the Bible does not even hint that the person now unmarried is not eligible to marry. But, as in the Old Testament, the woman can become another man's wife and the man can take another wife.

Is a man who is divorced and then remarried now "living in adultery"? Some would say so. The Bible does not say so. It is clear that fornication, that is, to continue in sex relations with someone else, would break the former marriage, and so to be married again, at least, whether it were right or wrong, would break the former marriage. Neither the first wife, nor the husband, nor the law of the land, nor the Bible regards the man as still married to the other woman who was divorced, if the second marriage has now taken place.

Must a man then divorce a second wife in such a case? No, two wrongs would not make a right. That would not restore the former marriage. What God does not require, no preacher has a right to require. Penitence for any former sins? Yes, of course. Humility, facing the measure of disgrace that always follows a divorce of a Christian? Yes, humility and penitence. Some sins and mistakes and failures can be forgiven but they cannot be undone. When David had Uriah killed, he could not bring him back to life. When one marriage is ruined, and there is another, and when now there is another woman and other children to consider, one may not restore the first marriage. One can be forgiven and face with humility whatever shame and questioning must follow when one has made such a mistake and has committed such a sin.

Then should a divorced person be allowed church membership? a place of responsibility in the church? Let us say first, if he proves himself humble, penitent, upright, with no excusing and no defense for his sin, he might be used when he gains the confidence of the people and proves his steadfastness and faithfulness. But always one who has been overtaken in grievous sin should walk humbly and prove himself before expecting people to trust him with spiritual leadership.

VERSES 19 — 26:

19 There was a certain rich man, which was clothed in purple and fine linen, and fared sumptuously every day:

20 And there was a certain beggar named Lazarus, which was laid at his gate, full of sores,

21 And desiring to be fed with the crumbs which fell from the rich man's table: moreover the dogs came and licked his sores.

22 And it came to pass, that the beggar died, and was carried by the angels into Abraham's bosom: the rich man also died, and was buried;

23 And in hell he lift up his eyes, being in torments, and seeth Abraham afar off, and Lazarus in his bosom.

24 And he cried and said, Father Abraham, have mercy on me. and send Lazarus, that he may dip the tip of his finger in water, and cool my tongue; for I am tormented in this flame.

25 But Abraham said, Son, remember that thou in thy lifetime receivedst thy good things, and likewise Lazarus evil things: but now he is comforted, and thou art tormented.

26 And beside all this, between us and you there is a great gulf fixed: so that they which would pass from hence to you cannot; neither can they pass to us, that *would come* from thence.

The Rich Man and Lazarus

We do not count this a parable, though some other commentators do call it so. Jesus does not call it a parable. There are definite people named in the story. Abraham was a historical character. It is probable that there was a real beggar named Lazarus and that the rich man was a real person whose name is not called so as to avoid offense and grief to loved ones and friends. Parables do not name particular people. Compare this with the parable of the prodigal son: *"A certain man"* represents God. There are two sons but neither name is given. The boy went into a *"far country."* What country? Any country where the sinner flees from God. One would like to reduce the awful impact of this story of the rich man and Lazarus by calling it a parable, but we cannot conscientiously do so.

What a contrast! The beggar, afflicted, an outcast, hungry, is now carried to Abraham's bosom and is comforted in Heaven with everlasting blessedness! The rich man who was clothed in purple and fine linen and fared sumptuously every day, in Hell is so poor that he cannot buy a drop of water to cool his tongue. How much better to be a beggar here and be rich in Heaven! Life here is so short compared with eternity that surely only a fool would lose his happiness, peace and pleasure for eternity for temporary pleasure here!

The rich man died; the beggar died. Hebrews 9:27 says, *". . . it is appointed unto men once to die."* This inevitable specter that faces every man had better be considered. How foolish to eat our meals, do our work, enjoy our pleasure, go to our rest at night, without knowing that our sins are forgiven and that we will meet God in peace. Death comes to young and old.

Here in this passage the well man died as well as the sick man. The rich man who could have all that money could buy and doctors and medicine, treatment, and comfort, still died. And God's preachers ought to continually face people with the question, "Are you prepared to meet God?"

Note that Heaven and Hell are the immediate distinations after death. There is no waiting for a judgment. The beggar, who knew the Lord and had his sins forgiven, is already known to be a child of God, with a home in Heaven waiting. So immediately he was carried by the angels to *"Abraham's bosom."* The child of God already *"hath everlasting life"* (John 3:36). To the penitent thief on the cross Jesus said, *"To day shalt thou be with me in paradise"* (Luke 23:43).

While this writer's mother was dying, she had us sing:

> **"How firm a foundation, ye saints of the Lord,**
> **Is laid for your faith in His excellent Word!"**

She lifted her hands in joy and said, "I can see Jesus and my baby now!" and fell asleep. I knew then that she was already with the Saviour.

The rich man died *"and in hell he lift up his eyes, being in torments."* There was no hesitation. The body is not cold but he is in the torments of Hell. Before the expensive funeral and the mourning of rich friends and the eulogy, the rich man was already being tormented in flames. God does not have to wait till judgment time to know that the sinner is unrepentant, unconverted, unforgiven.

Later, as Revelation 20 tells us, there will be a judgment when souls will be brought out of Hell and their bodies out of the grave, to be judged according to the records of God's books. Their bodies will be brought out of their graves or the sea, then *"both soul and body"* shall be cast into Hell, Jesus said in Matthew 10:28. But immediately at death the unrepentant, unconverted soul wakes in Hell.

Note that in Hell one has all his senses. The rich man saw and heard and prayed and was tormented. He was thirsty and pleaded for one to dip his finger in water so as to cool the parched tongue. All the senses in Hell! We know that his body was still in the grave, but the senses simply use organs of the body as servants and means but the senses are part, no doubt, of the person, the spirit. So in Hell one has all his senses.

Hades Here Really Means Hell

The word "*hell*" here is the Greek word *hades,* referring
to the unseen world. The word is about equivalent to
the Hebrew *sheol* in the Old Testament, meaning the
realm of the dead, the place of the departed. And the
word *sheol* is sometimes translated *grave,* but it never
refers to a particular sepulcher but only *grave* in the
symbolic sense as the realm of the dead. Originally, the
term primarily meant all departed spirits and so the
psalmist could cry, "*If I make my bed in hell, behold,
thou art there*" (Ps. 139:8), that is, if one should die.
Jonah, in the "*belly of hell*" and thinking of himself as already about gone to the unseen world, said,
"*Out of the belly of hell cried I, and thou heardest my
voice*" (Jonah 2:2). So, originally, the Hebrew *sheol*
and the Greek *hades,* used here, meant the unseen state,
the realm of departed spirits, and would include both
saved and lost.

However, terminology has a tendency to grow more
definite. And as there came to be very clear teaching
about Heaven and eternal life, through the Scriptures, the
general term *hades* came to refer to the place of the
unsaved dead. The Plymouth Brethren idea, taught by
Dr. Scofield and others, as a "place of departed human
spirits between death and resurrection," is not justified.
The Hell in this story in verse 23 is not simply a place
for both saved and lost but for the unsaved. Lazarus is
not said to be in *hades* but in a separate place, in
Abraham's bosom. Again we think the ultradispensation-
alists are wrong in supposing, as Scofield said, that

> . . . a change has taken place which affects paradise. . . .
> Paradise, therefore, is now in the immediate presence of
> God. It is believed that Eph. 4. 8-10 indicates the time
> of the change.

We do not think so. There is no consistent teaching

of Scripture, we think, that there has been any change in
Heaven and Hell. It is true that until the resurrection
Hell has only the souls, the spirits, of the unsaved and
not the bodies. It is clear that Heaven now does not
have the bodies of the saved, except those of Elijah and
Enoch, but there is no evidence for the Plymouth Brethren
teaching that when born-again people die they go at
once to a Paradise not Heaven.

Is There Literal Fire in Hell?

The Hell mentioned here is a place of fire and torment.
The rich man, "*being in torments*" (vs. 23), says, "*I
am tormented in this flame*" (vs. 24). Actual torment?
Yes. In the first place, sin brings its own pain. There
would be the torment of memory. There would be the
consciousness that the man had brought himself to this
ruin, that he had neglected the Scriptures (his brothers
had Moses and the prophets, and so did he). The inevitable wages of sin is death. And then we must remember that God Himself punishes sin. Hell is not
simply a place for rehabilitation but a place of eternal
punishment for men who go on without Christ and die
unsaved and so continue sinners.

Is the fire in Hell literal fire? We think so. It would
seem strange and hardly honest for God to use the term
again and again and again about Hell, unless He meant
it. He has warned again and again of the place "*where
their worm dieth not, and the fire is not quenched*"
(Mark 9:44,46,48). Jesus said that He Himself would
say to certain wicked ones, "*Depart from me, ye cursed,
into everlasting fire, prepared for the devil and his angels*"
(Matt. 25:41). We are plainly told in Revelation 20:15,
"*And whosoever was not found written in the book of
life was cast into the lake of fire.*" Revelation 21:8 tells
us, "*But the fearful, and unbelieving, and the abominable,
and murderers, and whoremongers, and sorcerers, and
idolaters, and all liars, shall have their part in the lake*

which burneth with fire and brimstone: which is the second death." Those in the tribulation time who decide forever against Christ and receive the mark of the Antichrist ". . . *shall drink of the wine of the wrath of God, which is poured out without mixture into the cup of his indignation; and he shall be tormented with fire and brimstone in the presence of the holy angels, and in the presence of the Lamb: And the smoke of their torment ascendeth up for ever and ever: and they have no rest day nor night. . ."* we are told in Revelation 14:10,11.

Sodom and Gomorrah were destroyed by literal fire and brimstone from Heaven, the Scripture tells us. And II Peter 2:6 tells us plainly that God thus *"condemned them with an overthrow, making them an ensample unto those that after should live ungodly."* And Jude says that those cities in their destruction *"are set forth for an example, suffering the vengeance of eternal fire"* (vs. 7). That indicates that God took a bit of the eternal fire of Hell and poured it on Sodom and Gomorrah. The indication is of literal fire.

Hell, then, is a literal place. People in Hell will have literal bodies after the resurrection. If the fire is figurative, then what about the smoke that ascends forever? Is that figurative smoke?

John the Baptist said about the Saviour that *"he will burn up the chaff with unquenchable fire"* (Matt. 3:12).

And what about the fire used in all the sacrifices and types in the Old Testament? Does not that picture the wrath and judgment of God? Was the fire that came down and destroyed Nadab and Abihu, Aaron's priestly sons, not literal fire (Lev. 10:1,2)? You say there are difficulties. You cannot understand how people who have literal bodies could continue tormented in flames in Hell. Of course we cannot understand it. I cannot understand how the three Hebrew children could walk in the flame of Nebuchadnezzar's fiery furnace and come out uninjured with not even the smell of smoke on their garments. Do

you really think that God cannot do anything but that
which fits within your limited understanding? How can
we understand that in Heaven resurrected bodies can live
on forever without sickness, without growing old, without
decay, without pain? You must understand that when we
walk into the realm of infinity and eternity, we deal with
matters beyond what the human mind knows. Of course,
if the fire were only figurative, it could not mean less
than awful pain and eternal torment. But if God did not
mean fire, why did He say fire so often?

The Punishment of Hell Is Eternal

And here is the fact that the punishment in Hell is
eternal. A great gulf is fixed between Heaven and Hell.
It cannot be crossed. Those in Hell remain in Hell.
The rich man died impenitent. Tormented in Hell,
there is still not a touch of penitence. There is no sorrow
for sin, no love for Christ, no pleading for mercy:
"Where the tree falleth, there it shall be" (Eccles. 11:3).
One who goes to Hell unrepentant, will stay unrepentant,
will stay hardened and sinful in Hell, will remain punished and miserable because of his sin. People go to Hell
simply because they ought to go there, because they
would not take the only way a good God could provide
for men to escape Hell and that is through trusting the
atoning death of Christ, His substitutionary sacrifice.
A good and honest God must punish sin. If one will not
take the suffering of Jesus as paying the debt, he must
pay it himself.

Some argue that the term "everlasting punishment"
means simply "age lasting" or "lasting indefinitely,"
not necessarily lasting forever. But the same word is
used for everlasting fire and everlasting punishment in
Matthew 25:41,46 as is used for everlasting life in John
3:16; John 3:36; John 5:24 and elsewhere. If Heaven
is to be eternal, everlasting, then Hell is to be eternal,
everlasting.

How gently Abraham talks to his descendant in Hell
and calls him *"son."* How God loves the sinner who
goes to Hell and grieves over him! And those of us who
go to Heaven will grieve that loved ones and neighbors
are in Hell. But everybody who comes to the judgment
time will openly declare that God does right, that the
punishment of the wicked is just. And the men of Nineveh will rise in the judgment to condemn those who did
not repent.

VERSES 27—31:

27 Then he said, I pray thee
therefore, father, that thou would-
est send him to my father's house:
28 For I have five brethren; that
he may testify unto them, lest they
also come into this place of torment.
29 Abraham saith unto him, They
have Moses and the prophets; let
them hear them.
30 And he said, Nay, father Abraham: but if one went unto them
from the dead, they will repent.
31 And he said unto him, If they
hear not Moses and the prophets,
neither will they be persuaded,
though one rose from the dead.

Brothers of the Man in Hell

The rich man in Hell had five brothers. We suppose
they were younger than he, that they admired and
patterned after their older brother. It would seem likely
that they, too, either did clothe themselves in fine linen
and fared sumptuously every day or aspired to do so,
like their rich brother. Note that these had *"Moses and
the prophets,"* that is, they had the Old Testament (vs.
29). So they had the many invitations such as Isaiah
1:18 and Isaiah 55:6 and 7. They had the sweet, tender
message about the dying Saviour who would bear our
iniquity and through whose stripes we are to be healed
(Isa. 53). They would have had the word from Joel
2:32 that *"whosoever shall call on the name of the Lord
shall be delivered."* They would have had that sweet
call from Isaiah, *"Look unto me, and be ye saved, all*

the ends of the earth: for I am God, and there is none else" (Isa. 45:22).

We think Jesus won Nicodemus with His sermon on the serpent on the pole which was lifted up by Moses in the wilderness; surely these people would have known about that Scripture and could have gotten that lesson.

Let us say then that every lost man in the world could get the Gospel. If he followed what light he had, God would give more light. If one, like that Roman centurion in Acts, chapter 10, who had never heard the Gospel, prayed with all his heart and sought God, God would surely make some way for him to hear the Gospel. And every lost man will be judged: if he has the Scriptures, by the law, i.e. the Scriptures, and if he does not have the law, he will be judged by his own conscience—the conscience either accusing or excusing (Rom. 2:12-16).

But if Lazarus arose from the dead to preach to these five brothers, would they not repent? No. If they would not repent through the hearing of the Word of God, they would not repent *"though one rose from the dead"!* We have the life-giving message. Oh, let us depend upon the Word. *"Is not my word like as a fire? saith the Lord; and like a hammer that breaketh the rock in pieces"* (Jer. 23:29). *"It pleased God by the foolishness of preaching to save them that believe,"* that is, the preaching of the Word of God (I Cor. 1:21). So I Peter 1:23 says, *"Being born again, not of corruptible seed, but of incorruptible, by the word of God, which liveth and abideth for ever."* The Word of God has the saving Gospel and people will not be saved without it.

Why did the rich man go to Hell? Some foolishly have thought because he was rich. No! Some have thought because he did not share his goods with the poor beggar. No! Jesus does not even hint that in this Scripture. He knew why he was in Hell! He went to Hell because he would not repent, for the rich man says, *"But if one went unto them from the dead, they will repent."* He was mistaken in thinking anything but the Word of God would lead them to repent, but he knew that people went to Hell because they did not repent. So Jesus plainly said in Luke 13:3 and 5, *"I tell you, Nay: but, except ye repent, ye shall all likewise perish."* And in Acts 17:30 Paul preached at Athens; *"And the times of this ignorance God winked at; but now commandeth all men every where to repent."*

The rich man in Hell was stirred with deep concern for his lost brothers. Isn't it strange and sad that in Hell people are so concerned about lost sinners and that up in Heaven there is more joy *"over one sinner that repenteth, more than over ninety and nine just persons, which need no repentance"* (Luke 15:7), but we here who have the opportunity to help people be saved do so little about it?

Oh, God, help that we may see the awful ruin that comes to people in Hell and let us heed the cries of those in Hell and go to win their loved ones.

LUKE 17

THEN said he unto the disciples, It is impossible but that offences will come: but woe *unto him*, through whom they come! 2 It were better for him that a millstone were hanged about his neck, and he cast into the sea, than that he should offend one of these little ones.

3 Take heed to yourselves: If thy brother trespass against thee, rebuke him; and if he repent, forgive him. 4 And if he trespass against thee seven times in a day, and seven times in a day turn again to thee, saying, I repent; thou shalt forgive him.

Offenses and Forgiveness

Jesus gave a companion passage to verses 1 and 2 in Matthew 18:6 after setting up a little child as an example. There is a similar passage also in Mark 9:42. To "*offend*" means to cause to stumble. If we do right we will sometimes displease other Christians and they may feel offense. That is not the point. But to hinder one in his Christian life and cause him to be disillusioned, cause him to stumble or to sin, would be a terrible sin and bring great punishment. With this in mind Paul was inspired to exhort us to take heed that our liberty become not a stumblingblock to them who are weak, as when a Christian might eat meat in the idol's temple, knowing that the idol was nothing, but a weaker brother might not know so and he might do that which he thought was wrong, following the Christian, and thus sin as he went against his conscience. So I Corinthians 8:13 says, "*Wherefore, if meat make my brother to offend, I will eat no flesh while the world standeth, lest I make my brother to offend,*" to stumble. We are not only to be honest but we are to "*provide things honest in the sight of all men"* (Rom. 12:17). We are not only to do no evil, but we are to *"abstain from all appearance of evil"* (I Thess. 5:22).

But if some brother trespass against us, we should be quick to forgive. May I tell my brother when he has wronged me? Yes I may, but with the aim to restore fellowship. And as often as one repents he is to be forgiven, even seven times a day.

Now, it is true that the Christian should have a forgiving heart, with longsuffering and without enmity, even if the one who has wronged him does not repent. *"Be ye kind one to another, tenderhearted, forgiving one another, even as God for Christ's sake hath forgiven you"* (Eph. 4:32).

Sometimes a brother may repent and want to treat right the one he wronged, even though he may not abjectly confess his wrong. Oh, Christians should be quick to forgive if anyone is sorry for his wrong toward us.

But what if the brother or friend will not undo the wrong? Instructions are given in Matthew 18:15-17. First, one should *"go and tell him his fault between thee and him alone: if he shall hear thee, thou hast gained thy brother."* Gaining him should be the object of the loving approach.

"But if he will not hear thee, then take with thee one or two more, that in the mouth of two or three witnesses every word may be established." In other words, one should enlist others to help win the friend who has done wrong and bring him to do right. If, then, he will not hear the matter (we consider here, we suppose, a very serious offense), then we are to tell it to the church and the church will try to advise the man what is right and get him to right his wrong. If he will not do so, then his fellowship is lost with the church and with Christian brethren. Remember that the plan all along is not for one simply to get justice for himself but for one to keep his friend and to restore him who does wrong. *"Breth-*

ren, if a man be overtaken in a fault, ye which are spiritual, restore such an one in the spirit of meekness; considering thyself, lest thou also be tempted" (Gal. 6:1).

VERSES 5, 6:

5 And the apostles said unto the Lord, Increase our faith.
6 And the Lord said, If ye had faith as a grain of mustard seed, ye might say unto this sycamine tree, Be thou plucked up by the root, and be thou planted in the sea; and it should obey you.

The Prayer of Faith

This matter of faith in God is so important that it comes up again and again in the language of Jesus. When the disciples asked Jesus why they could not cast the devil out of the demon-possessed boy, *"Jesus said unto them, Because of your unbelief: for verily I say unto you, If ye have faith as a grain of mustard seed, ye shall say unto this mountain, Remove hence to yonder place; and it shall remove; and nothing shall be impossible unto you"* (Matt. 17:20).

In connection with this same event, we are told that Jesus said to the anguished father, *"If thou canst believe, all things are possible to him that believeth"* (Mark 9:23). In Matthew 21:22 Jesus said, *"And all things, whatsoever ye shall ask in prayer, believing, ye shall receive."* Perhaps the nearest approximation to this statement in Luke is that in Mark 11, in connection with the cursing of the fig tree. There Jesus said in verses 22 to 24:

"And Jesus answering saith unto them, Have faith in God. For verily I say unto you, That whosoever shall say unto this mountain, Be thou removed, and be thou

cast into the sea; and shall not doubt in his heart, but shall believe that those things which he saith shall come to pass; he shall have whatsoever he saith. Therefore I say unto you, What things soever ye desire, when ye pray, believe that ye receive them, and ye shall have them."

We are commanded to have faith. Note what leads to faith:

1. We should pray like the disciples, *"Lord, Increase our faith."*

2. We should find what God says in His Word about answers and then claim what God has promised: *"So then faith cometh by hearing, and hearing by the word of God"* (Rom. 10:17). Faith is believing God will do what He said.

3. We can increase our faith by trying God out and proving how wonderfully He keeps His Word. So one is commanded to have faith.

In some particular matters not clearly promised in the Bible, faith must be a gift of God (see I Cor. 12:9). If God does not give faith in such a case, we cannot have it. So when James 5:15 says, *"The prayer of faith shall save the sick, and the Lord shall raise him up,"* we must understand that if God does not give the faith, then we cannot pray the prayer of faith. So we should pray, *"Lord, Increase our faith."*

Compare the word of Jesus in Matthew 17:20 and Mark 11:23 with Luke 17:6. Jesus illustrates that one may pray for either a tree or a mountain to be cast into the sea and Jesus means, as He says in Matthew 17:20, *"and nothing shall be impossible unto you,"* if you have faith. So in Mark 16:17, *"And these signs shall follow them that believe,"* that is, these particular signs named will follow for those who have faith for these particular signs or miracles.

VERSES 7 — 10:

7 But which of you, having a servant plowing or feeding cattle, will say unto him by and by, when he is come from the field, Go and sit down to meat? 8 And will not rather say unto him, Make ready wherewith I may sup, and gird thyself, and serve me, till I have eaten and drunken; and afterward thou shalt eat and drink? 9 Doth he thank that servant because he did the things that were commanded him? I trow not. 10 So likewise ye, when ye shall have done all those things which are commanded you, say, We are unprofitable servants: we have done that which was our duty to do.

At Best We Are Unprofitable Servants

Paul knew that because of the abundance of the revelations he might be exalted above measure, so there was given him a thorn in the flesh. When all we have and are is bought and paid for at such awful cost, and when we are forever in debt to the dear Saviour, how presumptuous to think that we are especially worthy and that we put God under obligation by whatever meager service we can give!

Dr. Bob Jones, Sr., used to say, "Don't say that some man does ten men's work. Every man's work is all that he can do for Jesus." And God, who judges the heart and keeps the record, will see to it that all who serve Him do not fail of a reward! *"In due season we shall reap, if we faint not"* (Gal. 6:9).

VERSES 11—19:

11 And it came to pass, as he went to Jerusalem, that he passed through the midst of Samaria and Galilee. 12 And as he entered into a certain village, there met him ten men that were lepers, which stood afar off:

13 And they lifted up *their* voices, and said, Jesus, Master, have mercy on us.

14 And when he saw *them*, he said unto them, Go shew yourselves unto the priests. And it came to pass, that, as they went, they were cleansed.

15 And one of them, when he saw that he was healed, turned back, and with a loud voice glorified God,

16 And fell down on *his* face at his feet, giving him thanks: and he was a Samaritan.

17 And Jesus answering said, Were there not ten cleansed? but where *are* the nine?

18 There are not found that returned to give glory to God, save this stranger.

19 And he said unto him, Arise, go thy way: thy faith hath made thee whole.

Ten Lepers Healed or Cleansed

Jesus is still going through cities and towns in Samaria and Galilee, headed eventually to Jerusalem. It is not surprising, then, that in a certain village, of ten lepers He met, one of them would be a Samaritan.

The lepers "*stood afar off*" (vs. 12). They were following the requirement of the Mosaic Law as given in Leviticus 13:4 5,46:

"*And the leper in whom the plague is, his clothes shall be rent, and his head bare, and he shall put a covering upon his upper lip, and shall cry, Unclean, unclean. All the days wherein the plague shall be in him he shall be defiled; he is unclean: he shall dwell alone; without the camp shall his habitation be.*"

These poor afflicted men cried out, "*Jesus, Master, have mercy on us.*" When He said, "*Go shew yourselves unto the priests,*" He meant for them to follow the instructions of Leviticus 14. And as they went they were cleansed. Surely they had some faith that Christ would heal them and they took His Word for it and went to let the priest examine them and see the evidence that they were cleansed. The cleansing happened miraculously as they went.

Strangely, sadly, only one of the ten returned to give glory and thanks to God. Jesus was sad, for He said,

"*Were there not ten cleansed? but where are the nine?*"
There is a sad usual pattern in the fact that so many,
greatly blessed beyond measure, did not even return to
thank Christ! Many now do not even regularly thank
God for their food. And it is wickedness beyond measure
for those who take God's mercies, His sunshine, His air,
His food, family, friends, work, pleasure, to never turn
to give any thanks to Christ, to God, or to love and
trust the Saviour.

Why just the Samaritan who returned to give thanks?
I should think possibly because the Samaritans were
underprivileged, despised by the Jews, more conscious
of their own need, and thus the Samaritan would be
more sensitive to the blessing that Christ had given him.
Oh, we favored people who come from Christian families,
who grow up in comfort, and all our lives live in pleasant places. I think we do not love the Lord as much
nor feel as grateful for His blessings as others less for-
tunate. So the woman who was a sinner in the house of
the Pharisee, who knelt at the feet of Jesus and kissed
them and washed them with her tears and dried them with
her hair, was forgiven so much, so she loved Jesus much,
while the Pharisee loved Him little (Luke 7:36-50). Also,
the reaction of one in a lower position socially was the
more noticeable, we think. So Jesus used the Samaritan
in the parable of the Good Samaritan as the one who
helped the man assaulted and wounded by thieves on
the road from Jerusalem to Jericho.

The word stranger in verse 18 and as used throughout the Bible, means foreigner. The Samaritan people
were not fully Jews but half-breeds. And it was the
Samaritan's faith that made him whole.

VERSES 20, 21:

20 And when he was demanded of the Pharisees, when the kingdom of God should come, he answered them and said, The kingdom of God cometh not with observation: 21 Neither shall they say, Lo here! or, lo there! for, behold, the kingdom of God is within you.

When Would the Kingdom of God Come?

The Jews well knew that God had promised that He would restore the kingdom to Israel. Second Samuel 7:10-16 tells us how that promise was made to David. It is told also in I Chronicles 17:4-15. David's kingdom is to be restored. Isaiah 11 tells about the king to come as a "*root*" or sprout from the stump of Jesse who will restore the tree of God's kingdom (Isa. 11:1-10). Jeremiah 33:3-8 tells so clearly about the return and salvation of Israel and "*THE LORD OUR RIGHTEOUSNESS*" who would reign. Ezekiel 37: 24,25 tells of the return to Israel, "*And David my servant shall be king over them.*" And Zechariah told of the day of the Lord when Christ will come to deliver Israel from the nations that will surround Jerusalem, "*And the Lord shall be king over all the earth: in that day shall there be one Lord, and his name one*" (Zech. 14:9).

It is not surprising that even the apostles would ask the risen Saviour, "*Lord, wilt thou at this time restore again the kingdom to Israel*" (Acts 1:6). They well knew that God had planned a kingdom. And they may have known, though the Pharisee probably would not, that the Angel Gabriel had promised to Mary this about Jesus: "*And the Lord God shall give unto him the throne of his father David: And he shall reign over the house of Jacob for ever; and of his kingdom there shall be no end*" (Luke 1:32,33). Jesus had spoken often in para-

bles, saying, "*The kingdom of heaven is likened unto
. . .*" or had spoken about "*the kingdom of God.*"   Nor
is it surprising, then, that the Pharisees wanted to know
when the kingdom would come.   You see, they expected
a kingdom that would be purely a physical regathering
of Israel, and they thought that Jews, as Jews, would inherit the promises.   They did not know, though they
should have known, that God required a new heart for
those who would be in this kingdom. And Jesus had to
tell Nicodemus, a ruler of the Jews, "*Except a man be
born again, he cannot see the kingdom of God,*" and
"*Except a man be born of water and of the Spirit, he
cannot enter into the kingdom of God*" (John 3:3,5).

Jesus answered in two ways: First, the kingdom of
God is now in a spiritual form and not a thing one can
observe as he could observe a great revolution and a
change in government.   Now, the born-again ones are in
the kingdom of God and God has "*translated us into the
kingdom of his dear Son*" (Col. 1:13). And the parables
about the kingdom of God or the kingdom of Heaven
usually speak of the sphere of Christian profession, for
in the kingdom area are those who do not accept the
King nor serve Him.   The kingdom, in the time of these
Pharisees, "*cometh not with observation.*"   Rather, the
kingdom of God "*is within,*" that is, truly it is an inward matter.

Perhaps in some sense the meaning is as Dr. Scofield
thinks:

> Gr. *entos* = "in the midst."   It could not be said of a
> self-righteous, Christ-rejecting Pharisee, that the kingdom
> of God, as to its spiritual content, was within him.   Our
> Lord's whole answer, designedly enigmatic to the Phari-
> sees (cf. Mt. 13. 10-13), has a dispensational meaning.
> The kingdom in its outward form, as covenanted to
> David (2 Sam. 7. 8-17) and described by the prophets
> (Zech. 12.8, note), had been rejected by the Jews; so that,
> during this present age, it would not "come with observa-
> tion" (lit. "outward show") but in the hearts of men (cf.

Lk. 19.11,12; Acts 1.6-8, note; Rom. 14.17). Meantime, the kingdom was actually "in the midst" of the Pharisees in the persons of the King and His disciples. Ultimately the kingdom of heaven *will* come, with outward show. (See v. 24.)

Eventually, Christ will come openly, publicly at His return to reign with all the saints and angels, but at present, and until then, the kingdom grows as people are converted, and the kingdom is not with outward observation. Eventually, as Paul happily anticipated, "*. . . the Lord shall deliver me from every evil work, and will preserve me unto his heavenly kingdom*" (II Tim. 4:18).

VERSES 22— 25:

22 And he said unto the disciples, The days will come, when ye shall desire to see one of the days of the Son of man, and ye shall not see *it*.
23   And they shall say to you, See here; or, see there: go not after *them*, nor follow *them*.
24 For as the lightning, that light-eneth out of the one *part* under heaven, shineth unto the other *part* under heaven; so shall also the Son of man be in his day.
25 But first must he suffer many things, and be rejected of this generation.

Jesus Speaks Further About the Kingdom

There could be no open manifestation of the kingdom of God on earth, with Christ to sit on David's throne and rule the whole earth, until the Scriptures first be fulfilled. He must be crucified and rejected by that generation, the Jewish nation as such. The disciples would long to see Jesus, long for Him to come, and would remember the days when they walked with Jesus in the flesh. But they were not to be misled by false prophets and those who would teach that Jesus was coming at a certain time or in a certain way, for the return of Christ would be so

certain and sudden that there would be no mistaking of
it.   It would be as sudden as the lightning flash.   But
first must come the crucifixion and other things.   It is
good for us to be reminded that Jesus spoke frequently
about His second coming.   The discussion that follows
in this chapter is different from the Olivet Discourse, part
of which is repeated in Luke 21.

VERSES 26—32:

26 And as it was in the days of
Noe, so shall it be also in the days
of the Son of man.
27 They did eat, they drank, they
married wives, they were given in
marriage, until the day that Noe
entered into the ark, and the flood
came, and destroyed them all.
28 Likewise also as it was in the
days of Lot; they did eat, they
drank, they bought, they sold, they
planted, they builded;
29 But the same day that Lot

went out of Sodom it rained fire
and brimstone from heaven, and
destroyed *them* all.
30 Even thus shall it be in the day
when the Son of man is revealed.
31 In that day, he which shall be
upon the housetop, and his stuff in
the house, let him not come down
to take it away: and he that is in
the field, let him likewise not return
back.
32 Remember Lot's wife.

Warning From the Days of Noah and From Sodom

See the Olivet Discourse in Matthew 24, particularly
verses 37 and 38 about the days of Noah.   Some have
foolishly made the meaning here the exact opposite of
what Jesus stresses.   Jesus is not saying that life will get
as wicked as in the day of Noah and by that we will
know when the return of Christ approaches.   In contradiction of that, He is saying that so suddenly and unex-
pectedly came the flood and the people "*were eating and
drinking, marrying and giving in marriage, until the
day that Noe entered into the ark, And knew not until
the flood came, and took them all away; so shall also
the coming of the Son of man be*" (Matt. 24:38,39).   It

is the suddenness, the unexpectedness of His return which He stresses there and here. So also about the destruction of Sodom. The people went on with their normal life—eating, drinking, buying, selling, planting, building, and in one day the holocaust of fire from Heaven destroyed them all. So sudden, so unexpected, will be the coming of the Saviour even as a lightning flash, as verse 24 tells us. It will be "*In a moment, in the twinkling of an eye*" (I Cor. 15:52).

Even so, when Christ comes, a man will not have time to get his stuff from the house and will not return from the field. And to show the urgency, they are to remember Lot's wife who lingered.

Does not that mean, first, that all should be watching and ready for Christ's coming now? And it may have some special meaning, also about Jews and Jerusalem in the tribulation time, which is surely intended in a similar passage in Matthew 24:15-21.

The tribulation time will be after the rapture, and "*when the Son of man is revealed*" would mean the second phase of Christ's coming—when He returns to the earth to reign. However, the warning about the suddenness, the unpredictability of Christ's coming is about His coming into the air to receive His own. About that time Matthew 24:36 tells us, "*But of that day and hour knoweth no man, no not the angels of heaven, but my Father only.*" So also Mark 13:32.

After Christ calls His saints to meet Him in the air, however, there will be a measured, predicted period, Daniel's 70th week (Dan. 9:27). The Great Tribulation proper, the reign of the Antichrist on earth, will be three and a half years (Dan. 7:25;12:7;Rev. 12:14), or 42 months (Rev. 11:2), or 1,260 days (Rev. 11:3;12:6). So the coming end of that period can be foreseen (Matt. 24:33; Luke 21:28). But until the rapture, when Christ calls His own to meet Him in the air, there are no par-

ticular prophesied events, no way to predict when Jesus
will come.

VERSE 33:

33 Whosoever shall seek to save | shall lose his life shall preserve it.
his life shall lose it; and whosoever |

Save One's Life by Losing It

This great verse deserves separate treatment.   The
same teaching is given wonderfully by the Saviour in
Luke 9:24, Mark 8:35 and in Matthew 16:25. And in
each case the Lord Jesus asks the solemn question, "*For
what is a man profited, if he shall gain the whole world,
and lose his own soul? or what shall a man give in
exchange for his soul?*"
In each of these cases Jesus reminds us of the two
contrasting events: His own death on the cross and
His triumphant return to reign.   Jesus came meek and
lowly in heart, born and reared in abject poverty, in a
little village in an obscure province.   Foxes had holes
and birds had nests but He, the Creator, had not where
to lay His head.   He was hated by chief priests and
elders and Pharisees.   He was shunned by the learned.
One of His own disciples betrayed Him, and the rest
forsook Him and fled.   Nicodemus, a member of the
Sanhedrin, would come to Him only under cover of
darkness.   He died a shameful death as a criminal
between two thieves, amid the mocking of the crowd.
But He will come again in glory, crowned with many
crowns, to set up His kingdom and rule the whole earth.
Jesus gained all the future triumph by losing His life
and Himself.
Jesus tells the disciples that they would profit by giving
up things that other men value in this life to have the

great blessings in the next. They should give up earthly treasures for spiritual treasures. Is a man happier to be poor, with constant fellowship with Christ and joy in His service, than to be rich in this world? Millions have tried it, some on one side and some the other, and proved the Saviour's statement true.

In Mark 10:29 and 30 is this wonderful promise:

"And Jesus answered and said, Verily I say unto you, There is no man that hath left house, or brethren, or sisters, or father, or mother, or wife, or children, or lands, for my sake, and the gospel's, But he shall receive an hundredfold now in this time, houses, and brethren, and sisters, and mothers, and children, and lands, with persecutions; and in the world to come eternal life."

"An hundredfold now in this time"! Wonderful! Besides all the rewards of Heaven! So one gives up his own way, his own immediate pleasure and profit, gains wonderfully in this life besides the gains in the life to come.

And so this great Christian paradox is mentioned throughout the Bible. It is the meek who shall inherit the earth. Not one who hoards his goods but one who gives, increases, for Jesus said, *"Give, and it shall be given unto you; good measure, pressed down, and shaken together, and running over, shall men give into your bosom. For with the same measure that ye mete withal it shall be measured to you again"* (Luke 6:38). And we are told that *"the liberal soul shall be made fat: and he that watereth shall be watered also himself"* (Prov. 11:25). So one who would be chief among the disciples is to be servant of all. And Jesus said that when one goes to a wedding feast he should seek the lowest room and that he may be then invited up higher. So *"whosoever exalteth himself shall be abased; and he that humbleth himself shall be exalted"* (Luke 14:11). Those who suffer with Jesus now will reign with Him later (II Tim.

2:12). So it is more blessed to give than to receive, and one who saves his life will lose it.

How many people have eagerly sought for themselves the money, the houses, the pleasures, the luxuries of this life only to find them bitter to the soul! In the parable in Luke, chapter 12, that rich fool who laid by his goods and said, *"Soul, thou hast much goods laid up for many years; take thine ease, eat, drink, and be merry,"* was called a fool because he chose the fleeting and unstable things and had neglected the eternal things.

So when Jesus comes with all His holy angels, those who are ashamed of Jesus and His Word will find the Lord Jesus ashamed of them. But how blessed and happy will be those who can hear the words: *"Thou hast been faithful over a few things, I will make thee ruler over many things"* (Matt. 25:21,23).

"By faith Moses, when he was come to years, refused to be called the son of Pharaoh's daughter; Choosing rather to suffer affliction with the people of God, than to enjoy the pleasures of sin for a season; Esteeming the reproach of Christ greater riches than the treasures in Egypt: for he had respect unto the recompence of the reward. By faith he forsook Egypt, not fearing the wrath of the king: for he endured, as seeing him who is invisible." — Heb. 11:24-27.

Moses who forsook the palace of the king to spend forty lonely years in the desert, then to lead a nation from slavery; Paul the apostle, a scholar and spiritual giant who was glad to die, neglected in a Roman prison; Stephen who was battered to death as he witnessed for Jesus — how rich were these!

―――

VERSES 34—37:

34 I tell you, in that night there | shall be two *men* in one bed; the

one shall be taken, and the other shall be left.

35 Two *women* shall be grinding together; the one shall be taken, and the other left.

36 Two *men* shall be in the field; the one shall be taken, and the other left.

37 And they answered and said unto him, Where, Lord? And he said unto them, Wheresoever the body *is*, thither will the eagles be gathered together.

One Taken, the Other Left When Jesus Comes

This compares with Matthew 24:40 and 41 and it speaks, we think, about the rapture when *"we shall not all sleep, but we shall all be changed, In a moment, in the twinkling of an eye, at the last trump: for the trumpet shall sound, and the dead shall be raised incorruptible, and we shall be changed"* (I Cor. 15:51,52). And I Thessalonians 4:16 and 17 repeats the truth, in these words:

"For the Lord himself shall descend from heaven with a shout, with the voice of the archangel, and with the trump of God: and the dead in Christ shall rise first: Then we which are alive and remain shall be caught up together with them in the clouds, to meet the Lord in the air: and so shall we ever be with the Lord."

Here then will be the great division. Living saints will be changed and the Christian dead will be raised. The Christian will be taken and the unsaved person left. Even in that resurrection of the saved, the unsaved will be left behind: *"But the rest of the dead lived not again until the thousand years were finished. This is the first resurrection"* (Rev. 20:5).

Verse 34 indicates that in some parts of the earth it will be night when Jesus comes: two people in one bed, one taken and the other left. Verse 35 indicates it may be in the morning in some places: the women grinding the meal for the day, one taken and the other left. Verse 36 indicates that perhaps it will be midday or afternoon: two men in the same field, one taken and the other left.

Will the coming of Christ to receive His own be extended through day and night? Oh, no! It will be *"in a moment, in the twinkling of an eye,"* as I Corinthians 15:52 tells us. And Luke 17:24 says, *"For as the lightning, that lighteneth out of the one part under heaven, shineth unto the other part under heaven; so shall also the Son of man be in his day."* No, the Christ who said this knew the earth turns on its axis and that it is night at one place on the earth when it is morning at another and noonday at another. This Scripture clearly indicates the revolution of the earth, although it was not known then to the people.

And where will this gathering be of all the saints when the living are changed and the Christian dead are raised? Never mind where; the Lord answers, *"Wheresoever the body is, thither will the eagles be gathered together."* As birds of prey instinctively find a body, we may be sure that when Christ calls His own, we will know where to meet Him in the air!

LUKE 18

VERSE 1:

AND he spake a parable unto them *to this end*, that men ought always to pray, and not to faint;

"Men Ought Always to Pray"

It is not only that we would do well to pray but that we *ought* to pray. It is not only that we ought to pray often but that we ought *always* to pray. Christians ought not to be discouraged, ought not to faint, ought not to cease pleading with God for what they need.

Romans 12:12 says that the Christian should be *"patient in tribulation; continuing instant in prayer,"* that is, one should be always on the alert in prayer.

In Colossians 4:2 we are commanded, *"Continue in prayer, and watch in the same with thanksgiving."* Christians should have regular seasons of prayer, of course, seasons when they do nothing but pray. And then they should pray the rest of the time, whatever else they do. And as verse 7 here says, Christians should pray *"day and night."* Christians are to watch and pray, that is, stay awake in the night watches to plead with God. And prayer should be accompanied with thanksgiving.

Ephesians 6:18 says that the Christian should put on the whole armour of God, *"praying always with all prayer and supplication in the Spirit, and watching thereunto with all perseverance and supplication for all saints."*

Note the "alls": *"Always," "all prayer," "with all perseverance,"* and *"for all saints."* And note the continued pleading: "*Always... supplication... persever-ance... supplication....*" And perhaps even more boldly stated is I Thessalonians 5:17, "*Pray without ceasing.*" That is, Christians should simply pray all the time, day and night.

That means necessarily that the prayer life must flow from the subconscious as well as from the conscious. A mother grows such a natural concern and watchful-ness that she listens for the baby while she sleeps and she hears the slightest whimper. Should not a Christian be as concerned for the salvation of sinners for whom he prays as the mother is to keep her babe covered in the night?

It is said that Dr. George W. Truett, long-famous pastor of the First Baptist Church of Dallas, Texas, in the Baylor Hospital in his final illness, was sometimes delirious. Once he asked a nurse, "When I was un-conscious, did I say anything that a Christian ought not say?"

"No," she replied. "Sometimes you thought you were preaching, sometimes counselling with Christians, some-times pleading with sinners. No, you were just like you are when you are conscious."

He answered, "I would be so sad if, when I am de-lirious, anything comes out of my heart that would dis-honor the Lord."

Don't you see that one ought to be a good Christian subconsciously, whether he is thinking about it or not? And what good is the Pharisee's prayer that is simply a part of the public expression for all to see and hear, if it does not come from the depths of a heart that cries out day and night to God?

That means, then, that prayer with the things that ac-company prayer, such as abiding in Christ, is about the only thing we are commanded to do all the time.

VERSES 2—8:

2 Saying, There was in a city a judge, which feared not God, neither regarded man:
3 And there was a widow in that city; and she came unto him, saying, Avenge me of mine adversary.
4 And he would not for a while: but afterward he said within himself, Though I fear not God, nor regard man;
5 Yet because this widow troubleth me, I will avenge her, lest by her continual coming she weary me.
6 And the Lord said, Hear what the unjust judge saith.
7 And shall not God avenge his own elect, which cry day and night unto him, though he bear long with them?
8 I tell you that he will avenge them speedily. Nevertheless when the Son of man cometh, shall he find faith on the earth?

The Unjust Judge Answers: Will Not God Answer His Own?

In the parable of the unjust steward, the worldly man, acting perhaps without much principle, is held up as an example to Christians in the single fact that he used his money and offices now, to have a home for himself hereafter. So Christians should use money, things, posessions, position, to make sure that we have those to receive us gladly into everlasting habitations. So here an unjust judge is held up as an antithesis to God to show that if persistence gains its end even with a selfish and wicked man, would not the pleading of one of God's own children be heard and answered? The wicked judge did not fear God, had no moral convictions, had no compassion for a widow in her trouble, but lest he should be wearied by her continual coming, he answered the cry of the widow. In the American Standard Version, the judge is quoted as saying, "*lest she wear me out by her continual coming.*" And shall not our own Heavenly Father "*avenge his own elect, which cry day and night unto him, though he bear long with them? I tell you that he will avenge them speedily.*"

The Lord speaks here about "*day and night*" praying
(vs. 7). So it was that Nehemiah prayed: "*Hear the
prayer of thy servant, which I pray before thee now,
day and night*" (Neh. 1:6). Happy the Christian who
has sometimes prayed all night or who has sometimes
neglected food in order to seek the face of God! Colossians 4:2 says that a Christian should "*continue in
prayer, and watch in the same,*" that is, he should keep
the night watches in prayer.

Far too little we heed this oft-repeated command and
plea for continual pleading. In II Chronicles 7:14, in
God's promise for revival, the healing of the land requires that God's people "*seek my face.*" And Isaiah
40:28-32 says that God gives power to the faint and to
those who have no might He increases strength, for "*they
that WAIT UPON THE LORD shall renew their strength;
they shall mount up with wings as eagles; they shall
run, and not be weary; and they shall walk, and not
faint.*" In Psalm 37:7 we are told to "*wait patiently*" for
the Lord. Again in Psalm 27 we are to learn to "*wait,
I say, on the Lord.*"

When a man with an unexpected guest for whom he
had no food came pleading at midnight with a friend,
"*. . . lend me three loaves,*" he did not at first receive it.
But, Jesus said, "*I say unto you, Though he will not
rise and give him, because he is his friend, yet because
of his IMPORTUNITY he will rise and give him as
many as he needeth*" (Luke 11:8). All our faithfulness
in attending the house of God, or reading His Word, our
family devotions, our giving of tithes, does not get the
Bread for sinners like importunity!

Before Pentecost the disciples "*all continued with one
accord in prayer and supplication*" (Acts 1:14). And
twice Ephesians 6:18 emphasizes supplication.

It may well be that ofttimes if God does not withhold
the blessing for a season, we do not seek His presence
and do not enjoy His company. So if He withholds, for

a season, the blessing desired and needed, we are to plead all the more earnestly.

We are told that God will "*avenge his own elect*." The Christian is not to return evil for evil, and we are commanded, "*Avenge not yourselves, but rather give place unto wrath*" (Rom. 12:19). We are to do good to those who hate us and pray for those who despitefully use us and persecute us (Matt. 5:44). God says, "*Vengeance is mine; I will repay, saith the Lord*" (Rom. 12:19). So when King Hezekiah and Isaiah laid out before the Lord in the Temple the threatening letter of Sennacherib, God avenged them and Israel and punished the boastful heathen by slaying 185,000 in the camp of the Assyrians that night (Isaiah 37 and II Chronicles 32)! So with Korah and others who rebelled against Moses and conspired to oppose his leadership, at the word of Moses, God had the ground open up and they went down alive into the pit (Num. 16:33).

David could have God's help in avenging Ziklag and in getting restored his family and goods taken by the Amalekites (I Sam. 27). The Christian, even when he suffers some at the hands of men, can say, "*Let your conversation be without covetousness; and be content with such things as ye have: for he hath said, I will never leave thee, nor forsake thee. So that we may boldly say, The Lord is my helper, and I will not fear what man shall do unto me*" (Heb. 13:5,6). The God who counts all the hairs on the heads of His children and who watches with compassion the fall of a sparrow and who with careful delight clothes the wild flowers, will surely care for His own who trust Him!

Note again verse 8: "*Nevertheless when the Son of man cometh, shall he find faith on the earth?*" The Saviour seems to say that sadly. Note that here persistent praying is counted as faith. When the Lord Jesus returns, will He find many Christians with that kind of faith, those who persistently hold on to God? Our lack of power, our lack of soul-winning blessing, stems from our lack of persistent prayer.

VERSES 9— 14:

9 And he spake this parable unto certain which trusted in themselves that they were righteous, and despised others:

10 Two men went up into the temple to pray; the one a Pharisee, and the other a publican.

11 The Pharisee stood and prayed thus with himself, God, I thank thee, that I am not as other men *are*, extortioners, unjust, adulterers, or even as this publican.

12 I fast twice in the week, I give tithes of all that I possess.

13 And the publican, standing afar off, would not lift up so much as *his* eyes unto heaven, but smote upon his breast, saying, God be merciful to me a sinner.

14 I tell you, this man went down to his house justified *rather* than the other: for every one that exalteth himself shall be abased; and he that humbleth himself shall be exalted.

A Pharisee Prays

Note that he *"prayed thus with himself."* I think we might say this only pretends to be a prayer. It is prayer in the generally accepted term but not the kind of prayer the Bible teaches, for prayer means asking and this man asks nothing. Rather, he *"prayed thus with himself."* Was it rather a soliloquy? He congratulates himself. He enjoys his form of righteousness. What he calls a prayer is really his boasting. He said, *"I thank thee, that I am not as other men are. . . even as this publican."* True, outwardly he was righteous, and even formal ceremonial uprightness is better than sin. It is good to pray, to give, to be virtuous instead of adulterous; better to deal honestly in business than with extortion, as many tax collectors did and probably as did this one. But the righteousness that pleases God must be a heart-righteousness. Jesus said, *"Blessed are they which do hunger and thirst after righteousness"* (Matt. 5:6). To love God with all your heart and your neighbor as yourself fulfills the law (Matt. 22:36-40; Luke 10:25-28; Rom. 13:8-10).

But even so, all human righteousness fails to satisfy a perfect God. It is only relatively righteous compared to other men: as between the Pharisee and the publican, the Pharisee was righteous; as between him and God, he was a poor lost sinner with a corrupt heart. All his righteousnesses were as filthy rags (Isa. 64:6). Perhaps he did not steal but he coveted. Even if he did not commit adultery, he longed after some other woman who was not his wife. He did not kill but perhaps he hated someone and was a murderer in his heart (I John 3:15). Thus it turns out that good fruit cannot come from a corrupt tree and *"the plowing of the wicked, is sin"* (Prov. 21:4). None of his outward formal righteousness could please God when he had an impenitent heart, a corrupt nature not reborn.

The Pharisee could have been as outwardly blameless as Saul of Tarsus before he was saved (Acts 23:1; Acts 24:16; II Tim. 1:3; Phil. 3:4-6), but he would still be like Saul—a lost sinner. Or he may have been as superficial as most Pharisees, hypocrites, as Jesus called them repeatedly in Matthew 23, seeking to appear righteous unto men. He might have been like the whited sepulchers full of dead men's bones and all uncleanness, as Jesus charged about some (Matt. 23:27). At any rate, his prayer was not acceptable.

Paul said about good Jews, *"Brethren, my heart's desire and prayer to God for Israel is, that they might be saved. For I bear them record that they have a zeal of God, but not according to knowledge. For they being ignorant of God's righteousness, and going about to establish their own righteousness, have not submitted themselves unto the righteousness of God"* (Rom. 10:1-3). And Christ Himself *"is the end of the law for righteousness to every one that believeth,"* as the next verse says. So, when one is converted and has Christ, we Christians should have *"the righteousness of the law. . . fulfilled in us, who walk not after the flesh, but after the Spirit"* (Rom. 8:4).

This poor Pharisee was not justified, not saved, as was the publican, according to verse 14.

A Crooked Tax Collector Gets Saved

The publican was a tax collector.   The simple and effective way the Roman Empire had of collecting taxes was to simply farm out the taxes.   The man who took responsibility for the taxes in a given large area was required to turn in a certain amount.   He would agree with other men to take this village or that and the tax collector had authority to collect from the people.   All he could collect above the amount he was required to turn in, he kept for himself.   So it is not surprising that the Pharisees spoke of such tax collectors as *"extortioners"* (vs. 11), or that Zacchaeus, a chief among the tax collectors, was rich (Luke 19:2) and that his conscience required him to say, *"If I have taken any thing from any man by false accusation, I restore him fourfold"* (Luke 19:8).   Also, it is not surprising that the publicans were hated by the Jews, and the Pharisees thought it shocking that anyone would eat with these publicans and have fellowship with them (Matt. 9:11; Mark 2:16; Luke 5:30 and Luke 19:7).

Notice the term regularly used—*"publicans and sinners,"* indicating that the greedy and immoral tax collectors oppressed other people and so kept company with harlots and other gross sinners.   And when the publicans and sinners drew near unto Jesus to hear Him (as in Luke 15:1 and 2), the Pharisees and scribes murmured.   The publicans had generally earned the aversion of moral and religious people.

But here a publican comes to the Temple to pray.

Notice the contrast which Jesus has in this parable which He spake *"unto certain which trusted in themselves that they were righteous, and despised others."* One man, as far as we know, had the best reputation for morality and religion. The other was regarded as a great sinner against God and man, and he probably was.

Note how the publican prayed: He stood *"afar off."* We judge that he did not feel at home in the Temple and did not often come there to pray. He has none of the glib talk of the self-righteous Pharisee, none of the assurance of the Pharisee looking up to Heaven with confidence that God is greatly pleased with his outward morality. The deep penitence in his heart is noted by the phrase, *"but smote upon his breast."* He had godly sorrow which leads to repentance. Like a prodigal, he had come to himself and resolved to confess his sinfulness. And the prayer of the publican is no self-righteous cliche. He pleads, *"God be merciful to me a sinner."*

On this passage, Dr. Scofield thinks that

> "as an instructed Jew the publican is thinking, not of mere mercy, but of the blood-sprinkled mercy-seat (Lev. 16.5. . .). His prayer might be paraphrased, 'Be toward me as thou art when thou lookest upon the atoning blood.'"

But while God Himself, in having mercy on a sinner, looks at the atoning blood, we have little reason to suppose that this penitent publican was "an instructed Jew." I think the Lord Jesus put in the parable all He intended to put in, and that He meant to leave this clear impression that any poor sinner — well instructed or not — who comes to God for mercy can have mercy, if he admits his sinfulness. Romans 10:13 says, *"For whosoever shall call upon the name of the Lord shall be saved."* That implies that one may come without much information, without much knowledge of the Bible, just so he comes honestly to Jesus in his heart for forgiveness.

The Bible says it so often but in different words: *"All that the Father giveth me shall come to me; and him that cometh to me I will in no wise cast out"* (John 6: 37). And in still other words it is given in Revelation 3:20, *"Behold, I stand at the door, and knock: if any man hear my voice, and open the door, I will come in to him, and will sup with him, and he with me."* And Revelation 22:17 offers so sweetly and freely, *"And whosoever will, let him take the water of life freely."*

Did the publican have faith? Yes, the prayer itself is faith. He believes there is a God and he addresses Him. He hopes that that God will have mercy on him, and he asks for it. Whether he would understand very well the marvelous plan God has of an atoning Saviour who bore all of our sins in His own body on the tree, we do not know. When a sick man goes to the doctor, he need not know what medicine he needs. If he goes to the right doctor, he will get the right medicine. And a poor lost sinner need not understand fully all the doctrines of salvation, if he comes to the right Saviour and relies on Him.

Dr. H. A. Ironside told me how in a great seminary some of the students, with learned language, approached him about this parable. They thought that this prayer, *"God be merciful to me a sinner,"* ought not be taught as a model for lost people, since, they thought, the one who prayed this prayer must understand all the Mosaic law of sacrifices and the blood-sprinkled Mercy Seat in the Old Testament. And dear Dr. Ironside told me that he said to these young men, "Go down to a rescue mission and see how the outcasts of society—the drunks, the harlots, the infidels—are won, and you will see that this is a proper prayer for any sinner who wants forgiveness."

The pardon was instantaneous. Jesus said, *"This man went down to his house justified."* Already he is counted just. The mercy of God not only forgives sin but takes away the blame and a man is counted righteous, has righteousness put into his heart!

In how many hundreds, perhaps thousands of cases, I have taught sinners to pray this prayer, *"God be merciful to me a sinner."* And I have often taught them to add these words: *"and save me for Jesus' sake."* And such sinners who honestly seek that mercy of God and come to Him for it, receive it!

Now let us not forget the lesson of the parable mentioned in verse 14: *"For every one that exalteth himself shall be abased; and he that humbleth himself shall be exalted."* No one can be saved by his righteousness, no matter how confident he is of it. But the most sinful person can be saved if he comes as a sinner, relying on God for mercy, through Christ Jesus.

VERSES 15—17:

15 And they brought unto him also infants that he would touch them: but when *his* disciples saw *it*, they rebuked them.

16 But Jesus called them *unto him*, and said, Suffer little children to come unto me, and forbid them not: for of such is the kingdom of God.

17 Verily I say unto you, Whosoever shall not receive the kingdom of God as a little child shall in no wise enter therein.

Jesus Blesses Little Children

This incident is told also in Matthew 19:13-15 and in Mark 10:13-16. Matthew adds to the intent of their coming *"that he should put his hands on them, and pray,"* and Mark says, *". . . that he should touch them."* Matthew says, *"Then there were brought unto him LITTLE CHILDREN."* Mark says *"young children."* Here Luke says *"infants."* But the term in verses 16 and 17 is *"little children"* and *"little child."* Jesus would bless infants, but only responsible *"little children"* can turn to Christ for forgiveness. Some here were young enough to be taken in His arms. It would appear also that some were old enough to turn to Jesus, being conscious of their sin and trusting Him for salvation, that is, consciously *"to come unto me,"* as He says in verse 16.

What did they come for? For His touch? For Him to pray for them? For Him to bless them? Yes. All devout parents would wish that the dear Lord Jesus could put His hands upon their children and bless them, those wonderful healing hands which have touched blind eyes and made them see, those miracle-working hands which created enough loaves and fishes to feed five thousand.

Did Jesus baptize these? That is not mentioned, not even inferred. In fact, "... *Jesus himself baptized not, but his disciples*" (John 4:2). Not here nor anywhere else in the Bible is there a hint that unaccountable infants were baptized or that anybody was baptized except by immersion after professing faith in Christ.

But surely we should learn, as the apostles needed to learn here, to take time for little children. By rebuking the multitude, the disciples may have tried to save Jesus the stress and strain of constant pressure from the crowd. But I am so glad that just as Jesus received the sinful and the ignorant and the poor, He received little children also. And so He does today. Oh, little children should be taught the Bible, should be taught about Christ and sin and salvation; they should learn Scriptures by memory.

How triumphantly one of my six daughters used to say, "Chi'ren, go 'bey your parents for this is right!" One little daughter memorized John 3:15 and she said it, "... *that whosoever believeth in him should not perish but have INTERNAL life."* Oh, fill their little minds with Scriptures and with Christian songs and with the fundamental truths of the Bible! And teach them to pray.

I remember so well when one of my small daughters was shooting off tiny firecrackers, one exploded in her hand. Of course there was pain but no serious damage. She ran to me and said, "Pray, Daddy, pray!" And I did pray and then she said, "It's rell, now. It's rell."

Once I had started to my office and I was to take the children by school on a bitter winter morning. But the car would not start. I stopped in puzzlement, and my baby girl, going to the first grade, said, "Daddy, I know what we can do!"

I said, "Yes, we can call a taxi or have a garage man come and start the car and be late for work and school."

"No," she said, "I didn't mean that."

"Then what can we do, my dear," I said.

"We can pray!" she said.

And, rebuked in heart, I did pray and at the first touch of the starter the motor spun, and we were soon gone! Oh, teach little children about Christ and the Bible and sin and salvation and prayer!

How Young May Little Children Be and Yet Repent and Trust Christ and Be Saved?

God has no different way of salvation for little children or for hardened sinners. How young, then, can a child become conscious of sin and his need and honestly turn his heart from sin to trust in Christ? Some people have set the age as twelve, but there is no biblical foundation for that. In fact, the Bible sets no age limit. Let us say that as early as the child knows himself to be a sinner and that he needs forgiveness, then he should be taught to look to Jesus and trust Him for forgiveness and salvation.

I have often read with little children I John 3:20: *"For if our heart condemn us, God is greater than our heart,*

and knoweth all things." So I would say: If your
conscience tells you that you are a sinner and you need
forgiveness, then, of course, God knows you are a sinner, too, and He wants to forgive you. And I have told
little children as plainly as I have adults, that Christ
died for our sins, that He is ready to forgive and save
and change the heart. And I have had thousands of
little children turn to Christ and later show abundant
evidence that they have peace with God. My own six
daughters were each saved and claimed the Lord before
they were six years of age, some of them before they
were five. But remember, they had Bible reading in the
home every day; they went continually to revival services and heard revival preaching. The only songs they
ever sang were gospel songs. They were early punished
for wrongdoing and taught to confess sin and turn from
it. I would suppose that a child who never heard the
Gospel, who had no discipline to give him a consciousness of sin, who did not know from earliest day that
Christ died for sinners, might not become conscious of
his sins and thus become accountable, as soon as one
who had good, strict and loving Christian environment
and teaching. But surely any child who is old enough
to know that he sins or does wrong, is old enough to
ask for forgiveness and to trust Christ for salvation.

So here is a sweet command of Jesus: "*Suffer little
children to come unto me, and forbid them not: for of
such is the kingdom of God.*" This same good command
is given in Matthew 19:14, and that follows a similar
statement of Jesus in Matthew 18:3-6 which says:

"*And said, Verily I say unto you, Except ye be converted, and become as little children, ye shall not enter
into the kingdom of heaven. Whosoever therefore shall
humble himself as this little child, the same is greatest
in the kingdom of heaven. And whoso shall receive one
such little child in my name receiveth me. But whoso*

*shall offend one of these little ones which believe in me,
it were better for him that a millstone were hanged about
his neck, and that he were drowned in the depth of
the sea."*

I think that the woe pronounced here is for those who
would hinder a little child from coming to Christ —
either to forbid his coming or discourage him from
coming.

In my own case, when I was nine years old I heard
a sermon on the prodigal son and I trusted Christ and
went forward to confess Christ. No one took the Bible
to show me how I could know for sure I was saved.
My father, a godly man, doubted if I were old enough
to understand and so gave me no help but rather planted
in my mind a doubt. It was three rather sad years
before, reading the Bible for myself, I came to the certain
assurance that I had everlasting life the moment I had
trusted Christ.

Oh, parents, teachers, Christian workers, make sure
that you encourage little children to be saved! Do not
think you need to offer them any different plan of salvation. Do not think that you have to leave off Bible
teaching about sin and the wrath of God on sin and the
punishment of Hell that awaits Christ-rejecting sinners.
The Gospel is still *"the power of God unto salvation to
every one that believeth,"* and any child who sees himself a lost sinner needing forgiveness can turn to Christ
and be saved.

Note that the heart attitude of an adult to come to
Christ must become childlike (vs. 17). A child is accustomed to receiving his daily food and care and pro-
tection and love as the free gift of his parents. He has
not yet become proud and haughty and independent-
minded. And if he is being properly reared, he knows
that sin is rebuked and punished and that there is loving
mercy for the penitent heart. So one who is to be saved

is to receive Christ as a little child.

Over America, in dealing with great congregations, in hundreds of cities, I have found that more than half of all those who claim to have trusted Christ turned to Him before they were fifteen. We should remember that *"those that seek me early shall find me"* (Prov. 8:17). And so children should be taught, *"Remember now thy Creator in the days of thy youth, while the evil days come not. . ."* (Eccles. 12:1).

VERSES 18—23:

18 And a certain ruler asked him, saying, Good Master, what shall I do to inherit eternal life?

19 And Jesus said unto him, Why callest thou me good? none *is* good, save one, *that is,* God.

20 Thou knowest the commandments, Do not commit adultery, Do not kill, Do not steal, Do not bear false witness, Honour thy father and thy mother.

21 And he said, All these have I kept from my youth up.

22 Now when Jesus heard these things, he said unto him, Yet lackest thou one thing: sell all that thou hast, and distribute unto the poor, and thou shalt have treasure in heaven: and come, follow me.

23 And when he heard this, he was very sorrowful: for he was very rich.

The Rich Young Ruler

The parallel accounts are given in Matthew 19:16-22 and in Mark 10:17-22. Mark says of the young ruler that *"there came one running, and kneeled to him,"* showing his deep concern and his reverence for Jesus. And here he says, *"What shall I do to inherit eternal life?"* But the intent is made more clear in Matthew 19:16 when he said, *"Good Master, what good thing shall I do, that I may have eternal life?"* He was seeking eternal life by way of the commandments—the law—by doing good things. He addressed Jesus as *"Good Master,"* or *"Rabbi."*

To address Jesus as "Good Master" or "Rabbi" or

"Teacher" is not enough. If Jesus is only a rabbi, a teacher, a prophet, He is not good, for *"there is none good but one, that is, God."* If Jesus is not God then He is not good. The rebuke was proper.

The modern liberals who do not believe in the virgin birth and the actual deity and pre-existence of Christ pretend great admiration for the Lord Jesus. They would throw away the authority of the Bible but cling to the Jesus they have in mind, one largely of their own manufacture, not the God-Man, the Christ of the Bible. He is no true friend of Christ who does not believe that He is all He claims to be—God in human form. One who casts aspersion on the inspiration of the Bible or on the virgin birth or on the bodily resurrection or on the miracle-working power of Christ on earth, is no true friend of Jesus Christ. He wants no praises, no salutation less than His due as our Lord and Saviour.

Remember the plain words of Jesus to the Pharisees in John 8:23,24: *"And he said unto them, Ye are from beneath; I am from above: ye are of this world; I am not of this world. I said therefore unto you, that ye shall die in your sins: for if ye believe not that I am he, ye shall die in your sins."*

Here the pronoun *he* is not in the original. Jesus claims to be the *"I am"* who appeared to Moses in the wilderness, the Jehovah God of the Old Testament, and those who do not receive Him as such will die in their sins, He says.

On what basis does the young man seek eternal life? On the basis of his own righteousness, his own keeping of the law. So he must be measured by the Ten Commandments. Notice the five commands which Jesus gave of the ten. He does not remind the young ruler of the commands about God—to have no other gods but Jehovah, to not bow down to idols, to not take the name of the Lord in vain. In some sense these are intangible, not witnessed necessarily by men, and are more clearly heart matters. And the Sabbath command is not mentioned, perhaps because it is the only ceremonial command of the ten and simply sums up the law, that one who labors and does all his work for six days has earned a day of rest, and one who has done all that God required in his life deserves Heaven. So the Sabbath is not mentioned. But of the six commands concerning duty to man, only one is omitted — covetousness. Jesus did not mention that at first because He will put it to a practical test later. The covetousness, which is idolatry, was one besetting sin of the young man.

Perhaps as far as rather literal and surface obedience is concerned, he had not committed adultery, though he may have lusted; he had not killed, though he may have hated; perhaps he had not stolen, though he coveted. He does not recall perhaps that he bore false witness or at least has not admitted it. In some degree, according to his own standard he has honored his father and mother and he is well pleased with himself—"*All these have I kept from my youth up,*" said he. And now comes the acid test that will show that the man has not kept the commandments: "*Yet lackest thou one thing: sell all that thou hast, and distribute unto the poor, and thou shalt have treasure in heaven: and come, follow me.*"

That was too much. His righteousness had not changed his covetous heart. And I remind you that Jesus is not here giving a plan of salvation. He was not partly saved because he did not commit adultery and more near salvation because he did not kill, and Jesus does not mean that now his righteousness would be perfect if he sold his goods. No, no! He is answering the young man's question about a way to Heaven by keeping the law, and Christ is here using the law as it is intended — as a "*schoolmaster to bring us unto Christ*" (Gal. 3:24).

Ah, he had not kept the commandment about covetousness. And that makes it clear also that he had not loved

God with all his heart and mind and soul, for "*covetous-ness. . . is idolatry*" (Col. 3:5). No, he was a sinner as all the rest of us are and he needed to come, not seeking some good thing to do to earn eternal life but seeking unmerited forgiveness and mercy for his sinful heart and lost soul.

Would it be better for a Christian to "*sell all that thou hast, and distribute unto the poor*"? Not necessarily, not always; but sometimes, perhaps. We should love our neighbors as ourselves, it is true. But hard work and saving are not necessarily forbidden in the Bible but are often encouraged. Riches are dangerous, as the following passage makes clear, but the command of Jesus to the young man, "*Sell all that thou hast, and distribute unto the poor,*" is simply showing that man the state of his own heart, what is really his god, what is his first love. God never told Abraham nor David nor Solomon nor Job nor Joseph of Arimathaea to sell all they had and give to the poor. The possession of private property is clearly encouraged in the Bible, though anxiety over riches or any inordinate desire to be rich is not encouraged.

There is a principle throughout the Bible that when a man does not want the truth, God does not force it on him. He spake in parables so people who had no heart to see the truth would not get it. The rich young ruler did not say, "O Lord Jesus, I am such a sinner. How can I get forgiveness?" And Jesus did not tell him that, but on his own avowed plan of righteousness, Jesus answered him and showed him he had failed, that he was a sinner.

The young man was sorrowful; not sorrowful over his sins but sorrowful there was such a hard way, he thought, to get to Heaven. He was not willing to pay that price.

VERSES 24— 30:

24 And when Jesus saw that he was very sorrowful, he said, How hardly shall they that have riches enter into the kingdom of God!

25 For it is easier for a camel to go through a needle's eye, than for a rich man to enter into the kingdom of God.

26 And they that heard *it* said, Who then can be saved?

27 And he said, The things which are impossible with men are possible with God.

28 Then Peter said, Lo, we have left all, and followed thee.

29 And he said unto them, Verily I say unto you, There is no man that hath left house, or parents, or brethren, or wife, or children, for the kingdom of God's sake,

30 Who shall not receive manifold more in this present time, and in the world to come life everlasting.

How Riches Hinder the Gospel

Jesus said, "*How hardly shall they that have riches enter into the kingdom of God.*" It is certain that some rich men have been truly converted but it is clear here that riches may hinder and doubtless do hinder many from entering the kingdom. We think the rich young ruler of this chapter might have been saved had he not been so enamored of his riches but had been willing to see his covetousness and to come as a sinner for mercy. It would obviously be a miracle for a camel to go through a needle's eye, and so it is, of course, for anyone to be saved. And the parallel account in Mark 10: 24 gives an explanatory additional word, "*But Jesus answereth again, and saith unto them, Children, how hard it is for them that TRUST IN RICHES to enter into the kingdom of God!*" So, it is not the possession of riches that would keep a man from Heaven but the trust in those riches.

It seems that riches are used as a delusion of Satan to keep one's mind from heavenly things. One who lives in a mansion now, may not be as much attracted to a mansion in Heaven. One who dresses in purple and fine linen now, may not see how wonderful is the white robe of Christ's righteousness for the heavenly wedding feast! One who, because of his riches, is counted so much above poorer people about him and honored above them now, may find it very humbling to his pride to come as an unworthy sinner, poor in spirit. So the man who has riches has probably worked much and given up much to have them. Riches have brought him so much in this life that he is likely to trust in the standards of earthly wealth and honor and happiness.

In the story of the rich man and Lazarus, in Luke 16, the man who went to Hell was a rich man, and the man who went to Heaven was a beggar. The rich man did not go to Hell because he was rich, but he may have been proud and arrogant and with little sense of his need, because he fared sumptuously and was clothed in purple and fine linen. The beggar did not go to Heaven because he was a beggar, but in his poverty he may have seen what the rich man did not see—how vain are all earthly things and how much better to make sure of eternal riches.   And saved people are often warned about the deceitfulness of riches.

In the parable of the sower, Jesus explained in Luke 8:14:   "*And that which fell among thorns are they, which, when they have heard, go forth, and are choked with cares and riches and pleasures of this life, and bring no fruit to perfection.*"   So riches, along with being absorbed with other cares or being interested in pleasures, can draw the Christian away from spiritual fruitfulness after he is a child of God.

Paul was inspired to warn Timothy about those of corrupt minds "*supposing that gain is godliness.*" He was to withdraw from them, "*but godliness with contentment is great gain*" (I Tim. 6:5,6). And Paul continued:

"*For we brought nothing into this world, and it is certain we can carry nothing out.   And having food and raiment. let us be therewith content.   But they that will be rich fall into temptation and a snare, and into many foolish and hurtful lusts, which drown men in destruction and perdition. For the love of money is the root of all evil: which while some coveted after, they have erred from the faith, and pierced themselves through with many sorrows."* — I Tim. 6:7-10.

Yes, and Paul pressed further in the same chapter and charged *"them that are rich in this world, that they be not highminded, nor trust in uncertain riches, but in the living God, who giveth us richly all things to enjoy"* (I Tim. 6:17). They were to be rich in good works and giving, laying up in Heaven *"a good foundation against the time to come, that they may lay hold on eternal life"* (vss. 18,19).

Christians are specially instructed not to give more honor to a man with wealth than to the humble and are reminded, *"Hath not God chosen the poor of this world rich in faith, and heirs of the kingdom which he hath promised to them that love him? But ye have despised the poor. Do not rich men oppress you, and draw you before the judgment seats? Do not they blaspheme that worthy name by the which ye are called?"* (James 2:5-7).

Christians are to be honored for their godliness, their character, their giving, their service, but not for their wealth.

And let us remember that while it is as hard for a rich man to enter the kingdom as it is for a camel to go through a needle's eye, it is also a miracle of grace for anybody else to be saved. We do not wonder that in this connection the disciples were astonished, *"saying among themselves, Who then can be saved?"* And Jesus answered them, *" The things which are impossible with men are possible with God"* (Luke 18:26,27).

One does not go to Heaven because he is rich or poor and only God's miraculous intervention can bring us to repentance and regeneration.

It is in this connection that Peter brings up the great sacrifice the apostles have honestly made to follow Christ. Peter said, *"Lo, we have left all, and followed thee."* Is there here a gladness that he has left behind him the money-making? I think so. How often this writer has been constrained to say, "I am glad I am not working for a living any more, just working for Jesus. Let Him take care of the living." But there is also in Peter's mind the question of rewards. For in that parallel passage in Matthew 19:27 is a fuller account of Peter's statement: *"Behold, we have forsaken all, and followed thee; what shall we have therefore?"* And since the Gospel of Matthew has more dispensational flavor, more reference to God's plan for Israel, and more that Jesus is King of the Jews, the answer is given in more detail and directly to Peter: *"And Jesus said unto them, Verily I say unto you, That ye which have followed me, in the regeneration when the Son of man shall sit in the throne of his glory, ye also shall sit upon twelve thrones, judging the twelve tribes of Israel"* (Matt. 19:28). In the kingdom of Christ, when He sits on David's throne and when Israel as a nation lives again *"in the regeneration,"* the twelve apostles will sit on twelve thrones helping to judge Israel.

But here in Luke, which depicts Jesus more as the Son of mankind with a Gospel for all the world, the promise is more general and includes all of us. Everyone who has left house, or parents, or brethren, or wife, or children, for the kingdom's sake *"shall. . . receive manifold more in this present time,"* besides everlasting life in the world to come. The parallel account, Mark 10:30, gives more detail: *"But he shall receive an hundredfold now in this time, houses, and brethren, and sisters, and mothers, and children, and lands, with persecutions; and in the world to come eternal life."*

This writer lost his mother before he was six years old. But as a man of God, preaching the Gospel, winning souls, and bearing the cross for Jesus in some measure, many a godly woman has been like a mother to me and there are thousands, thank God, who would do for me what brothers and sisters would do. It was once a happy privilege, never regretted, to walk off and leave the brick home for Jesus' sake, but how many hundreds of homes are now open to me as my own. And one who leaves all for Jesus will suffer persecution as well as having all things. One such will prove himself as a minister of God *"by honour and dishonour, by evil report and good report: as deceivers, and yet true; As unknown, and yet well known; as dying, and, behold, we live; as chastened, and not killed; As sorrowful, yet alway rejoicing; as poor, yet making many rich; as having nothing, and yet possessing all things"* (II Cor. 6:8-10).

So, Elisha, having nothing, was fed by the widow of Zarephath (I Kings 17:8-16). So the *"great woman"* of Shunem had her husband build a prophet's chamber for Elisha, with bed and table and stool and candlestick for his own, when he came that way. He had gladly left a farm big enough to require plowing by twelve yoke of oxen (I Kings 19:19-21), to be a servant of the prophet Elijah. But God provides many a home for the man who gives up a home for Jesus.

The abundant reward in the heavenly kingdom is not discussed here in detail. It is enough that we will have eternal life, and all that God's love will provide.

VERSES 31 — 34:

31 Then he took *unto him* the twelve, and said unto them, Behold, we go up to Jerusalem, and all things that are written by the prophets concerning the Son of man shall be accomplished.

32 For he shall be delivered unto the Gentiles, and shall be mocked, and spitefully entreated, and spitted on:
33 And they shall scourge *him*, and put him to death: and the third

day he shall rise again.
34 And they understood none of these things: and this saying was hid from them, neither knew they the things which were spoken.

Jesus Foretells His Death and Resurrection

Jesus knew ahead of time that He came to die on the cross. When did Jesus know He was God in the flesh? Very early, certainly. Since it was revealed to Zacharias, to Elisabeth, Mary, Simeon, and Anna the prophetess (Luke 1), to Joseph (Matt. 1:18-25), to the shepherds on the hillside (Luke 2:8-20), to the wise men from the east (Matt. 2:1-12), that Jesus was the promised Messiah, it is surely unthinkable that the dear Saviour Himself would not know the main fact that He is God and that He came to be a Saviour. He knew His name was Jesus, Saviour. When He was twelve years old He visited the Temple at Jerusalem and told His troubled mother, *"Wist ye not that I must be about my Father's business?"* (Luke 2:49).

It was not until He was *"about thirty years of age,"* when Jesus was baptized, that the Holy Spirit came upon Him in a special anointing for His ministry, as told in Luke 3:21-23. Before that He had never preached a sermon, never won a soul, never worked a miracle. But the fullness of the Spirit, empowering them for witnessing and service, did not come upon the disciples until the day of Pentecost, although Jesus had breathed on them and they had received the Holy Spirit to dwell within, the day of His resurrection (John 20:19-21). And so we believe that Jesus Christ was never out of touch with the Spirit of God. If John the Baptist was *"filled with the Holy Ghost, even from his mother's womb,"* I think surely we might say that Jesus, in His consciousness of God's presence and in being perfectly in tune with God and doing the will of God, knew the comforting, enlightening work of the Spirit all His days.

In Luke 2:52 we are told that He *"increased in wisdom and stature, and in favour with God and men."* Perhaps that means that the details of His life and ministry and sacrifice became more and more clear to Him. I do not know. When the dear Lord Jesus laid aside the garments of deity in Heaven, made Himself of no reputation, humbled Himself, and became obedient unto death, even the death of the cross, as told in Philippians 2:5-8, we do not know how much of God's wisdom He intentionally shut out of His mind when He was born as a baby. But certainly all through His ministry Jesus knew that He came to die and He hastened toward that from the beginning.

But His Death and Resurrection Are to Be As Written by the O. T. Prophets

Jesus knew the Scriptures, and His questions and answers, at twelve years of age in the Temple, astonished all who heard Him (Luke 2:46,47). How many details were revealed to Jesus besides the part foretold in the Old Testament, we do not know. We know that He knew all that He wanted to know and He loved all that the Scriptures said.

He knew, no doubt, the year of the crucifixion. He knew the fulfillment of the 483 years to the coming of the Messiah in Daniel 9:25,26. Whether that referred to His birth or His crucifixion, He knew. He knew the day, since He knew He was the Passover Lamb and must be killed on the day of the preparation (John 19:14,31). He knew He should *"be delivered unto the Gentiles"* because the crucifixion must involve *"the kings of the earth. . . and the rulers,"* that they should *"take counsel together, against the Lord, and against his anointed. . ."* (Ps. 2:2). He knew He should be scourged because Isaiah 50:6 says, *"I gave my back to the smiters, and my cheeks to them that plucked off the hair: I hid not my face from shame and spitting."* And so He knew He would be *"mocked, and spitefully entreated, and spitted on."* And Isaiah 53:5 had foretold He would be *"bruised for our iniquities: the chastisement of our peace was upon him; and with his stripes we are healed."*

He knew, of course, that He must die a substitutionary death: did not the death of every animal sacrificed foretell His death? Was not the symbolic offering of Isaac by Abraham a picture of His real sacrifice? And He knew all the tragic pain foretold in the twenty-second Psalm and that cry, *"My God, my God, why hast thou forsaken me."* He knew that He should be *"numbered with the transgressors"* (Isa. 53:12) and die alongside the two thieves, so it would be that He would make *"his grave with the wicked, and with the rich in his death,"* that is, be buried in the tomb of Joseph of Arimathaea. He knew that He should rise from the dead, for it was written, *"Therefore my heart is glad, and my glory rejoiceth: my flesh also shall rest in hope. For thou wilt not leave my soul in hell; neither wilt thou suffer thine Holy One to see corruption"* (Ps. 16:9,10).

Oh, yes, and He knew of the many, many repeated promises that He should return in glory, that He should reign on David's throne.

Let no one think that Jesus did not know all the tortures and ignominy, pain and humiliation, that awaited Him at the crucifixion. And let no one think that He went grudgingly to the cross because that was what He came to the earth for, knowing all the pain and cost.

The disciples did not understand these things. When Jesus died, they did not really expect Him to rise from the dead. That they were finally convinced means that the evidence is so overwhelming for His resurrection that none could deny it.

VERSES 35— 43:

35 And it came to pass, that as he was come nigh unto Jericho, a certain blind man sat by the way side begging:

36 And hearing the multitude pass by, he asked what it meant.

37 And they told him, that Jesus of Nazareth passeth by.

38 And he cried, saying, Jesus, *thou* son of David, have mercy on me.

39 And they which went before rebuked him, that he should hold his peace: but he cried so much the more, *Thou* son of David, have mercy on me.

40 And Jesus stood, and commanded him to be brought unto him: and when he was come near, he asked him,

41 Saying, What wilt thou that I shall do unto thee? And he said, Lord, that I may receive my sight.

42 And Jesus said unto him, Receive thy sight: thy faith hath saved thee.

43 And immediately he received his sight, and followed him, glorifying God: and all the people, when they saw *it*, gave praise unto God.

Blind Bartimaeus Is Given His Sight

The parallel passages are in Matthew 20:29-34 and Mark 10:46-52. Verse 35 here says this healing occurred as Jesus "*was come nigh unto Jericho*." In the case of blind Bartimaeus, Mark 10:46 says, "*And they came to Jericho: and as he went out of Jericho with his disciples and a great number of people, blind Bartimaeus, the son of Timaeus, sat by the highway side begging*." The cases are similar but they need not have been the same. It is very probable that since the fame had gone out about Jesus and a great crowd followed Him everywhere He went and He healed so many blind people and afflicted that there would be blind men by the wayside as He entered into Jericho and blind men by the roadside also as He left. And it is also very likely that the fame of His entrance into the city and the healings that he had done would be spread over the whole city in a few moments.

We are not told how long He spent in Jericho. He might well have stopped for a meal or to rest in the

shade after a long walk into the city. There is no difficulty in supposing that friends of blind Bartimaeus
brought him the happy word that the Saviour had
healed another blind man as He entered Jericho. And
then, hearing the commotion, He may well have been
listening for it, expecting the coming of the Saviour that
way. And Jesus might have followed the same kind of
formula with Bartimaeus as He did with many others
when He asked, "*What wilt thou that I should do unto
thee?*" The obvious answer would be the same, so there
is no mistake in either the account in Luke or in Mark,
if there were two different cases — one entering into and
the other coming out from Jericho.

And the parallel passage in Matthew 20:29-34 tells us
that there were two blind men sitting by the wayside
who cried for mercy and were healed. It would be
perfectly in accord with the plan of the four Gospels, all
divinely inspired, for one to tell part of the story and
the other to tell more of the story. So there was another
blind man besides Bartimaeus. There was some reason
for Bartimaeus to be particularly named.

There were those who discouraged the blind man.
There was a great crowd surrounding Jesus: He was
preaching to them. He might not want a poor beggar to
disrupt His teaching, they thought. But Jesus had them
reassure him and He commanded the blind man to be
brought near Him. He asked for and received his sight.
"*And immediately he received his sight, and followed
him, glorifying God.*" We are glad that the heart of the
Lord Jesus is expressed in Matthew 20:34: "*So Jesus
had compassion on them, and touched their eyes.*" The
Lord Jesus did not work these miracles to convince
people that He was the Messiah. Out of the deep compassion of His heart He helped people in trouble. And
His ministry was foretold in Isaiah 61:1, "*The Lord
hath anointed me to preach good tidings unto the meek;
he hath sent me to bind up the brokenhearted, to pro-*

claim liberty to the captives, and the opening of the prison to them that are bound." And as Jesus interpreted that in Luke 4:18 it included *"recovering of sight to the blind."*

LUKE 19

AND *Jesus* entered and passed through Jericho.

2 And, behold, *there was* a man named Zacchæus, which was the chief among the publicans, and he was rich.

3 And he sought to see Jesus who he was; and could not for the press, because he was little of stature.

4 And he ran before, and climbed up into a sycomore tree to see him: for he was to pass that *way*.

5 And when Jesus came to the place, he looked up, and saw him, and said unto him, Zacchæus, make haste, and come down; for to day I must abide at thy house.

6 And he made haste, and came down, and received him joyfully.

7 And when they saw *it*, they all murmured, saying, That he was gone to be guest with a man that is a sinner.

8 And Zacchæus stood, and said unto the Lord; Behold, Lord, the half of my goods I give to the poor; and if I have taken any thing from any man by false accusation, I restore *him* fourfold.

9 And Jesus said unto him, This day is salvation come to this house, forsomuch as he also is a son of Abraham.

10 For the Son of man is come to seek and to save that which was lost.

A Tax Collector, Zacchaeus, Saved

Jesus has come down the Jordan valley and passes through Jericho, and now will go up to Jerusalem. Matthew 20:29 tells us, "*And as they departed from Jericho, a great multitude followed him. And, behold, two blind men sitting by the way side*" cried out to Jesus and were healed. Mark 10:46 says, "*. . . and as he went out of Jericho with his disciples and a great number of people. . .*" and it tells us that one of the two blind men who were healed was Bartimaeus. It is not surprising that in the "*great multitude*" and the "*great number*" of people who followed Jesus to hear Him speak, to see His wonders, and to be healed of sickness, there was one blind man healed "*as he was come nigh unto Jericho*" (Luke 18:35) and two blind men asking

for help in the same way as He left the city. And in all
this crowd (of thousands we suppose), in the great ex-
citement, there was at least one man who wanted to be
saved and he could not get to Jesus for the crowd.

Zacchaeus was *"little of stature."* He was *"chief
among the publicans,"* possibly over the tax collecting
in all Judaea. He was rich, since he would get a share
of all the taxes collected by the men he appointed.

Since he was chief of the publicans, he may have heard
how Jesus called Matthew or Levi the publican, and how
he had left his tax collecting to follow Jesus (Luke 5:
27-29). And he had very likely heard about the tremendous feast that Levi had prepared for other tax
collectors and friends when Jesus came with them.

What was the interest that Zacchaeus had? He did not
seek to be healed. He was not paralyzed, nor was he a
leper, nor blind. *"He sought to see Jesus who he was."*
It seems nearly certain that he was already fairly well
convinced that the Lord Jesus was the promised Messiah.
If so, then he longed to meet the Saviour and have his
sins forgiven.

Was he under conviction because of those he had
wronged in collecting taxes *"by false accusation"* and
because he was rich by making other people poor, as
is maybe indicated in verse 8?

We may be sure that the heart that was honest in
wanting to see Jesus, wanting to know Him, could find
Him. It is a part of God's plan and promise, *"Draw
nigh to God, and he will draw nigh to you"* (Jas. 4:8).
He said to Israel and He says to every penitent sinner,
*"And ye shall seek me, and find me, when ye shall
search for me with all your heart"* (Jer. 29:13).

The Seeker Is Sought

Was it a happy coincidence that the man who sought
Jesus found Him easily? Jesus came to the sycamore

tree and stopped and looked up. Ah, it was not only that Zacchaeus sought Jesus but Jesus sought Zacchaeus. He knew his name, knew the hunger of his heart and said, "*To day I must abide at thy house.*" When a sinner seeks the Saviour, he finds that the Saviour has been seeking him, too. John 6:37 says, "*All that the Father giveth me shall come to me; and him that cometh to me I will in no wise cast out.*" God had given to Jesus Zacchaeus, so the man whom God had already given to Jesus was happily received when he came.

When the prodigal son came home, the father saw him a great way off and ran to meet him. The father longed for the son before he "*came to himself*" and returned. And you may be sure that every poor sinner whose heart turns to seek the Lord will find the Lord right at hand seeking him.

Zacchaeus did not need to go through some particular rite to be saved. He did not pray for salvation, outwardly, as far as we know. He simply "*made haste, and came down, and received him joyfully.*" And anybody who receives Jesus joyfully from the heart is saved. John 1:12 says, "*But as many as received him, to them gave he power to become the sons of God, even to them that believe on his name.*" So we may be sure that Zacchaeus received Jesus and believed on Him.

And Zacchaeus repented, too. We can tell the penitence of his heart because he boldly declared, "*Behold, Lord, the half of my goods I give to the poor; and if I have taken any thing from any man by false accusation, I restore him fourfold.*" That was according to the Mosaic Law in Exodus 22:1. I think he does not mean that this has been his practice in the past. I think that here he is setting out to make right what was wrong, and is turning from sin. "*And Jesus said unto him, This day is salvation come to this house.*"

And Jesus said, "*Forsomuch as he also is a son of Abraham.*"

He was already a son of Abraham according to the flesh. Now, born again, he is the spiritual son of Abraham. Galatians 3:7 says, *"Know ye therefore that they which are of faith, the same are the children of Abraham."* And Galatians 3:29 says, *"And if ye be Christ's, then are ye Abraham's seed, and heirs according to the promise."* And again the Scripture says, *"For he is not a Jew, which is one outwardly; neither is that circumcision, which is outward in the flesh: But he is a Jew, which is one inwardly; and circumcision is that of the heart, in the spirit, and not in the letter; whose praise is not of men, but of God"* (Rom. 2:28,29).

I am sure that verse 10 was not only assurance to Zacchaeus but it was the answer to scribes and Pharisees who so often murmured that *"This man receiveth sinners, and eateth with them"* (Luke 15:2; Luke 5:30; Mark 2:16; Matt. 9:11). But in each case Jesus had reassured them that He came not to call the righteous but sinners to repentance, that He would have mercy and not sacrifice (Matt. 9:13; Mark 2:17; Luke 5:31,32). And this blessed truth, that Jesus came to save sinners, is often repeated. In Matthew 18:11 He said, *"For the Son of man is come to save that which was lost."* And in I Timothy 1:15 we read that this is a *"faithful saying . . . that Christ Jesus came into the world to save sinners."*

VERSES 11—27:

11 And as they heard these things, he added and spake a parable, because he was nigh to Jerusalem, and because they thought that the kingdom of God should immediately appear.

12 He said therefore, A certain nobleman went into a far country to receive for himself a kingdom, and to return.

13 And he called his ten servants, and delivered them ten pounds, and said unto them, Occupy till I come.

14 But his citizens hated him, and sent a message after him, saying, We will not have this *man* to reign over us.

15 And it came to pass, that when he was returned, having received the kingdom, then he commanded these servants to be called unto him, to whom he had given the money, that he might know how much every man had gained by trading.

16 Then came the first, saying, Lord, thy pound hath gained ten pounds.

17 And he said unto him, Well, thou good servant: because thou hast been faithful in a very little, have thou authority over ten cities.

18 And the second came, saying, Lord, thy pound hath gained five pounds.

19 And he said likewise to him, Be thou also over five cities.

20 And another came, saying, Lord, behold, *here is* thy pound, which I have kept laid up in a napkin:

21 For I feared thee, because thou art an austere man: thou takest up that thou layedst not down,

and reapest that thou didst not sow.

22 And he saith unto him, Out of thine own mouth will I judge thee, *thou* wicked servant. Thou knewest that I was an austere man, taking up that I laid not down, and reaping that I did not sow:

23 Wherefore then gavest not thou my money into the bank, that at my coming I might have required mine own with usury?

24 And he said unto them that stood by, Take from him the pound, and give *it* to him that hath ten pounds.

25 (And they said unto him, Lord, he hath ten pounds.)

26 For I say unto you, That unto every one which hath shall be given; and from him that hath not, even that he hath shall be taken away from him.

27 But those mine enemies, which would not that I should reign over them, bring hither, and slay *them* before me.

Parable of the Pounds

Note carefully the purpose and setting of this parable. Jesus was approaching Jerusalem. Some people thought He would go to Jerusalem to seize an earthly kingdom and re-establish Israel and sit on David's throne. They knew that such a restoration of the kingdom had been promised to David in II Samuel 7:10-17 and in I Chronicles 17:7-17. It was not promised that the succession of David's line would be continuous but that in the future God would establish the throne forever.

Isaiah 11 foretold such a kingdom to be set up by the "*rod out of the stem of Jesse, and a Branch shall grow out of his roots*" (vs. 1). The kingdom blessing was told beautifully in Isaiah, chapter 35. Jeremiah 23:1-8 tells of the restoration of that wonderful kingdom by "*THE LORD OUR RIGHTEOUSNESS.*" A number of times in Ezekiel, chapters 34, 36 and 37 particularly tell of this restoration and there are allusions to it throughout all the Old Testament.

The angel, in announcing to the virgin Mary that she would bear a Son, said, "*The Lord God shall give unto him the throne of his father David: And he shall reign over the house of Jacob for ever; and of his kingdom there shall be no end*" (Luke 1:32,33).

So the people were not wrong to suppose that there would be a kingdom of God on earth and that Jesus would reign. They were wrong in supposing "*that the kingdom of God should immediately appear.*" So in Luke 17:20,21, "*when he was demanded of the Pharisees, when the kingdom of God should come, he answered them and said, The kingdom of God cometh not with observation,*" that is, it would not be a political development that people could trace and see it develop. He said, "*The kingdom of God is within you,*" that is, one could now enter the kingdom of God spiritually by trusting in Christ but that the public manifestation and completion of the kingdom and the day of the Lord when Christ reigns on earth awaits a future return of Christ.

It is interesting that the twelve apostles, too, were thinking that Christ would now restore Israel and set up His kingdom. So in Acts 1:6 "*when they therefore were come together, they asked of him, saying, Lord, wilt thou at this time restore again the kingdom to Israel?*" and there He told them plainly, "*It is not for you to know the times or the seasons, which the Father hath put in his own power.*" They were not to seek to know the time of Christ's return which cannot be known but rather, they were to be concerned mostly about soul winning: "*But ye shall receive power, after that the Holy Ghost is come upon you: and ye shall be witnesses unto me both in Jerusalem, and in all Judaea, and in Samaria, and unto the uttermost part of the earth,*" He said (Acts 1:7,8).

Here in verse 12 is the simple outline of God's plan about the kingdom: *"A certain nobleman went into a far country to receive for himself a kingdom, and to return."* Jesus is gone to Heaven. There at the hand of the Father, in due time, He will receive the kingdom and will return. So the kingdom in its public manifestation and completion awaits the personal, bodily return of Jesus Christ to the earth.

We who now live in this New Testament age are like the ten servants occupying for the Nobleman, our Master, while He has gone to Heaven, occupying until He shall return to take us with Him for the honeymoon and wedding feast and judgment seat of Christ and then return for the kingdom.

The word *"pound"* is a translation of the Greek word *mina,* twelve and a half ounces, and that much gold would be valuable. Each must use the pound in trading in business and see how much he can gain for the master. Then the accounting when the nobleman returned, having received the kingdom, is like the judgment seat of Christ when Christians must face the Lord. That judgment seat of Christ is pictured in I Corinthians 3: 11-15. Of course, this is only for Christians who are built on the foundation of Jesus Christ. And every man's work shall be tried by fire. The gold and silver and precious stones will remain. The wood, hay and stubble will be burned. *"If any man's work shall be burned, he shall suffer loss: but he himself shall be saved; yet so as by fire."*

Second Corinthians 5:10 tells us, *"For we must all appear before the judgment seat of Christ; that every one may receive the things done in his body, according to that he hath done, whether it be good or bad."* Paul labored to *"be accepted of him"* (vs. 9) and he knew *"the terror of the Lord"* of Christians whose works would be burned and who would receive in their bodies that which was done, bad as well as good.

The Rewards

One servant had so used the money given him that he had gained ten pounds and the nobleman who had now become a king said, "*Because thou hast been faithful in a very little, have thou authority over ten cities,*" that is, the daily handling of some money for his lord was not nearly so great as the privilege now of ruling over ten cities. And we think that the ten cities here means literally that when Jesus comes to reign Christians will help Him reign on earth. We are told that the twelve apostles will sit on twelve thrones judging the twelve tribes of Israel (Matt. 19:28). And Paul wrote Timothy that "*if we suffer, we shall also reign with him*" (II Tim. 2:12).

The second servant's pound gained five pounds and the nobleman, now king, said, "*Be thou also over five cities.*" Let us emphasize again that the eternal blessedness and usefulness of a Christian in Heaven will depend somewhat on his service here. Salvation is free and all alike are saved by the blood of Christ, by grace and without works. But after He saves us, God will reward us for our service also.

The third servant reported. He brought back the pound. He had kept it laid up in a napkin. He did not respect the nobleman but called him an austere man and accused him of dishonesty. He had a rebellious heart. Then the king asked kindly, "*Wherefore then gavest not thou my money into the bank, that at my coming I might have required mine own with usury?*" Doesn't every man have a right to the interest on money invested? And does not God have a right to some profit on all He has invested in us, His children? So the man had taken from him the pound that he had and he would represent, we suppose, the Christian who at the judgment seat of Christ sees all his works burned up and he is saved, "*yet so as by fire.*"

The Citizens Hated Him

This nobleman had an estate and servants. But citizens of the country *"hated him, and sent a message after him, saying, We will not have this man to reign over us"* (vs. 14). Now the parable speaks not of Christians but of Christ-rejecting sinners. And the end promised them is tragic: *"But those mine enemies, which would not that I should reign over them, bring hither, and slay them before me"* (vs. 27).

Here is a wonderful outline of the return of Christ in glory, after the rapture, and of the battle of Armageddon in which He destroys the armies of His enemies, and the judgment of Gentiles, as foretold in Matthew 25: 31-46, and Christ-rejecting sinners must go to Hell, and those alive on the earth after Christ's return will evidently be destroyed immediately.

VERSES 28— 40:

28 And when he had thus spoken, he went before, ascending up to Jerusalem.

29 And it came to pass, when he was come nigh to Bethphage and Bethany, at the mount called *the mount* of Olives, he sent two of his disciples,

30 Saying, Go ye into the village over against *you;* in the which at your entering ye shall find a colt tied, whereon yet never man sat: loose him, and bring *him hither.*

31 And if any man ask you, Why do ye loose *him?* thus shall ye say unto him, Because the Lord hath need of him.

32 And they that were sent went their way, and found even as he had said unto them.

33 And as they were loosing the colt, the owners thereof said unto them, Why loose ye the colt?

34 And they said, The Lord hath need of him.

35 And they brought him to Jesus: and they cast their garments upon the colt, and they set Jesus thereon.

36 And as he went, they spread their clothes in the way.

37 And when he was come nigh, even now at the descent of the mount of Olives, the whole multitude of the disciples began to rejoice and praise God with a loud voice for all the mighty works that they had seen;

38 Saying, Blessed *be* the King that cometh in the name of the Lord: peace in heaven, and glory in the highest.

39 And some of the Pharisees from among the multitude said unto him, Master, rebuke thy disciples.

40 And he answered and said unto them, I tell you that, if these should | hold their peace, the stones would immediately cry out.

The Triumphal Entry Into Jerusalem

The parallel passages are Matthew 21:1-9; Mark 11:1-10; John 12:12-19. No doubt Jesus very consciously and with deliberate planning fulfilled the prophecy of Zechariah 9:9, *"Rejoice greatly, O daughter of Zion; shout, O daughter of Jerusalem: behold, thy King cometh unto thee: he is just, and having salvation; lowly, and riding upon an ass, and upon a colt the foal of an ass."*

Jesus had now arrived at the eastern side of the Mount of Olives opposite Jerusalem. Two villages on the mountain were Bethany and Bethphage. I do not suppose that Jesus had prearranged it but with the supernatural revelation of the Spirit of God, He knew that there would be an ass tied and that when the disciples should say, *"The Lord hath need of him,"* the owner would gladly surrender the ass and the colt. Matthew 21:2 says, *"Ye shall find an ass tied, and a colt with her."* They brought both the ass and the ass's colt. Matthew 21:7 says, *"And brought the ass, and the colt, and put on them their clothes, and they set him thereon."* Did Jesus ride both the animals? At least He rode the younger, the young ass that had never been ridden before, so he is the one particularly mentioned here in Luke: *"They cast their garments upon the colt, and they set Jesus thereon"* (vs. 35). The multitude began to sense that Jesus was fulfilling prophecy and *"the whole multitude of the disciples began to rejoice and praise God with a loud voice for all the mighty works that they had seen; Saying, Blessed be the King that cometh in the name of the Lord"* (vss. 37,38). And Mark 11:8 says, *"And many spread their garments in the way: and others cut down branches off the trees, and strawed them in the way.''* So says Matthew 21:8. They could not now cut down branches from the trees, for devastating wars through the century have denuded the country around Jerusalem of trees. Except for the eight ancient olive trees in the Garden of Gethsemane and olive orchards further away, there is only an occasional tree around Jerusalem now.

Jesus knew the owner of the donkey would send him. Thousands loved Jesus. Some good women *"followed Jesus from Galilee, ministering unto him: Among which was Mary Magdalene, and Mary the mother of James and Joses, and the mother of Zebedee's children''* (Matt. 27:55, 56). Some such godly woman, no doubt, had made that garment, that coat, *"without seam, woven from the top throughout''* (John 19:23) which pictured the perfect righteousness of Christ. I think Simon of Cyrene will be forever honored in Glory because he was allowed to bear the cross of Jesus (Matt. 27:32). Joseph of Arimathaea furnished the tomb, and Nicodemus the hundred pound of spices with the white linen, as they prepared the body of Jesus for burial (John 19:38-42). Oh, that the dear Lord Jesus may take our hands, our feet, our voices, our influence, our tears, and all of our heart's love and someway use them, for, as with the donkey, *'the Lord hath need of them.'*

The love of those about Him pleased the Saviour greatly. Some put garments on the donkey on which Jesus sat and others *"cut down branches from the trees, and strawed them in the way''* (Matt. 21:8).

John 12:13 tells us that the people *"took branches of palm trees, and went forth to meet him, and cried, Hosanna: Blessed is the King of Israel that cometh in the name of the Lord.''* It is true that even the disciples did not fully understand about the coming crucifixion, but many Jews looked for the Messiah, the King, and many must have recognized the fulfillment of Zechariah 9:9 in this triumphal entry and so they could shout,

"*Blessed is the King of Israel that cometh in the name of the Lord.*" What a rejoicing and praise of the multitude there! (vs. 37). Some of the Pharisees who did not love Jesus and did not want to recognize Him as the Son of David and coming King, said, "*Master, rebuke thy disciples.*" Ah, but it was a time of praise, and it must be, and the praise must come forth! "*And he answered and said unto them, I tell you that, if these should hold their peace, the stones would immediately cry out.*" It was proper that people recognize Him as the Son of David, fulfilling the Scripture here.

It is interesting to note that with what infinite detail God controls all the inanimate objects — the earth, the sea, the air — as well as the animals. So the rocks rent when Jesus died. So the storm and the sea stopped at His word. So a fish provided a coin for taxation. So a cock (a rooster) crowed at His bidding to remind Peter of his sin. God could have a whale to swallow Jonah, and to vomit him up. He could have a gourd vine to cover him and a worm to destroy the vine. God could send hornets to drive out the Canaanites before Israel. He could stop the sun in its course, to prolong Joshua's day. And we are told that "*the stars in their courses fought against Sisera*" (Judg. 5:20).

And when Jesus returns to the earth in that glad day, "*all the trees of the field shall clap their hands*" (Isa. 55:12). We know that at Mount Sinai "*the mountains skipped like rams, and the little hills like lambs*" (Ps. 114:4). And in the millennial reign of Christ, "*the cow and the bear shall feed; their young ones shall lie down together: and the lion shall eat straw like the ox. And the sucking child shall play on the hole of the asp, and the weaned child shall put his hand on the cockatrice' den,*" and "*the desert shall rejoice, and blossom as the rose.*"

Oh, this poor, old, accursed world is still in the hands of God! He who knows every sparrow's fall has His

mighty hand on all nature. And Jesus Christ will yet
be glorified in His creation. We do not wonder that
Psalm 103:22 says, *"Bless the Lord, all his works in all
places of his dominion."*

Notice the contrast in this triumphal entry, just as the
contrast in the parable of the pounds. A nobleman went
away. He had ten servants. There are citizens of the
country whom he wants to rule, but they hate him. He
comes back with power, with the kingdom belonging to
him, and he slays his enemies, and magnificently rewards
faithful servants. So here the Lord Jesus rides into
Jerusalem on a donkey, and He goes in knowing He is
soon to be scourged and crucified. But He will come
again crowned with many crowns, riding upon a white
horse, with the armies of Heaven following Him! (Rev.
19:14). And that group that shouted, *"Hosanna to the
son of David"* as they walked down the hillside into the
city, pictures, oh, so slightly the time when Jesus will
return and *"Behold, he cometh with clouds; and every
eye shall see him. . ."* (Rev. 1:7), and that time is foretold by Enoch, the seventh from Adam and from Jude,
when, *"Behold, the Lord cometh with ten thousands of
his saints,"* or more literally, tens of thousands (Jude 14).

Note the praises of the people: *"Blessed be the King
that cometh in the name of the Lord."* Some time before
when *"he went through the cities and villages, teaching,
and journeying toward Jerusalem,"* He lamented over
Jerusalem (Luke 13:34,35) and said, *". . . verily I say
unto you, Ye shall not see me, until the time come when
ye shall say, Blessed is he that cometh in the name of
the Lord."* That, of course, had a double meaning.
Jerusalem would not see Him again until He made that
triumphal entry, as foretold. But surely He looked forward to another triumphal entry, foretold in Zechariah
14:4-9, when, after the battle of Armageddon, Jesus shall
stand again on the Mount of Olives and set up His
kingdom with the throne in Jerusalem.

In verse 37 we are told that *"the whole multitude of
the disciples began to rejoice and praise God with a loud
voice."* That was a fulfillment of Zechariah 9:9, *"Rejoice
greatly, O daughter of Zion; shout, O daughter of Jerusalem: behold, thy King cometh unto thee: he is just, and
having salvation; lowly, and riding upon an ass, and
upon a colt the foal of an ass."* So they must rejoice!

The Pharisees objected. The Gospel of John tells us
that between the events in Luke 19, that is, between the
conversion of Zacchaeus at Jericho and the entrance to
Jerusalem, came the events of John, chapters 11 and 12,
the raising of Lazarus and the supper at Bethany where
Lazarus sat at the table with Him and Mary anointed
Jesus with ointment. And the Pharisees plotted then to
kill Jesus, as we see in John 11:47-57. They were
greatly disturbed at the popular clamor for Jesus, and
John 12:19 tells us, *"The Pharisees therefore said among
themselves, Perceive ye how ye prevail nothing? behold,
the world is gone after him."*

But the Pharisees could not stop the praises of the
people. Praises were prophesied in the Scriptures and
they must come, even if the very stones must cry out to
fulfill the Scriptures (vs. 40)!

VERSES 41—44:

41 And when he was come near, he beheld the city, and wept over it,
42 Saying, If thou hadst known, even thou, at least in this thy day, the things *which belong* unto thy peace! but now they are hid from thine eyes.
43 For the days shall come upon thee, that thine enemies shall cast a trench about thee, and compass thee round, and keep thee in on every side,
44 And shall lay thee even with the ground, and thy children within thee; and they shall not leave in thee one stone upon another; because thou knewest not the time of thy visitation.

Jesus Weeps Over Jerusalem

The parallel passage is Matthew 23:37-39 and there the lament is given in different words. It is probable that Jesus said a great deal more than is recorded in either account. There Jesus said:

"O Jerusalem, Jerusalem, thou that killest the prophets, and stonest them which are sent unto thee, how often would I have gathered thy children together, even as a hen gathereth her chickens under her wings, and ye would not! Behold, your house is left unto you desolate. For I say unto you, Ye shall not see me henceforth, till ye shall say, Blessed is he that cometh in the name of the Lord."

There He said, *"Your house is left unto you desolate."* That is, the Shekinah Glory was gone from the Temple. It was no longer the house of God. And this is a larger repetition of the lament He gave when He was still going through the cities and towns, coming toward Jerusalem, recorded in Luke 13:34,35. So here again He says, *"Ye shall not see me henceforth, till ye shall say, Blessed is he that cometh in the name of the Lord."* This time in Matthew 23 He must, of course, refer to His second coming.

Jerusalem had missed her opportunity. She had missed *"the things which belong unto thy peace."* Had Jerusalem, with its leaders, joyfully received the Saviour, we have reason to believe that the awful destruction under Titus in A. D. 70 would have been avoided.

Notice the solemn warning in verse 43. Jesus foretells the siege of Jerusalem by Titus, the Roman general, when the city would be taken and utterly destroyed and the Jewish people scattered. The warning will be repeated in Luke 21:20, but there it has the double meaning of the siege and destruction under Titus and the future destruction by the armies of the Antichrist in the tribulation time. All these sorrowful things Jesus had on His mind, no doubt, so He wept.

The city could have been spared. Israel's people could have turned to the Saviour but they did not. They did not know that their rejection of the Saviour meant the ruin of the city, war and captivity. We in America who grieve over the worldliness and sin and Christ-rejection, do not weep enough for the awful doom that is certain to come when people, with great light and great opportunity, continue to reject the Saviour in increasing wickedness and rebellion.

So the Jewish nation before had failed to listen to the prophets, and at last destruction and captivity were inevitable and they were carried to Babylon. Rome, we believe, could have listened to the Apostle Paul and the destruction been long postponed.

Nineveh did listen to the Prophet Jonah and was spared. England, at least in some large measure, listened to Wesley and Whitefield and the great revival and were spared from the anarchy and reign of terror that came to France. England was given a new period of prosperity and blessing.

So Jesus wept. He had wept also at the grave of Lazarus a week before (John 11:35). I am not surprised. I wonder if there were not tears in the heart of Christ all the years! In truth, Jesus is "*the Lamb slain from the foundation of the world*" (Rev. 13:8). Sinners, long rejecting the Saviour, even now still "*crucify to themselves the Son of God afresh, and put him to an open shame*" (Heb. 6:6). I think this is one of the glorious mysteries of the atonement — an infinite Christ, through infinite centuries, has suffered for an infinite number of sinners. And the broken heart of God, who gave His Son, as pictured in the crucifixion, has been broken through all the centuries for the men He would save and the Saviour has suffered and wept in His heart over all the sinners. Do not think, then, that the six hours on the cross are all of the sufferings of Christ or complete all the meaning of the crucifixion. O, weeping Saviour!

> Weeping, weeping o'er the city
> On the Mount of Olives Jesus stood
> Grieving o'er His sore rejection
> And the doom impending on the city loved so well.

Or as another poet has said:

> The Son of God in tears,
> And shall my tears be dry?
> Let tears of penitential grief
> Flow forth from every eye.

If we would enter into the compassion of Christ for the multitude who are like sheep having no shepherd, we like Paul would "*fill up that which is behind of the afflictions of Christ in my flesh for his body's sake, which is the church*" (Col. 1:24). We must enter into His heart-broken weeping for sinners.

Oh, let us who read today not miss, as did Jerusalem, "*the time of thy visitation.*"

VERSES 45—48:

45 And he went into the temple, and began to cast out them that sold therein, and them that bought;
46 Saying unto them, It is written, My house is the house of prayer: but ye have made it a den of thieves.

47 And he taught daily in the temple. But the chief priests and the scribes and the chief of the people sought to destroy him,
48 And could not find what they might do: for all the people were very attentive to hear him.

Second Cleansing of the Temple

In John 2:13-17 we are told how, at the very beginning of His ministry, Jesus

"*found in the temple those that sold oxen and sheep*"

*and doves, and the changers of money sitting: And
when he had made a scourge of small cords, he drove
them all out of the temple, and the sheep, and the oxen;
and poured out the changers' money, and overthrew
the tables; And said unto them that sold doves, Take
these things hence; make not my Father's house an house
of merchandise. And his disciples remembered that it
was written, The zeal of thine house hath eaten me up.*"

That reference is to Psalm 69:9. And that zeal Christ
still has for the Temple in this second cleansing. In that
first cleansing, He made a scourge. We suppose He
used the scourge on men as well as on sheep and oxen.
He did not gently ask them to leave but *"poured out
the changers' money, and overthrew the tables."* Oh,
the holy indignation of Jesus!

Here He came into the Temple and cast out those who
bought and sold. It is not only that they sold merchandise, that is, oxen and sheep and doves used for sacrifices, and that they changed money into the Temple
money which was required, but they had made it a *"den
of thieves,"* making a profit on the exchange of money
by requiring that no money could be given except in the
Temple coinage. Since some people must come a long
way to Jerusalem to offer sacrifices, they must buy whatever is available and at whatever price. So dishonesty
and greed were apparent in the Temple, and the priests
and Levites themselves had part in it.

In Matthew 21:12,13 and in Mark 11:15-17 are
parallel passages to this one. And Matthew tells how
*"the blind and the lame came to him in the temple; and
he healed them."* Then there were children in the Temple
still crying, *"Hosanna to the son of David."* Jesus had
first cleansed the Temple, as recorded in John 2:13-17.
The Jews were displeased and demanded what evidence
He could give for authority in these matters. But now,
after two or three years, they hated Him and wanted to

kill Him: "*But the chief priests and the scribes and the chief of the people sought to destroy him.*" They could not just now but they will find a way soon, with Judas betraying Him for money.

We should remember that the Temple has no counterpart in church buildings today. There where the Shekinah Glory lived in the holy of holies, there where every sacrifice must be brought and where anointed priests carried on the ceremonies picturing the Saviour's death, the prophet could say, "*The Lord is in his holy temple: let all the earth keep silence before him*" (Hab. 2:20). But now though the house is left desolate by the Spirit, it still ought to have been the house of prayer.

Now, the body of a Christian is the temple of the Lord, and now the love of money and making merchandise an idol and using this temple of God for thievery is a sin just like that of the Jews who sold and cheated in the Temple. And now, "*Know ye not that ye are the temple of God, and that the Spirit of God dwelleth in you? If any man defile the temple of God, him shall God destroy; for the temple of God is holy, which temple ye are*" (I Cor. 3:16,17).

Verse 47 tells us that He taught daily in the Temple. Other Scriptures such as Mark 11:12-20 indicate that in the evenings they walked out to Bethany, perhaps to the home of Mary and Martha and Lazarus, for the night, and then would return to Jerusalem in the day for His teaching. But the chief priests and scribes and leaders were dead set on seeing Jesus killed.

LUKE 20

VERSES 1—8:

AND it came to pass, *that* on one of those days, as he taught the people in the temple, and preached the gospel, the chief priests and the scribes came upon *him* with the elders,

2 And spake unto him, saying, Tell us, by what authority doest thou these things? or who is he that gave thee this authority?

3 And he answered and said unto them, I will also ask you one thing; and answer me:

4 The baptism of John, was it from heaven, or of men?

5 And they reasoned with themselves, saying, If we shall say, From heaven; he will say, Why then believed ye him not?

6 But and if we say, Of men; all the people will stone us: for they be persuaded that John was a prophet.

7 And they answered, that they could not tell whence *it was*.

8 And Jesus said unto them, Neither tell I you by what authority I do these things.

"By What Authority Jesus?"

The corresponding passages in the synoptics are Matthew 21:23-27 and Mark 11:27-33. Mark says, "*As he was walking in the temple....*" Matthew says, "*As he was teaching....*" Here Luke says, "*As he taught the people in the temple, and preached the gospel....*" The Temple here means not just strictly and simply the Holy Place and Most Holy Place, but the courts and colonades about the Temple where the people gathered, where they bought sacrifices and had money changed, where they heard arguments and teaching, gathered informally about some speaker. Here Jesus taught and preached to the milling crowds. It was much like a supermarket, a central gathering place but with no auditorium, no pulpit or pews.

Note that there is a deliberate agreement, a conspiracy among the priests, scribes and elders. They hate Jesus. They would trap Him, or bring Him into disrepute

with the people or into conflict with the Roman authorities, or find some slip by which they could accuse Him.
They say, *"By what authority doest thou these things?"*

Well, why did Jesus not tell them that He has the
authority of His Father, that He is the Messiah, the
Lamb of God foretold, even the Creator, the promised
Son of Abraham and of David through whom all the
world would be blessed? Do you suppose their's was
an honest question?

Did they not have abundant evidence that this miracle-
working One is from God! Multitudes were already
convinced that He was the Saviour. Perhaps the dis-
courses in John, chapters 8 and 9, had already taken
place. He had already said to them, *"I am the light
of the world"* (John 8:12), and they had accused Him
of lying. He told them, *"Ye neither know me, nor my
Father: if ye had known me, ye should have known
my Father also."* And He had said to them, *"Ye are
from beneath; I am from above: ye are of this world;
I am not of this world"* (John 8:23). He had said
unto them, *"When ye have lifted up the Son of man,
then shall ye know that I am he"*—literally, *"I am the
I AM"* (John 8:28). He had already told them, *"Before Abraham was, I am"* (John 8:58). The claims
of Jesus to be one with the Father, that God had given
all judgment into His hands, that He is the Light
of the world, did not convince these scoffers. You see,
their unbelief was wicked. It was an intentional, determined unbelief of wicked hearts set against the truth
because they loved their sin. It was true of them, as
Jesus said in John 3:19-21:

*"And this is the condemnation, that light is come into
the world, and men loved darkness rather than light,
because their deeds were evil. For every one that doeth
evil hateth the light, neither cometh to the light, lest
his deeds should be reproved. But he that doeth truth*

*cometh to the light, that his deeds may be made man-
ifest, that they are wrought in God."*

Why should Jesus here give further evidence to these
who would not receive it? There is clear teaching
throughout the Bible that God does not reveal Himself
fully to those who go on in deliberate, willful rejection
and willful blindness. That is why Jesus often spoke
in parables, as He Himself carefully explained (Matt.
13:10-15).

But here was a proper answer for their wicked hearts.
Jesus and John the Baptist were closely identified, John
being the forerunner of Jesus. His principal message
was, *"Behold the Lamb of God, which taketh away the
sin of the world,"* and, *"Repent ye: for the kingdom
of heaven is at hand"* (that is in the person of the King
Himself). All who listened to John willingly would
listen to Jesus. All who trusted in the Saviour John
preached, trusted in Jesus and loved Him. So He asked
these religious leaders, *"The baptism of John, was it
from heaven, or of men?"* That meant not only John's
baptism but his preaching repentance, his announcement of the coming Messiah, the John the Baptist revival.
They dared not answer — they would convict themselves.
If John's message and announcement and baptizing
were from Heaven, why did they not believe John?
But they dared not say it was not from Heaven. The
overwhelming conviction of the multitude was that John
was the prophet of God.

They would reject every proof that Jesus gave, and
even when He arose from the dead, they would bribe
the soldiers to say that someone had stolen His body
(Matt. 28:12-14).

In moral and spiritual matters, the intellect is controlled by the heart and blinded by deliberate, wicked
rejection of truth.

VERSES 9—18:

9 Then began he to speak to the people this parable; A certain man planted a vineyard, and let it forth to husbandmen, and went into a far country for a long time.

10 And at the season he sent a servant to the husbandmen, that they should give him of the fruit of the vineyard: but the husbandmen beat him, and sent *him* away empty.

11 And again he sent another servant: and they beat him also, and entreated *him* shamefully, and sent *him* away empty.

12 And again he sent a third: and they wounded him also, and cast *him* out.

13 Then said the lord of the vineyard, What shall I do? I will send my beloved son: it may be they will reverence *him* when they see him.

14 But when the husbandmen saw him, they reasoned among themselves, saying, This is the heir: come, let us kill him, that the inheritance may be our's.

15 So they cast him out of the vineyard, and killed *him*. What therefore shall the lord of the vineyard do unto them?

16 He shall come and destroy these husbandmen, and shall give the vineyard to others. And when they heard *it*, they said, God forbid.

17 And he beheld them, and said, What is this then that is written, The stone which the builders rejected, the same is become the head of the corner?

18 Whosoever shall fall upon that stone shall be broken; but on whomsoever it shall fall, it will grind him to powder.

The Parable of the Vineyard

Parallel passages are Matthew 21:33-46 and Mark 12:1-12. Here Israel is likened to a vineyard, God's vineyard, rented out or put in charge of scribes, Pharisees and chief priests. No doubt Jesus had in mind that of which the others would be reminded—the Old Testament teaching that Israel was the Lord's vineyard as in Isaiah 5:1-7. The loving care of God for His people and their land, prosperity and happiness, is recounted, but instead of bringing forth good grapes it brought forth wild grapes. And for that reason God allowed the vineyard to be trampled down.

God means that He allowed judgment on the people and captivity in Babylon. Remember Isaiah 5:7: "*For the vineyard of the Lord of hosts is the house of Israel,*

and the men of Judah his pleasant plant." These scribes
and Pharisees are counted the renters, the husbandmen
who were put in charge of the land and the people,
and they should have fruit brought to God, the fruits
of righteousness and godly teaching, but they did not.
They did not regard the vineyard as belonging to the
Lord, but as their own province, as other worldly rulers
do.   You need not wonder then at the eight woes pronounced by the Saviour on the scribes and Pharisees
in Matthew 23.

In verse 10 we find the servant was sent to the husbandmen to collect the rental for the fruits.   That meant
prophets were sent to Israel to plead for the people to
love , and serve the true God, give Him the fruits of
obedience, and worship and allegiance.   Prophet after
prophet was sent and each rejected.   Then the owner
sent his beloved son.   That meant that God now sends
Christ the Saviour.   Jesus knew that they would say,
*"Come, let us kill him, that the inheritance may be
our's."*   Thus the Lord Jesus reveals the heart of these
wicked men.   He knew that they hated Him and would
kill Him.

Then what would become of these husbandmen? They
would be destroyed and the vineyard given to others.
That meant that in A. D. 70 Titus and his Roman
army would destroy Jerusalem and the people would
be scattered throughout the world.   The Gospel would
be given to Gentiles, and God would have other spiritual leaders instead of the Jewish hierarchy.

The quotation in verse 17 is from Psalm 118:22.
Christ is often pictured as a stone or rock.   The
great rock in the wilderness which was smitten and gave
out water for the multitude pictured Christ, for I Corinthians 10:4 says that Israel *"drank of that spiritual
Rock that followed them: and that Rock was Christ."*

According to the interpretation of Nebuchadnezzar's
dream of empires, that *"stone. . . cut out without hands"*

which was to fall down upon the feet of the great image and grind it to powder, then the stone fill the whole earth—that rock was to be Christ in His kingdom (Dan. 2:44, 45). We suppose Jesus had that picture in mind when He said, *"Whosoever shall fall upon that stone shall be broken; but on whomsoever it shall fall, it will grind him to powder."*

Those who attack that Stone shall be broken, but in the day of judgment Christ shall grind to powder those who hate Him and reject Him. Christ is that *"living stone, disallowed indeed of men, but chosen of God, and precious"* (I Pet. 2:4), we as living stones are built upon that foundation, *"a spiritual house."*

Christ is also the *"chief corner stone"* as well as the *"head of the corner, And a stone of stumbling, and a rock of offence"* to the wicked (I Pet. 2:4-8). Christ, not Peter, not some confession, is the foundation of the church. *"For other foundation can no man lay than that is laid, which is Jesus Christ"* (I Cor. 3:11).

Let all who are put in places of responsibility consider the awful judgment that will come on those who misuse places of spiritual leadership. What terrible punishment must come to those who pervert the Gospel. Some wear sheep's clothing *"but inwardly they are ravening wolves,"* Jesus said in Matthew 7:15. Some infidels wear bishop's robes. Professors of religion in the seminaries and colleges are in reality often enemies of Christ and the Bible, husbandmen who would refuse the fruits of the vineyard to the owner and who would kill the son. The wicked scribes and Pharisees who would not believe in the deity and authority of Jesus Christ have many in the religious world who follow in their steps and they will come to like judgment under the anger of God.

Verses 19 and following tell us that the chief priests and scribes *"perceived that he had spoken this parable against them."*

VERSES 19—26:

19 And the chief priests and the scribes the same hour sought to lay hands on him; and they feared the people: for they perceived that he had spoken this parable against them.

20 And they watched *him*, and sent forth spies, which should feign themselves just men, that they might take hold of his words, that so they might deliver him unto the power and authority of the governor.

21 And they asked him, saying, Master, we know that thou sayest and teachest rightly, neither acceptest thou the person *of any*, but teachest the way of God truly:

22 Is it lawful for us to give tribute unto Cæsar, or no?

23 But he perceived their craftiness, and said unto them, Why tempt ye me?

24 Shew me a penny. Whose image and superscription hath it? They answered and said, Cæsar's.

25 And he said unto them, Render therefore unto Cæsar the things which be Cæsar's, and unto God the things which be God's.

26 And they could not take hold of his words before the people: and they marvelled at his answer, and held their peace.

Should Jews Pay Tribute to Caesar?

The parallel passages are in Matthew 22:15-22 and Mark 12:13-17.

We have seen before, in Luke 19:47 that *"the chief priests and the scribes and the chief of the people sought to destroy him."* They sought some way to embarrass Him, to get Him in trouble with the Roman authorities, or to turn the people against Him. Now that He has clearly spoken the parable of the vineyard, accusing them as untrue to God and disloyal to the vineyard they kept, they *"the same hour sought to lay hands on him,"* but they feared the people.

These wicked leaders sent spies who pretended to be His friends. With flattering words they pretended to admire Jesus for His frankness and honesty so that He would commit Himself openly. They asked the question, *"Is it lawful for us to give tribute unto Caesar, or no?"*

If He took the part of the Roman tax collectors, the leaders thought the common people then would be against Jesus. Tax collectors are never popular. The tax collecting in Israel was more unpopular because it was done by the Roman Empire; the Jews were a conquered people, supporting their conquerors. More unpopular yet it was because the tax collectors were often exorbitant and unfair, requiring more than was just. If Jesus approved the tax gathering, surely, thought these wicked men, common people who loved Jesus would be offended at Him. And if He spoke against paying taxes, as they hoped, then *"they might deliver him unto the power and authority of the governor"* (vs. 20).

Jesus saw through their trickery. He said, *"Why tempt ye me?"* He said more, for Matthew 22:18 reports it thus: *"But Jesus perceived their wickedness, and said, Why tempt ye me, ye hypocrites?"* They were hypocrites, of course.

How often Jesus charged people with hypocrisy! Giving alms to be seen of men is *"as the hypocrites do"* (Matt. 6:2). When Pharisees and others prayed standing in the streets to be seen of men, they were *"as the hypocrites are"* (vs. 5). When people fast to be seen of men, putting on a show with a sad countenance, that is *"as the hypocrites,"* Jesus said (vs. 16). A hypocrite judges others but does not see his own sins, Jesus said in Matthew 7:5 and Luke 7:42. A ruler of the synagogue who watered his ox or ass and objected to a woman being healed was *"Thou hypocrite"* (Luke 13:15). Those who talk religious language and do not draw near to God with their hearts are hypocrites, Jesus said (Matt. 15:7). And Pharisees were hypocrites in demanding a sign or miracle to prove His deity when it was obvious to the multitude (Matt. 16:3). The disciples were warned, *"Beware ye of the leaven of the Pharisees, which is hypocrisy"* (Luke 12:1). And seven times in Matthew 23 Jesus said, *"Woe unto you, scribes and Pharisees, hypocrites!"* In religion, evidently the great temptation is to make an impression on men, to do religious matters to *"be seen of men,"* to be a hypocrite.

Patriotism and Christianity Go Together

Yes, the Christian is to *"render therefore unto Caesar the things which be Caesar's, and unto God the things which be God's."* Paul is inspired to give detailed instructions thus in Romans 13:1-7: *"The powers that be are ordained of God. Whosoever therefore resisteth the power, resisteth the ordinance of God."* The ruler is *"the minister of God to thee for good."* He *"beareth not the sword in vain: for he is the minister of God, a revenger to execute wrath upon him that doeth evil."* The ruler is *"the minister of God"* as truly as the preacher in the pulpit. One is a minister in government and order; the other is a minister of the Gospel — but both represent God. One who would be a good Christian must be a patriot.

It is interesting that Jesus offers allegiance to Caesar as represented by Governor Pilate, though Pilate, knowing He is innocent, is the one who will condemn Jesus to death! It is interesting that when Nero was emperor at Rome and would be the same man who would have Paul beheaded, Paul would say that he is the minister of God and *"the powers that be are ordained of God."* Children ought to obey parents whether the parents are always right or not. A wife is to be subject to her husband *"in every thing"* (Eph. 5:22-24), even if he is unsaved (I Pet. 3:1,2). Servants are to be obedient to their masters, *"not only to the good and gentle, but also to the froward"* (I Pet. 2:18). Citizens are to *"honour the king,"* are to *"submit yourselves to every ordinance of man for the Lord's sake: whether it be to the king, as supreme; Or unto governors, as unto them*

that are sent by him for the punishment of evildoers,
and for the praise of them that do well" (I Pet. 2:13,
14).

It is remarkable that we never hear Christ sneering
or railing at the Roman government. No, nor at Pilate
the governor. The Lord Jesus was tried and condemned
and the governor knew He was innocent. Paul rebuked
the high priest sharply for commanding that he be smitten contrary to the law, but he spoke not knowing that
he addressed the high priest. And Acts 23:4, 5 tells us,
"And they that stood by said, Revilest thou God's high
priest? Then said Paul, I wist not, brethren, that he was
the high priest: for it is written, Thou shalt not speak
evil of the ruler of thy people." Paul admitted it was
wrong to speak so sharply to the high priest even when
the high priest was wrong.

Note the plain teaching that it is a sin to *"speak evil*
of dignities," to *"despise dominion,"* to *"bring. . . rail-*
ing accusation" against rulers, leaders (Jude, vss.
8 and 9, and II Pet. 2:10, 11). Christians have a right
to express their opinions, to differ with other people,
to vote for a change in government, but their opinion
should be expressed with respect for those who are the
ministers of God in government. Unrestrained language,
accusations and abuse ill become a Christian anywhere
and they are particularly forbidden when spoken of
rulers. One who really has disrespect for our government, like the anarchists, one who brings railing accusations against rulers and speaks evil against dignities,
is not a good Christian, no matter how fundamental
in doctrine he claims to be nor how ardent a defender
of Americanism he appears to be.

VERSES 27—38:

27 Then came to *him* certain of the Sadducees, which deny that there is any resurrection; and they asked him,

28 Saying, Master, Moses wrote unto us, If any man's brother die, having a wife, and he die without children, that his brother should take his wife, and raise up seed unto his brother.

29 There were therefore seven brethren: and the first took a wife, and died without children.

30 And the second took her to wife, and he died childless.

31 And the third took her; and in like manner the seven also: and they left no children, and died.

32 Last of all the woman died also.

33 Therefore in the resurrection whose wife of them is she? for seven had her to wife.

34 And Jesus answering said unto them, The children of this world marry, and are given in marriage:

35 But they which shall be accounted worthy to obtain that world, and the resurrection from the dead, neither marry, nor are given in marriage:

36 Neither can they die any more: for they are equal unto the angels; and are the children of God, being the children of the resurrection.

37 Now that the dead are raised, even Moses shewed at the bush, when he calleth the Lord the God of Abraham, and the God of Isaac, and the God of Jacob.

38 For he is not a God of the dead, but of the living: for all live unto him.

Jesus Answers the Sadducees About the Resurrection

Parallel passages are Matthew 22:23-33 and Mark 12:18-27, and the wording is slightly different.

The Sadducees bring this question. More often it has been the Pharisees who were opposing Jesus. They were a religious sect that more or less held to the orthodox position professedly but were worldly minded and covetous. They kept the form and ceremony without a heart change, and so were unconverted religionists. The Sadducees were another sect—unitarians, modernists, liberals of the day who *"deny that there is any resurrection"* (vs. 27). They did not believe in either angels or spirits (Acts 23:8). Though the Sadducees and the Pharisees were bitter enemies, they were together in their hatred of Jesus Christ. When Paul was arrested and brought before the Sanhedrin, he caused division and an upset among them by saying, "*Men and brethren, I am a Pharisee, the son of a Pharisee: of the hope and resurrection of the dead I am called in question*" (Acts 23:6). That dissension caused Paul to be rescued by the Roman officer.

Here the Sadducees came to Jesus, hoping to reduce the question of the resurrection to an absurdity. The Mosaic Law in Deuteronomy 25:5 provided that when a brother died, his brother living with him would take his wife to raise up seed. Now the Pharisees, to make it ridiculous, carry this to the seventh time. When the woman dies at last, in the resurrection whose wife will she be of the seven? There mistake was in supposing that people are the same in Heaven as they are here. They erred not knowing the Scriptures or the power of God, Jesus said.

The answer was that there will be no marriage in Heaven. Christians will have resurrection bodies and will be children of God in body as well as spirit, and, like the angels, they will never die. And since there will be no death, no thinning of the population, there will be no need to multiply and replenish the earth, no need for procreation; so there will be no marriage in Heaven.

Does that mean that in Heaven we will all be sexless beings of the same kind, made after one pattern? I do not think so. It seems to me that our personality will carry over into Heaven but purified and made perfect and fit for sinless eternal beings. We think that men will have a man's personality and women will have a woman's personality. There are many reasons why men and women were made to complement each other. And there are many joys of fellowship between the sexes that do not involve marriage or sex relations.

Will I not know and have sweet fellowship with my wife, after being one on earth? Will I not know and love my dear mother in Heaven and know that she is my

mother? Will not my six daughters still be my daughters, and dear? Will they be changed into some strange
and unknown beings with whom I will have no ties of
love, no affection or sweet memories?

In wonderful ways, beyond the knowledge of men,
the joys, the associations, the fellowships in Heaven
will be perfect and complete among sinless beings.
Abraham in Heaven will still be *"Father Abraham"*
to Jews (Luke 16:22-24).

Paul the apostle was inspired to write, *"It is good for
a man not to touch a woman. Nevertheless, to avoid
fornication, let every man have his own wife, and let
every woman have her own husband"* (I Cor. 7:1, 2).
With no necessity and with no temptation, in Heaven
we suppose that all Christians would agree with Paul.
There is a certain wonderful freedom without the burdens
and cares of married life, so Paul said:

*"But I would have you without carefulness. He that
is unmarried careth for the things that belong to the
Lord, how he may please the Lord: But he that is
married careth for the things that are of the world,
how he may please his wife. There is difference also
between a wife and a virgin. The unmarried woman
careth for the things of the Lord, that she may be
holy both in body and in spirit: but she that is married
careth for the things of the world, how she may please
her husband. And this I speak for your own profit;
not that I may cast a snare upon you, but for that
which is comely, and that ye may attend upon the
Lord without distraction. But if any man think that he
behaveth himself uncomely toward his virgin, if she
pass the flower of her age, and need so require, let him
do what he will, he sinneth not: let them marry. Nevertheless he that standeth stedfast in his heart, having no
necessity, but hath power over his own will, and hath
so decreed in his heart that he will keep his virgin,*

doeth well. So then he that giveth her in marriage doeth well; but he that giveth her not in marriage doeth better." — I Cor. 7:32-38.

Paul was happier and content not to be married, though he had wonderfully sweet fellowship with many Christian women and rejoiced in knowing them, as we learn from that list in Romans, chapter 16. Jesus had the loving help of many good women and rejoiced in their love. So in Heaven, no doubt, without temptations and sex and the burdens of marriage, all the sweetness and goodness of perfect heart-fellowship will be the part of all Christians where they neither marry nor are given in marriage.

So the Pharisees' argument fell to the ground. But Jesus stopped their mouths by reminding them of the recorded statement of Moses in Exodus 3:5 where God said, *"I am the God of thy father, the God of Abraham, the God of Isaac, and the God of Jacob."* Notice that Jesus here insisted even on the present tense — even that is inspired in the Scripture. So God was still the God of Abraham, Isaac and Jacob. That meant that they were still in existence. They were not dead but living, although their bodies were in the grave.

"For he is not a God of the dead, but of the living: for all live unto him," that is, those who have gone on before are alive and Christians are with God as are Abraham, Isaac and Jacob.

VERSES 39—47:

39 Then certain of the scribes answering said, Master, thou hast well said.

40 And after that they durst not ask him any *question at all.*

41 And he said unto them, How say they that Christ is David's son?

42 And David himself saith in the book of Psalms, The LORD said unto my Lord, Sit thou on my right hand,

43 Till I make thine enemies thy footstool.

44 David therefore calleth him

Lord, how is he then his son?
45 Then in the audience of all the people he said unto his disciples,
46 Beware of the scribes, which desire to walk in long robes, and love greetings in the markets, and the highest seats in the syna- gogues, and the chief rooms at feasts;
47 Which devour widows' houses, and for a shew make long prayers: the same shall receive greater damnation.

Why Did David Call Christ "Lord"?

The scribes were impressed with the answer Jesus gave to the Sadducees, when Jesus proved by the Scriptures that Abraham, Isaac and Jacob were still alive and with God.

However, all the scribes, students and copyists of the Old Testament Scriptures knew that the Messiah (Hebrew), the Christ (Greek), that is, the Anointed One, was promised. He reminded them of the second Psalm where verse 2 prophesied that "*the kings of the earth set themselves, and the rulers take counsel together, against the Lord, and against his ANOINTED....*" Isaiah 61:1 prophesied also about this Anointed One, Jesus, "*The Spirit of the Lord God is upon me; because the Lord hath anointed me to preach good tidings unto the meek....*" Jesus quoted this Scripture in the synagogue at Nazareth, saying it has been fulfilled (Luke 4:18).

You see, the people were looking for the coming of the Messiah, the Christ. That we see from John 1:41; John 4:25-29; John 6:69; Luke 2:26; Luke 3:15. Now Jesus poses the question: If the promised Christ is descended from David, how could David call Him Lord as he did in Psalm 110:1? The answer, of course, has to be that the Messiah, the Anointed One, is really God in human form, and Jesus is not only the Son of David but the Son of God, born of a virgin, and the Creator of the world who humbled Himself and became a man. So Jesus was the Messiah or Christ, (that is, anointed of God) but He is also Lord, Lord of David and of all of us, and the Lord Jesus Christ, and Son of God, and Creator.

Then Jesus solemnly warned the disciples, *"Beware of the scribes, which desire to walk in long robes, and love greetings in the markets, and the highest seats in the synagogues, and the chief rooms at feasts."* They were unconverted. They were covetous. They devoured widow's houses. But their long prayers were simply to make an impression on people. Jesus warned about this hypocrisy in Matthew 6:1-7 and 16-18. Giving alms or saying prayers or fasting or going through any other religious ceremony *"to be seen of men,"* or to impress men, is hypocrisy and is here forbidden. Oh, may the dear Lord speak to and rebuke the pride that comes so easily to our poor hearts, and let us seek in the inmost heart to please God and not men.

LUKE 21

VERSES 1—4:

AND he looked up, and saw the rich men casting their gifts into the treasury.

2 And he saw also a certain poor widow casting in thither two mites.

3 And he said, Of a truth I say unto you, that this poor widow hath cast in more than they all:

4 For all these have of their abundance cast in unto the offerings of God: but she of her penury hath cast in all the living that she had.

The Widow Gives Two Mites

"Jesus sat over against the treasury, and beheld how the people cast money into the treasury," is the way Mark 12:41 tells it. He watched rich men cast their gifts into the treasury, and here came a certain poor widow and she put in two mites, which was only a fraction of a penny but it was *"all the living that she had."* She gave all she had.

Does the Lord Jesus care about how people give? Oh, yes He does, for the giving is somewhat a measure of our heart's devotion. And *"God loveth a cheerful giver"* (II Cor. 9:7). You see, giving is a measure of trust. God told the Jews in Malachi 3:10-12:

"Bring ye all the tithes into the storehouse, that there may be meat in mine house, and prove me now herewith, saith the Lord of hosts, if I will not open you the windows of heaven, and pour you out a blessing, that there shall not be room enough to receive it. And I will rebuke the devourer for your sakes, and he shall not destroy the fruits of your ground; neither shall your vine cast her fruit before the time in the field, saith the Lord of hosts. And all nations shall call you blessed: for ye shall be a delightsome land, saith the Lord of hosts."

Now the ceremonial Temple at Jerusalem, the Levites and priesthood, are gone and the only temple God has on earth is the human body of a Christian. But God's principle is the same. All things belong to God. Those who love Him and trust Him to repay, as He said, will give. God has promised, "*The liberal soul shall be made fat: and he that watereth shall be watered also himself*" (Prov. 11:25). Jesus said, "*Give, and it shall be given unto you; good measure, pressed down, and shaken together, and running over, shall men give into your bosom. For with the same measure that ye mete withal it shall be measured to you again*" (Luke 6:38). Paul was inspired to say again, "*He which soweth sparingly shall reap also sparingly; and he which soweth bountifully shall reap also bountifully*" (II Cor. 9:6). So giving represents faith and love and obedience. And how pleasing it is to God when the heart trusts Him and knows that He will provide in return. So the Lord made this widow famous to all the millions who read the Scriptures because she gave all she had — two little mites!

VERSES 5, 6:

5 And as some spake of the temple, how it was adorned with goodly stones and gifts, he said, 6 *As for* these things which ye behold, the days will come, in the which there shall not be left one stone upon another, that shall not be thrown down.

The Olivet Discourse

Here begins and extends through the chapter what is called the Olivet Discourse because Matthew 24:1-3 tells us that Jesus departed from the Temple and went into the Mount of Olives and gave this teaching. It extends through Matthew 24 and through Mark 13, in the

parallel passages. In viewing the Temple, one of the
disciples had said to him, "*Master, see what manner of
stones and what buildings are here! And Jesus answering said unto him, Seest thou these great buildings?
there shall not be left one stone upon another, that shall
not be thrown down*" (Mark 13:1,2). So here Jesus
plainly foretells the destruction of Jerusalem in A. D. 70
when Titus, a Roman general, would take the rebellious
city and destroy it. And perhaps it looks further toward
the second destruction of the city which would take place
in the year A. D. 135 when Jerusalem would again be
destroyed to the ground and all the Jews scattered to the
four winds.

VERSE 7:

7 And they asked him, saying, Master, but when shall these things be? and what sign *will there be* when these things shall come to pass?

When Would This Destruction Come to Pass?

The question in more detail is given in Matthew 24:3,
"*And as he sat upon the mount of Olives, the disciples
came unto him privately, saying, Tell us, when shall
these things be? and what shall be the sign of thy coming, and of the end of the world?*" The disciples asked
about three things and presumably had them connected
in their minds: 1. When would be the destruction of
Jerusalem, when not one stone of the Temple would be
left upon another? 2. What would be the miraculous
manifestation, "*sign*" of Christ's coming? 3. Would it
be the same as "*the end of the world,*" that is, the
consummation of this age?

The disciples, like other intelligent Jews, were concerned
about the prophesied future of Jerusalem and the nation

Israel.   And they will ask after Christ's resurrection, *"Lord, wilt thou at this time restore again the kingdom to Israel?"* (Acts 1:6).   The destruction of Jerusalem in A. D. 70 was not connected with the second coming of Christ, which is yet future, but the apostles might well have expected it.   The Old Testament prophecies in Zechariah 14 foretell another destruction of Jerusalem by the armies of the Antichrist at the *"day of the Lord"* and the literal return of Christ, to defeat the demon-possessed armies of the Antichrist (Zech. 14:1-7). And the rest of the chapter tells of the personal reign of Christ.   But that destruction, mentioned in the Olivet Discourse, was to come within the lifetime of many of those present.

VERSES 8—19:

8   And he said, Take heed that ye be not deceived: for many shall come in my name, saying, I am *Christ;* and the time draweth near: go ye not therefore after them.

9   But when ye shall hear of wars and commotions, be not terrified: for these things must first come to pass; but the end *is* not by and by.

10   Then said he unto them, Nation shall rise against nation, and kingdom against kingdom:

11   And great earthquakes shall be in divers places, and famines, and pestilences; and fearful sights and great signs shall there be from heaven.

12   But before all these, they shall lay their hands on you, and persecute *you,* delivering *you* up to the synagogues, and into prisons,

being brought before kings and rulers for my name's sake.

13   And it shall turn to you for a testimony.

14   Settle *it* therefore in your hearts, not to meditate before what ye shall answer:

15   For I will give you a mouth and wisdom, which all your adversaries shall not be able to gainsay nor resist.

16   And ye shall be betrayed both by parents, and brethren, and kinsfolks, and friends; and *some* of you shall they cause to be put to death.

17   And ye shall be hated of all *men* for my name's sake.

18   But there shall not an hair of your head perish.

19   In your patience possess ye your souls.

The Course of This Age

This passage, and particularly the companion passages

in Matthew 24 and Mark 13, have often been wrongly used, as if they give signs showing when the return of Christ could be seen coming immediately. Thus every great war has been cited by some as a sign that the coming of Christ would immediately follow. The earthquakes and famines and pestilences (vs. 11) have been cited as certain evidences that Jesus must come right away.

That is not the intention here, as is made clear, we think, in verse 9: *"These things must first come to pass; but the end is not by and by,"* or *"the end is not yet"* as given in Matthew 24:6. The Bible clearly teaches again and again the return of Christ is imminent, that is, it may be at any time, but that no one can possibly foretell when it will be. Of the whole matter of Christ's coming in the air for His saints and His later return to earth to set up the kingdom and related events, *"of that day and hour knoweth no man, no, not the angels of heaven, but my Father only"* (Matt. 24:36. See also Mark 13:32,33). And Jesus had already said to them, *"The kingdom of God cometh not with observation,"* that is, one could not see it approaching (Luke 17:20). And Jesus told the disciples later, in Acts 1:7, *"It is not for you to know the times or the seasons, which the Father hath put in his own power."* That referred to the return of Christ and the restoration of Israel.

Jesus has said, *"An evil and adulterous generation seeketh after a sign,"* but the word *"sign"* refers to a miraculous manifestation and not, as some would like to believe, to events in history and in nature indicating the approach of Christ's return. And the question in verse 7, *"What sign will there be when these things shall come to pass?"* simply means, What will be the marvelous manifestation, the miraculous appearance, the *"sign of thy coming, and of the end of the world?"* as Matthew 24:3 states it. Remember, the word *"sign"* is in the singular and does not refer to a series of evidences before

Jesus comes but simply the one spectacular, miraculous appearance of Christ at His Second Coming to reign.

Matthew 24:29,30 tells us that *"immediately after the tribulation of those days... shall appear the sign of the Son of man in heaven... and they shall see the Son of man coming in the clouds of heaven with power and great glory."* There are to be no "signs" in the sense of evidences that Jesus will come within any set limit of time.

Again and again in this Olivet Discourse the disciples are commanded to watch (Matt. 24:42-44; Mark 13:32-37). Following the clear teachings of the Saviour to watch, Paul expected the return of Christ while he was alive, as we see in I Corinthians 15:52 and in I Thessalonians 4:16,17. And following this teaching, the Thessalonian Christians, as all others, were saved and taught *"to wait for his Son from heaven, whom he raised from the dead, even Jesus, which delivered us from the wrath to come"* (I Thess. 1:10).

Then the course of this age will naturally have these features: wars and commotions (vs. 9), earthquakes, famines, pestilences, perhaps comets, falling stars, and sometimes an eclipse of sun or moon (vs. 11). There will be persecutions of Christians as in apostolic times, as in the Roman Church, the Spanish Inquisition, and as happens now in Latin American countries, in China and Russia (vs. 12). And Christ will be an issue to bring division in families, in denominations and among friends (vss. 16,17). Just as Jesus had said before, *"I came not to send peace, but a sword. For I am come to set a man at variance against his father, and the daughter against her mother, and the daughter in law against her mother in law"* (Matt. 10:34,35).

In all this, the Christian is to remember that God wonderfully preserves us. He will give us what to say in time of persecution. Some shall be put to death. Others who are true shall be hated, but there will be no perma-

nent, eternal loss to a hair of our head, for resurrection
is coming (vs. 18).   But we are to run the race with
patience (vs. 19; Heb. 10:35,36; Heb. 12:1,2).

VERSES 20 — 24:

20 And when ye shall see Jerusalem compassed with armies, then
know that the desolation thereof is
nigh.
21 Then let them which are in
Judæa flee to the mountains; and
let them which are in the midst of
it depart out; and let not them
that are in the countries enter
thereinto.
22 For these be the days of vengeance, that all things which are
written may be fulfilled.
23 But woe unto them that are
with child, and to them that give
suck, in those days! for there shall
be great distress in the land, and
wrath upon this people.
24 And they shall fall by the edge
of the sword, and shall be led away
captive into all nations: and Jerusalem shall be trodden down of
the Gentiles, until the times of the
Gentiles be fulfilled.

The Destruction of Jerusalem Foretold

It is clear that Jesus had in mind primarily the destruction of Jerusalem and the scattering of all the Jews which
took place in A. D. 70. However, in that Olivet Discourse
He made many clear references to the future destruction
of Jerusalem in the close of the tribulation period, as you
see from Matthew 24:14 and following. In the Scripture,
God often has one event to be repeated in intensity and
thus the same Scripture may have in mind one event and
yet picture another. So the destruction of Jerusalem under Titus was a type and picture, perhaps, of the terrible
tribulation time when the abomination of desolation will
take place, when the Man of Sin will claim to be God
and seek to kill all who will not take his mark or serve
him.   And Jerusalem will be surrounded by armies and
ravished, then delivered by the personal return of Christ,
as told in Zechariah 14.

But the discussion here is simpler.   Jerusalem is to be

destroyed in the lifetime of some of these present, perhaps in from seventeen to twenty-one years. The book
of Hebrews, written while the Temple was still standing
and while the offerings were being offered (Heb.
13:10), was preparing the Jews everywhere for the destruction
of Jerusalem, and it was this same destruction pictured
in Luke 21:20-24 which is told in Hebrews 10:25, *"Not
forsaking the assembling of ourselves together, as the
manner of some is; but exhorting one another: and so
much the more, as ye see the day approaching."* One
cannot see the day of Christ's coming approaching and
that is not the meaning. But when Jerusalem was compassed with armies and seized by Titus, people were to
"know that the desolation thereof is nigh" (vs. 20).
They would see the day approaching.

   "These be the days of vengeance." Oh, awful punishment on a nation that cried out to Pilate, *"His blood be
on us, and on our children"* (Matt. 27:25). Jesus had
predicted awful judgment on the cities that heard Him
but rejected Him, particularly Chorazin, Bethsaida, Capernaum, and He had said that *"it shall be more tolerable for the land of Sodom in the day of judgment, than
for thee"* (Matt. 11:20-24). So the judgment of God here
is on the whole nation Israel for rejecting her Saviour.

   Note the worldwide dispersion foretold in verse 24.
Jews will go all over the world. And note the specific
prophecy in the last half of verse 24: *". . . and Jerusalem shall be trodden down of the Gentiles, until the times
of the Gentiles be fulfilled."* As this is being written,
Jews have control of the old city of Jerusalem, but it is
inhabited primarily by Arabs and we would think from
this Scripture that the Jewish control is only temporary
and limited. Yet, according to this verse, it seems that
an independent Jewish nation cannot have undisputed
claim to and possession of the city of Jerusalem proper
"until the times of the Gentiles be fulfilled," that is, when
the last Gentile rulers will be put down with the destruc-

tion of the Antichrist in the tribulation time and when Christ Himself shall return and "*the God of heaven set up a kingdom,*" the Jewish kingdom of Christ in Palestine, although it will be a kingdom of the whole world (Dan. 2:44,45). If we understand verse 24 correctly, then the ownership and control of Jerusalem is likely to be put into international hands and not left permanently under the control of Israel.

VERSES 25—28:

25 And there shall be signs in the sun, and in the moon, and in the stars; and upon the earth distress of nations, with perplexity; the sea and the waves roaring;
26 Men's hearts failing them for fear, and for looking after those things which are coming on the earth: for the powers of heaven shall be shaken.
27 And then shall they see the Son of man coming in a cloud with power and great glory.
28 And when these things begin to come to pass, then look up, and lift up your heads; for your redemption draweth nigh.

The Return of Christ in Glory

Pay particular attention to the fact that the rapture of the saints, the coming of Christ in the air to receive His own, foretold in I Thessalonians 4:14-18 and in I Corinthians 15:51,52, is not mentioned here. God does not let His timetable be known: the rapture of the saints is an event kept secret until it occurs. No one knows or can know when that will occur, and Jesus does not tell or give any hint here as to just when it will occur.

In verse 20, Jews in Jerusalem, surrounded by Titus' army, were able to know that the desolation was near. After the tribulation time (as Matt. 24:29 plainly says) there will be tremendous signs in the sun, moon and stars, and awful trouble on the earth, then people will see Christ in His glory coming to fight the battle of

Armageddon and set up His kingdom on earth. They will see Him coming in clouds, as pictured in Revelation 19:11-16 and Jude, verse 14, and in Zechariah 14:3,4. Then Jews and others converted in the tribulation time will see these things begin to come to pass and they will look up, for their redemption from the Antichrist and from the troubles of the tribulation will be drawing near!

VERSES 29—33:

29 And he spake to them a parable; Behold the fig tree, and all the trees;
30 When they now shoot forth, ye see and know of your own selves that summer is now nigh at hand.
31 So likewise ye, when ye see these things come to pass, know ye that the kingdom of God is nigh at hand.
32 Verily I say unto you, This generation shall not pass away, till all be fulfilled.
33 Heaven and earth shall pass away: but my words shall not pass away.

The Parable of the Fig Tree

Compare this passage with Matthew 24:32,33; Mark 13:28,29. Do not confuse the time intended. This is *"immediately after the tribulation of those days"* (Matt. 24:29). This is after they shall *"see the Son of man coming in a cloud with power and great glory"* (Luke 21:27). Remember that the great concern of Jewish believers was for the restoration of Israel and this is the blessing promised here. When the Saviour appears, then according to Matthew 24:31, *"he shall send his angels with a great sound of a trumpet, and they shall gather together his elect from the four winds, from one end of heaven to the other"* and bring them back to Palestine. That is the regathering of Israel foretold in Isaiah 11:10-16, in Jeremiah 23:1-8, in Deuteronomy 30:1-6, and in Acts 15:16.

What is *"this generation"* which *"shall not pass away,*

till all be fulfilled" in verse 32? Dr. Scofield says about
"this generation" in the parallel passage, Matthew 24:34:

> Gr. *genea,* the primary definition of which is, "race,
> kind, family, stock, breed." (So all lexicons.) That the
> word is used in this sense here is sure because none of
> "these things," i. e. the world-wide preaching of the king-
> dom, the great tribulation, the return of the Lord in
> visible glory, and the regathering of the elect, occurred
> at the destruction of Jerusalem by Titus, A. D. 70. The
> promise is, therefore, that the generation--nation, or
> family of Israel--will be preserved unto "these things";
> a promise wonderfully fulfilled to this day.

VERSES 34 — 38:

34 And take heed to yourselves, lest at any time your hearts be overcharged with surfeiting, and drunkenness, and cares of this life, and so that day come upon you unawares.
35 For as a snare shall it come on all them that dwell on the face of the whole earth.
36 Watch ye therefore, and pray always, that ye may be accounted worthy to escape all these things that shall come to pass, and to stand before the Son of man.
37 And in the day time he was teaching in the temple; and at night he went out, and abode in the mount that is called *the mount* of Olives.
38 And all the people came early in the morning to him in the temple, for to hear him.

Christians Are to "Take Heed" and to "Watch" Until Christ Returns

How anxious good Christians become for Christ's
return! So there is a tendency, a bad tendency, to set
dates for His coming. And these efforts to foretell when
Christ will come have always ended in disappointment,
disillusionment and trouble. Others have felt that the
coming of Christ is so far away that it has no practical
meaning for us, so they have a tendency to go along
with the worldliness about them, with their hearts being
"overcharged with surfeiting, and drunkenness, and

cares of this life," and on some surely the day of Christ will come unawares! What about the persecutions, the troubles, the wars, foretold as the course of this age? We are to watch and to pray, to be counted worthy to escape all these things.

Jerusalem was jammed with multitudes for the coming passover season.   In the daytime Jesus was in the Temple teaching.   At night He went out *"and abode in the mount that is called the mount of Olives."*   Compare this with John 7:53 and John 8:1 ignoring the chapter division.   *"And every man went unto his own house. Jesus went unto the mount of Olives."* Does that mean that Jesus slept on the ground, probably in the Garden of Gethsemane, where He *"ofttimes resorted thither with his disciples"*? (John 18:2).   We remember that Jesus had said to a would-be disciple, *" The foxes have holes, and the birds of the air have nests; but the Son of man hath not where to lay his head"* (Matt. 8:20).   I have no doubt He often slept on the ground among the Olive trees. He was hungry, so He sought to pluck a fig from a barren fig tree (Mark 11:13). Perhaps He, like the disciples, sometimes rubbed out wheat from the husk (*corn* here means small grain, not our Indian corn), and ate it when He was hungry (Luke 6:1).

The time is short before His arrest and crucifixion, so Jesus will early in the morning be in the Temple teaching the people.

LUKE 22

VERSES 1 — 6:

NOW the feast of unleavened bread drew nigh, which is called the Passover.

2 And the chief priests and scribes sought how they might kill him; for they feared the people.

3 Then entered Satan into Judas surnamed Iscariot, being of the number of the twelve.

4 And he went his way, and communed with the chief priests and captains, how he might betray him unto them.

5 And they were glad, and covenanted to give him money.

6 And he promised, and sought opportunity to betray him unto them in the absence of the multitude.

Judas Agrees With Jewish Leaders to Betray Jesus

See Matthew 26:2, 14-16; Mark 14:1,2,10,11, parallel passages. The hatred of Jesus by the chief priests and scribes has increased until they have a passionate desire to kill Him. They had had abundant evidences that God was with Christ and that He was the promised Messiah, but they would not heed. They knew that He cast out devils but they wickedly said that He cast out devils through Beelzebub. Jesus knew their thoughts (Luke 11:17 and Matt. 12:25) and gave them the solemn warning about the unpardonable sin (Matt. 12:31,32; Mark 3:29,30) and we think they committed that unpardonable sin.

It was not in the words they said but in their thoughts. They said He cast out devils by Beelzebub, prince of devils, but, no doubt, in their hearts they knew: "He is bound to be the Son of God, as He claims to be. I don't care, I still hate Him; I will not serve Him." So after great enlightenment and conviction they blaspheme the Spirit of God in their hearts and in their thoughts; and that was the unpardonable sin, if they then committed it, as it seems sure. I think they had reached the state of great enlightenment, had tasted the evidences of the heavenly gift. They had gone along in the present and had seen the power of the Holy Spirit, according to Hebrews 6:4, and falling away from all conviction, it was impossible for them to repent. Concerning the awful wickedness before the flood, the Lord said in Genesis 6:3, *"My spirit shall not always strive with man."* So there came a time when Noah need preach no more, but judgment should come. It was so, we think, with Pharaoh when he hardened his heart and God hardened his heart and rushed him on to his death. Now these wicked men, hardened in sin, plan how they may kill Jesus.

We think it is these same chief priests and scribes who will *"see the Son of man sitting on the right hand of power, and coming in the clouds of heaven,"* as Jesus warned them in Matthew 26:64, in the prophesied time, when at the name of Jesus every knee shall bow to Christ in Heaven and earth and Hell! (Phil. 2:10,11).

It is probable also that Judas committed the unpardonable sin. He had had enlightenment such as could come to only few people in the world. Judas had never trusted in Christ, for Jesus said, *"But there are some of you that believe not. For Jesus knew from the beginning who they were that believed not, and who should betray him,"* and He said, *"Have not I chosen you twelve, and one of you is a devil? He spake of Judas Iscariot . . . ."* (John 6:64, 70, 71). He had seen the miracles, he had heard the teachings, he had seen a multitude saved. It is impossible but that he had felt the deep conviction of the Spirit of God and had rejected it. We cannot but think that he had become so hardened and so set in his rebellion against the Spirit that he had insulted and driven away that Spirit.

It had been prophesied in Psalm 41:9, *"Yea, mine own familiar friend, in whom I trusted, which did eat*

of my bread, hath lifted up his heel against me." And
in John 13:18 Jesus quoted that Scripture about Judas
Iscariot.· That does not meant that Judas was compelled
to betray Jesus. It means only that God knew ahead
of time Judas would do so. The only predestination
God makes is based upon His foreknowledge, as we
are plainly told in Romans 8:29 and in I Peter 1:2.
How sad is the story of Judas, intimate companion
and chosen helper of Jesus, who persistently rejected
the Saviour and came to hate Him and finally betrayed
Him for thirty pieces of silver.

Note verse 3: "*Then entered Satan into Judas.*"
Already Jesus had said of Judas that he "*is a devil*"
(John 6:70). And now, in a stronger attack, Satan
came in to master Judas and get him definitely to act
in selling Jesus.

The immediate occasion here for Judas' anger and
rebellion was the anointing of Jesus by Mary of Bethany,
as told in Matthew 26:6-13; Mark 14:3-9 and John 12:
1-8, where covetous Judas protested that the ointment
could have been sold for money and since as treasurer
of the twelve, he carried the bag, he would have gotten
part of it. He was rebuked by the Saviour. Others
of the disciples, perhaps, agreed with Judas, but John
12:4-6 tells us that it was Judas who made the protest
"*because he was a thief, and had the bag, and bare
what was put therein.*" And both the accounts in Mark
14:10 and in Matthew 26:14, 15, show that immediately
after this incident Judas went to the chief priests and
asked for a price to deliver Jesus. The price the chief
priests agreed to pay Judas was "*thirty pieces of silver*"
(Matt. 26:15). Is not this the fulfillment of the prophecy
in Zechariah 11:12 and 13:

"*And I said unto them, If ye think good, give me my
price; and if not, forbear. So they weighed for my price
thirty pieces of silver. And the Lord said unto me,*

Cast it unto the potter: a goodly price that I was prised at of them. And I took the thirty pieces of silver, and cast them to the potter in the house of the Lord."

But Judas must find occasion to lead the soldiers of the high priest to Jesus in secret, away from the multitude. He would find the opportunity tonight as Jesus goes to the Garden of Gethsemane.

VERSES 7—13:

7 Then came the day of unleavened bread, when the passover must be killed.

8 And he sent Peter and John, saying, Go and prepare us the passover, that we may eat.

9 And they said unto him, Where wilt thou that we prepare?

10 And he said unto them, Behold, when ye are entered into the city, there shall a man meet you, bearing a pitcher of water; follow him into the house where he entereth in.

11 And ye shall say unto the goodman of the house, The Master saith unto thee, Where is the guest-chamber, where I shall eat the passover with my disciples?

12 And he shall shew you a large upper room furnished: there make ready.

13 And they went, and found as he had said unto them: and they made ready the passover.

Preparation for the Passover

A careful study here will show, we believe, that Jesus did not eat the passover lamb. He Himself was God's Passover, the fulfillment of the prophetic type, so He must die at the time when passover lambs are being slain.

Verse 7 says, *"Then came the day of unleavened bread, when the passover must be killed."* In Matthew 26:17 the King James Version mistakenly adds certain words: *"Now the first day of the feast of unleavened bread. . . ."* But in the Greek, leaving out the added words, that verse literally says, *"Now the first of the unleavened bread the disciples came to Jesus."*

God had given very, very strict rules about the pass-over season. The passover lamb was to be eaten with unleavened bread, and they were to eat only unleavened bread the seven days of the feast of unleavened bread. Exodus 12:15 says, "*Seven days shall ye eat unleaven-ed bread; even the first day ye shall put away leaven out of your houses: for whosoever eateth leavened bread from the first day until the seventh day, that soul shall be cut off from Israel.*" That command and the penalty were so severe that we understand Jews regularly had only leavened bread preceding the passover feast because the passover feast and the feast of unleavened bread would begin at sundown and so the bread must be prepared before that.

If we understand verse 7, that it is now about sun-down and the day when they will bake the unleavened bread for the feast and the passover lamb will be killed, on this day between sundown now and sundown on the morrow, then after sundown tomorrow the passover feast will be eaten with unleavened bread. So this is the "*day of the preparation*" beginning now at sundown, and simple preparations were made for a simple meal which would include bread, perhaps a sour wine or vinegar, into which Jesus will dip the sop. And so in Matthew 26:20 we read, "*Now when the even was come, he sat down with the twelve,*" or literally, "re-clined" with the twelve.

You will note that while in the Old Testament the term "*passover*" referred to the particular meal of a lamb roasted with fire and eaten with bitter herbs, here in the New Testament the term "*passover*" is a general term referring to the whole celebration: the feast including the preliminary day with unleavened bread before the passover feast itself and the feast of unleavened bread for seven days. So in verse 13, where they "*made ready the passover,*" the disciples simply prepared for the whole week, that is, they were settled in the upper room and had whatever was necessary for the first preliminary meals of the season.

Since the day began at sundown, and they were eating in this evening, the passover lamb had not yet been killed and tomorrow afternoon, while Jesus is on the cross, it will still be the day of *"the preparation of the passover,"* as we see from John 19:14, 31.

Was it prearranged that the man bearing a pitcher of water would appear at a certain time? I think not. I have no doubt that Christ, who knew all things that He wanted to know, knew about that and simply told the disciples they would see such a man and to follow him to the proper house. And they did. No doubt that good man of the house knew Jesus and when the disciples said, *"The Master saith unto thee, Where is the guestchamber, where I shall eat the passover with my disciples?"* he was glad to furnish for Jesus that upper room.

VERSES 14—20:

14 And when the hour was come, he sat down, and the twelve apostles with him.

15 And he said unto them, With desire I have desired to eat this passover with you before I suffer:

16 For I say unto you, I will not any more eat thereof, until it be fulfilled in the kingdom of God.

17 And he took the cup, and gave thanks, and said, Take this, and divide *it* among yourselves:

18 For I say unto you, I will not drink of the fruit of the vine, until the kingdom of God shall come.

19 And he took bread, and gave thanks, and brake *it*, and gave unto them, saying, This is my body which is given for you: this do in remembrance of me.

20 Likewise also the cup after supper, saying, This cup *is* the new testament in my blood, which is shed for you.

The Preliminary Meal of the Feast: the Lord's Supper Given

The order of events on the night of this last supper

is given by Dr. Scofield in the Scofield Reference Bible,
as follows:

> (1) The taking by our Lord and the disciples of their
> places at the table; (2) the contention who should be
> greatest; (3) the feet-washing; (4) the identification of
> Judas as the traitor; (5) the withdrawal of Judas; (6) the
> institution of the supper; (7) the words of Jesus while
> still in the room (Mt. 26.26-29; Lk. 22.35-38; John
> 13.31-35; 14.1-31); (8) the words of Jesus between the
> room and the garden (Mt. 26.31-35; Mk. 14.26-31;
> John 15., 16., 17.); it seems probable that the high-
> priestly prayer (John 17.) was uttered after they reached
> the garden; (9) the agony in the garden; (10) the be-
> trayal and arrest; (11) Jesus before Caiaphas; Peter's
> denial.

Again, the term *"passover"* is referring to the whole
passover and feast of unleavened bread celebration,
including this preliminary day, literally the *"day of
the preparation."* What did they have to eat? We
know only that they had bread and *"the fruit of the
vine."* They did not have a passover lamb. The
passover lamb had not been killed. They had not had
any time to roast that lamb. It would not have fitted
in with the prophecies, since the killing of the passover
lamb pictured the killing of Jesus who will die tomorrow
afternoon on the cross — tomorrow to us, but to them
the same day which had already begun at sundown.

Jesus loved His own and had longed for this time with
them. And the tender affection and fellowship here is
told in John 13 when He washed the disciples' feet.
There we are told that *"having loved his own which
were in the world, he loved them unto the end,"* even
as the Garden of Gethsemane, the betrayal and crucifixion, rushed upon Him! Jesus will eat again broiled
fish and honeycomb before His disciples after He is
raised from the dead (Luke 24:42,43). He will no more
eat of this passover feast *"until it be fulfilled in the
kingdom of God"* (vs. 16). He will not drink of the

fruit of the vine *"until the kingdom of God shall come"* (vs. 18).

Now supper being ended, Jesus instituted the Lord's Supper.   On this we suggest you read Matthew 26:26-29; Mark 14:22-25 and John 13. Now He took bread that remained from the meal and broke it and gave to each, saying, *"This is my body which is given for you: this do in remembrance of me."* Obviously this is figurative language just as when He said in John 10:7, *"I am the door of the sheep,"* and again in verse 9, *"I am the door,"* and when He said, *"I am the way"* or road (John 14:6). Jesus literally sat before them, in His body, so the bread was not His body but it pictured and illustrated His body. In John 6:53 Jesus said, *"Verily, verily, I say unto you, Except ye eat the flesh of the Son of man, and drink his blood, ye have no life in you."*   But again that was figurative language and had no reference to the Lord's Supper, the communion.   For in the same chapter, verses 28 and 29 say, *"Then said they unto him, What shall we do, that we might work the works of God? Jesus answered and said unto them, This is the work of God, that ye believe on him whom he hath sent."*

So the way to be saved is to *"believe on him"* (Christ). No, the Lord's Supper is a testimony, not a saving ordinance. Jesus said, *"This do in remembrance of me."* Salvation is not in rites and ceremonies but in repentance and faith in the heart.

VERSES 21—23:

21 But, behold, the hand of him that betrayeth me *is* with me on the table.

22 And truly the Son of man goeth, as it was determined: but woe unto that man by whom he is betrayed!

23 And they began to enquire among themselves, which of them it was that should do this thing.

"Lord, Is It I?"

The parallel passages are Matthew 26:21-25; Mark 14:18-21; and John 13:18-30. The parallel Scriptures give more detail. There are five verses on this in Matthew, five in Mark, and fifteen in John. Matthew and Mark say that the disciples said to Him one by one, "*Is it I?*" And John tells us that as he (the beloved disciple) leaned on Jesus' breast, Peter motioned to him that he should ask Jesus who it was that should betray Him. And Jesus answered, "*He it is, to whom I shall give a sop, when I have dipped it.*" He gave the sop to Judas. John tells further, "*And after the sop Satan entered into him. Then said Jesus unto him, That thou doest, do quickly.*" The other disciples did not understand and thought Judas was sent to buy something for the feast.

Verse 22 tells us that Jesus knew that it was clearly prophesied that He should die and be betrayed exactly as had been prophesied in the Old Testament and "as it was determined" of God.

In the prayer in Acts 4:27, 28 the Jerusalem Christians reminded that Herod, Pontius Pilate, the Gentiles and the people of Israel "*were gathered together, For to do whatsoever thy hand and thy counsel determined before to be done.*" And what woe was to come upon Judas by whom Jesus knew He would be betrayed! Matthew and Mark both add to that pronouncement of woe upon Judas: "*Good were it for that man if he had never been born.*"

Here is striking proof that Judas Iscariot will be forever in Hell, with no restoration, with no end to the eternal punishment and destiny. If Judas should spend a thousand years, or ten thousand, in Hell and then be restored to peace and fellowship with God and Heaven's joys for all the millions of years of eternity, it would still be better for him to be born. But the awful woe on a sinner who goes to Hell is that through all the millenniums of eternity he will wish he had never been born.

VERSES 24—30:

24 And there was also a strife among them, which of them should be accounted the greatest.

25 And he said unto them, The kings of the Gentiles exercise lordship over them; and they that exercise authority upon them are called benefactors.

26 But ye *shall* not *be* so: but he that is greatest among you, let him be as the younger; and he that is chief, as he that doth serve.

27 For whether *is* greater, he that sitteth at meat, or he that serveth? *is* not he that sitteth at meat? but I am among you as he that serveth.

28 Ye are they which have continued with me in my temptations.

29 And I appoint unto you a kingdom, as my Father hath appointed unto me;

30 That ye may eat and drink at my table in my kingdom, and sit on thrones judging the twelve tribes of Israel.

Jealousy Among the Apostles

Who shall be greatest among the apostles? It was most natural that twelve people, all preachers, all destined to be leaders and teachers, all specially trained in the work, with some three years of personal contact and teaching of Jesus, should have some natural competition and some jealousy. The mother of James and John had come to Jesus before asking that her two sons should be on His right hand and on His left, in His kingdom (Matt. 20:20-24; Mark 10:36-41). In the following verses there, Matthew 20:25-28 and in Mark 10:42-45, Jesus had told them that places of honor in the kingdom could not be given simply on application but must be earned. And He told them that one who was to be greatest of all must be servant of all. And here the question comes up again.

It is not surprising. There are many things that would naturally cause the apostles to look to the future and wonder what position, what work, what honor, they could expect. And Peter, James, John and Andrew were the first of the apostles called and all along they took some pre-eminence. When the apostles are named, Peter was always named first and the list in Matthew 10:2-4 starts off, "*Now the names of the twelve apostles are these; The first, Simon, who is called Peter....*" It was Peter who answered, "*Thou art the Christ, the Son of the living God*" (Matt. 16:16), and was greatly praised because God had revealed this to him. It was Peter to whom it was promised that he would be given the keys of the kingdom, which some think means he was to be the first to preach at Pentecost to the Jews and the first to carry the Gospel to the Gentiles, in Acts 10. It was Peter who asked for all the apostles, "*Behold, we have forsaken all, and followed thee; what shall we have therefore?*" And Jesus promised them that they "*shall sit upon twelve thrones, judging the twelve tribes of Israel*" (Matt. 19:27, 28).

When Jesus went into the house to raise up the twelve-year-old girl who had died, "*he suffered no man to go in, save Peter, and James, and John, and the father and the mother of the maiden*" (Luke 8:51). Probably the others were envious or a little jealous.

It was Peter, James and John who went aside to pray with Jesus and they were with Him on the mount of transfiguration (Matt. 17:1; Mark 9:2; Luke 9:28). These same three would be asked to go a little further and pray with Jesus in the Garden of Gethsemane.

John, too, had had special favors and he calls himself "*one of his disciples whom Jesus loved,*" and at the Last Supper he was "*leaning on Jesus' bosom*" (John 13:23), and the special intimacy John had with Jesus was recognized when Simon Peter beckoned to John "*that he should ask who it should be of whom he spake*" that should betray Him.

There are deep-seated currents in every man's life

and it is not unnatural that a man should want to succeed, should want to have loving favor, should want to earn and have some authority. So, among Christian workers, all of us need to continually beware lest we should be jealous or envious of others. It has been very commonly observed that it is difficult for an assistant pastor or music director or associate to remain loyal to the pastor being criticised and not to seek some preference for himself at the expense of the pastor who does the plain, sharp preaching for God.

So here Jesus reminds the disciples, "*The kings of the Gentiles exercise lordship over them: and they that exercise authority upon them are called benefactors. But ye shall not be so: but he that is greatest among you, let him be as the younger; and he that is chief, as he that doth serve.*" And He reminded them of His own example, being "*among them as he that serveth.*"

Luke does not give all the story but at about this time would come in that tender experience and lesson when Jesus washed the disciples' feet. He laid aside His garments and did the work of a common servant and said, "*For I have given you an example, that ye should do as I have done to you*" (John 13:15). But we are to serve others, are to restore others when they fall into sin, are to forgive others when they wrong us, and we are to help Christians to have their spiritual feet washed again and again by the mercy of Christians who love them. All of us walk in a dirty world.

Here again Jesus repeats the promise that He gave to Peter in Matthew 19:27, 28. And again Jesus tells us that those who suffer with Him now will reign with Him later (II Tim. 2:12). And the apostles will sit on twelve thrones judging the twelve tribes of Israel.

VERSE 31—34:

31 And the Lord said, Simon, Simon, behold, Satan hath desired *to have* you, that he may sift *you* as wheat:

32   But I have prayed for thee, that thy faith fail not: and when thou art converted, strengthen thy brethren.

33 And he said unto him, Lord, I am ready to go with thee, both into prison, and to death.

34 And he said, I tell thee, Peter, the cock shall not crow this day, before that thou shalt thrice deny that thou knowest me.

Peter's Denial Foretold

It is in connection with the preceding verses, intentionally, that Peter's denial is mentioned. Peter must remember that he is weak and frail and while he is honored, he will bring great disgrace on the call. All the others of us must remember that, too.

Satan had especially selected Peter for temptation: *"Satan hath desired to have you, that he may sift you as wheat."* We know that Satan had especially selected Job also for trial and temptation. First his wealth, then his children and honors were taken away, and when still he loved and praised the Lord, Satan requested and God gave to him the right to torment Job's body with sickness and sores. It is blessed to remember that even in that testing, Satan could go only as far as God particularly allowed him. First, God said to Satan, *"Behold, all that he hath is in thy power; only upon himself put not forth thine hand"* (Job 1:12). And Satan had accused God, *"Hast not thou made an hedge about him, and about his house, and about all that he hath on every side?"* (Job 1:10). Then Satan thought that if he could touch Job's body he would curse God: *"And the Lord said unto Satan, Behold, he is in thine hand; but save his life"* (Job 2:6). With God's children, Satan can go only as far as God allows. So Satan had desired to tempt and sift Peter, and Jesus had permitted it. Perhaps Satan felt that he could bring Peter to disgrace and ruin. And God, who knew all things, may have known that the proud and haughty spirit that would be greatly exalted some day needed testing for his own humility, even as Paul would need the thorn in the flesh, *"lest I should be exalted above measure,"* as he said in II Corinthians 12:7.

Make sure you understand that Peter did not have to sin. He could not avoid the temptation but he could have avoided sin. It is promised, *"There hath no temptation taken you but such as is common to man: but God is faithful, who will not suffer you to be tempted above that ye are able; but will with the temptation also make a way to escape, that ye may be able to bear it"* (I Cor. 10:13). And Jesus tells Peter here the sad truth, that before the cock crows at daybreak (they are now in the night) Peter would deny Him thrice.

Oh, but there is a glad light in the midst of this darkness, joy in the midst of this sorrow. Jesus said, *"But I have prayed for thee, that thy faith fail not: and when thou art converted* [or turned back], *strengthen thy brethren."* If Satan thought he could get Peter's soul, he was mistaken. Jesus has prayed for him, and the prayers of Jesus are always answered. He said, *"Father, I thank thee that thou hast heard me. And I knew that thou hearest me always"* (John 11:41, 42).

Yes, Jesus prayed for all the twelve. In John 17:9 in the High Priestly prayer, He said, *"I pray for them: I pray not for the world, but for them which thou hast given me; for they are thine."* And in John 17:20, the Lord Jesus prayed for all the rest of us: *"Neither pray I for these alone, but for them also which shall believe on me through their word."* So, even as Satan could not get Peter, so Satan cannot get any born-again child of God. He may lead us to sin, as he did Peter, if we do not watch and pray; but Christ will never lose one of His own who is bought with His blood. It was a proud claim that Jesus could make in that High Priestly prayer when He asked the Father to "*keep through thine own name those whom thou hast given me,*" and then said, "*While I was with them in the world, I kept them in thy name: those that thou gavest me I have kept, and none of them is lost, but the son of perdition; that the scripture might be fulfilled*" (John 17:11, 12). Judas was never saved, so he was lost. But those who had been converted were not lost and could not be. O Peter, you will weep bitterly over your sins, but Jesus Christ will go to seek you out and call you back into His blessed service.

VERSES 35—38:

35 And he said unto them, When I sent you without purse, and scrip, and shoes, lacked ye any thing? And they said, Nothing.
36 Then said he unto them, But now, he that hath a purse, let him take *it*, and likewise *his* scrip: and he that hath no sword, let him sell his garment, and buy one.

37 For I say unto you, that this that is written must yet be accomplished in me, And he was reckoned among the transgressors: for the things concerning me have an end.
38 And they said, Lord, behold, here are two swords. And he said unto them, It is enough.

The Disciples Warned: Trouble Ahead

It is remarkable that in these last hours before Jesus went to the crucifixion He kept on loving and thinking of His disciples, even as John 13:1 says. So now He must warn them again. Before He had sent them out on brief, hasty journeys to the cities and towns whither He Himself would come. And He had told them, "*Take nothing for your journey, neither staves, nor scrip, neither bread, neither money; neither have two coats apiece*" (Luke 9:3). Now He tells them that those rules for that simple, hasty journey are not meant for a lifetime. Still God will provide for people, but it is not wrong to have a change of garment, not wrong to provide for our daily needs.

And again He must lay on their hearts the solemn truth that they will face opposition, persecution, false accusation and sometimes a martyr's death. So He said, "*He that hath no sword, let him sell his garment, and buy one.*" We judge that was figure of speech for when the disciples said, "*Lord, behold, here are two swords,*" He let the matter pass. They had misunderstood His meaning. But when Peter cut off the ear of the servant of the high priest, Jesus healed his ear with a touch and said to Peter, "*Put up again thy sword into his place: for all they that take the sword shall perish with the sword*" (Matt. 26:52). He had not meant that they should take a sword to defend Him, so He explained, "*Thinkest thou that I cannot now pray to my Father, and he shall presently give me more that twelve legions of angels?*" (Matt. 26:53). Oh, Jesus wants us to know that there is trouble and persecution ahead for godly, soul-winning Christians and He wants our hearts prepared.

There is no indication that any of the apostles, when they were arrested or beaten or put in jail or falsely accused, offered physical resistance. Stephen did not fight back when he was stoned to death, nor did Paul when he was stoned at Lystra.

The place for the sword is in the hands of the government, as Romans 13:1-7 plainly teaches us, and the policemen or the soldiers may serve God as they serve the government and the people in punishing crime, and in defending the country. According to the law of Moses, it is perfectly proper for men to defend their property from theft and burglarly. And self-defense is not wrong. But it is another matter when one is persecuted for Jesus' sake. Always one must remember that the man must be "*no striker . . . but patient, not a brawler*" (I Tim. 3:3).

Now Jesus knows that He must be "*numbered with the transgressors*" according to Isaiah 53:12; He must die at the time of killing the passover: the time is at hand.

VERSES 39 — 46:

39 And he came out, and went, as he was wont, to the mount of Olives; and his disciples also followed him.

40 And when he was at the place, he said unto them, Pray that ye enter not into temptation.

41 And he was withdrawn from them about a stone's cast, and kneeled down, and prayed,

42 Saying, Father, if thou be willing, remove this cup from me: nevertheless not my will, but thine, be done.

43 And there appeared an angel unto him from heaven, strengthening him.

44 And being in an agony he prayed more earnestly: and his sweat was as it were great drops of blood falling down to the ground.

45 And when he rose up from prayer, and was come to his disciples, he found them sleeping for sorrow,

46 And said unto them, Why sleep ye? rise and pray, lest ye enter into temptation.

Jesus in Gethsemane

Jesus "*went as he was wont*" to the mount of Olives. The parallel passages in Matthew and Luke say "*unto a place called Gethsemane.*" The Garden of Gethsemane, now on the slopes of the mount of Olives, seems to be a part of the original Garden of Gethsemane. There are eight very ancient olive trees and a church has been built around a great stone protruding from the ground which is called "the Rock of Agony." However, the Scripture says nothing about Jesus kneeling or praying on the rock, and that is simply unfounded tradition. In Matthew 26:36-41 and in Mark 14:32-38 we are told that He took Peter, James and John with Him a little farther than the place where the other disciples sat.   The four of them left the other disciples and then Jesus went farther yet.   Matthew says He *"began to be very sorrowful and very heavy.   Then saith he unto them, My soul is exceeding sorrowful, even unto death."*

Here we learn He was *"withdrawn from them about a stone's cast"* and kneeled down and prayed.   Mark 14:35 says He *"fell on the ground, and prayed."*   What was His prayer?   *"Father, if thou be willing, remove this cup from me: nevertheless not my will, but thine, be done"* (vs. 42).   Mark says that He repeated the same words a second time, and Matthew says, *"And he left them, and went away again, and prayed the third time, saying the same words"* (vs. 44).

We believe the prayer of Jesus has been greatly misunderstood.   He surely was not praying to miss the crucifixion.   He came to the world for that.   He prophesied it again and again and looked forward to it.   And knowing the Old Testament, He, of course, knew that men could not be saved except as the Scripture should be fulfilled literally.   The saving Gospel is that *"Christ died for our sins according to the scriptures; And that he was buried, and that he rose again the third day according to the scriptures"* (I Cor. 15:3,4).   No, He was not praying to miss the crucifixion.   On the contrary, He was praying that He might die according to the Scriptures at the proper time and place and not here in the Garden at the wrong time and place and way.   His soul was *"exceeding sorrowful, even unto death,"* that is, He was literally about to die at the wrong time and place.   Satan wanted to kill Jesus and thus thwart the Gospel.   And when Jesus said, *"Nevertheless not my will, but thine, be done,"* He meant, "I am not praying against the will of God but in the will of God and according to the Scriptures."

That time of prayer is recorded in Hebrews 5:7, which

speaks about Jesus and says, "*Who in the days of his flesh, when he had offered up prayers and supplications with strong crying and tears unto him that was able to save him from death, and was heard in that he feared.*" So Jesus prayed to be delivered from death that night in the Garden and was heard. He was supposed to die on the cross, not in the Garden. He was supposed to die on the next afternoon when passover lambs were dying, and He was fulfilling the prophetic type. He was to be mocked on the cross. He was to be scourged and spit upon. He is to have nail wounds in hands and feet and be pierced with a spear. He was to cry out according to the 22nd Psalm, "*My God, my God, why hast thou forsaken me?*" He was to have His garments parted among the soldiers and they were to cast lots upon His vesture. People were to mock Him on the cross, saying, "*He trusted on the Lord that he would deliver him: let him deliver him, seeing he delighted in him*" (Ps. 22:8).

We think it impossible that Jesus should have thought there was any other way to save sinners and fulfill the Scriptures literally. There is not any evidence that Jesus ever prayed contrary to the will of God. In fact, Jesus plainly said, "*Father, . . . I knew that thou hearest me always.*" Jesus never prayed for anything out of the will of God. He got every prayer answered. He and the Father were perfectly united in what They wanted and did. So in Gethsemane Jesus, overwhelmed with suffering, was about to die and He prayed for strength and deliverance and He was delivered so that He could go on to the morrow to fulfill the Scriptures and die at the proper time and way.

In answer to His prayer, He did not die that night. Verse 43 tells us, "*And there appeared an angel unto him from heaven, strengthening him.*"

He had said to the disciples when He went to pray, "*Pray that ye enter not into temptation*" (vs. 40). He

came back and *"found them sleeping for sorrow."*
Matthew 26:40 and 41 tells us that He spoke particularly to Peter, *"What, could ye not watch with me one
hour? Watch and pray, that ye enter not into temptation:
the spirit indeed is willing, but the flesh is weak."* So
if Peter had prayed as he ought, he would not have
fallen into the temptation to deny Jesus.

Will you note the agony of Jesus in verse 44, *"His
sweat was as it were great drops of blood falling down
to the ground."* We suppose that the pressure, the
tension, the sorrow, the burden of the sins of the world,
were about to kill Him. The capillaries were about to
burst. Perhaps the blood was oozing out through the
sweat glands. Some medical authorities think that the
water that came out with the blood, when the soldier
pierced His side with a spear (John 19:34), was an
indication of the same awful pressure, and that Jesus
literally died of a broken heart.

At any rate, let us remember that the sufferings of
Jesus for the sins of the world were not simply the
sufferings on the cross alone, but all the shame and pain,
the unjust trial, the mockery, the public nudity and the
Father turning His face away, were part of the agelong
suffering of Jesus as a Lamb slain from the foundation
of the world. The physical pain of the cross was terrible,
but the pain of heart was worse than all else. Dear
loving, suffering, dying Jesus, paying for my sins and
yours!

VERSES 47—53:

47 And while he yet spake, behold a multitude, and he that was
called Judas, one of the twelve,
went before them, and drew near
unto Jesus to kiss him.
48 But Jesus said unto him,
Judas, betrayest thou the Son of
man with a kiss?
49 When they which were about
him saw what would follow, they
said unto him, Lord, shall we smite
with the sword?
50 And one of them smote the
servant of the high priest, and cut

off his right ear.

51 And Jesus answered and said, Suffer ye thus far. And he touched his ear, and healed him.

52 Then Jesus said unto the chief priests, and captains of the temple, and the elders, which were come to him, Be ye come out, as against a thief, with swords and staves?

53 When I was daily with you in the temple, ye stretched forth no hands against me: but this is your hour, and the power of darkness.

Judas and the Kiss of Betrayal

You should read here also Matthew 26:47-56; Mark 14:43-50 and John 18:3-11. What awesome hypocrisy when Judas betrayed Jesus with a kiss! That was to be the sign for the soldiers and the mob that came with him. *"Whomsoever I shall kiss, that same is he: hold him fast"* (Matt. 26:48). And according to Matthew, Jesus said unto him, *"Friend, wherefore art thou come?"* (vs. 50). Isn't it strange that He called Judas *"friend"*? When Peter, with anguish of heart over the thought that Jesus would die on the cross, said, *"Be it far from thee, Lord: this shall not be unto thee,"* Jesus turned and said unto Peter, *"Get thee behind me, Satan: thou art an offence unto me. . ."* (Matt. 16:22,23). Judas, the wicked, awful sinner, was called *"friend"* when he helped Jesus to go on to the cross to save sinners; and Peter, dearest apostle, when he would hinder Jesus from going to the cross, was addressed as *"Satan"*!

We remember that Jesus had it inspired in Isaiah 50:6, *"I gave my back to the smiters, and my cheeks to them that plucked off the hair: I hid not my face from shame and spitting."* We remember that before Pilate, Jesus uttered not a word in defense when He could have. We remember that Jesus could have called twelve legions of angels to deliver Him but He did not. He had said, *"I have a baptism to be baptized with; and how am I straitened till it be accomplished!"* Oh, Jesus went headlong on to the crucifixion gladly, determinedly, to do the will of God, to purchase salvation for sinners. Those who went forward with that plan, which for man's part was diabolical, were yet counted friends; any who would oppose it, though they be the dearest friends, were counted as the instruments of Satan.

Even as this night He loved His own, washed the disciples' feet, tenderly taught them about the heavenly mansions, the coming blessed Comforter and Teacher, the Holy Spirit, and the fruit-bearing He had in mind for them (recorded in John, chapters 14, 15 and 16), so even now, in the shameful incident of His betrayal, He takes time to tenderly restore the ear of the servant of the high priest, cut off by Peter's sword (vs. 50). It was the servant's RIGHT ear. Perhaps Peter was lefthanded and as he swung to cut off the man's head, he dodged and the ear was sliced off! We do not know that, but the Scriptures had a reason for specifying it was the right ear which Jesus restored.

And what a gentle rebuke Jesus gave to the chief priests and captains of the Temple: Why should they come against Him as against a thief? He had never resisted them. He was daily in the Temple. They could have arrested Him at any time. It shows their wickedness that they must get Him in a private place lest the mass of people would insist that Christ be delivered. But Jesus said, "*This is your hour, and the power of darkness.*" Jesus, who knew no sin, is made sin for us and He must suffer as a sinner. And as the second Psalm has foretold, the kings and rulers are combined to put Jesus to death.

––––––––

VERSES 54—62:

54 Then took they him, and led *him*, and brought him into the high priest's house. And Peter followed afar off.

55 And when they had kindled a fire in the midst of the hall, and were set down together, Peter sat down among them.

56 But a certain maid beheld him as he sat by the fire, and earnestly looked upon him, and said, This man was also with him.

57 And he denied him, saying, Woman, I know him not.

58 And after a little while another saw him, and said, Thou art also of them. And Peter said, Man, I am not.

59 And about the space of one hour after another confidently affirmed, saying, Of a truth this *fellow* also was with him: for he is a Galilæan.

60 And Peter said, Man, I know not what thou sayest. And imme-diately, while he yet spake, the cock crew.

61 And the Lord turned, and looked upon Peter. And Peter remembered the word of the Lord, how he had said unto him, Before the cock crow, thou shalt deny me thrice.

62 And Peter went out, and wept bitterly.

Peter Denies the Lord

Parallel passages are Matthew 26:57,69-75; Mark 14:53,54,66-72; and John 18:12,15-18, 25-27.

The account in John's Gospel says that the "*officers of the Jews took Jesus, and bound him, And led him away to Annas first; for he was father in law to Caia-phas, which was the high priest that same year*" (John 18:12,13). And John 18:24 tells us, "*Now Annas had sent him bound unto Caiaphas the high priest.*" Tradition says the "*high priest's house*" (vs. 54), the "*palace of the high priest*" (Mark 14:54) stood over the ruins where is now built the Church of the Crowing Cock, on the hill formerly called Zion, south of the present walled city of Jerusalem. In those ruins were found weights and measures of the Temple, and there were rings cut in the stone where prisoners might be bound and where they might be scourged. This, then, may have been the place where Jesus came, first before Annas, the father-in-law, and then before Caiaphas the high priest.

John tells us that Peter followed afar off. One disciple, presumably John, was known to those at the high priest's house and then he came back and brought Peter in. This was, we suppose, on the lower floor, where the servants and soldiers of the high priest stayed. There Peter came to warm himself by the fire (John 18: 15-18).

A number of people challenged Peter, saying that he

was one of Jesus' disciples. Since it was clear they intended to kill Jesus, it was dangerous to be a disciple of Jesus.

First, "*the damsel that kept the door* [said] *unto Peter, Art not thou also one of this man's disciples? He saith, I am not*" (John 18:17). Again, Matthew 26 tells us:

"*Now Peter sat without in the palace: and a damsel came unto him, saying, Thou also wast with Jesus of Galilee. But he denied before them all, saying, I know not what thou sayest. And when he was gone out into the porch, another maid saw him, and said unto them that were there, This fellow was also with Jesus of Nazareth. And again he denied with an oath, I do not know the man. And after a while came unto him they that stood by, and said to Peter, Surely thou also art one of them; for thy speech bewrayeth thee. Then began he to curse and to swear, saying, I know not the man. And immediately the cock crew. And Peter remembered the word of Jesus, which said unto him, Before the cock crow, thou shalt deny me thrice. And he went out, and wept bitterly.*" -- Matt. 26:69-75.

One of the group that especially charged Peter was a servant of the high priest who was a kinsman of Malchus (John 18:10) whose ear Peter had cut off (John 18:26), and we suppose there was a general clamour and a number accusing Peter. Peter had warmed himself by the fire with these enemies of Christ (vs. 55) and stayed there for more than an hour (vs. 59), and he had been talking to them, too, for they recognized his Galilean accent which indicated he was one of the twelve, since all came from Galilee (Matt. 26:73; Luke 22:59). After Peter had denied Jesus at least three times, the cock crowed twice—a reminder of what Jesus had foretold (Mark 14:30,72).

I have listed the following estimates of how bad was Peter's sin.

1. The sin itself: He denied Christ, he cursed and swore, he quit the ministry.
2. He was the best Christian and principal preacher in the world; first of the apostles; appointed to preach first to Jews and Gentiles.
3. His case followed the sad list of Christians falling into terrible sin: Moses, Samson, David, Solomon, and many today, proving the fallen nature of man and a personal Devil.

The following elements had part in Peter's fall into sin.
1. He was specially chosen for sifting by Satan.
2. He neglected prayer in the garden.
3. He sat with the wrong crowd, warmed by their fires.
4. Peter had an old carnal nature, as all of us have, and he should have been aware.

The following elements led to Peter's return to fellowship and cleansing.
1. Jesus prayed for him, as He does for all the saved. Satan could not have him.
2. Peter had a new nature, born again, and a rebuking in his heart against sin, a longing for cleansing. The Spirit of God would not leave him alone.
3. The Lord controlled the cock and had him crow to remind Peter; and the fish at Galilee (John, chapter 21), to call Peter back to penitence and forgiveness.
4. Jesus sought him personally in John 21.
5. Certain unbreakable promises and calls of God: "*For the gifts and calling of God are without repentance*" (Rom. 11:29). Jesus had promised about born-again people, "*And I give unto them eternal life; and they shall never perish, neither shall any man pluck them out of my hand*" (John 10:28).

The fact that Peter went out and wept bitterly indicates

that he had a saved heart and could not be content in sin.

VERSES 63—71:

63 And the men that held Jesus mocked him, and smote *him*.

64 And when they had blindfolded him, they struck him on the face, and asked him, saying, Prophesy, who is it that smote thee?

65 And many other things blasphemously spake they against him.

66 And as soon as it was day, the elders of the people and the chief priests and the scribes came together, and led him into their council, saying,

67 Art thou the Christ? tell us.

And he said unto them, If I tell you, ye will not believe:

68 And if I also ask *you*, ye will not answer me, nor let *me* go.

69 Hereafter shall the Son of man sit on the right hand of the power of God.

70 Then said they all, Art thou then the Son of God? And he said unto them, Ye say that I am.

71 And they said, What need we any further witness? for we ourselves have heard of his own mouth.

Jesus Then Buffeted Before the Sanhedrin

The hatred of the chief priests and scribes and elders against Jesus was so great that they were willing to bribe any kind of witnesses to get Him killed. Matthew 26:59 says, *"Now the chief priests, and elders, and all the council, sought false witness against Jesus, to put him to death."* That settles forever that they were not honest, not sincere. They were consciously and deliberately fighting God when they rejected Jesus. Hence, we need not be surprised that they allow the servants and soldiers to mock Jesus and strike Him and blindfold Him. They would strike Him on the face and say, *"Prophesy, who is it that smote thee?"* Prophecy means, of course, speaking in the power and wisdom of God. If He were Christ, could He not tell who hit Him, though blindfolded? Yes, but Jesus did not set out to prove Himself the Son of God to people who did not want to believe and would not have believed. This abuse of Jesus was told in Isaiah 50:6: *"I gave my back to the smiters, and my cheeks to them that plucked off*

the hair: I hid not my face from shame and spitting."
And Isaiah 52:14, speaking of Christ, Jehovah's Servant, says, *"As many were astonied at thee; his visage
was so marred more than any man, and his form more
than the sons of men."* His face was so bruised and
perhaps so bloodied that it did not look like the normal
face of a man! Oh, Jesus must bear whatever shameful
things all us poor sinners in the world deserve, so all
kinds of blasphemy and mockery went on about Him
(vs. 65).

Jesus had been up all night. It was evening, after
dark, when Jesus and the disciples had that preliminary
meal in the upper room. Then He took time to give
them the Lord's Supper, with instructions. He told how
Judas would betray Him, how Peter would deny Him.
Then Jesus washed the disciples' feet and gave them the
lesson of humility and on restoring a sinful brother.
Then Jesus gave the teaching in the fourteenth chapter
of John, and at that time He said, *"Arise, let us go
hence."* As the little group moved slowly through the
darkness, Jesus was teaching them what is recorded for
us in the fifteenth and sixteenth chapters of John, and
perhaps much more. Somewhere they stopped along the
way while Jesus prayed that High Priestly prayer,
interceding for all of us (John, chapter 17).

They came to the Garden of Gethsemane (John, chapter 18), and there was that extended period of time
while Jesus prayed again and again and sweated bloody
sweat and nearly died. Then while the disciples slept
an angel came and comforted Him and strengthened
Him.

Then came the arrest. Taken before Annas, father-
in-law of the high priest, then before Caiaphas the high
priest—that interrogation went on for some time, more
than an hour, the Scripture indicates. Now it was probably far into the wee small hours, toward morning.
Jesus may have spent an hour or two or three in one

of the dungeons which are found in the ruins of the old high priest's palace.

Now, as soon as it is day, *"the elders of the people and the chief priests and the scribes came together, and led him into their council."* Here was a called meeting of the Sanhedrin and they asked Him plainly, *"Art thou the Christ?"* He knew that they will not believe Him; they simply wanted some excuse to accuse Him of blasphemy.

Two principal charges they had against Jesus. John 5:18 tells us, *"Therefore the Jews sought the more to kill him, because he not only had broken the sabbath, but said also that God was his Father, making himself equal with God."* So now, insisting on an answer, the high priest put Him on oath, as we read in Matthew 26:63-66:

> *"But Jesus held his peace. And the high priest answered and said unto him, I adjure thee by the living God, that thou tell us whether thou be the Christ, the Son of God. Jesus saith unto him, Thou hast said: nevertheless I say unto you, Hereafter shall ye see the Son of man sitting on the right hand of power, and coming in the clouds of heaven. Then the high priest rent his clothes, saying, He hath spoken blasphemy; what further need have we of witnesses? behold, now ye have heard his blasphemy. What think ye? They answered and said, He is guilty of death."*

And to vent their anger and their hate, they smite Him and slap Him and abuse Him.

Now they have condemned Him to death. If they can get Pilate, the Roman governor to carry out their sentence, Jesus will die.

LUKE 23

AND the whole multitude of them arose, and led him unto Pilate. 2 And they began to accuse him, saying, We found this *fellow* perverting the nation, and forbidding to give tribute to Cæsar, saying that he himself is Christ a King. 3 And Pilate asked him, saying, Art thou the King of the Jews? And he answered him and said, Thou sayest *it*. 4 Then said Pilate to the chief priests and *to* the people, I find no fault in this man. 5 And they were the more fierce, saying, He stirreth up the people, teaching throughout all Jewry, beginning from Galilee to this place. 6 When Pilate heard of Galilee, he asked whether the man were a Galilæan. 7 And as soon as he knew that he belonged unto Herod's jurisdiction, he sent him to Herod, who himself also was at Jerusalem at that time. 8 And when Herod saw Jesus, he was exceeding glad: for he was desirous to see him of a long *season*, because he had heard many things of him; and he hoped to have seen some miracle done by him. 9 Then he questioned with him in many words; but he answered him nothing. 10 And the chief priests and scribes stood and vehemently accused him. 11 And Herod with his men of war set him at nought, and mocked *him*, and arrayed him in a gorgeous robe, and sent him again to Pilate. 12 And the same day Pilate and Herod were made friends together: for before they were at enmity between themselves.

Jesus Before Pilate and Herod

Parallel passages are Matthew 27:2,11-14; Mark 15:1-5; John 18:28-38.

The accusation against Jesus before the Sanhedrin was the point that He had made Himself the Son of God and so equal with God, and in their minds that involved disrespect for their traditions and the things they had added to the law, also their interpretation of the Sabbath. In John 19:7 they said, "*We have a law, and by our law he ought to die, because he made himself the Son of God.*" But before Pilate they made false accusations saying, "*We found this fellow perverting the nation, and forbidding to give tribute to Caesar, saying that he himself is Christ a King"* (vs. 2).

Now in truth they had tried hard to get Jesus to say that very thing but He would not. In answer to their questions about tribute to Caesar, He said, *"Render therefore unto Caesar the things which be Caesar's, and unto God the things which be God's"* (Luke 20:25). They say that Jesus claimed to be *"Christ a King."* Evidently they knew and understood that He claimed to be the Son of God, the Messiah and a fulfillment of prophecy, and thus Son of David, Son of Abraham, Son of God.

Again, on this matter of the kingdom they had earnestly tried to get Him to take the stand of a rebel against the Roman Empire, hoping thus to get Him executed by the Romans.

Luke 17:20,21 tells us: *"And when he was demanded of the Pharisees, when the kingdom of God should come, he answered them and said, The kingdom of God cometh not with observation: Neither shall they say, Lo here! or, lo there! for, behold, the kingdom of God is within you."*

Would Jesus raise an army and set out to overcome the Roman soldiers who were holding Palestine for Rome? Would He re-establish Israel as an independent nation? He answered them, *"The kingdom of God cometh not with observation."* He said, *"The kingdom of God is within you,"* that is, at least it would be a spiritual kingdom, as far as the present time was concerned. So Jesus was no threat to the Roman Empire. They accused Him falsely when they said in verse 5, *"He stirreth up the people, teaching throughout all Jewry, beginning from Galilee to this place."*

On this matter Pilate questioned Him, *"Art thou the King of the Jews?"* Jesus answered, *"My kingdom is not of this world: if my kingdom were of this world, then would my servants fight, that I should not be*

*delivered to the Jews: but now is my kingdom not
from hence."* That is, Jesus' kingdom is not of this
world order, this present world system. His kingdom
will come only when the *"times of the Gentiles"* are fulfilled, when Christ returns to set up His kingdom and
destroy all the kingdoms of the world.

Nevertheless, Pilate saw the insincerity of it and *"knew
that for envy they had delivered him"* (Matt. 27:18).
Yet the Jews kept stressing this point: Jesus was an
enemy of Caesar, He might start a revolution. *"If
thou let this man go, thou art not Caesar's friend: whosoever maketh himself a king speaketh against Caesar"*
(John 19:12).

But the Jews said that Jesus *"made himself the Son
of God,"* and *"When Pilate therefore heard that saying,
he was the more afraid"* (John 19:7,8).

But now the claim that Jesus is the King of the Jews
becomes a principal issue and even Pilate will call Him
"the King of the Jews," and the superscription over
His head on the cross will be *"THIS IS THE KING
OF THE JEWS"* (vs. 38).

Pilate Seeks a Way to Avoid His Dilemma

He knows that Jesus was innocent, that the charges
were false, that He claimed to be and doubtless is the
very Son of God. There is also the remarkable evidence
that in a dream his wife learned that Jesus is the Saviour, and sent word to Pilate, *"Have thou nothing to do
with that just man: for I have suffered many things
this day in a dream because of him"* (Matt. 27:19).
His conscience and even his fear of the wrath of God
bid him not to put Jesus to death. But what about the
uproar of the people? How keep down the riots that
are threatened? How would he defend himself before
Caesar if they falsely charge that he is favoring another
King?

But here is a possible escape! The people say, *"He stirreth up the people, teaching throughout all Jewry, beginning from Galilee to this place."* Then Pilate found He was a Galilean. He was in King Herod's jurisdiction, in the province of Galilee, so he would send Him to Herod and Herod would take the responsibility. So he did.

Herod had long wanted to see Jesus (vs. 8). He had beheaded John the Baptist and Herod *"heard of the fame of Jesus. . . and said unto his servants, This is John the Baptist; he is risen from the dead; and therefore mighty works do shew forth themselves in him"* (Matt. 14:2). Wicked Herod who had seduced and taken his brother's wife, then at her behest had slain John the Baptist, was greatly troubled at John's preaching, and somewhat conscience stricken, he thought Jesus may be John risen from the dead. Here was his chance to see Jesus and some of the wondrous things he has heard of Him! Now King Herod of Galilee was visiting in Jerusalem at this time (vs. 7), so Pilate sent the Saviour down before him, along with the chief priests and scribes who went along to accuse Jesus. But when Herod questioned Him again and again, Jesus *"answered him nothing."* So it had been at first when He was before Pilate (Matt. 27:12-14). Again, after He was scourged by Pilate's order, and crowned with thorns, *"Jesus gave him no answer"* (John 19:9).

There was abundant answers which Jesus could have given. Oh, no doubt He could have pressed the matter and have spoken so plainly and have so confused the wicked men who charged Him that inevitably He would have been released; but why should He? He came to die! If He had wanted to be released, He could have called for twelve legions of angels (Matt. 26:53). When He was arrested, Jesus asked that if He should deliver Himself, *"how then shall the scriptures be fulfilled, that thus it must be?"* (Matt. 26:54). No, Jesus was taking the place of a guilty sinner. If He proves Himself innocent, that proves that you and I, the writer and reader and all the other millions of the earth, are the guilty ones who must pay for our own sins. So Jesus stands in the place of sinners and makes no defense of Himself.

But is Pilate free from his awful dilemma? No! After Herod and his men of war had set Jesus *"at nought, and mocked him, and arrayed him in a gorgeous robe,"* then he *"sent him again to Pilate"* (vs. 11). Pilate again has Jesus on his hands!

VERSES 13 — 26:

13 And Pilate, when he had called together the chief priests and the rulers and the people,
14 Said unto them, Ye have brought this man unto me, as one that perverteth the people: and, behold, I, having examined *him* before you, have found no fault in this man touching those things whereof ye accuse him:
15 No, nor yet Herod: for I sent you to him; and, lo, nothing worthy of death is done unto him.
16 I will therefore chastise him, and release *him*.
17 (For of necessity he must release one unto them at the feast.)
18 And they cried out all at once, saying, Away with this *man*, and release unto us Barabbas:
19 (Who for a certain sedition made in the city, and for murder, was cast into prison.)
20 Pilate therefore, willing to release Jesus, spake again to them.

21 But they cried, saying, Crucify *him*, crucify him.
22 And he said unto them the third time, Why, what evil hath he done? I have found no cause of death in him: I will therefore chastise him, and let *him* go.
23 And they were instant with loud voices, requiring that he might be crucified. And the voices of them and of the chief priests prevailed.
24 And Pilate gave sentence that it should be as they required.
25 And he released unto them him that for sedition and murder was cast into prison, whom they had desired; but he delivered Jesus to their will.
26 And as they led him away, they laid hold upon one Simon, a Cyrenian, coming out of the country, and on him they laid the cross, that he might bear *it* after Jesus.

Jesus Again Before Pilate; Barabbas Released; Jesus Condemned

Parallel passages are Matthew 27:15-26; Mark 15:6-15; John 18:39,40.

Again Pilate tries to convince these angry Jewish leaders. There is no evidence that Jesus had perverted the people (vs. 14). Pilate had examined and said, "*I . . . have found no fault in this man touching those things whereof ye accuse him: No, nor yet Herod.*" So Pilate suggests that to appease them, he will scourge the innocent Jesus and release Him (vs. 16).

Here Pilate sees another possible escape from his dilemma. It is the Passover season. It is a custom every year for Pilate to pardon and release one prisoner. So, even if Jesus is counted guilty, He can be pardoned in accordance with the accepted custom. So he offers the people a choice of two: There is Barabbas, a rebel and murderer (vs. 19) who is not likely to have many friends; or they may take Jesus. Surely, Pilate thinks, they would choose to release Jesus instead of the known murderer! And perhaps they would have asked for Jesus, "*But the chief priests and elders persuaded the multitude that they should ask Barabbas, and destroy Jesus*" (Matt. 27:20).

Passions were hot! The lying charges had confused many people. An unsaved multitude is easily led to violence and killing. So "*Pilate therefore, willing to release Jesus, spake again to them. But they cried, saying, Crucify him, crucify him*" (vss. 20,21). And no matter his argument, they would not be changed. Jesus was to be crucified.

But how will Pilate live with his conscience? What answer will he give to his troubled wife who was warned in a dream and sent him word not to crucify Jesus? He will disavow his own responsibility and lay the blame on the people. So "*when Pilate saw that he could prevail nothing, but that rather a tumult was made, he took water, and washed his hands before the multitude, saying, I am innocent of the blood of this just person: see ye to it. Then answered all the people, and said, His blood be on us, and on our children.*"

From John 19:1-13 we find that even after Pilate had
Jesus beaten with the Roman cat-o'-nine-tails and
crowned with a crown of thorns by the soldiers and had
a purple robe put on Him, Pilate brought Him out to
the people and said, *"Behold the man!"* Again Pilate
sought to have Him released, but on the insistence of
Jewish leaders *"then delivered he him therefore unto
them to be crucified"* (John 19:16). So Barabbas the
murderer was released, and Jesus, the Substitute for
Barabbas and for every poor sinner in the world, was
led away to be crucified.

John 19:17 says about Jesus, *"And he bearing his
cross went forth into a place called the place of a skull,
which is called in the Hebrew Golgotha."* But He did
not bear the cross all the way. Jesus, rent and torn with
the sins of the world that had almost killed Him last
night in the Garden of Gethsemane, sweating a bloody
sweat, had now been kept up all night, tried and mocked.
Then He was beaten so that His face did not look like
a man's face (". . . *his visage was so marred more than
any man, and his form more than the sons of men"* so
that people were astonished [Isa. 52:14]). He was
scourged with a Roman cat-o'-nine-tails (the lashes
having bits of lead or bone on their end that would
cut into the flesh, with a scourging under which people
sometimes died). Now, tradition says the weakened
Jesus fainted under the cross. At any rate, the soldiers
compel *"one Simon, a Cyrenian, coming out of the
country,"* to bear the cross (vs. 26). What honor came
to Simon that he should bear the Saviour's cross and so
suffer some with Jesus! It is probably that he became
a well-known Christian, for Mark 15:21 explains that
he was *"the father of Alexander and Rufus."* And those
names would have meaning to New Testament Christians.

VERSES 27— 38:

27 And there followed him a great company of people, and of women, which also bewailed and lamented him.

28 But Jesus turning unto them said, Daughters of Jerusalem, weep not for me, but weep for yourselves, and for your children.

29 For, behold, the days are coming, in the which they shall say, Blessed *are* the barren, and the wombs that never bare, and the paps which never gave suck.

30 Then shall they begin to say to the mountains, Fall on us; and to the hills, Cover us.

31 For if they do these things in a green tree, what shall be done in the dry?

32 And there were also two other, malefactors, led with him to be put to death.

33 And when they were come to the place, which is called Calvary, there they crucified him, and the malefactors, one on the right hand, and the other on the left.

34 Then said Jesus, Father, forgive them; for they know not what they do. And they parted his raiment, and cast lots.

35 And the people stood beholding. And the rulers also with them derided *him*, saying, He saved others; let him save himself, if he be Christ, the chosen of God.

36 And the soldiers also mocked him, coming to him, and offering him vinegar,

37 And saying, If thou be the king of the Jews, save thyself.

38 And a superscription also was written over him in letters of Greek, and Latin, and Hebrew, THIS IS THE KING OF THE JEWS.

The Saviour Crucified

Shocked at the brutality and wickedness in condemning a Good Man to die, some godly women, and perhaps others, bewailed and lamented Jesus. Note the solemn warning. They should be weeping for themselves, for their children, for Jerusalem, since Jerusalem will soon be destroyed. This people Israel who have cried out, "*His blood be on us, and on our children*" (Matt. 27: 25), will soon come to awful tribulation at the siege and destruction of Jerusalem when, Josephus says, over a million Jews were slain, and all the trees in the area were cut down to make crosses for Jews, and Jews were sold as slaves until the slave markets of the world were glutted. They should well weep for their children. Women should be glad that they had no children. Jews will

cry out for mountains to fall on them because of the
awful raping, torture, murder, dislocation that will come
to them because of their sins. Jesus must have foreseen
also the awful spiritual darkness and blindness that
have come to Jews through the centuries since. If they
would crucify the dear Saviour who was present among
them, what would be done when the record was old
and disputed, and a matter of legend and false report
and the guilt denied by leaders, as it has been for
centuries?

Two other *"malefactors,"* that is, criminals, would be
crucified with Him, one on either side (vs. 33), because
Jesus was to be numbered with the transgressors and
make His grave with the wicked (Isa. 53:9,12). The
soldiers were entitled to whatever clothing would be left
by the prisoners; so, *"they parted his raiment, and cast
lots,"* fulfilling Psalm 22:18. John 19:23 and 24 tell
us that Jesus had one seamless garment, woven without
a seam throughout, and that they did not tear it and
divide it but cast lots for it.

Oh, Jesus laid aside the seamless garment which
pictures His perfect righteousness, in order that a poor,
wicked soldier might wear it, and, yes, that all of us
may wear that white robe. Surely that pictures the
righteousness of Christ with which the believer is clothed,
*"for he hath clothed me with the garments of salvation,
he hath covered me with the robe of righteousness"* (Isa.
61:10). Does that not picture the wedding garment
which the King provides for His guests at the heavenly
wedding (Matt. 22:11,12)?

Read again in Psalm 22 the scorning of the multitude:
*"All they that see me laugh me to scorn: they shoot out
the lip, they shake the head, saying, He trusted on the
Lord that he would deliver him: let him deliver him,
seeing he delighted in him"* (vss. 7,8). Note the suffering of the Saviour: poured out like water, bones out of
joint, heart like wax, strength dried up, tongue cleaving

to His jaws (pictured in Ps. 22:14,15). The Saviour must have been very worn and thin, and on the cross He could say, *"I may tell all my bones: they look and stare upon me."* And the piercing of His hands and feet is foretold in Psalm 22:16.

The   soldiers mocked Him, offering Him vinegar. Some have thought that they intended this to be a sedative to ease the pain. No, they *"mocked him."* John 19:28 tells us that Jesus cried out, *"I thirst."* This was to fulfill Psalm 22:15, *"My strength is dried up like a potsherd; and my tongue cleaveth to my jaws."*

The superscription over the cross was written in Greek, Latin and Hebrew — in Greek, the universal language of the empire and of cultured people; in Latin, the official language of the law, the Roman Empire; in Hebrew, the official language of the learned Jews.

The four accounts of the title over the cross do not conflict but simply supplement each other.

Matthew 27:37, *"THIS IS JESUS THE KING OF THE JEWS."*

Mark 15:26, *"THE KING OF THE JEWS."*

Luke 23:38, *"THIS IS THE KING OF THE JEWS."*

John 19:19, *"JESUS OF NAZARETH THE KING OF THE JEWS."*

Obviously the full quotation was *"THIS IS JESUS OF NAZARETH THE KING OF THE JEWS."* The wording might have been slightly different in the three languages without affecting the absolute accuracy of the report in all the four Gospels.

What was the time of the crucifixion and when was it over? Mark 15:25 tells us *"it was the third hour, and they crucified him."* According to Jewish reckoning, the third hour of the day was about 9:00 in the morning — when Jesus was crucified. Three hours Jesus hung on the cross with the mocking multitude about Him and Luke 23:44 tells us, *"And it was about the sixth hour, and there was a darkness over all the earth until the*

ninth hour." So after three hours under the pitiless
sun, there were three hours of midnight blackness, and
the veil of the Temple was rent and Jesus gave up the
ghost (Luke 23:45,46). We suppose, then, that the
crucifixion began about 9:00 in the morning and that
Jesus died about 3:00 in the afternoon. Sometime thereafter, and before sundown, His body was taken down
from the cross.

John, writing long after the destruction of Jerusalem,
used the Roman computation for time, not the Hebrew.
So John 19:14 tells us that *"it was . . . about the sixth
hour"* before the crucifixion.

VERSES 39—43:

39 And one of the malefactors which were hanged railed on him, saying, If thou be Christ, save thyself and us.
40 But the other answering rebuked him, saying, Dost not thou fear God, seeing thou art in the same condemnation?
41 And we indeed justly; for we receive the due reward of our deeds: but this man hath done nothing amiss.
42 And he said unto Jesus, Lord, remember me when thou comest into thy kingdom.
43 And Jesus said unto him, Verily I say unto thee, To day shalt thou be with me in paradise.

The Penitent Thief Saved

There were two criminals crucified with Jesus and both
of them railed at Him. When the crowd said, *"He
trusted in God; let him deliver him now, if he will have
him: for he said, I am the Son of God,"* the thieves
also, which were crucified with him, *"cast the same in
his teeth"* (Matt. 27:43,44).

But through the long hours of suffering and shame,
the Spirit of God worked on one thief. Did he remember
that in the synagogue he had heard rabbis tell of the
wonderful time of a kingdom when the eyes of the blind
would be opened, the ears of the deaf would be un-

stopped and the tongue of the dumb should sing, and when sorrow and sighing would flee away (foretold in Isaiah 35)? At any rate, God's Spirit brought deep conviction on the man. Now one thief rebuked the other sinner and asked Jesus for mercy.

As far as we know, this is the only person converted during those six awful hours of the crucifixion. If there were others, they are not recorded. God wanted this thief to be an example for all of us who are sinners alike. And the way one is saved is the way all are to be saved.

1. He confessed his sinfulness and condemnation: *"And we indeed justly; for we receive the due reward of our deeds."*

2. He acknowledged the sinless deity of Christ: *"This man hath done nothing amiss."* The sinless purity of Jesus marked Him as deity, and as the crowd had all accused Jesus of claiming to be the Son of God, the thief knew in his heart that it was true.

3. The thief surrendered to Jesus as Lord. He did not use that term lightly. He did not speak as to a fellow criminal but with heart surrender he gave himself to Jesus.

4. He simply called on the Lord. It was a rather foolish prayer but it was enough. If Jesus had taken that prayer literally, He might have said, "Yes, I am coming back to set up a kingdom on the earth in two or three thousand years. You go on to Hell now and then when I come back to My kingdom I will remember you."

Oh, but never mind the wording—here is a penitent heart that wants mercy! So the thief did call on the Lord, and that was enough to get saved. Romans 10:12 and 13 says, *"For there is no difference between the Jew and the Greek: for the same Lord over all is rich unto all that call upon him. For whosoever shall call upon the name of the Lord shall be saved."* He did not have

to call very intelligently, but he did call sincerely. And
John 6:37 says, *"Him that cometh to me I will in no
wise cast out,"* and so in his heart he came. James 4:8
says, *"Draw nigh to God, and he will draw nigh to
you."* Oh, never forget it: The poorest, most ignorant
person in the world can draw near to Jesus, can call
on Him for salvation, trust Him and in a moment have
it settled forever!

When one goes to a doctor, he need not know what
medicine he needs. He just needs to come to the right
doctor and the doctor will see that he gets the right
medicine. And a sinner does not need to know all the
theology — Christ as our Substitute, the atoning death of
Christ, all the sacrifices fulfilled, and prophecies that are
made true in Jesus. No, if a penitent sinner, confessing
his sinfulness, comes to Jesus for mercy, he gets it! The
thief called on the Lord and he was saved.

Note: he had no good works to offer, *"For by grace
are ye saved through faith; and that not of yourselves:
it is the gift of God: Not of works, lest any man should
boast"* (Eph. 2:8,9). It is *"not by works of righteousness which we have done, but according to his mercy he
saved us, by the washing of regeneration, and renewing
of the Holy Ghost"* (Titus 3:5).

This man was saved, forgiven, without any religious
rites. There was no baptism, no communion supper, no
learning of the catechism, no confession to a priest. He
simply turned his heart to Jesus for mercy, and he received it. So, thank God, the vilest sinner may be
saved instantly, if in repentance and faith he comes to
Jesus. Now, in a moment, the man who is not fit to
live on earth, is made fit for Heaven! And that day
Jesus took him along to Paradise, Heaven.

It is very sweet and suggestive that one who comes to
Jesus gets far more than he had anticipated or can
understand in his poor, frail, finite knowledge.

VERSES 44 — 49:

44 And it was about the sixth hour, and there was a darkness over all the earth until the ninth hour.

45 And the sun was darkened, and the veil of the temple was rent in the midst.

46 And when Jesus had cried with a loud voice, he said, Father, into thy hands I commend my spirit: and having said thus, he gave up the ghost.

47 Now when the centurion saw what was done, he glorified God, saying, Certainly this was a righteous man.

48 And all the people that came together to that sight, beholding the things which were done, smote their breasts, and returned.

49 And all his acquaintance, and the women that followed him from Galilee, stood afar off, beholding these things.

The Death of Jesus

Could the Creator of this universe give up His spirit and the just judgment of God on a wicked race of sinners be fulfilled, and could God the Father Himself turn away His face for a bit from His beloved Son and let Him die at the hands of wicked men, without nature mourning over its Creator? We are not surprised that about the sixth hour *"there was a darkness over all the earth until the ninth hour."* The sun hid its face from the sufferings of Jesus and the whole earth trembled in agony at the death of Christ. *"The veil of the temple was rent in twain from the top to the bottom; and the earth did quake, and the rocks rent; And the graves were opened. . ."* (Matt. 27:51,52). Dr. Bob Jones, Sr., has said that the rocks looked upon the suffering of their Creator and their hearts broke! We don't wonder that Jesus had said at the triumphal entry if the disciples had ceased to cry out, *"Hosanna to the son of David,"* the very rocks would have cried out. And we know that there was a time *"when the morning stars sang together, and all the sons of God shouted for joy"* (Job 38:7). And when Jesus returns to this glad earth, *"the desert shall rejoice, and blossom as the rose. It shall blossom*

abundantly and rejoice even with joy and singing" (Isa.
35:1,2). And "*in the wilderness shall waters break out,
and streams in the desert*" (Isa. 35:6). Then we learn,
"*the mountains and the hills shall break forth before
you into singing, and all the trees of the field shall clap
their hands*" (Isa. 55:12). Oh, if the inspired command
is, "*Bless the Lord, all his works in all places of his
dominion*" (Ps. 103:22), then surely it is only suitable
that nature should show her pain and grief at the death
of the Creator!

So "*the veil of the temple was rent in the midst*" (vs.
45). And Hebrews 10:19,20 refers to that torn veil thus:
"*Having therefore, brethren, boldness to enter into the
holiest by the blood of Jesus, By a new and living way,
which he hath consecrated for us, through the veil, that
is to say, his flesh.*" Oh, the way into the presence of
God is open! All the barriers between God and man are
torn down! It was true before, because in the mind and
plan of God, Jesus was "*the Lamb slain from the
foundation of the world.*" But now it is manifested to
all the world.

Walk in, dear, troubled, guilty sinner, to the presence
of God through the torn veil, that is, His flesh. For
when Jesus died, then every sinner can count that his
debt is paid and through Christ anyone may come to
Him boldly. Jesus said, "*I am the way, the truth, and
the life: no man cometh unto the Father, but by me*"
(John 14:6).

Heretofore at Jerusalem there was the court of the
Gentiles: people dare not come closer to the Temple.
There was a court of the Levites: they could not enter
into the holy place itself until the fixtures were covered.
Only the high priest could enter into the most holy place
and he only once a year could lift a corner of the veil,
go into that room with no door, and sprinkle the blood
of the lamb of atonement on the mercy seat.

Oh, but now, thank God, the middle wall of partition

is torn down and *"ye who sometimes were far off are made nigh by the blood of Christ,"* for Jesus *"abolished in his flesh the enmity, even the law of commandments"* and now we are *"no more strangers and foreigners, but fellowcitizens with the saints, and of the household of God"* (Eph. 2:13-19). In Matthew 27:51 the Holy Spirit takes pains to tell us that *"the veil of the temple was rent in twain FROM THE TOP TO THE BOTTOM."* It was not done by man but by the finger of God.

Before He died, Jesus cried with a loud voice, *"Father, into thy hands I commend my spirit."* About the ninth hour Jesus had, according to the prophecy of Psalm 22:1, cried out, *"My God, my God, why hast thou forsaken me?"* There He spoke as a poor, lost sinner for all the rest of us who have no right to call God "Father" until the debt is paid. But now Jesus could cry out, *"It is finished"* (John 19:30). Now the suffering is over, the atonement is made, and He can again approach God as His own Father and commend His spirit to the Father, for He is to rise again after three days.

Was that centurion, captain of the Roman army, saved? We do not know. He was convinced, *"Certainly this was a righteous man."* More than that, Matthew 27:54 quotes him as saying, *"Truly this was the Son of God."* He glorified God, and I wonder if that means that in his heart he saw Jesus as the Saviour and put his trust in Him. I hope so.

It was a sad group of people who lingered around the cross after the bodies were still and the suffering was over. Even the most wicked must have been sad, and depressed. They must have felt guilty. And *"all his acquaintance, and the women that followed him from Galilee, stood afar off, beholding these things,"* and they thought that the whole thing was over and Christ was dead and gone and their hope dead with Him! For, as far as we know, none of these really expected that Jesus would rise from the dead, for their hearts had not yet been open to that truth.

VERSES 50—56:

50 And, behold, *there was* a man named Joseph, a counsellor; *and he was* a good man, and a just:

51 (The same had not consented to the counsel and deed of them;) *he was* of Arimathæa, a city of the Jews: who also himself waited for the kingdom of God.

52 This *man* went unto Pilate, and begged the body of Jesus.

53 And he took it down, and wrapped it in linen, and laid it in a sepulchre that was hewn in stone, wherein never man before was laid.

54 And that day was the preparation, and the sabbath drew on.

55 And the women also, which came with him from Galilee, followed after, and beheld the sepulchre, and how his body was laid.

56 And they returned, and prepared spices and ointments; and rested the sabbath day according to the commandment.

The Saviour Buried in Joseph's Tomb

Two strange men now took responsibility of burying the body of Jesus—Nicodemus and Joseph of Arimathaea. Nicodemus was that *"man of the Pharisees, named Nicodemus, a ruler of the Jews,"* who came to Jesus by night (John, chapter 3). He was *"a ruler of the Jews";* he was *"a master of Israel,"* or teacher (John 3:10). He was a member of the Sanhedrin. And in John 7:50,51 we read that Nicodemus took up for Jesus before the other Pharisees: *"Nicodemus saith unto them, (he that came to Jesus by night, being one of them,) Doth our law judge any man, before it hear him, and know what he doeth?"* Nicodemus is mentioned only three times in the New Testament—those three times by John—and each time we are reminded that he is the man who *"came to Jesus by night."* The third time is in John 19:39 where we find that he joined with Joseph of Arimathaea for the burial of Jesus.

But the principal character in the burial of Jesus was

Joseph of Arimathaea. He was "*a counsellor*" and thus perhaps a member of the Sanhedrin. He was "*a good man, and a just*," who "*waited for the kingdom of God.*" John 19:38 tells us that he was "*a disciple of Jesus, but secretly for fear of the Jews.*" We do not know whether Nicodemus was saved after that wonderful little sermon with Jesus that night, but we hope so. We do know he had never before plainly committed himself publicly for Christ as a Christian.

Now Joseph went to Pilate and begged the body of Jesus. Mark 15:43 says that he "*went in boldly unto Pilate, and craved the body of Jesus.*" Pilate was surprised that Christ was dead so early, but the centurion verified it and Pilate gave the body to Joseph. Now Joseph bought fine linen (Mark 15:46). Nicodemus came and "*brought a mixture of myrrh and aloes, about an hundred pound weight. Then took they the body of Jesus, and wound it in linen clothes with the spices, as the manner of the Jews is to bury*" (John 19:39,40).

They laid the body "*in a sepulchre that was hewn in stone, wherein never man before was laid*" (vs. 53). But Matthew 27:60 tells us that it was "*his own new tomb, which he had hewn out in the rock.*" So they put the body of Jesus in Joseph's own sepulchre.

We think that the Garden Tomb in Jerusalem, near the hill, the "*place of a skull*" on the north side of Jerusalem, is the real tomb and not that in the Church of the Holy Sepulchre which was chosen by Queen Helena, the mother of Emperor Constantine. And it is interesting that that already prepared tomb seemed to have been too short, for at the foot extra length was chiseled out. We judge that the body of Jesus was longer than Joseph's, and as they wrapped it with linen clothes and the spices, found it necessary to chisel out the tomb and make it longer for the body of Jesus. And then Joseph "*rolled a great stone to the door of the sepulchre, and departed,*" says Matthew 27:60.

Chief priests and Pharisees had Pilate set a guard at
the grave to keep the disciples from stealing His body.

The day Jesus died was "*the preparation*" (vs. 54), so
called also in John 19:14,31. That means it was the
day of the killing of the passover lambs. They were
getting ready for the passover feast which would come
on the new day, that is, on the new day today which
would begin at sundown, with the annual seven days'
feast of unleavened bread. Here we are told that "*the
sabbath drew on*" (vs. 54). But that was not the weekly
Sabbath, Saturday. The Saturday approaching was that
annual Sabbath beginning always at sundown, after the
passover lamb was killed, on the fourteenth day of
Nisan (Exod. 12:18), and included that night and the
next day, the first day of the feast of unleavened bread.
Exodus 12:15,16 tells us about this Sabbath on the first
day and the seventh day of the feast of unleavened
bread in these words:

"*Seven days shall ye eat unleavened bread; even the
first day ye shall put away leaven out of your houses;
for whosoever eateth leavened bread from the first day
until the seventh day, that soul shall be cut off from
Israel. And in the first day there shall be an holy convocation, and in the seventh day there shall be an holy
convocation to you; no manner of work shall be done
in them, save that which every man must eat, that only
may be done of you.*"

So that Sabbath was not the usual weekly Sabbath but
the annual Sabbath of the passover, "*for that sabbath
was an high day*" (John 19:31). So, as we understand
the Scriptures, Jesus was crucified on Wednesday. He
was buried and was in the grave Thursday, Friday and
Saturday (the day beginning at sundown and ending at
sundown). Then sometime Saturday night He arose
from the dead and was in the grave, as He had specifically said, "*three days and three nights*" (Matt. 12:40).

Now the godly women who followed Him from Galilee and ministered to Him (see Matt. 27:55,56) watched the burial of the body and *"prepared spices and ointments; and rested the sabbath day according to the commandment,"* that is, according to the commandment in Exodus 12:16 that *"no manner of work shall be done in them, save that which every man must eat, that only may be done of you,"* and also according to the commandment about the weekly Sabbath which followed on Saturday. The first day of the week, mentioned in the next chapter, would be a weekly Sabbath, but that annual Sabbath must have come that day on Thursday.

Sleep on, dear bruised body of the Lord Jesus, the resurrection is coming in three short days!

LUKE 24

VERSES 1 — 12:

NOW upon the first *day* of the week, very early in the morning, they came unto the sepulchre, bringing the spices which they had prepared, and certain *others* with them.

2 And they found the stone rolled away from the sepulchre.

3 And they entered in, and found not the body of the Lord Jesus.

4 And it came to pass, as they were much perplexed thereabout, behold, two men stood by them in shining garments:

5 And as they were afraid, and bowed down *their* faces to the earth, they said unto them, Why seek ye the living among the dead?

6 He is not here, but is risen: remember how he spake unto you when he was yet in Galilee,

7 Saying, The Son of man must be delivered into the hands of sinful men, and be crucified, and the third day rise again.

8 And they remembered his words,

9 And returned from the sepulchre, and told all these things unto the eleven, and to all the rest.

10 It was Mary Magdalene, and Joanna, and Mary *the mother* of James, and other *women that were* with them, which told these things unto the apostles.

11 And their words seemed to them as idle tales, and they believed them not.

12 Then arose Peter, and ran unto the sepulchre; and stooping down, he beheld the linen clothes laid by themselves, and departed, wondering in himself at that which was come to pass.

The Resurrection of Jesus Christ

This story is told also in Matthew 28:1-6; Mark 16:1-8; and John 20:1-17.

Now it is the first day of the week. We understand that Jesus was in the grave Thursday, Friday and Saturday, that is, with the "high Sabbath," the annual Sabbath, on Thursday, and the weekly Sabbath on Saturday. As Dr. R. A. Torrey said, Jesus could have remained in the grave more than seventy-two hours but He could not be in the grave less than seventy-two hours and fulfill literally the exact prophecy of "*three days and three nights*" of Matthew 12:40.

The good women had "*prepared spices and ointments*"

very possibly on Friday. They had rested again on Saturday, the Sabbath, and now the first day in the week they come to bring these sweet spices and odors to perfume the dear dead body of Jesus, they think, that the decay of the body be not so obvious. Yes, and to express again their love for Him. Evidently they do not expect Him to rise from the dead. The women who came to the sepulchre, mentioned in Luke 23:55, are Mary Magdalene, and Mary the mother of James, and Salome (Mark 16:1). These women were "*much perplexed*" (vs. 4), not understanding about the resurrection.

When these good women and the other women of the company told these things to the apostles, "*Their words seemed to them as idle tales, and they believed them not.*" The two on the way to Emmaus, now that Jesus is dead, think of Him as "*a prophet mighty in deed and word,*" but they do not say He is the Son of God and they say, "*We trusted* [past tense] *that it had been he which should have redeemed Israel.*" And later, when Jesus appears to the group in Jerusalem, "*they were terrified and affrighted, and supposed that they had seen a spirit*" (vs. 37), and they "*believed not for joy*" (vs. 41).

Let no one suppose that the disciples were easy to convince about the resurrection. Thomas was not convinced until a week later when he could put his fingers in the nail prints and his hand in the wounded side in order to see for himself that Jesus was alive (John 20: 24, 28). The resurrection of Jesus is more a proven fact of history than nearly anything else that is recorded. For forty days He appeared to His disciples, talked with them, ate before them, had their hands upon Him. Paul says as evidence of the resurrection:

"*. . . that he was buried, and that he rose again the third day according to the scriptures: And that he was seen of Cephas, then of the twelve: After that, he was seen of about five hundred brethren at once; of whom the*

*greater part remain unto this present, but some are
fallen asleep. After that, he was seen of James; then of
all the apostles. And last of all he was seen of me also,
as of one born out of due time.*" — I Cor. 15:4-8.

As far as we can tell, none of the disciples expected
Jesus to rise from the dead, with the possible exception
of Mary of Bethany who had anointed Him for His
burial (Matt. 26:6-13; Mark 14:3-9; John 12:1-8). She
seemed worthy of some special praise, her name to be
lauded wherever the Gospel is preached, Jesus said. Dr.
Scofield says about this:

> No contradiction of John 12.3 is implied. The ordinary
> anointing of hospitality and honour was of the feet (Lk.
> 7.38) and head (Lk. 7.46). But Mary of Bethany, who
> alone of our Lord's disciples had comprehended His
> thrice repeated announcement of His coming death and
> resurrection, invested the anointing with the deeper mean-
> ing of the preparation of His body for burying. Mary
> of Bethany was not among the women who went to the
> sepulchre with intent to embalm the body of Jesus.

More detail is given in Matthew 28: "*Behold, there
was a great earthquake: for the angel of the Lord descended from heaven, and came and rolled back the
stone from the door, and sat upon it. His countenance
was like lightning, and his raiment white as snow: And
for fear of him the keepers did shake, and became as
dead men*" (Matt. 28:2-4). Matthew tells also how the
soldiers came and reported the matter to the chief priests
and were given large sums of money and were bidden to
tell that the disciples came by night and stole the body
away. The wickedness of the chief priests, scribes and
elders is obvious: they must have known that Jesus was
the Son of God. They still hated Him. They did not
want others to know that He was risen from the dead,
and that resurrection is the principal evidence of His
deity which He Himself had foretold in Matthew 12:40,
41. Romans 1:4 says that Jesus was "*declared to be the*

Son of God with power, according to the spirit of holiness, by the resurrection from the dead."

The soldiers who watched at the sepulchre of Jesus were accountable to the chief priests and the Sanhedrin and reported to them, after the resurrection (Matt. 28: 11-15). It was the chief priests who had the apostles arrested and put in jail, then tried before the Sanhedrin (Acts 4:1-22). The high priest, acting for the Sanhedrin, gave Saul of Tarsus letters to the synagogues at Damascus that he might arrest and bring to Jerusalem for trial any Christians (Acts 9:1,2).

The tender story of Mary Magdalene's grief is told in John, chapter 20, when she and the other Mary saw the sepulchre empty and she ran to tell Peter and John: *"They have taken away the Lord out of the sepulchre, and we know not where they have laid him."* Mary, Peter and John went to the sepulchre and saw it empty and with the cloth with which He was wrapped, laid in order. When the disciples went away Mary still stood by the sepulchre weeping. And to the angel she said she was weeping *"because they have taken away my Lord, and I know not where they have laid him."* And when she turned back, she saw Jesus and supposing Him to be the gardener, said, *"Sir, if thou have borne him hence, tell me where thou hast laid him, and I will take him away."* Then Jesus called her name and she knew Him!

The Order of Events of the Resurrection

Liberal churchmen and other infidels have foolishly said that there are irreconcilable contradictions in the Bible accounts of the resurrection. But every honest, believing person who takes time to study these Scriptures knows that that is not true. Since God planned to have four different Gospels, each with some slightly different

color and purpose, He intended that each one should
tell some things that the other did not tell. One Gospel
will tell of two wild men in Gadara, but Luke will tell
only of the one with a legion of devils which caused the
destruction of two thousand hogs. One will tell of two
blind men who begged for healing as Jesus came out of
Jericho the last time, but for special reasons Mark will
tell only of blind Bartimaeus. Luke will tell the story
of the prodigal son when the others do not. Matthew
will tell certain kingdom of Heaven parables that the
others do not tell. Luke will tell the parable of the
pounds and Matthew will tell the parable of the talents,
with similar applications but on different occasions.
Each one of the Gospels is sweet and wonderful reading
in the account of the resurrection. But the order of
events of the resurrection as Dr. Scofield gives them in
the Scofield Reference Bible is as follows:

> The order of events, combining the four narratives, is
> as follows: Three women, Mary Magdalene, and Mary
> the mother of James, and Salome, start for the sepulchre,
> followed by other women bearing spices. The three find
> the stone rolled away, and Mary Magdalene goes to tell
> the disciples (Lk. 23.55-24.9; John 20.1,2). Mary, the
> mother of James and Joses, draws nearer the tomb and
> sees the angel of the Lord (Mt. 28.2). She goes back to
> meet the other women following with spices. Meanwhile
> Peter and John, warned by Mary Magdalene, arrive, look
> in, and go away (John 20.3-10). Mary Magdalene re-
> turns weeping, sees the two angels and then Jesus (John
> 20.11-18), and goes as He bade her to tell the disciples.
> Mary (mother of James and Joses), meanwhile, has met
> the women with the spices, and, returning with them, they
> see the two angels (Lk. 24.4,5; Mk. 16.6). They also
> receive the angelic message, and, going to seek the
> disciples, are met by Jesus (Mt. 28.8-10).

VERSES 13—35:

13 And, behold, two of them | went that same day to a village called

Emmaus, which was from Jerusalem *about* threescore furlongs.

14 And they talked together of all these things which had happened.

15 And it came to pass, that, while they communed *together* and reasoned, Jesus himself drew near, and went with them.

16 But their eyes were holden that they should not know him.

17 And he said unto them, What manner of communications *are* these that ye have one to another, as ye walk, and are sad?

18 And the one of them, whose name was Cleopas, answering said unto him, Art thou only a stranger in Jerusalem, and hast not known the things which are come to pass there in these days?

19 And he said unto them, What things? And they said unto him, Concerning Jesus of Nazareth, which was a prophet mighty in deed and word before God and all the people:

20 And how the chief priests and our rulers delivered him to be condemned to death, and have crucified him.

21 But we trusted that it had been he which should have redeemed Israel: and beside all this, to day is the third day since these things were done.

22 Yea, and certain women also of our company made us astonished, which were early at the sepulchre;

23 And when they found not his body, they came, saying, that they had also seen a vision of angels, which said that he was alive.

24 And certain of them which were with us went to the sepulchre,

and found *it* even so as the women had said: but him they saw not.

25 Then he said unto them, O fools, and slow of heart to believe all that the prophets have spoken:

26 Ought not Christ to have suffered these things, and to enter into his glory?

27 And beginning at Moses and all the prophets, he expounded unto them in all the scriptures the things concerning himself.

28 And they drew nigh unto the village, whither they went: and he made as though he would have gone further.

29 But they constrained him, saying, Abide with us: for it is toward evening, and the day is far spent. And he went in to tarry with them.

30 And it came to pass, as he sat at meat with them, he took bread, and blessed *it*, and brake, and gave to them.

31 And their eyes were opened, and they knew him; and he vanished out of their sight.

32 And they said one to another, Did not our heart burn within us, while he talked with us by the way, and while he opened to us the scriptures?

33 And they rose up the same hour, and returned to Jerusalem, and found the eleven gathered together, and them that were with them,

34 Saying, The Lord is risen indeed, and hath appeared to Simon.

35 And they told what things *were done* in the way, and how he was known of them in breaking of bread.

The Risen Christ Appears to Two on the Road to Emmaus

The end of the world appeared to have come to the disciples. Jesus was dead! Hopes were blighted. Sadly, two of them went that day to a village called Emmaus.

Threescore furlongs would be a little more than two miles. They walked along sadly, reasoning, wondering. Then Jesus appeared walking along with them, *"but their eyes were holden that they should not know him."* Their sadness was obvious. Why?

Cleopas seemed astonished that anyone should ask! Ought not everybody in the world be sad that Jesus is dead? But Jesus insisted that they explain. Yes, Jesus was a mighty prophet, but now He is crucified. They had trusted that He would be the Redeemer, but now He is dead and has been in the grave three days. Oh, yes, certain women came and said His body was gone; they had seen a vision of angels who said that He was alive —but you know how women are! Yes, we found the tomb was empty, as the women said, but we didn't see Jesus.

Then came the most wonderful thing: Jesus rebuked them soundly. They were *"fools and slow of heart to believe all that the prophets have spoken."* They should have expected Jesus to suffer these things and then in His glory rise from the dead! So beginning with the Pentateuch, the writings of Moses, and all the Old Testament prophets, *"he expounded unto them in all the scriptures the things concerning himself."*

They still did not know that it was Jesus, but this wonderful Person had wrought faith in their hearts. Then Jesus WAS alive! And this good Messenger— surely He would stop and eat with them. As He sat down to eat and as He took bread and blessed it and broke it and gave to them, they saw at once He was Jesus, the same Saviour!

Oh, how their hearts burned within them as He talked and opened to them the Scriptures (vs. 32). Yes, that is where is found the comfort in sadness, the light in darkness, the information to the ignorant—in the Scriptures. The burning heart is found when the blessed Spirit of God makes the Scriptures real to us! Never mind now their mission down to Emmaus—"*They rose up the same hour, and returned to Jerusalem, and found the eleven gathered together, and them that were with them*" (vs. 33). And they found that others there, too, had had assurance: "*The Lord is risen indeed, and hath appeared to Simon.*"

"Fools, and Slow of Heart to Believe All That the Prophets Have Spoken"

Jesus said that. We are reminded that "*the fool hath said in his heart, There is no God*" (Ps. 14:1; 53:1). So only a fool is slow to believe the Bible, too. The evidences for the supernatural accuracy and authority of the Bible are so obvious to every seeking heart that only a perverse spirit, only a wicked determination to go on in sin, would keep people from knowing that the Bible is the Word of God and that it is true. And so Jesus could say in John 7:17, "*If any man will do his will* [or chooses to do His will], *he shall know of the doctrine, whether it be of God, or whether I speak of myself.*" Those who draw nigh to God find that God draws nigh to them and makes the truth clear. Those who have sinned and hate the light, do not come to the light (John 3:19-21). Any man with an honest, open heart who sets out to find for himself whether or not the Bible is the Word of God and whether or not Christ is the Son of God, will certainly find out that They are all They claim to be. God will not leave a seeking heart in darkness, but a perverse and wicked heart has no claim on God for light.

Mary and some of the women had been convinced by the angels who reminded them of the words of Jesus, that He would be crucified and rise again (vss. 6 and 7). And now other apostles are expectant, glad. The evidence increases: Jesus is alive again!

VERSES 36—45:

36 And as they thus spake, Jesus himself stood in the midst of them, and saith unto them, Peace *be* unto you.

37 But they were terrified and affrighted, and supposed that they had seen a spirit.

38 And he said unto them, Why are ye troubled? and why do thoughts arise in your hearts?

39 Behold my hands and my feet, that it is I myself: handle me, and see; for a spirit hath not flesh and bones, as ye see me have.

40 And when he had thus spoken, he shewed them *his* hands and *his* feet.

41 And while they yet believed not for joy, and wondered, he said unto them, Have ye here any meat?

42 And they gave him a piece of a broiled fish, and of an honeycomb.

43 And he took *it*, and did eat before them.

44 And he said unto them, These *are* the words which I spake unto you, while I was yet with you, that all things must be fulfilled, which were written in the law of Moses, and *in* the prophets, and *in* the psalms, concerning me.

45 Then opened he their understanding, that they might understand the scriptures,

The Lord Jesus Appears to Ten Disciples

This passage is paralleled in Matthew 28:16,17; Mark 16:14; John 20:19-23. In John we are told that Jesus showed the disciples His hands and feet and then gave to them the Great Commission, saying, "*As my Father hath sent me, even so send I you. And when he had said this, he breathed on them, and saith unto them, Receive ye the Holy Ghost*" (John 20:21,22).

Here only in Luke is given the story of how He ate before them and assured their doubting hearts: This is Jesus risen from the dead, with His flesh-and-blood body.

Does it seem strange that it was so hard for the disciples to believe? When Jesus appeared they were "*terrified and affrighted*" and supposed it was a ghost. But He had them see the wounds in His hands and feet. He had them put their hands upon Him and feel His flesh and bones. Because Jesus here mentioned that they could feel His flesh and bones but did not mention blood, some have thought that our resurrection bodies will have no blood. True, I Corinthians 15:50 says that *"flesh and blood cannot inherit the kingdom of God."* But that verse continues, *"Neither doth corruption inherit incorruption."*

So let us say that one does not enter the kingdom of God by earthly, family inheritance. That does not mean either that flesh cannot enter the kingdom or that blood cannot enter the kingdom in the resurrected bodies, but it is not by fleshly and corruptible human line that people inherit Heaven. It is true that when He died the blood of Jesus was poured out as the spear was thrust in His side. But it is also true that *"he hath poured out his soul unto death"* (Isa. 53:12), but His soul returned. Since Jesus ate literal, physical food, there is every reason to believe that the physical processes of digestion were carried on and that the body that had flesh and bones, also had blood to carry on these natural processes.

Some have supposed that John 20:19, which tells how Jesus came into the room where the disciples were assembled *"when the doors were shut,"* meant that the body of Jesus was ghostly and spiritual, not material. They are mistaken. It is true that the resurrected Jesus could go through a door without opening it if He wished, but could not Jesus do that at any time? He who walked on the water, He who someway, unobserved and uncaught, passed through the midst of those who wanted to kill Him in Luke 4:29,30 — could He not go through a door if He wished? After His resurrection the body of Jesus was a flesh-and-bone body, with normal processes. It was a body that could eat and digest food, a body one could feel. We suppose that when God created Adam in the Garden of Eden (and He created him perfectly and just as he ought to be), we see no reason why the glorified, resurrected body could not be restored like the body of Adam and live forever, as Adam would have lived had he not sinned. In the heavenly Jerusalem, the tree of life will have twelve manner of fruits, a fruit for each month, and the leaves will be for the healing of the nations (Rev. 22:2). There will be fluids in the bodies of resurrected Christians, as in the body of Jesus, for Jesus said, "*For I say unto you, I will not drink of the fruit of the vine, until the kingdom of God shall come*" (Luke 22:18).

"*Then opened he their understanding, that they might understand the scriptures.*" Oh, for the blessing of those who are tuned to the Word of God! And the blessed privilege of the Christian is that "*the Comforter, which is the Holy Ghost, whom the Father will send in my name, he shall teach you all things, and bring all things to your remembrance, whatsoever I have said unto you*" (John 14:26).

VERSES 46—49:

46 And said unto them, Thus it is written, and thus it behoved Christ to suffer, and to rise from the dead the third day:

47 And that repentance and remission of sins should be preached in his name among all nations, beginning at Jerusalem.

48 And ye are witnesses of these things.

49 And, behold, I send the promise of my Father upon you: but tarry ye in the city of Jerusalem, until ye be endued with power from on high.

The Great Commission

The Great Commission, which Jesus gave the disciples after His resurrection, is repeated for us five times, as we understand it—in Matthew 28:19,20; Mark 16:15,16; John 20:21-23 (with slightly different words); here in Luke 24:46-49; and in Acts 1:8. However, it seems likely that the Lord may have mentioned the Great Commission in different wordings twenty-five or possibly